# Hobbled Stirrups

# Hobbled Stirrups

by Jane Burnett Smith

*Caxton Press*
Caldwell, Idaho
2006

Library of Congress Cataloging-in-Publication Data

Smith, Jane Burnett, 1919-
Hobbled stirrups / by Jane Burnett Smith.-- 1st ed.
p. cm.
ISBN 0-87004-454-0
1. Smith, Jane Burnett, 1919- 2. Cowgirls--United States--Biography. 3. Wild west shows. I. Title.

GV1833.6.S55A3 2006
791.8'4092--dc22

2005026477

Lithographed and bound in the United States of America by
*CAXTON PRESS*
Caldwell, Idaho
172933

## ACKNOWLEDGEMENTS

I would never have been brave enough to tackle this rewrite of the original "Hobbled Stirrups" autobiography that was written some thirty-five years ago if I had not been encouraged and helped by all the members of my immediate family.

Special thanks to my daughter Camille who not only guided me through all of the technicalities of transferring my work from the old typewritten pages onto my computer but also reproduced the photographs and clippings from my scrapbook that she had organized several years before.

Other family members who prodded me along when I felt the project was more than I could handle include Loren, Tony, Dana and Pam. Without their urging I doubt if I would have succeeded in this undertaking so special thanks goes to them for having more faith in me than I had in myself at times.

Wayne Cornell at Caxton Press has guided me through the rough spots and should be commended for his efforts.

Christen Cavanaugh and Camille Smith of Color Inc. are also acknowledged for the distinct cover design.

# PROLOGUE

My grandfather, William Clinton Burnett, and his brother W. P. (Perkins) Burnett settled in Montana in the 1880s after having been part of several cattle-drives north from Texas. Bill divided his time between Wyoming and Montana after he had purchased a saloon and livery stable in Buffalo, Wyoming, and another bar in Sheridan. He married Elsie Newell in 1890 and, although he joined his brother in Montana to work as a cowhand on several established cattle ranches for six to eight months each year, Elsie remained in Wyoming with their children. Over a period of years, the brothers gradually accumulated cattle herds of their own by accepting livestock in lieu of wages. With their half-brother, Henry, in 1892 they obtained ownership of three separate cattle ranches in the Gilt Edge/Fort Maginnis area in Montana. These were deemed a single unit until disagreements among the brothers induced them to eventually divide the livestock and separate the ranches with one deed of ownership going to each brother.

In 1913, Bill Burnett moved my grandmother, Elsie, teenage son Clinton and older daughters Minnie and Gladys, from Wyoming to the Daniels Ranch on Chippewa Creek.

Some time later, Minnie, the elder Burnett daughter, while living with her husband in one of the homestead cabins on the Burnett ranch, died during the birth of their only son. The other daughter Gladys, moved to Billings with her mother when their parents separated in 1917.

It was understood that my father, Clint, would eventually take over his share of the responsibility for running the ranch after he attended college in Lincoln, Nebraska. However, on his return to Montana it was soon evident that his interests leaned more in the direction of having a good time than worrying about the mundane chores required of a ranch manager. With his outgoing personality and a penchant for being the center of attention, he soon realized that spending time with any available drinking or gambling group was more to his liking than herding cattle. He had the background and talent to be a good cattleman but this was merely a job to him and not something to which he would devote his entire life. Away from the ranch, he took control of most situations, partly because of his tremendous sense of humor but more than likely because he rarely let anyone else "pick up the tab" for drinks, food or any other expenses.

The ranch remained almost entirely the responsibility of my grandfather although Clint always made himself available during various critical times of each year such as putting up hay twice in the summer, branding calves in the spring, or trailing steers to the railroad in the fall, but ranching would never be a lifetime career for him. He fulfilled his obligations at the crucial times and then proceeded to carry on with his separate life of gambling and having fun.

There were few clues as to how I was destined to become part of this strange Burnett world, but one of my earliest recollections is of a cold December morning a few days before my seventh birthday.

Daddy, Grandpa, and I were eating breakfast. Mother was in the kitchen. No one spoke, as usual. The wind howled and the forge in the blacksmith shop wailed its eerie reply. There was no livestock visible in the corral or around the feedracks and I could see nothing through the frosted windows except drifting snow. Visions of eating hot popcorn and stretching out on the calf-hide rug near our pot-bellied coal stove in the living room were quickly squelched when Grandpa rose from the table and spoke.

He stood there, a tall, handsome, austere, uncompanionable man, who lived only for the cattle ranch he had built from nothing after the long trek to Montana from Texas. He had a West Point look to his stature, even though his fighting had been confined solely to Indians, rustlers, outlaws and Montana winters.

"Clinton," Grandpa said. "You'd better pick up those colts today. They're with Hedman's horses." Never a wasted word. His conversations always sounded like Western Union messages.

I knew what was coming. I shivered.

"Well?" Daddy turned to me. "Wanna go along?"

It was not really a question. There was only one acceptable reply.

"Sure."

The sub-zero weather seemed a minor issue in comparison to the idea of being considered unable to "take it."

What a miserable trip! My Shetland pony jogged along beside Daddy's horse, nearly high-centering on many of the deeper drifts. At times I wished I had been weak and feminine enough to remain with Mother (that popcorn idea seemed better by the second) or strong enough to admit I did not really want to go in the first place.

After opening a wire gate nearly ten miles from the ranch house, Daddy walked and led his horse for half a mile or so.

"Wanna get off and warm up a little?"

I shook my head "no," although I knew walking was supposed to help me stay warm, it was too cold to dismount for any reason.

Time was also frozen. I have no idea how much later it was when we found the horses we wanted. To head off a bunch of loose horses with a fat Shetland pony would be an inconceivable feat even if your arms were not stiff with cold, and too many jackets, so Daddy did most of the work of lining them out and pointing them in the right direction. When we had spooked the herd toward a narrow lane that led to a set of old abandoned corrals, Daddy indicated with a nod of his head that I was to sit near the entrance and wait while he sorted them. In case the horses got away from him, I could head them off at that end of the lane before they reached open country again. I nodded that I understood.

Several degrees later, I was still sitting at the end of the lane, huddled over the saddle-horn, icicles hanging from the end of my nose. (Probably from the end of my stirrups, also. As already mentioned, it was too cold to dismount for any reason.) The sound of horses running on frozen ground brought me around stiffly in the saddle, icicles snapping. For a second I was afraid the colts had gotten away from Daddy, but soon saw they were the Hedman horses so I let them pass.

Daddy rode over to me. He never questioned if I were frozen, could I make it all right, how I felt. He simply asked matter-of-factly, "You hired out as a tough hand, didn't you?"

Nothing else was necessary.

I nodded, elated that I was considered a tough hand. I reined my pony around and fell in beside Daddy, riding proudly. We returned to the corral to pick up the penned colts and headed for home.

Neither Daddy nor I could have known the events that were to develop from that one incident. In the years to come I was to get in and out of fights, hospitals, jails and marriages; ride in rodeos from the Canadian border to Mexico City, Los Angeles to Madison Square Garden, Gilt Edge to Hollywood; get whipped in several different states, bucked off in a few of them, and divorced in a couple of others. And all because I had "hired out for a tough hand" and thought I had to follow through without complaining. I asked for no sympathy and gave no excuses.

*We can't all be champions. In the rodeo business, as in every competitive sport, there are a select few who become truly great. Just as inevitably, there will be the many who make up the group from which these champions arise.*

*From the scared kid riding his first steer, to the crippled old saddle-bronc rider who is going to try it just one more season, each individual secretly believes himself capable of developing into one of the "greats." Without this belief there would be no competition.*

*I consider myself a charter member of these forever hopefuls who doggedly struggled in the shadows of the champions. During my rodeo years I had a few more disappointments than some, a great deal more fun than most, and never at any time doubted that I would eventually hold the title of World's Champion Woman Bronc-Rider.*

*It seems I was the only person who was genuinely surprised when this failed to occur.*

# Chapter One

During various interviews through the years I have managed to dodge any questions regarding my childhood. For one reason, any research on my part discloses that my role in the Burnett family was primarily as a mini-adult and rarely as a child. This first became evident to me when I began a family of my own and was surprised to learn there were certain childhood activities such as the Halloween "trick or treat" tradition that were completely alien to me. Birthday celebrations in my honor consisted entirely of adult guests who briefly toasted me with the drink in his/her hand before returning to their bridge games or other forms of entertainment. This situation may have been a result of the isolation of Montana cattle ranches but I have to assume that much of the problem had to do with the lifestyle of my parents.

Bits and pieces of the early years gradually trickled down to me and I learned that the brief courtship and marriage of my parents in 1917 was a typical example of the old axiom "opposites attract." My mother, Agnes Weiss, was the daughter of the Ashtabula County Doctor in Jefferson, Ohio. One of three girls in the family of four, she was a beautiful young woman, very shy, elegant and extremely refined who had led a very sheltered life prior to attending Valparaiso Normal College in Indiana. This was her first actual venture away from a family of educated, religious, cultured people who were surprised, and mildly disappointed at her decision to travel to Montana immediately after graduation. This was acceptable only because she accompanied Mable Gilkerson, her college roommate, on their trek to Montana, which was considered by the Weiss family to be a part of the Wild West. With brand new teaching certificates in hand, the two graduates arrived safely in Lewistown where they were welcomed by the rest of the Gilkerson family.

From their very first meeting, Clint was mesmerized by the beautiful, quiet, sedate young woman who remained in the background of whatever group of young people they found themselves, and who made no effort to attract his attention. Rumor has it that Agnes was "swept off of her feet" by the personable young cowboy but, being extremely shy, she was determined to hide any indication of these feelings. Sharing a penchant for finding humor in any given situation, they soon overcame the obvious hurdles of their diverse backgrounds and became engaged a short time later.

The early years of their marriage was an on-again off-again ranching lifestyle interrupted by their excursions to any location (poker game) that was easily reached in their new Studebaker coupe. In December, 1919, when it was time for my birth, Agnes returned to Ohio briefly so my Grandpa Weiss could deliver their child. Clint joined her there and was widely accepted by the Weiss family who I am sure did not realize that this young westerner with the magnetic personality was not the "cattle baron" they believed him to be but was in reality an "on again/off again" rancher only during spells between poker games and parties.

Within a year after my birth, the entire country entered a bleak period (1920-1933) known as "Prohibition–The Noble Experiment." The idea behind this project was to reduce crime and corruption, solve social problems, and reduce the tax burden created by poorhouses and prisons. Aside from the fact that none of these problems were solved, it was soon evident that the reverse was true even though it was thirteen years before this law was finally repealed. Not only were more people drinking alcohol than ever before, but the "home made" versions were dangerous to consume. Crime actually increased due to the illegal production of liquor and the roots of organized crime became evident during that period of time.

A single black woman named "Nigger Bertie" (an adjective acceptable during that era) lived in a cabin near the old Fort Maginnis and was the major supplier of bootleg whiskey throughout the years the restrictive law was in effect.

Prohibition had its effect on my family, as well, when it offered the opportunity for Clint and a gambler friend of his to haul bootleg whiskey from Canada to Salt Lake City, Utah, off and on for more than three years. This of course was in between intervals at the ranch due to irrigating, branding and/or haying. I recall hearing rumors that this was the one time Mother influenced my father in any regard, and that was when she insisted he stop bootlegging when I reached the age of four because it would be too dangerous and was no way to "bring up a child."

In later years, as told to me during a conversation with my mother's female companion of that particular adventure, I learned something that proved, to my surprise, at what age I began to exhibit my independence. It seems that each winter, between "treks" from Canada to Utah, Clint and his friend Burt often spent three or four months in Butte, Montana, at the Board of Trade, where the two men ran several gambling games. Burt's wife told me that during the evenings while the men were at work, she and Agnes remained in the hotel where they took turns playing solitaire or reading to me, with Mother teaching me to read and write the alphabet. The part that surprised me was when she recalled that each morning, while my parents slept, I took several coins from the table where they had been tossed by Clint the night before, and would go to the Board of Trade to have breakfast. This was in December of the year I had my fourth birthday! She said I would be bundled up in my winter clothing and after breakfast went out in the street to play with children of other employees of the "Trade" until my parents finally appeared around noon.

It was after that one particular winter that Agnes finally convinced Clint to return to my Grandpa Burnett's ranch on an almost permanent basis. Our lives assumed a moderate stability at that time but the unfamiliar sense of "belonging somewhere" did not last very long. There were still occasional weekend treks to nearby towns where rumors of a hot poker game had been passed on to my father, and of course the local bootleggers kept their whiskey supply intact.

One winter my grandfather leased a ranch about three miles north of the home place where my folks and I were to spend the next few months. They were going to winter some cows and calves on that land and the move almost proved disastrous for me. The first night we spent in our new residence, our gasoline lantern was accidentally knocked off of a table, and because it was not lit at the time, the damage was not evident. The following evening a local ranch hand stopped by. His excuse was that he had just picked up a bottle of booze from "Bertie" and wanted Mother to make him a hot toddy because whenever he made his own, he used so much booze that the drink was no longer hot. He was quite drunk and was slumped over in a chair just inside the front door with his coat across his lap. Mother was unpacking some of their newly purchased groceries and Clint started lighting the lantern.

With the natural curiosity of a child, I stood right beside the table and when he struck a match, flame shot out through a crack in the side of the lantern and set me on fire. My parents were both blinded by the flash and the drunken cowboy jumped out of the chair and threw his coat over my head and shoulders and completed doused the fire!

I was quite severely burned but because my Grandfather Weiss was a doctor, Mother remembered hearing him tell a patient, on the phone, to mix soda and vinegar and apply it as a poultice until he could get there to tend to the injured patient. Because she had just unpacked the groceries, Mother was able to dump a new package of soda into a bowl, add vinegar, and apply this to my face and neck.

When they took me straight into Lewistown that night, the doctor claimed her quick thinking was the only thing that saved me from being very badly scarred for life. We also had the cowboy to thank for quite possibly saving my life. He later claimed that every time he got drunk he had visions of me in flames, but I am forever thankful that he was able to come out of his stupor in time to douse the fire before it did any further damage.

I guess I always took it for granted that our lifestyle during my childhood was much the same as that of the neighboring ranchers' families but on looking back I can see that there was a great deal of difference.

The gold mining town of Gilt Edge, which was about seven miles north of our ranch, had at one time during its "boom" years been the home of as many as thirteen saloons, but by the time Prohibition came into effect, only one such business remained amid the few active establishments that included a post office where all of the ranchers in the area received their mail.

I understand that during those years, there were many "get-togethers" of local families, often held in the large Gilt Edge school house that remained standing following the days when the mines had been active. As a family, we did not attend any of these gatherings so I had no opportunity to spend time with children of my own age except during my on-again/off-again schooling at the Pleasant Plains School three miles from our place. Other ranchers, including our nearest neighbors, no doubt attended many of these festivities on some weekends and on various holidays, but my parents never attended. Their parties away from the ranch were generally held at friends' homes in Lewistown or at the Elks Club which was twenty-one miles away. This was in no way a matter of the Burnetts being exclusive, and it may have been considered snobbish by some, but in reality it was simply a product of diverse lifestyles.

Most of my schooling progressed through the early years in four-five-month sessions, probably due to our "junkets" to various towns where there were gambling opportunities for Clint during the winter months. Because one of the students at our school made fun of me for referring to my father as "Daddy," from that point on he would be "Clint," except in my own mind.

The result of this irregular education was my spending about one-half of a year in each class and often finishing in a more advanced grade. This was partially due to home-teaching by my mother and/or her semesters as a substitute teacher. Also, I was once advanced from the second grade to the fourth when there were only eight students in all, and they found it easier to combine the grades. The outcome was that I graduated from grade school at age eleven and assumed I was ready for high school the following September.

Our only games at Pleasant Plains were either "tag" or tossing rubber balls into an empty wastebasket during recess, so there was little camaraderie among the students and I always felt very much the outsider. I did spend one night with Lulu Swift, a schoolmate my age with whom I felt comfortable, but she was never allowed to stay at our ranch, no doubt influenced by rumors of my parents' habits. On one occasion when all of the students were "snowed in" at school we were forced to spend the night with a rancher and his family who lived very near the school house. I remained there for two days because my only transportation was my Shetland pony and I was unable to go home during the storm. Their older son rode to our ranch to let my parents know that I was safe. The incident was all but forgotten when several weeks later my parents received a letter from that family stating that I had stolen the husband's watch! The note said if it was returned, they would not report the incident.

This came as a real shock to me but I assured my parents that it was untrue and the subject was dropped. However, what little acceptance I had developed to that point was immediately destroyed. I felt alienated even more from our neighbors despite a note that was mailed to my parents several weeks later admitting that the husband had actually pawned the watch himself and had been reluctant to admit it to his wife.

It was difficult for me to see any humor in the situation but my parents considered the whole thing to be hilarious, which was the way most incidents were viewed in our family. I do not recall ever hearing them gossip about anyone or degrade them in any manner, which I tried to remember if and when I ever considered myself maligned in some way. I was not always quite as broad-minded as they were about such things and at times it was difficult to see humor in certain adverse situations.

There was no evidence of affection among the Burnetts. On the one occasion when I tried to hug Clint as thanks for a birthday gift, he appeared so embarrassed when he shrugged away from me that I never again repeated such a gesture. His persona as life of the party did not include anything that might be interpreted as a weakness and he seemed to consider such action on behalf of others to be an indication that they wanted something from him. It seemed strange, however, that he did not seem aware that he was being hustled for free drinks wherever he went.

By the time I was in my teens, Clint and I had developed a kind of a "cat and mouse" relationship, with an undercurrent of "one-upmanship" that was both playful and serious at the same time. I was treated the same as any other cowhand and I responded to orders the same way, neither getting nor expecting special treatment.

There were no such things as family meetings, per se. Grandpa Burnett gave the orders, and we followed them. He was not a severe person in any sense of the word, but when he issued an order, it was understood that you would obey. As a rule, I obeyed Clint's orders even on various occasions when they were issued in one of his sarcastic moods. During one incident I remember when I returned to the ranch after attending a rodeo in Wyoming, Clint and I were roping some yearling steers that needed closer inspection of their brands. I was riding a high-strung Arabian horse of mine named Cricket that had a tendency to come apart at the seams in any tight situation. I had just roped a steer by both hind legs when I realized my saddle was beginning to slide sideways, indicating a loose cinch. Rather than have Cricket throw one of his fits, I released my rope, stepped down and was getting ready to tighten the cinch when Clint hollered at me from the other side of the corral.

"What the hell you doing?" he asked, sarcastically. "If you don't want to work, why don't you just turn your horse loose?"

Under ordinary circumstances I would have just ignored this ridiculous outburst, but for the first time in my life I thought, "to hell with it."

Instead of tightening the cinch, I unhooked it completely, set my saddle on the top rail of our pole-fence, removed Cricket's bridle, crawled through the fence and walked across the yard to our house.

I was told sometime later that the various ranchers who were helping us that day had to hide their delight because they had all been victims of Clint's sarcasm at one time or another and could barely resist cheering out loud.

The incident was never discussed between Clint and me.

I am sure tenderness and/or familiarity had been part of my Mother's childhood but this was not carried over into her life in Montana, quite possibly as a result of having also been rebuffed by the Burnett family early in her marriage. She and I were close, to the extent that we were able to exchange a hug or "peck on the cheek" when not in the presence of other family members, but my interests lay specifically in the man's world of ranching, and later in the world of rodeo.

Through the years I was never comfortable with the way the various hangers-on took advantage of Clint's generosity and I made a special effort to get by with a minimum of requests for money if I could handle the situation by myself. However, on a few occasions in later years, such as the time I was stranded in Mexico, I was mighty glad to be able to wire home for help.

A few people shared my opinion of the groupies who hovered around Clint at the Burke Hotel Bar or the Montana Tavern, waiting on him hand-and-foot in order to be assured they were included in the next round of drinks.

A certain young man who was the son of one of the very few sheepmen in our area was noticeably present any time drinks were being ordered. He ran the errands, took the phone calls, pulled out a chair for Clint to be seated, and never spent a nickel of his own money. In deference to his family, I will just call him "Moochie."

On one rainy afternoon while we were waiting for Mother to do the grocery shopping, I was seated on a bar stool next to a wheat farmer from Stanford who did not know I was in any way affiliated with the group in the corner booth.

He nudged me in the ribs, and grinned. "If anyone ever kicked Burnett in the rear-end, they'd break that young man's nose, wouldn't they?"

I did not identify myself but I shared his laughter.

My grade school years must have been a lonely time for Mother. Outside of the schoolroom, I recall spending very few hours with her, and then only when Clint and Grandpa Burnett were away from the ranch. If either of the men were there, I was kept busy riding, haying, fixing fence, breaking colts, cleaning horse stalls or whatever was required to keep me treading in Burnett bootprints. Looking back, I am ashamed that I resented any time I had to spend washing windows, dusting furniture, drying dishes or any other household chores, especially if I had already put in a full day's work chasing cattle or driving a buck-rake while gathering hay. From my mother's Holland Dutch ancestry, she had inherited this overwhelming need to clean, clean clean.

Knowing that a bunch of cowhands could not care less if there might be a smudge on one of the windows or a speck of dust on a kitchen chair, it all seemed like a waste of time to me, and I felt that the "outside" work I had done on any given day should exempt me from any menial household chores. To this day I resent having to do any housework.

Somewhere along the line the few scattered hours with Mother had some effect, inasmuch as I can behave like a lady if I have to (maybe only when wearing a dress but rarely if I am in Levis). It is obvious that she struggled to undermine the totally male influence as much as possible. She saw to it that I attended Bible classes at the Episcopal Church in Lewistown although I would never reach the point where I read from the Bible every single day, as she did. Because of Mother's tranquil expression, clear hazel eyes, and good-humored mouth, her soft-spoken instructions concerning manners or grammar penetrated despite my resistance.

My character definitely conformed to the outline of the Burnett mold, although any physical resemblance to Clint's lanky frame, thin face, big ears, and perpetually uncombed hair was not in evidence. A sense of humor, certain mannerisms and blue eyes were the only visible factors of my paternal heritage.

Proving myself gradually became almost an obsession with me. Why, in what way, or to whom, I have never been quite sure, but it has ruled my entire life.

# Chapter Two

I seldom accompanied my parents on their gambling trips by the time I reached the age of eleven. During each hiatus between spring branding and the two sessions of mowing and stacking hay for the coming winter, I often remained at the ranch with my grandfather and Nate, our permanent hired hand at the time. When my parents were away, Grandpa always took over the job of cooking our meals when we were with a regular crew, and I washed the dishes. The sparse dialogue between the two men pertained almost entirely to everyday ranch work.

Music was my salvation. A beautiful spinet piano in our living room that had belonged to my Aunt Gladys was my one and only form of entertainment. I managed to keep myself occupied for hours at a time attempting to play tunes I remembered from our gambling trips around Montana. There was a single battery-operated radio in Grandpa's room, but once the news was broadcast morning or evening, this sole connection to the outside world was shut off. Sometimes when he was out of the house, I sneaked in and listened to music for a few minutes but managed to shut it off before his return so he could not tell the radio had been used.

Although I was the designated horse wrangler during haying or prior to any of the various cattle roundups, I helped with a few small chores during each hiatus. I gathered eggs from the henhouse, tossed hay to Grandpa's saddle-horse whenever he kept it overnight in the barn, and even made one feeble attempt to get milk from our only Guernsey cow. I had always assumed there was no particular talent involved in convincing a dairy cow to release a stream of the white stuff if you just gave her the opportunity. Otherwise, why were they called dairy cows. Right? However, after nearly an hour of "squeeze and pull" I had less than four inches of liquid in the bucket to show for my trouble and Nate declared that hereafter he would resume that particular chore.

When Nate was shoeing one of the horses or performing ranch jobs, there was little else for me to do during the day. I had found a "Ranch Romances" magazine in our hotel room in Billings one weekend, and I read it cover to cover until it was in shreds. I even penned a few stories of my own with similar plotlines only I made sure the story centered around a "cowgirl." This appealed to my sense of justice since most ranching stories of the era portrayed the protagonist as a tall, handsome, curly-headed blonde male who had no faults and was unstoppable in his quest for whatever.

To occupy myself during the afternoon, I often saddled my horse and rode the three miles south over the hills to the main highway. To date, my only contact with automobiles had been our 1930 Studebaker, Grandpa's Ford coupe and our aging Ford Model-A pickup that I had learned to drive that summer, so it was exciting for me to watch the various models of strange new vehicles traveling that route between Lewistown and Billings. Sometimes I would dismount and let my horse graze while I re-read my own stories for entertainment. In order to keep my horse from running away, in case I dozed, I put "hobbles" on his legs so he could move slowly away from me but was always available. Hobbles are specially made so you can buckle one end around each of the horse's front ankles, and the sixteen- or eighteen-inch strap between his front legs was sufficient to allow him to move around. At the time, I did not realize that a version of these contraptions (the "hobbles") would play a very important role in my future.

On my way back to the ranch, I sometimes stopped to survey the ranch buildings sprawled in a brushy curve of Chippewa Creek. Long before my birth, additions to the original single tiny log cabin had gradually expanded, one room at a time, to accommodate the growing Burnett family, until now the L-shaped eight-room house was a model worthy of representing our 20,000 acre ranch. The completed structure had one continuous roof and siding with a covered porch that ran all along the front and the short side of the "L". A great deal of time and money had been put into making this an attractive well-constructed single-level building. There were separate outside entrances to the bedroom area, the living room, dining room and kitchen, and there was a standing joke in the family concerning the fact that only one of these outside doors had been furnished with a lock, and that lock was on backwards! You could lock yourself IN that area of the house, but could not keep anyone OUT.

The history of that lock was often told to new guests solely for the humor factor because at that time ranchers had no reason to lock any doors to their homes. Often when we returned from a trip, either from Lewistown or from one of Clint's other junkets, there would be a note on the kitchen table indicating that some cowboy had stayed over-night in the bunkhouse, had fed his horse, and himself (always in that order) and thanked us for the accommodation.

During the summer months I always slept on our front porch where I shared a narrow cot with my Collie dog, Pal. He seemed to accept the fact that he was never allowed to sleep inside the house, but any time I was at the ranch we were practically inseparable.

Because of my sleeping arrangements, at least once or twice each year when I was awakened at dawn with Pal occupying more than his share of our cot, I would be amazed to see a familiar scene that appeared near one of our windmills about three miles from the house. A small cluster of mini-mountains named "Three Buttes" that I knew to be twenty miles or more from the ranch, appeared to be right there on our pasture-land near a windmill within walking distance of the house. The first time or two when this happened, I did not mention it to anyone because I was afraid they would accuse me of dreaming the entire incident. When I finally discussed it with one of our hired men he confirmed that I was actually witnessing a mirage that he had seen a few times himself.

At dawn on that particular Fourth of July, the mirage again appeared at daylight. As Nate approached the house for breakfast, I intercepted him and we discussed the mirage phenomenon and the actual location of Three Buttes. He confirmed that they were at least twenty miles or more east of our ranch, and added that, in fact, if there was any way to get my grandfather to take us to the annual celebration at Valentine that afternoon, we could see the exact location of Three Buttes a short distance from the rodeo.

I rarely ate breakfast during the summer unless there was a reason to wrangle the horses, but I joined the two men that morning to add moral support to Nate when he broached the subject of our attending the festivities. Grandpa indicated with a nod of his head that it might be possible and an hour or so later he pulled his car around to the front of the house, honked the horn, and we were on our way.

Because Grandpa insisted on rising at 4 a.m. summer or winter, we were always the first arrivals wherever we went but I was happy just to be going anywhere. As Nate had promised, we could actually see Three Buttes a few miles north of Valentine and for a few seconds I had a strange illusive feeling that this scene was not real.

Almost immediately I became preoccupied with the rodeo site. The only clue to the actual location of the performances that afternoon was a small white school house squatting forlornly in the center of a dusty sagebrush flat. A closer inspection disclosed one lone bucking-chute hiding behind the school as though dreading its annual day in the limelight, and as was the norm with those prairie rodeos, there was no fenced-in arena. Only open range.

Two sweltering hours after our arrival, the first of the rodeo fans began to arrive. No official parking instructions were required since each car was automatically parked on an imaginary line to form an oval-shaped arena. Doors flew open and the cars seemed to boil over with people. Picnic lunches were spread on blankets and calls of "Come and get it!" sounded in every direction.

Despite the strong odors of sagebrush and horses, I felt weak from the predominating smell of other people's food. Four a.m. breakfasts have a tendency to do that. Just as I was tempted to invade one of the picnic groups, a two-wheeled sheepherder's wagon was towed in and parked near Grandpa's car. The unmistakable aroma of frying wieners reached us just as a scrawled home-made sign appeared on the wagon stating they had "Hot Dawgs Fer Sale. 15-cents with mustard included." No rescuing Saint Bernard ever received a warmer welcome.

After handing me a quarter for a hot dog and lemonade, Grandpa began chatting with a rancher who was sitting in the front seat of a Model-T Ford parked next to us. I was amazed to hear Grandpa actually providing his share of the dialogue, considering how rarely he spoke in anything other than four- or five-word sentences at home.

Nate had wandered away and from my viewpoint I could see him with two other men on the far-side of a pickup truck several cars away. Even with his back to me, the motion of his head tipping back toward me, then forward, suggested that he had already located someone with a jug.

There was a tug at my sleeve and I recognized the older brother of Lulu, my sometimes-friend from grade school. At his suggestion, we went over to the single chute where he asked permission for us to ride a couple of steers. Two giggling teenagers had already tried to complete rides even before the various vehicles had entirely encircled the "arena" and the animals ran through the gaps between cars and took off at a dead run across country. We were informed they would pay us fifty cents per mount, and because the event was not a "contest" we would not be required to complete the ride in order to receive payment. There was a brief delay until a few more cars completed the circle that would keep the animals from running away and then we were told it was time to start the first event.

I was not all that anxious to take part in the rodeo, especially after seeing the first two cowboys get bucked off right in front of the chute but the prospect of being the only person to make a qualified ride took precedence over my cowardice and I agreed to ride at least one steer if they said it was okay. When it was my turn, I felt a little bit better as soon as Nate appeared at the top of the chute beside me. He patted me on the shoulder when I crawled down onto a short, stocky Hereford yearling steer. I could feel my shaking knees knocking against the inside of the chute. The steer's hair was soft and curly like the calf-hide rug at the ranch, and when Nate pulled the rope tight with my hands under it, palms facing upwards, I could feel twitching nerves running through the hide like escaping air bubbles. I peeked through the gate poles at the waiting crowd, then took a deep breath and nodded.

At the first glimpse of "daylight" when the chute gate opened, the steer exploded into the arena. I had an eerie sensation of being catapulted backwards over a steep cliff, but there was no mistaking the instant I made contact with that hard-packed gumbo dirt. A noise something like "Whooosh!" escaped from me. I sounded and felt like a punctured balloon.

The rodeo clown rushed over to me. His Indian-like facial decorations might have startled me under other circumstances, but I just grabbed him by the front of his fringed shirt and gasped, "Did I ride him? Did I? Did I?"

"You bet!" He lied. "Just like a real little cow-hand!"

Although greasepaint alone is often associated with the term "ham" (as in performer), a mouthful of gumbo dirt is just as effective if car horns are honking, people are applauding and cheering voices can be heard. The fact that I was thrown only a few jumps from the bucking-chutes in no way dampened my enthusiasm.

I was a hand! That's what the man said.

Since this was my very first attempt at riding bucking stock, I did not know anything about using what is known as a "loose rope." This is actually a braided soft rope that encircles the animal (steer or bareback bronc), with the long end threaded through a loop at the other end, and doubled back to be grasped by the rider. Your hands gripping the two layers of rope is all that keeps you on top of the animal. Anyone strong enough to ride with one hand, using the other arm for balance, will not be whipped forward and back as violently as the rider with both hands under the rope, but since I did not have the strength to ride one-handed, I would have been snapped forward and back severely had I remained aboard long enough to experience this problem. However, with a ride lasting only one or two jumps out of the chute, it made almost no difference either way.

Before we had a chance to see any of the calf roping, Grandpa sent Nate to tell me we were leaving. I had ridden (bucked off of) two more steers, but even the huge sum of a dollar and fifty cents was not as exciting to me as the fact that I was actually accepted as a rodeo hand on my very first try.

The following day I was alone at the ranch. Grandpa and Nate had gone to Lewistown, and I was seated in an alfalfa patch letting my saddlehorse graze at the end of a thirty foot picket rope. I had a note pad in my lap and continued to write figures of all sizes on the paper.

Three dollars and fifty cents. Three and one-half dollars. Three hundred fifty cents. $3.50.

Any way I wrote it, the rodeo money plus my first two dollar check for raking hay that summer now constituted a bankroll that just would not quit.

More than usual, by the end of the week I found myself watching the road that led to the main highway, hoping my parents would be coming home and I could share my experience with them. On Sunday morning, Grandpa told me to check on a barbed-wire gate north of the house at the far end of our holding pasture. Once or twice in recent weeks someone had left that gate open and, although we had no way of knowing who might be doing this, it was important to check occasionally since our saddle horses at times had access to that pasture.

It was early morning and as I approached the gate in question I was surprised to see a pickup truck chugging along the narrow lane from the northwest. They were on the single dirt road that led to Gilt Edge. The truck pulled up to where I was tightening the top wire on the gate in question, and I recognized one of the La Fountain clan with a pickup full of little La Fountains.

We exchanged greetings and once it was determined that they were headed for a rodeo "off in the direction of Grass Range," I began probing for more information about the event. They asked if I wanted to join them, and naturally that was all I needed to send me off on another wild experience. Although they said they would not be coming back past our place after the rodeo, I said I could surely catch a ride home with someone within walking distance. They followed me back to the ranch and after turning my horse loose and telling Grandpa I was headed for Flat Willow, I was on my way again.

Grandpa simply shook his head and walked away from me, but I was too excited about the rodeo to be concerned.

I crawled into the back of the pickup truck and was soon surrounded by an assortment of little dark-eyed children and even more dogs. One of the little boys peed on my boots and although they smelled pretty bad, they did take on a nice shine until I stepped out into the dust later on after a long, long, long ride across country. I thought I might get a gate count on kids and dogs when we arrived, but the instant the tailgate dropped there was a flood of indistinguishable bodies that could not be separated into definite groups.

The site for the rodeo grounds was almost identical to Valentine, with a single bucking chute out in the middle of a sagebrush flat, not chosen for its beauty. In every direction there were just miles and miles of nothing but miles and miles. Sagebrush and dust. Grey dotted with darker grey.

Parked cars again formed the temporary arena. The rodeo promoters always hoped the horses and steers would not buck over the top of one of the parked cars but the spectators did not seem concerned. Women and children picnicked in the shade of cars and trucks. Most of the men, and all of the contestants, were still gloriously drunk from the rodeo dance the night before.

I strolled in the general direction of the bucking-chutes and heard greetings from several cowboys, some who knew my name and others who just called out, "Hi, cowgirl!"

I spent nearly an hour trying to convince someone around the chutes that I was serious. "I want to ride steers," I kept repeating. "Who's in charge?"

A big rawboned bewhiskered cowboy with his chaps on backwards and his hat on sideways grabbed me off of my feet and held me in the air over his head. "You don't need to see nobody else, little Cowmamma! Big George'll set you on one of these yearlin's an' you can test his air right now—howzat?"

"You bet," I agreed. Anything to get back on the ground. "That'd be great."

I don't believe my feet even touched the ground before Big George lifted me over the chute gate and set me on top of a shaggy black yearling steer.

"Hey! What about a surcingle—or rope—or something?" After all, there was a limit to humoring this jerk.

"Don' worry 'bout nothin' girlie," he laughed. "Ever-thing's under control."

Before I could protest, a young cowboy swung the gate open, Big George jerked my hat down over my eyes, and away I went! In the wild churning darkness I grabbed for the steer's short hair and got nothing but Montana air as I sailed through it and lit with a THUD that jarred me clear to my toes. I struggled to sit up, gasping for air, and tugged the hat from my eyes. The first sight I saw was Big George lumbering toward me, a huge grin on his face.

"Atta girl!" he crowed. "Couple a more like that an' you'll ride like a pro!"

I scrambled toward the nearest car and crawled beneath it. I had no idea where I was headed except away from George. I could hear him puffing right behind me but I was saved by his size. He could not get far enough under the car to reach me before I scooted out the back and was gone.

I found a round-about way back to the bucking chute hoping to find someone sober enough to discuss the steer riding without getting me killed first. There were two cowboys leaning against the back of the chute who seemed somewhat sober despite each of them having their own individual bottle of what smelled like dandelion wine. When one of them offered me a drink, I tried to explain that all I wanted was a chance to ride a couple of steers for practice.

One of them grinned. "If ya wanna ride steers, we'll see that ya ride 'em without bein' hassled—right, Chick?"

"That's right, Tom. That's right."

Chick scrambled out and stood beside Tom. "I'll run 'em in—you and Janie take turns riding 'em—and I'll keep that big bastard George away from you!"

He turned to me. "Okay, Janie?"

"Let's go! I'm ready."

Rodeo promoters and spectators are always screaming for a faster show. That day we formed a trio that gave them their money's worth. In between attempted rides by two teenagers, Tom and I each rode two more steers out of the chute so fast that no one, least of all we three, really realized how many there were. Several things helped to speed up operations. The parked cars had not yet completed a solid line to serve as a temporary fence around the arena, and stupid as it may seem, we were still riding with no rope or surcingle, so it never took us long to get back to the chutes and there was no delay in returning the steers to the chute since most of them were escaping through the gap between the parked cars. As a matter of fact, on one of my rides I bucked off so fast they had to move me out of the way in order to close the gate! But it was fun.

By what would have been my fourth steer, Chick and Tom were still giggling while they ran cattle into the chutes. Since I had no wine consumption to put me on a par with their go-to-hell attitude, those hard falls were taking their toll on me and for once I was mighty glad to see the rodeo manager running across the arena, waving his arms and shaking his fists in the air.

"Somebody stop 'em!" he yelled. "Fer chrissakes somebody stop 'em! We ain't got enough stock left to put on a show."

This time I was leaning against the chute gate when I looked up at the big angry man standing beside me. I actually felt sorry as I watched him wipe away a few tears with a red bandana handkerchief.

"**Get out of here**—get out of here—*get out. . .*"

During the delay while several cowboys with saddlehorses combed the distant coulees for the escaped rodeo stock, a cowboy I had seen talking to my parents at one of our brandings, stopped by to say, "Hello."

After we exchanged greetings, he said, "Saw Clint in Lewistown last night. Did he make it out to the ranch? He was pretty much under the weather when we talked."

I didn't want to admit that I was unaware that they had returned from their July Fourth trip, so I just mumbled, "No, not yet."

Up to that point, I had considered the day to be pretty much of a success, but I felt betrayed hearing that my parents had returned and it was necessary for me to learn about it from someone I barely knew. I asked several people if they were going into Lewistown when the rodeo ended, thinking I might catch a ride with them, but had no luck. I was relieved, however, when Lulu's brother invited me to ride with them as far as their ranch.

On the way home, I kept thinking about the fact that my parents were actually only a short distance from the ranch and had not come home or at least sent for me to join them. We had no telephone communication that far from Lewistown except in the Gilt Edge Post Office, but I felt that someone could have come to take me into town.

Actually, my disappointment was unfair. They had gone away so often without my knowing when they might return that I had no right to expect any word until they actually walked in the front door, but I was feeling kind of sorry for myself and wanted an excuse to be angry.

The Swifts dropped me off at the gate to our land and as I walked the remaining three miles to our house, I was in a rebellious mood. The more I thought about it, the more I felt like I had been deserted, and by the time I got home I had decided on a solution.

If my parents were not at the ranch by bedtime, I was going to take the pickup truck and go to Lewistown by myself! The very fact that I had never driven on the highway did not interfere with my plans. Could it be any different than driving along the twin tire-tracks that led from our house past several Dunn family ranches to Gilt Edge, where I had picked up our mail on numerous occasions? I was convinced I could handle the problem and my mind was already made up by the time it was dark outside.

Water was piped into our house from a well located in the first section of the building next to the bunk house. With electricity supplied by a gasoline engine in the basement of the house, a "real bathroom" had been installed that summer. It was located just off of the kitchen area, and we could actually fill the tub with hot water right out of the faucets which was quite a treat. Although I had taken my weekly bath the day before, this time I repeated the process while killing time until Grandpa went to bed. It was nearly dark by the time I finished and because his room was on the far end of the house from where we parked the pickup, I felt sure he would not hear me leave.

The Ford was fairly noisy when you first started up but I drove slowly out of the yard in order to be as quiet as possible. The only reaction to my departure was Pal who stood on the porch watching me leave and Nate who came to the door of the bunkhouse when I drove past. I could only hope that Grandpa was not part of that audience.

I had no problems with the truck during the first few miles until I reached a lane that led to the main highway. There was a very steep downgrade on the south side of the hill that I had to maneuver in order to reach what we called the "main road." It was a winding trail through timber land and at times I wondered if I had over-estimated my ability to drive when the switchbacks through the trees forced me to creep along at under ten miles an hour. By the time I finally did reach the highway, I had convinced myself that everything was under control and, although I was probably still only driving about fifteen miles an hour, the exhilaration from my accomplishment made me feel like I was flying through the clouds.

I crept along until I was about seven or eight miles from Lewistown and for the first time I saw oncoming lights and really began to panic. There was rarely any traffic on the road at night in those days, and all I could think about was giving the other car plenty of room to pass by. It was fortunate that I was traveling so slow because in an effort to provide ample space for the other car to pass, I pulled over too far to the right and suddenly felt the ground give away under the right front wheel and almost like in a dream, the truck rolled over on its right side in the ditch and settled there.

Because this entire accident happened in slow motion, I was not even frightened. At first. The other car had long since travelled on down the road, so when I crawled out through the door on my side my main concern was how do I get to Lewistown from here?

I was not hurt, and it did not appear that the truck was really damaged, but all I could think about was, "What's Grandpa going to think?"

I sat down on the side of the road and began to whimper.

# Chapter Three

I'm not sure how long I sat by the side of the road, but when I eventually stood and looked around, I noticed that the mailbox and a narrow lane to the Skaggs ranch was almost directly across the highway from me. There were so few ranchers in the area at that time, it was common practice to help each other with branding and other jobs that required extra man power. We had eaten dinner in their house during their branding that spring and I remembered seeing one of the "cranking" telephones on their wall. No doubt they were already in bed, but I felt I had no choice but to waken them so I walked the half-mile or so from the highway and stepped onto their front porch. Before I had a chance to knock, Mrs. Skaggs barely opened the door at first. I'm sure she was startled to see someone there since no car-sounds had been heard.

As soon as she recognized me and I explained what had happened, Mr. Skaggs placed a call to the sheriff's office in Lewistown. He assured them that I was not injured but that I would need transportation. The police station and sheriff's office shared the same building, so a deputy and one of the policemen arrived about thirty minutes later to see what could be done about the truck. And me.

With Mr. Skaggs' help, the two officers were able to tip the truck back into an upright position and push it back onto the road. I stood off to one side, watching and wondering what would happen next.

With very little exchange of dialogue other than my thanking the Skaggs for their help, I was told to ride into town with the sheriff and the deputy would follow in the truck. There was no explanation as to what would happen when we arrived in town, but when the sheriff told me that Clint had been notified about the accident I was confused even more as to why he had not come with them to be sure I was all right.

When we arrived, I was ordered to wait in the sheriff's office while they decided if there were going to be any charges against me. Still no Burnetts. I was becoming more scared by the minute. Then, after about thirty of those minutes, Clint arrived. I saw him talking to the sheriff in the outer office before finally motioning for me to follow him to his car and we drove to their hotel. In silence.

At first I felt like crying. Then I got mad. The least he could do was ask if I was okay!

At their hotel room, Mother was really upset. She put her arms around me and kept pulling away to look at me, then hugging me again. Periodically she asked if I was sure I was okay and this made me feel a little better about the whole situation. That is until I thought about Grandpa again and wondered what would happen when he learned what I had done.

Clint had gone back to bed and rolled over to face the far wall. Mother whispered in my ear that he acted the way he did because, in fact, he really had been worried about me until the sheriff assured him on the phone that I had not been hurt. In a town as small as Lewistown, even the sheriff knew that the Burnetts stayed at the Fergus Hotel when they were in town so he had contacted them immediately after the Skaggs phone call.

Mother whispered that as soon as Clint heard I was okay, he simply did not want anyone to "fuss over me," as she put it. She said he mainly wanted me to sweat for awhile at the sheriff's office which also explained the lack of conversation between the law officers and myself.

The next morning, just before dawn, we headed for the ranch. Clint drove the pickup and I rode in the car with Mother. When we arrived, she dropped me off in front of the house and I slipped under the covers on my cot and hoped that Grandpa had not as yet missed the truck. The incident was never mentioned again.

The next two weeks found us busy with the second cutting of hay, so there were no discussions about going anywhere. I had hoped we might begin making some decisions about living arrangements that fall when I entered high school but one Saturday in mid-August Clint announced that he and Mother were going away for the weekend and that it was not possible for me to go because I had to stay home and see that the Guernsey was milked twice a day!

With haying over, the crew had already left, but I assumed Nate would remain as always. I also knew better than to question Clint's decision. He and I had a strange relationship with both of us accepting the fact that I was to follow orders, if and when they were explicit, but occasionally I was able to find loopholes that gave me a slight edge. There were a couple of protests that came to mind such as the disastrous results of my previous attempt at milking, and also the fact that the cow and her calf could be put in a pasture together for a few days as was often done when no-one would be home for any period of time.

Clint predicted the protests I might make, even if I had dared, so he mentioned almost immediately that Nate was going into Lewistown with them and would be gone for at least a week. He also pointed out that Grandpa would remain in Billings at a cattlemen's convention that entire weekend and this left me with no grounds for an argument.

Mother had packed a small suitcase, indicating they would definitely be gone for several days and when I looked at her questioningly, she just shrugged and turned away. There was a hint of tears in her eyes.

George Smith, a young cowboy from Gilt Edge, better known as "Sonny," had helped us with the haying and sometime in the past few days he had mentioned a rodeo in Stanford that would take place that weekend. I hoped Clint had not been listening but I suspected that was not the case when his final action before driving away was to open the corral gate and drive all of the saddle horses out into a twenty acre pasture south of the horse barn. The key word here is all. My saddle horse was part of that herd.

Now, while I watched my folks drive away, I sat on the front porch scratching Pal's ears as he lay next to me. I felt real sorry for myself.

This was Saturday afternoon and I was in such a bad mood I did not even play the piano. That evening after struggling once more with the Guernsey cow, I kicked her in the butt after a less than cooperative effort on her part at chore time, and dumped the measly cup or so of milk out onto the dirt. By Sunday morning I had decided I was not going to be forced to stay home just to prevent me from going to the rodeo, so I hatched what I considered to be a brilliant plan. Actually, I could have just turned both the cow and calf into the pasture with the horses but that solution did not occur to me. I prided myself on following orders when they pertained to handling cattle on the range, or even at home as was the case this time. A time or two, I had been told by other people that Clint, and/or Grandpa, had occasionally suggested (when I was not present) that I was a "natural" when it came to that particular job. In this case, I felt all that was necessary to complete my instructions, or at least my version of same, was to see to it that the cow was milked twice a day by someone. (Clint had slipped up, this time!)

I might have been stretching it a bit when I arrived at a solution but I walked to Brown's small farm which was about one mile closer than Lulu Swift's house, and convinced their oldest boy to take over my milking chores with the understanding that I would pay him one dollar a day for Sunday and Monday if he agreed to also give me a ride to the highway on his horse. He wanted the money in advance so when we rode "double" back to the ranch, I gave him two dollars from my "cache" under the mattress on my cot. He had actually helped with the milking chore a time or two when all of us were gone overnight, so he was already familiar with which corral and holding pen we used for the cow and calf before and after the milking was done.

I packed a small satchel with a change of underwear, a tooth brush, and whatever cash remained in my cache. (Cash in my cache?? Had a nice ring to it!)

We headed for the highway and I was on my way.

I was not sure how soon I would be able to catch a ride but fortunately the elderly couple who picked me up were going to Great Falls, on the other side of Lewistown, and would go right through Stanford so it was possible I might get there in time, after all.

On arrival at the rodeo grounds I saw that the rodeo was at least half over, and I rushed behind the chutes looking for the rodeo promoter.

"They haven't ridden all the steers yet, have they?" I asked breathlessly.

"No, they haven't, Jane," he laughed. I wondered how he knew my name until he added, "Clint told us to save one for you. He said he didn't know how you'd get here, but he figured you'd make it before too long!"

I borrowed some spurs and a two-handhold surcingle and a couple of cowboys placed it on the little roan steer they had saved for me. (The surcingle was a wide leather rigging that was occasionally used on steers and/or bareback broncs at that time. In general, it replaced the "loose rope" entirely and eventually the single hand-hold version became the bareback bronc-riders' required piece of equipment).

In the rush, the surcingle was not cinched tight enough but we did not realize it at the time. Just as I was squirming down onto the steer, working my legs carefully down on either side, I heard a familiar voice coming from the top of the chute gate behind me.

"Spur him in the neck, Skipper!" It was Clint. He rarely used that nickname, but I was too busy to be surprised. He was grinning at me when I grabbed the handholds and nodded to the gate-man.

Those words were fresh in my mind. I leaned back as far as possible, and still hang on. I knocked small tufts of roan hair right out of the top of the steer's neck on the first jump. The next jump, the surcingle began to slip forward and my spurs hit the points of his shoulders, then his ears, and finally I sailed out over his head and landed with a WHOOOF!

Clint ran over to me. I was sitting in the dirt, spitting small bits of gumbo dirt out of my mouth, and I was still hanging onto the surcingle.

He didn't even ask if I were hurt. "Why the hell didn't you spur him in the neck like I told you?"

I looked up at him and knew I had to get mad or I would start blubbering. "Goddammit, I did 'til I ran out of neck!"

We must have been shouting because I suddenly realized that everyone around us was laughing. I crawled to my feet and after handing the surcingle and borrowed spurs to someone next to the chutes, I went toward our car with Clint.

Mother was completely surprised when they announced my name over the loud speakers. Apparently Clint had not confided in her that possibly I would arrive at the rodeo some time that afternoon. She had been sitting on the fender of our car and when the chute gate opened, it startled her so much that she fell off even before I did, and she missed my entire ride, brief as it was. A woman from Lewistown whose car was parked next to ours had apparently been talking, talking, talking ever since since my parents' arrival. Both her husband and Clint managed to escape by heading for the chutes immediately after parking their cars but Mother was trapped with no chance of escape.

The husband arrived at the same time as we did, and his wife immediately grabbed him by the arm and squealed, "Did you know these are the Burnetts from Gilt Edge? We've heard so much about them from the Tom Stout family. And about your wonderful parties!"

Mother was already opening the door on her side of the car and she showed visible signs of collapsing if we did not get away now!

Not to be outdone, the woman moved over to block Mother's entry and gushed, "I've heard so much about your positively gorgeous ranch house. . .and your rugs! I've heard you sink into them at least four inches!"

Just before Mother finally escaped and was pulling the door closed, she looked at the woman with disgust. "Good Lord, woman, we don't even have beds like that!"

It so happened the "locals" in Stanford had decided against having any gambling in town that evening so I rode back to Lewistown with my parents and the next day they began making plans for my entry into high school.

Parents of most of the Gilt Edge teens who attended high school in Lewistown made arrangements for these students to live in a hotel owned by Susie Dunn Johnson and her husband Harry. Since there were several families of Dunns who owned ranches in the Gilt Edge area, it was natural that most of the students opted for "board and room" with the Johnsons during the school week. They would return home on weekends. At one time, such an arrangement had been contemplated for me but Mother felt it might be best if we had a place of our own for my freshman year.

I did not mention to my parents that I had really hoped to stay with the Johnsons, also. I really wanted the opportunity to become further acquainted with some of the Gilt Edge teens who might possibly include me in some of their summertime activities if things worked out well. Early that spring I had nearly accomplished this on my own. One afternoon right after the various country schools were dismissed for the summer, I had gone to Gilt Edge to pick up our mail and I struck up a conversation with a local girl who appeared to be about my age.

During the course of our conversation, this girl sounded interested in coming to one of our brandings and although she had other obligations on the first occasion, she said she would love to spend the day with us at the second branding which generally turned into sort of an overgrown family picnic.

It so happened that during our first branding, Grandpa had injured his hand when he accidentally slammed the car door on several fingers. Because his main job at the brandings was to castrate the bull calves, his injuries made this impossible. It so happened that we had been short of help for that particular weekend due to a misunderstanding about the date and a neighbor had also scheduled his branding for that same day. I for one was happy about this conflict because it gave me the opportunity to learn the "grown up" job of castrating calves. I was quite flattered when Grandpa assigned me to this new job to be done in conjunction with my regular chore of vaccinating the calves. He showed me how to perform that task, and it was really quite simple but in my mind this moved me up a notch or two into the "big people" category.

At no time did it ever occur to me that this new one-afternoon-job would be anything other than a step in the direction of adulthood, and in fact I was quite proud of my "promotion."

However, and this is a big however, the girl who had accepted my invitation to our second branding did not attend. No explanation. No apology. Nothing. And the next time I saw her, which was actually in one of our classes in high school that fall, she barely spoke to me.

I did not understand what was happening and felt I was being snubbed for no reason, so I was totally shocked when one of her brothers finally admitted to me that their mother would not allow her to come to our branding because she heard I had been castrating calves, and she thought this was not proper for a girl to do!

Once I recovered from the shock of this ridiculous revelation, I was finally able to give it the "Burnett treatment" and laugh about it when I related the story to my family.

Mother had a glorious time shopping for my clothes for the next few days after we found an apartment. It was actually her first and last act of rebellion against the male domination. My new wardrobe consisted entirely of organdie dresses with wide belts, huge bows, and puffed sleeves. When I tried on the first one, Mother stood back, smiling.

"Now you look like my own sweet little girl," she glowed.

Who? ME?

Tears filled my eyes. Mother gave me a hug, completely misinterpreting my reaction as tears of gratitude over my new wardrobe when actually I was thinking how ridiculous I looked in dresses that were appropriate for what I really was, an eleven-year-old girl who was being thrust into a world of more sophisticated fourteen- and fifteen-year-olds who had long since passed the age when they wore ruffles.

Mother gave me a hug. Lucky for me, she could not see the expression on my face.

When school started, I wore the organdie dresses for a few months because I loved my mother very much, but most of the time I longed for my Levis. As quickly as possible after my last class of the day, I would make a mad dash to our nearby apartment where I changed into more comfortable clothes, offering the explanation that I was going to the gym for an hour or so. Or perhaps I said I was going to the gym in an HOUR or so.

I made no attempt to invade the world of the "town girls" but because I had my first real crush on one of the football players, my after-school hours were often spent watching their practice in a large lot behind the school. Even without the organdie dresses, it was soon apparent that I was making a fool of myself and if he was ever aware of the smitten child who kept following him around, he gave no indication.

When football season ended, I again began a search for a niche that might allow me to become a small part of something, anything, if only to occupy my time between the end of the classroom hours and the time I returned to our apartment for supper and my evening study period. All of the big plans for a normal family life soon went by the wayside when my parents again began spending as much time out of town as they did in their new roles as model parents. On occasion, I stayed with my mother's friend Mabel, sometimes a night at Johnson's Hotel, and other times with a woman friend who was paid by the hour to "baby sit."

Even when my folks were home, I had a problem with being able to study at night. Almost daily they had friends over to play cards, drink home-brew (or even some of the recently "legalized" booze now that Prohibition had ended), or just "party" until late at night. The one-bedroom apartment had a kitchen, dining area and an enormous closet next to the living room in which they had inserted a narrow two-layered mattress. That was my room. It was difficult to study when their company became too noisy, and it was actually kind of a relief for me whenever my folks were gone for a few days.

I was fascinated with Spain for some reason, even though I did not know exactly where it was located. Because of this, I took the two years of Latin that was required before they would allow me to take any other foreign language. Somewhere in Mother's background there had been instilled the idea that only Latin was appropriate for a young woman's proper education so I was stuck with a Home-Ec class which was a total waste of time. (Even with this road-block, I did eventually write several Spanish/English puzzle books and a History of Mexico in Spanish, all of which were published by a text-book company later in my life, although I still have never attended a class in Spanish!)

I struggled with algebra but did extremely well in geometry and actually had the second highest score in the state in the geometry test given to all Montana students enrolled in that subject. I have never been sure what this accomplished but it was good for my ego.

Still searching for a niche, I signed up for band. The only opening was for a coronet player and my folks did buy me one, although they (and several other apartment dwellers) complained so much about my evening practice hours at the apartment, I eventually dropped out. My gym classes were also pretty much of a disaster. In my first attempt at playing basketball, with the courts divided into thirds according to the rules in the '30's, the ball was passed to me and I tucked it under my arm and ran toward the basket. I had been watching the boys play football and thought that was what I was supposed to do. I was ashamed to admit to the gym teacher that I had never seen a basketball game and I was more or less "benched" even during class hours.

For the past year or so when we had come to town for supplies, I had dabbled at learning to play eight-ball at a place called The City Billiards. I discovered I was fairly good at the game, despite the strange looks in my direction the first few times I rented a table, but before long the other patrons accepted me as one of the gang. My first stop at CB's, as I soon began to think of that establishment, was a month or so after I started high school. I would play for about an hour giving Mother, or whoever was responsible for me that week, the excuse that I was again at the gym, and this gradually grew into mid-day excursions when I skipped the classes that were too boring to hold my attention.

John Brooks, owner of CB's, had long since stopped charging me for use of the tables because he stirred up a certain amount of interest in the game by setting up games for me to play against some of his other patrons. I won fairly often, but win or lose, it was a good promotional gimmick for him and a cheap way for me to practice.

I did make friends with another freshhman girl, Barbara, whose parents owned a small grocery store and who never considered herself as one of the "in" group, either, so we had that in common from the start. She played pool with me a few times until her parents caught on to the fact that the blue chalk that appeared on her blouses did not come from art class at school. Their first clue was when they remembered that she had not signed up for art.

I invited her to a movie one Sunday afternoon and her parents said she could go if we would lock up the store before we left because they were going on a picnic. The store was an extension of their home with a doorway at the back of the store that led into their kitchen. I watched her go through a very complicated procedure of locking doors and windows, placing a metal rod through some kind of gadget across the front door of the store, taking the money out of the cash register and hiding it in a bag which she placed in the corner of her clothes closet under her gym bag. Then she sat down to write a note to her parents. As I read over her shoulder, I could not believe what she was doing. She not only left the key to the store right there on the table with her note but she wrote this very detailed letter explaining where she hid the money bag. I had a rough time keeping a straight face as I realized this was their standard procedure for locking the store and they saw nothing wrong with the way they did it. It would be bad enough if someone broke into the house but as it was, she did not even lock the front door when we left. To this day I've often wondered if I should not have pointed out to her that she was "aiding and abetting" but at the time I figured it was none of my business.

Barbara did spend one weekend at the ranch with me when my parents were away. Grandpa put each of us on one end of a two-man saw and we cut logs nearly all day Saturday and Sunday. She did not visit me again.

That entire winter I dreamed of becoming a professional rodeo rider. I subscribed to *Hoofs & Horns*, a rodeo magazine, and saw my image in each picture of the glamorous girls in fringed leather skirts or bell-bottomed pants and hand embroidered blouses. My drab home-life seemed unbearable after only two or three brief experiences in the arena. There had been the rather awesome attitude of the spectators toward the contestants, whether the performance was good or not, that made me feel special. Even the minimum sums I had earned completely outweighed the memory of the hard ground.

In a few months it was rodeo time again. Sneaking away was more complicated that summer with my folks spending more time at the ranch, but I did manage to ride a few steers and earn enough to make me feel almost professional. Already that life was beginning to get under my black-and-blue skin.

During my sophomore year, "rodeo" was treated like a nasty word in our house. Before that, someone was always discussing past-present-and-future shows around the state because of gambling opportunities available to Clint and his friends, but things got so bad in their attempts to keep the information from me that they were practically passing notes under the table whenever a trip was planned.

I thought maybe I should go along with my folks' wishes and at least consider an alternate profession. During those years, pool playing offered little future for women except as a hobby, especially when Clint managed to beat me every time we played which was a real blow to my ego. I did think there might be a future in some form of show business but when I mentioned ballet, Mother objected, saying that toe-dancing would make my legs too muscular! The very fact that I was almost as light on my feet as a buffalo cow was not included in this protest, and being a real lady, she sincerely believed her protest to be valid.

Becoming a musician did not sound quite so disastrous so I began considering a future in that field, instead. I felt I could sing fairly well, but there was little opportunity to prove it.

Piano lessons in high school might have helped but I was soon discouraged because I found I was absolutely tone-deaf to the cardboard keyboards that the school furnished for us to practice on in class. One evening at the ranch, I mentioned that I had heard about a high school senior in Lewistown who was giving private lessons on a real piano, and to my surprise, Grandpa staked me to five dollars which was enough for my first ten lessons of one-half hour each. The following Friday evening my folks volunteered to escort me to my first lesson before we were to head for the ranch for the weekend. They were aware that my piano teacher's mother was still selling home brew even though drinking was now legal and this no doubt influenced their cooperation in waiting for me. My lesson was delayed because the student ahead of me decided to extend his session to a full sixty minutes for that one day. By the time it was my turn, and that first glorious lesson ended, I found Mother and Clint in the kitchen with empty bottles stacked all over the table to show where my other $4.50 had gone!

As the saying goes, "It was nice while it lasted!"

Each winter during school I managed to trade someone out of an assortment of used musical instruments: a guitar, a harmonica, and an accordion. Then, in the spring, about the time I learned to play Saint Louis Blues on each of them, I would hear about a rodeo someplace. The coronet from band class was the first to go.

The nearest actual "hock shop" was in Billings, a hundred or so miles from our ranch, but I had worked out a deal with the music store owner in Lewistown whereby I could sell my instruments back to him for half price providing I buy the next one from his store, so off I would go in search of traveling money. I think it's safe to say I could play Saint Louis Blues on a greater number of instruments than any other non professional musician in the Northwest. Due to its size, and lack of transportability, I did finally manage to become a pretty fair piano player.

I departed from home one morning before daylight with my accordian in my arms after having left my standard note: GONE TO A RODEO. LOVE, JANE.

As mentioned before, it was about three miles to the main highway at the south edge of our range land, so my usual routine was to ride one of my horses, bareback, to the highway, hang the bridle on a fence post and spook the horse toward home before stepping onto the side of the road to hitch a ride.

On this particular trip to the hock shop, having no accordion case, I wrapped the instrument in a gunny sack and led my horse over to a water trough in the corral by the barn so I could mount with as little struggle as possible. My current saddle horse was pretty much a colt so carrying that cumbersome package while astride a bareback half bronc presented untold difficulties.

I was finally within sight of the highway and elated at my progress up to that point when the leather hook on the accordian came loose allowing it to spread-eagle in my arms. Besides jerking the reins from my hand, the eerie wail from inside the sack sounded like a den of coyotes and the colt went crazy. He reared in the air, nearly going over backwards, then he landed on all fours, doubled in a knot and began bucking.

The first lunge unseated me completely but my main concern was for the shockable accordian. I hugged the unwieldy squawk-box close to my flat little bosom and took the brunt of the fall myself. I have never hit the ground harder. I blacked out.

When I came to, my back ached, my forehead was skinned, and my arms were cramping from my death-like grip on the gunny-sack. Surprisingly, the colt was grazing nearby. And the accordian was safe.

It was impossible to catch the colt again, let alone mount him without something to stand on. Besides which, he was bound to be suspicious of anyone capable of making such weird noises so I was unable to slip his bridle off before he headed home. I regretted that his arrival at the ranch would surely give the impression that I had been thrown and I hated for Mother to be needlessly more concerned than ever, but at that point there was little I could do about it. Because all of my departures were during pre-dawn hours, Mother often admitted that she never knew whether she would find me in my bed, or a note on my pillow.

After a short walk along the highway I was fortunate in stopping a car that was headed toward Lewistown so I decided to deal with the music store this time even though they did not pay as well as the Billings pawnshop. The only local rodeo I knew for sure was being held that weekend was Winifred, a small town northwest of Lewistown. That appeared to be my best bet.

The young couple who gave me a ride must have wondered about a teenager with a bruised forehead who was hitchhiking at least fifteen miles from the nearest town and carrying a gunny sack that periodically emitted strange squawking noises. However, in keeping with true western customs they never questioned my situation or motives.

It was still early morning when my "ride" stopped at the Milwaukee train depot as we pulled into Lewistown. It so happened they were from Grass Range and had been notified of a crate at the depot that had been shipped to them in Lewistown, their nearest freight station. I waited around until they made arrangements for their crate to be sent to Grass Range on the mail truck, and I struck up a conversation with a different railroad employee inside the depot.

I asked him how often there were trains going to Winifred, trying to give the impression that my parents wondered about shipping something to relatives in that town. He assured me there was a freight train scheduled three times a week, and in fact there was one due that day. He said it would be leaving in about two hours. I thanked him for the information and said I would pass it on to my parents. I did not own a watch but I hurried toward the center of town thinking it was almost time for the music store to open.

Shortly after I collected a few dollars for my accordian, I headed back to the depot. Riding a freight train sounded like a good idea to me. I could ride for an hour or so straight through to my destination without having to stand out on the highway where I might be seen by any number of local people including ranchers I knew, or even teachers from high school.

At the depot, no railroad employees were visible, and I slipped along the far side of the boxcars that had been pointed out to me as the ones headed for Winifred. While I was wondering how to go about boarding one of them, I heard voices coming from inside the one closest to where I was standing. The door was only partially closed and I stuck my head around the corner to see who was inside. There were four young cowboys in the middle of the car arguing about whether or not they should ride the freight train to Winifred or go back out on the highway and hitch-hike. When they saw me, two of them jumped out of the boxcar on the far side. The other two came to the doorway, both talking at the same time and asking my impression of the pros and cons of "riding the rails." When I said I thought this would be an easy cheap way to make the trip, they finally decided to stay where they were and take a chance on the fact that I might be right. One of them motioned to two other cowboys who were climbing into a different boxcar when they were stopped by a railroad employee and told to leave. We ducked out of sight and stayed hidden until the train pulled out of the station about thirty minutes later. No one asked about my facial bruises so I offered no explanation.

In a short time I had begun to envy those who were kicked off before the train chugged toward its destination with a maddening lack of speed. About fifteen miles from Lewistown we puffed to a stop near some loading corrals out on the prairie. The doors on both sides of our cattle-car were wide open so we were pretty scared when someone slid just one of them closed, indicating their intentions of loading livestock into that car. We did not dare come out of our corners to see how many head were climbing the ramp, but the shouting, whip-cracking and mooing indicated the loading of a large herd. I almost laughed out loud when two old cows, two calves, a short-yearling steer (not yet one year old), a nanny-goat, and a sow pig trudged through the doorway and the panel slid closed behind them.

We immediately made a deal with the livestock to stay at their end of the car and we would do the same.

After a few more miles across the plains we felt the train jar to a stop again. We waited. It was mid-morning and the sun was beating down on the smelly stockcar. It was impossible to take a deep breath. The odor was powerful.

Bud, a young cowboy with blue eyes and a crooked grin, climbed high enough to peek out through the boards.

"I'll be a son-of-a-bitch!" Bud shouted.

Toby, the thin-faced one, was rolling a cigarette over in the corner of the boxcar. "I'm convinced," he mused. "But what's new?"

Even through the dust and grime on his face Bud looked pale when he turned around.

"We're stranded!" he squeaked. "Them bastards has gone and left us."

It was my turn to feel pale. I ran over to climb up beside Bud and peek out. In the distance I saw an engine pulling seven or eight cars. It puffed away from us laughing hah-hah-hah-hah.

My first concern was about missing the rodeo. Toby's next words reminded me we had more to think about than that.

"Kee-rist! I wonder if they'll come back here today at all?" He sounded scared and I shared the feeling.

An attempt to open the doors proved we not only had been dumped but were also locked in. Toby and Bud slumped onto the dirty straw dejectedly. I got sick in the corner. They ignored me.

When I felt better I went over to sit beside them. "They probably just dropped this car off while they went on into Roy. It's only about twenty miles."

I tried to sound cheerful.

They both glared at me. "If we'd gone ahead and hitch-hiked like we wanted to, this wouldn't have happened!" Bud snapped.

"Yeah," Toby agreed in the same tone.

I moved over near the friendly cow. "At least we know they won't leave this livestock here too long."

To avoid being completely ostracized, I came up with an idea to keep us occupied while we awaited our fate.

"Why don't we ride these cows and calves?" I suggested. "Might as well get some practice. There's nothing else to do."

To my surprise they approved. They still weren't speaking to me but we took turns riding everything but the pig. Even the goat. Most of the stock just trotted around the cattle-car, but the bigger calf, a spooky bawling steer, bucked me off over his head into a corner where the old sow had been standing. Recently. If anyone thinks pig manure smells terrible in a corral, they should wear it! I got sick again but at least my companions were speaking to me again once they stopped laughing.

Even I was getting tired of me before the engine finally returned for us several hours later and we completed the trip in a sulky smelly silence.

In Winifred, we pooled our meager finances and sent Bud into town to get us some food and inquire about entering in the riding events. While we waited, Toby got a bucket of water and helped wash the pig smell off of me as much for his own benefit as for mine.

Bud didn't come back. We knew the rodeo was getting underway because the announcer's voice carried across the flats to the freight yard where we waited.

"Well, hell!" Toby sounded disgusted. "Let's go into town anyway. Bud must know something by now. Besides, I 'm hungry."

"Okay," I agreed, trying to shake myself dry.

There was one block of saloons that actually was the town. With Prohibition recently repealed, it seemed that nearly every building was turned into a saloon. Someone had smuggled a grocery store into the area but he probably sold some leftover moonshine under the counter.

Toby and I naively checked the food dispensing establishment first, in search of Bud, then continued from bar to bar where I heard Bud before I saw him.

"This is Janie's roast beef sandwich," Bud chuckled, sipping a shot of whiskey in one hand and an' this is Bud's hamburger," he said of the drink in his other hand. We watched him order two more of our sandwiches before either of us trusted ourselves to speak.

"Dammit, Bud!" I finally exploded. I was holding Toby's arm to keep him from attacking. "You knew that was all the money we had."

Bud choked on the ice from one of our "sandwiches" when he spun around toward us. His face turned almost purple.

"But- - -but- - -but. . ." he stammered. "I did get you some food. Honest!" He handed each of us a hard-boiled egg and a small package of peanuts. See?"

I heard a snorting sound behind me and Toby shoved me aside to take a full swing at Bud. An unshaven sheepherder stepped into the punch and was knocked flat. At this point, four "locals" jumped on Toby but Bud moved in and took care of two of them. A bar-maid who had been making moves on the sheepherder for his bankroll clobbered me over the ear with her drink tray. In a daze, I took a swing at her with a beer bottle from the bar but Bud jerked me toward the door, spoiling my aim.

When my vision cleared, Toby, Bud, and I were on the street in front of the bar where noises of the free-for-all still sounded inside.

"Let's get the hell out of here," Bud suggested. He was almost sober by then.

Toby laughed, wiping blood from his nose. "With any luck, they won't even remember who started it."

We walked to the rodeo grounds. They had a makeshift rodeo office under the announcer's stand so we made our way toward it to sign up for the riding events.

A little grey-haired lady who lived in Gilt Edge where Grandpa got his mail was there with some of her nieces and nephews and she called out as soon as she recognized me. "What're you doing over here, Jane?"

"I came to ride in the rodeo," I explained, with no attempt at humility.

"Ooooh! My goodness, isn't that dangerous?"

I looked at Toby and Bud limping ahead of me, mopping blood from their bruises.

"No, ma'am," I replied. We're just getting to the easy part now."

The boys heard me and started laughing.

The rodeo promoters would not let me to sign up for the steer riding competition but they agreed to run one critter back in the chute after the other events were over and we could take up a hat-collection from the audience at that time.

Bud had won some saddle-bronc riding money that afternoon and Toby, although he bucked off of his bareback bronc, did manage to win third place in the steer riding. The purses were settled after each event, for some reason, and neither of the boys offered to share their meager winnings, so after I made a fairly good ride on a Black Angus heifer and collected a "goodly amount" of change from the audience, I did not feel bad about keeping that money for myself.

I was able to catch a ride back to Gilt Edge with the family of the grey-haired woman I talked to earlier. Several times I noticed that she was sniffing the air and I suspected that some of the pig smell remained but nothing was actually said about it.

Sonny Smith gave me a ride, double, back to the ranch from Gilt Edge, and for once I was actually relieved to be home.

# Chapter Four

With the end of prohibition, there were not as many changes in Lewistown activities as one would imagine. Where almost continuous parties were accepted as normal in some private homes, the new center of activity had moved to various new saloons, one of which was the Montana Tavern. It was common knowledge that more cattle sales and other ranch financial deals were made in that locale than any other place in town. Of the 5,000 plus residents of Lewistown, it was natural that there would be some non-drinking families but they definitely made up the minority. It was a standing joke that a certain traveling salesman had been instructed by his bosses to plan his schedule with no overnight layovers in Lewistown because he often would not get out of town for three or four days on what should have been an eight-hour stop once a month.

Mother realized she had no choice but to go along with whatever activity Clint was involved in. If, on occasion, she stayed at the ranch to finish such chores as doing the family laundry, it simply meant that Clint went into town anyway, and might not return for several days. She eventually began drinking along with the crowd and over the years it took a great toll on her health. However, during those early years she learned to adapt and quite often she even did her grocery shopping from the Montana Tavern by paying some local teenager, or a barfly, to purchase and deliver the items on her list to the first booth on the right.

Clint was always the center of attention, mostly due to his outgoing personality but I suspected the fact that he bought most of the drinks had a great deal to do with it. Although my age was never questioned. I still only drank on occasion. It was not that I was averse to the idea, but I simply did not like the taste of beer or whiskey, and I did not feel the need to prove to anyone that I could actually walk up to a bar and place my order as though I were of age. In fact, the first time a bartender asked my age I was already nearly twenty years old and had been drinking since age thirteen! I spent a lot of time hanging around the drinking crowd because during the summer months I really had no other place to go when we were in town except for a bar or the pool hall.

My impressions of Clint mainly stemmed from his attitude that it was permissible for him to do just about anything he wanted to do. I remember us heading for our parked car as we were headed for the ranch and he was carrying a paper bag full of bottled beer. About fifty feet from the car, the bag began to split open. One bottle fell out and crashed to the sidewalk. Then another. By the time the third bottle was slipping away, Clint tossed the entire bag over his head and walked on down the street as though nothing had happened.

Because of his small stature, he always managed to have a "sidekick" along to do his fighting if the occasion arose. This was fairly often since Clint had a tendency to grow weary of people as the evening progressed and his alcoholic consumption increased. One of these men who did his fighting for him, a large easy-going man named Bill Hinkley, happened to be absent on one such occasion and Clint was forced to handle the problem by himself. We were in a small bar in Roy, Montana, and as we were settling into a corner booth, a mountain of a man at the bar turned around, staggered, and slammed his beer mug across the room. It crashed into the wall right by Mother's head.

Clint jumped out of the booth after he saw Mother was not injured, squared his shoulders and straightened to his full five-foot-eleven. He patted Mother on the arm and headed for the bar.

Without saying a word, Clint stood on his tiptoes and brought a swing straight up from his knees with every ounce of his 120 pounds behind it.

The glass thrower never stopped talking.

Another from-the-knees windup caught the man right on the point of his chin.

Mother and I both flinched, but Clint's opponent kept talking.

At that point, Clint looked completely bewildered.

"God-dammit, pay attention!" he whined. "I just hit you!"

For the first time, the man seemed to realize what had happened.

"Hell, that's all right, fella! It's rodeo time. Let's have a drink."

Clint dragged himself back to the booth, looking dejected.

"Sorry, Honey! But I suppose we might as well have that drink anyway. Right?"

Although the occasional bar-room fight was fairly common, it had never occurred to me that I would have a reason to actually hit someone with my fists so the first time it happened, I was as surprised as the recipient of my action. This event was brought about when I overheard a couple of cowboys who were playing pool on a table next to mine. They were laughing about seeing Clint at the local road house where he was "making a play for" a local woman who was the secretary of the town's leading attorney. I recognized the lawyer by name because he had been Grandpa Burnett's attorney for many years. This conversation took place during late afternoon hours when I was killing time until we would leave for the ranch. I had no specific plan when I left there after finishing that particular eight-ball game, but I automatically headed across the street to the office building where I went straight to the fourth floor and headed down the hall to the lawyer's office. The secretary in question had just stepped into the hallway and was turning to lock the door when I approached. I knew her by name but asked her identity just to confirm it.

"Are you Ruth?" I asked. "I'm Clint's daughter."

She turned toward me and her face began to turn red.

"I know."

With no warning I doubled up my fist and hit her in the face. When she fell backwards into the open doorway, I think I was even more surprised than she was. I just turned and walked away without looking back.

I never discussed any of this with Mother but I'm sure somewhere down the line she must have heard about it and I often wondered if she was as pleased with the incident as I was.

I had enough credits to graduate after my junior year but at age fourteen that seemed a bit ridiculous and although I never did develop an interest in Shakespeare that year, I was still enjoying the more advanced mathematics so I stayed in school. One thing I remember about my graduation was that we were issued "cap and gown" attire and for the first time I was not self-conscious about the way I was dressed. The second thing I remember about the event was that Clint did not attend. Mother explained that he was not much interested in "that sort of thing" but I felt bad about what I considered his lack of interest.

She had tried to convince Clint that the rodeo phase of my life might end if I were to go to college, although he claimed there was no reason for a woman to have a college education.

For a while it appeared that Clint's attitude about my further education would be supported by our lack of finances until I actually had the misfortune (or fortune) to be riding on a Greyhound bus on my way home from a rodeo when we collided with a truck-load of sheep on their way to market. Sonny Smith's sister Fern also happened to be on that same bus, and the $200 reimbursement for my medical expenses for minor back injuries made it possible for me to enter Montana State University in the fall. Because Grandpa Burnett found reason to criticize anything involving sheep ranchers, he insisted that the accident had somehow been the fault of the sheep.

I am afraid the sororities and college parties did not bring about the desired magical changes my mother hoped for. The first Saturday night I returned to the dormitory a few minutes late after playing pool and drinking a couple of beers, and was not nearly ready for bed. Since the outside door was locked, I interpreted this to be an indication that no one cared whether I returned to my room or not so I returned to the pool hall and along toward dawn when my "Big Sister" from the Delta Gamma sorority located me, I was almost convinced that college life was great. Had the bartender known I was only fifteen, he probably would have been as shaken over the incident as were the college officials who allowed me to move into the sorority house the next day so they could keep an eye on me. Due to the fact that to date I was the youngest freshman ever to attend Montana University, they had made kind of a fuss over me and were willing to make allowances.

The all-night episode got me off to a bad start but I set out to seriously overcome it and I was not allowed off of the campus for several weeks. After my parole ended, I took things more seriously. I really liked journalism, had a crush on a senior from Great Falls, and could easily beat most of my opponents at Joe's Billiard Room. I made no more impression in one case than I did in the others, but I was reasonably happy until I ran out of money which actually did not take long with only a $200 bankroll to start with!

I could have worked my way through school had it seemed important enough at the time. As it was, I returned to the ranch with one-half of a semester of college to my credit. I still had one-half of a semester credit many years later when I enrolled in several classes at two Arizona junior colleges.

My parents rented another apartment in Lewistown because Clint ran a blackjack game at one of the local night clubs each weekend. By February I was getting restless and after several months of corresponding with an ex-bronc-rider, a woman who lived in Wyoming, I decided to accept her offer to break some colts at her ranch. With a new trumpet and case tucked under my arm, I caught the Billings bus. Fifty miles short of the hock shop I was forcibly evicted from the bus by the local sheriff at Roundup. Clint had been tipped off about my intentions via a phone call from the mother of one of my high school friends and he arrived in Roundup soon afterward to haul me back to the ranch. He never spoke a word to me on the entire trip.

I was banished to the ranch for a few months and each time I stuck a pitchfork into a bale of hay, I imagined the bale to be the ample back-side of that Lewistown do-gooder who had squealed about my planned excursion. Such fervid fantasies made life bearable until spring.

Once the calves were branded and the herd moved to summer pasture, there was a brief period of time before we were to begin cutting and stacking hay. When my folks suggested we attend a western celebration in Billings for a few days, I was extremely grateful for this sign that I was out of the "dog house."

For four days it rained so hard they were unable to have the rodeo in Billings so indoor sports were encouraged. I had been wearing a brand new pair of hand-made boots, which I deposited at the bar in the hotel. I had already decided they were much too pretty to wear in the rain so for our entire stay in Billings, I remained barefooted, with my pants legs rolled to my knees.

On Thursday, Clint said we might as well go home the next morning because the arena would not dry out enough for the riding events even if it did stop raining.

While we were eating breakfast at the Stockman's Café, I deliberately kept Clint's head turned away from a poster advertising a rodeo in Red Lodge, Montana, that would begin in two days. On our way to the hotel, both of us were unusually quiet.

Finally we both spoke at the same time, "Maybe I'll just hang around for one more day."

For some time we had developed a habit of tossing a coin to determine which one of us would be responsible for certain undesirable tasks at the ranch and for quite a while I went along with the fact that Clint's choice of "heads" always seemed to determine him to be the winner. This time, before he could protest, I said, "I'll take heads this time and see if it brings me luck!"

The toss won me the privilege of staying over one extra day before returning to Gilt Edge. Somehow Clint was not as moody as might be expected when he and Mother climbed into their car to depart for the ranch.

"I'll take off first thing tomorrow," I promised, carefully avoiding mention of my destination.

"Okay, Skipper," Clint agreed. "We'll hold down the fort 'till you get there."

The following morning I retrieved my boots and put them on before I headed for Red Lodge. Another week of rain and I would have been web-footed.

I caught a ride with two cowboys and their wives who made room for me in the back of their pickup truck. We arrived in Red Lodge about noon and they went straight through town to the rodeo grounds without stopping.

The Greenoughs had the entire show pretty well under control. Turk and Bill were entered in every event. When their sisters, Alice and Margie, finished riding their own broncs, they stood in front of the chutes, arms crossed, looking extremely regal and aloof as they peered out from under their ten-acre hats. (As opposed to ten gallons such as the ones worn by us peons.)

Although I was allowed to ride one wild cow, I could have carried her piggy-back and not received any attention in Greenough's home town. However, I was as awed by the famous family as everyone else was, so I just trailed around behind them, staring.

A round-faced cowboy with sad eyes had apparently been watching me. He tapped me on the shoulder and inquired, "Somethin' eatin' you, little one?"

"Sure is," I sighed. "Just hope I can be a great woman bronc-rider, someday."

His pale eyes were thoughtful when he said softly, "Maybe you won't ever be a bronc-rider, little one, but you're sure gonna be a woman! Just remember, sometimes that's more important than you'd think."

Alice Greenough motioned to him. Without another word he turned away, and followed her from the arena.

"Who's the guy with the sad eyes?" I asked a bull-rider standing nearby.

"Ain't you ever met Mister Alice Greenough?" he laughed. "Well, that's him!"

Several of my friends were leaving so I hurried to catch up with them. I thought they were going into town but instead they led me to a wild west show that was part of the carnival. The others volunteered their services, and mine, to ride the bucking stock for five dollars mount-money per head. I found myself crawling down onto a shaggy old buffalo before it even occurred to me to rebel. It was not really too difficult to keep from being thrown, but after eight seconds of straddling that razor-backed beast, I knew the in-seam measurement on my levis had increased at least six inches. It was several years before I could look at a buffalo nickel without flinching.

When all of us had collected our money, we left. Again I mistakenly assumed we were headed for town. Even though the cowboys seemed to have formed a protective circle around me, I was still jostled along the midway. I was only vaguely aware of the sing-song chant of the barkers until one of their whiskey-tenors hoarsely promised "a crisp nee-ew ten dollar bill to any young woman that climbs into the ring with Shady-Sadie-The-Wrestling-Lady." At the exact second I glimpsed frizzie-haired, 180-pound Sadie flexing her muscles for the crowd, I realized I was being maneuvered to the slaughter.

"Not today, fellas," I yelped, as I broke through the circle and disappeared into the crowd. I could hear laughter somewhere in the background, but I had no desire to stop and investigate whether the whole thing had been a joke. Best to play it safe.

I ran all the way to the nearest saloon. It was smoky-dark inside the jammed-to-capacity establishment. Using the cash-register sounds as a guide, I elbowed my way to the base of operations.

Even though I never did actually develop a taste for beer, at some point I had discovered that mixing Jim Beam with Coca-Cola produced a delightful drink that indeed improved my outlook in any given situation.

I was trying to get the bartender's attention when a one-eyed bulldogger named Ted McCrory stopped to say hello.

"Buy you a drink, Ted?" I asked, after exchanging greetings.

"No. I'll buy you one. I've got a couple of highballs waiting at my corner of the crap table."

"Craps? Here?"

"Yeah. They got craps and blackjack both—over against that far wall." His good eye rolled to indicate the direction while the glass eye pinned me down until his gaze returned to me. "Come on over. You can order your drink at the tables."

"Okay," I replied. "Maybe I'll even play one hand of blackjack."

Ted cleared a path for me on his way to the crap table. I was unable to see past him until he stepped aside to indicate an open spot for me at the blackjack table. I laid out a five-dollar bill.

"Two hands at a buck each," I said. "Okay?"

"Only room for one hand," the dealer answered. Then his head jerked up at the same time as mine did. It was Clint!

"Oh, no!" I moaned. "How. . . ?"

"Jane!" His surprise equaled mine this time. "What're you doin' here? I thought you went home."

"Nope. But I didn't know you saw that poster, too. It's a good thing Grandpa's at the ranch."

"Well, what the hell?" Clint said, grinning. "It's still raining at the ranch so there's no haying, anyway!"

I nodded agreement when he added, "Place your bet, sucker. Your money's as good as anybody's."

"I don't know about that. Is it okay if I play a two-headed quarter on the next hand?"

"What. . . ?" He sucked in his cheeks, making kind of a whooshing sound. I am sure he was beginning to think about our "coin toss" in Billings where we determined who was to return to the ranch the day before.

While Clint dealt the cards he looked from one player to the other and asked plaintively, "What's a man to do when he can't even trust his own kid?" He turned to me. "And just where the hell did you find such a coin? I could make use of one of those."

"I just got lucky. When I swiped some of your change last week, I happened to find that strange looking two-bit piece. It's no wonder I've been doing all the piddling little jobs all summer whenever we tossed to see who had to do them."

Clint pulled his hat down with the brim touching his nose and dealt the next round without saying another word.

I detoured past the crap table long enough to watch Ted lose thirty or forty dollars, then I continued on to the bar and told the bartender I had a free one coming, as promised to me by the friendly blackjack dealer.

Later in the evening Mother arrived with some friends who lived in Red Lodge. They took us to dinner, then Mother and I returned to the hotel where she and Clint had a large corner room with double beds.

"You waiting up for Dad?"

"Yes, dear," Mother answered. "He'll be here soon. . .whenever the bar closes. He said he would."

One of Mother's most admirable traits was her loyalty to Clint—or her poor memory. I was never quite sure which.

Later, when I awoke, I thought it was still night time until I uncovered my face and saw Clint sitting cross-legged in the middle of the floor with his hat tipped forward to keep the rays of sunshine out of his eyes. He had both hands full of money.

Mother was sitting in bed with two pillows at her back, her arms crossed, and her eyes snapping. Rarely did she question his actions so I was somewhat surprised.

"All right, Clint. Where were you all night?"

The hat nodded but did not reply. Mother turned to face the wall and pulled the covers over her head.

I stumbled from my bed and stood beside Clint while he stacked and counted the crumpled bills.

"How about a fiver, ol' buddy?"

He stuck out his tongue, and continued counting. I figured he was making an issue of the money to square himself with Mother, but I was also reasonably sure all of the bars had closed several hours before, except maybe the local nightclub at the edge of town.

Clint finished tallying the fives and the tens. He was just beginning on the twenties when I took a wild gamble.

"Twenty- - -forty- - -sixty- - -eighty."

"Where'd you get the lipstick?" I spoke softly so Mother could not hear me.

Without looking up, he raised his arm over his head and handed me the next twenty. He continued counting, "One hundred, one-hundred-twenty."

By the time Clint discovered there were no lipstick smudges, I was already down stairs spending some of my blackmail loot on breakfast.

On our way to Lewistown, we stopped in Billings for lunch and a gambler friend of Clint's approached him with an offer to run the gambling in a new night club at the edge of town. I was not aware of it at the time but it was soon evident that we were moving when Mother began packing most of our clothing as soon as we arrived at the ranch. It was difficult to know how Grandpa Burnett felt about their leaving since he rarely had much to say, anyway, but I had to assume he was not happy with the deal.

Our move to the city became a turning point in my life in more ways than one. It was not unusual for me feel like the odd man out because I had no contact, at first, with anyone my own age and when I finally did "connect," it is safe to say that my life was not improved by the changes that came about.

We stayed in a hotel for the first few weeks and it did not take long for me to become restless. Working jigsaw puzzles with Mother when she was not playing solitaire, and finding something to read did not keep me entertained for long. I kept the current copy of *Hoofs & Horns* folded inside a *Saturday Evening Post* but I doubt that anyone was fooled even though I read it from cover to cover until the pages were ragged.

When I expressed an interest in learning to use a typewriter, Mother enrolled me in a six-week course at a business school that was within walking distance of our hotel. The classes were from seven to nine o'clock in the evening and this gave me something to look forward to. Before the course was completed we had moved into a nice duplex in another area of town so Clint now dropped me off at the school on his way to work and I called a cab when it was time to go home. A few times I had the cabbie wait for me while I checked out a local pool hall but it was evident that they did not like the idea of a woman hanging around their establishment. Most of the players appeared to be much better than I, anyway, so I gave up.

Our new landlady lived in the other half of the duplex and the few glimpses I had of her daughter Jeri encouraged me to believe that I might at last have a friend my own age but this turned out to be more complicated than I ever imagined. Jeri was an outstandingly beautiful blonde, tall with curves in all the right places, and blue eyes that could turn icy cold when she was angry. My problem was that Jeri showed no interest whatsoever in being my friend and when my occasional attempts at a conversation were rudely rejected, I decided to forget the whole thing.

On the weekends, I was working part-time as an usherette at one of the local theaters. One evening after the last show I stopped in at a café and bar nearby to get something to eat before going home. I was surprised to see Jeri standing at the bar, completely surrounded by five or six handsome young men who were literally fighting among themselves for her attention. My first impulse was to stop and say something to Jeri. No doubt my ulterior motive was to make one more attempt at a friendship, and quite possibly set myself up to catch some of the "overflow" of good-looking admirers. As I was elbowing my way in their direction, another teenage girl stopped to say something to Jeri and with no warning whatsoever, Jeri doubled up her fist and knocked the girl down! No-one made an attempt to help the girl to her feet and they just continued to drink as though nothing had happened.

I was so shocked I just climbed onto a barstool near where I was standing and tried to understand what I had just witnessed. After a few minutes I stopped one of the waitresses who was walking past and asked her about Jeri's surprising actions.

"Oh, that's just Jeri!" she laughed. "She ain't lettin' nobody get near her bunch of pretty boys! If you got any notions along those lines, I suggest you forget about it!"

When the waitress disappeared among the crowd at the bar I did the same thing in the opposite direction. I called for a cab and decided it was wise for me to wait outside until it arrived to haul me to the safety of hearth and home."

Actually I had no intentions of trying to cultivate a friendship with Jeri, even if she happened to be a Romeo-magnet, but a few days later I learned that Mother and Jeri's mother had thought it would be nice if their girls became friends. How could I divulge the fact that I would feel safer on a steer, any time, than I would on a planned invasion of Jeri's territory? Completely without my approval the two mothers cooked up a scheme whereby Jeri and I would be taken to a party at the local Elks' Club the following weekend so we could "become friends."

The entire project was out of my hands. I had nothing that even remotely resembled party attire so Mother dressed me in her new black floor-length gown that she had never worn. Since we were almost the same size, she insisted this would be a perfect solution to the problem and I actually began to believe that maybe this party would finally give me an opportunity to meet some teens of my own age. The party was designed specifically as a get-together of teenage children of Elks' members. Jeri's father (divorced) was an Elk as were Clint and Grandpa Burnett so everything appeared to be on track at the time a taxi pulled up in front of our duplex.

I was still a bit uneasy when we arrived at the beautiful lodge that was built on a small tree-lined lake. The serenity of the entire scene soon convinced me that my fears were probably unfounded.

Yeah.

Everything was going well except that I had never learned to dance so when a nice young man about my age asked if I would like to go for a walk out on the pier, I was more than eager to accept. I had been drinking wine with the others and was feeling a bit giddy as we walked toward the end of the pier and had no reason to suspect that we were being followed. The first I knew anything was wrong was when I felt two hands grabbing my shoulders from behind and I was being hurled into the lake! As I fell, I recognized Jeri's laughter from somewhere in the middle of the teenage on-lookers.

It was fortunate that I knew how to swim because no-one made an attempt to help me crawl back onto the pier. The young man who had been walking with me apparently was not part of the "prank" but in any event he also was not going to interfere with the action that caused me to be dumped into the lake.

When I finally crawled back onto the pier and managed to stand, I had lost both of my shoes and Mother's nice new dress was already shrinking, becoming shorter and shorter by the minute. All I could think of was how to explain the incident when I went home so I sat on one of the benches located at the end of the pier and drank as much wine as I was able to wheedle from the waitresses. By the time I finally caught a cab and went home alone, all I could do was cry while trying to explain to Mother what happened to her dress, and then I vomited in the kitchen sink and passed out.

The saying, "If you can't lick 'em, join em" is not just an adage, it is the very essence of survival. Despite the disaster at the Elks' Club, I had decided it might be safer to have Jeri on my side and not antagonize her. Besides, the remote chance of capturing some of her boyfriend overflow still had its merits.

Just to be on the safe side, I signed up to work out in a local gym and even received instructions on how to punch one of those heavy leather bags that hang from the ceiling. I was really more interested in footwork, just in case.

One afternoon Jeri and I were sitting on the front steps of our duplex when I mentioned that my current *Hoofs & Horns* magazine indicated a rodeo was going to be held at Wolf Point, Montana the following week and that I really wanted to go there. Actually, I was just making conversation so I was surprised when Jeri announced that she was going with me.

"I'd like to meet some of those handsome cowboys, anyway!" she said. "When do we leave?"

Being a coward at heart when it came to women with a great right cross, I agreed to try and work something out and said I would keep her posted.

The following week I explained to my folks, "I've been thinking, I'd like to go see Grandpa this weekend. Jeri might go with me. Is that okay?"

This may sound like an out-and-out lie unless the statement is broken down into individual words. I did want to see Grandpa. But actually, I was going to a rodeo.

I had built up a small bankroll from my job as an usher and with the Burnett donation for the trip to Lewistown, the trip began to appear possible. Amazing that the ticket was almost the exact amount of the round-trip fare to Wolf Point. Such coincidences never ceased to amaze me.

Our first difficulty on arrival in Wolf Point was finding a room. Before we even left the lunchroom at the bus station, we were informed that no housing was available, even in private homes. While I was in a booth, studying the menu, I became aware that there really was an advantage to having a beautiful girl as a traveling companion. Two young highway patrolmen were hovering over Jeri while she retrieved our luggage, and they gallantly offered their hotel accommodations to her for the entire weekend.

"We'll be glad to sleep on the cots at the 'department' office," they assured her. Then one of them jerked his thumb over his uniformed shoulder toward my booth, and added resignedly, "And she can stay, too."

At the rodeo headquarters I began to question my decision to travel this far with no assurance of a job, and with the extra responsibility of another mouth to feed (to say nothing of her taste for expensive Scotch whiskey). The only encouragement offered was that I might possibly work out something in their "mount money" bareback riding event. One of the cowboys who dragged himself away from the huddle around Jeri, explained to me that there was not an actual bareback bronc riding event offered, but each saddle-bronc rider was required to ride at least one bareback bronc every day for one dollar each. This had been designed to fill out their list of events and none of them really wanted to participate.

"You oughta find at least one bronc-rider, or more, who'd be glad to turn his bareback over to you and let you have the money."

I knew that the term "mount money" referred to cash paid for just coming out of the chute on any mount. There was no judging and no competition, per se. However, the prospect of only one dollar each was certainly not very inviting but in the back of my mind I kept thinking that just maybe I could finagle one of those hat collections, or something. Also, my decision to bring Jeri along on the trip seemed to be working out great! I had never been surrounded with so many good-looking young cowhands as I was from the very beginning of that rodeo.

At the performance on Saturday afternoon, I drifted from cowboy to cowboy, asking each bronc rider if I could ride his bareback mount. Without mention of the measly amount of cash offered, I used the excuse that I needed the practice, which in fact was true.

The transactions turned out to be surprisingly easy. By the time I slowed down and took a re-count I discovered I had agreed to ride a total of eight broncs during the two-day show. Four each day. It seemed like a good time to stop negotiations. I leaned against the fence, still somewhat dazed at what I had done as I watched some cowboys shooting craps on a saddle-blanket behind the bucking chutes.

"Can you imagine them birds thinkin' we'd be stupid enough to ride them chute-fightin' barebacks fer a buck apiece?" one of the dice shooters laughed.

I walked away. No wonder it had been so easy.

By questioning different contestants, I learned that each year just prior to their annual rodeo, the cowboys in the Wolf Point area scanned the open country for green broncs that had never been inside of a corral, much less a bucking chute. No professional bucking horses for those people. From the moment the first chute gate flew open, the horses fell over backwards, ran into fences, bit, kicked, and snorted in rebellion against their treatment.

Before my first ride, Jeri arrived at the arena in time to offer a few words of encouragement(?). Her exact words were, "Ride 'em good, Jane. I'm running out of beer money."

The one-woman rodeo I put on during the bareback riding was pretty wild. I came out of the chute, bucked off, stumbled back and prepared to mount another bronc. At one point in the confusion, a tall Indian boy on a big sorrel horse loped over to me and hollered, "Hey, keed. Thet bronc you wanted is in chute number seex."

"Wait your turn, boy. Wait your turn," I gasped, and scrambled to the top of chute number four.

We stayed at the rodeo grounds until the steer riding was over and I had collected my $4 for the day.

As I limped toward the exit where we could catch a ride into town, I suggested we get cleaned up before the big dance that evening.

Jeri glanced toward my money pocket and said, "Okay. Whatever."

A hot bath soothed my poor punished body. When I stepped out of the shower, Jeri was already dressed. She was now wearing the new black Stetson that Clint bought for me in Billings. The pocket of my Levi's was turned wrong-side-out and Jeri simply glared at me defiantly. She was not aware of my cache of cash in the toe of my left boot.

For a second, I felt a wave of wild anger, then I rubbed my glass jaw thoughtfully and reached for my old brown hat to see what could be done to make it look presentable

So far, Jeri had pretty much behaved herself. That is to say, she had not yet attacked anyone or poured her drink over anyone's head, and to date my "dunk" in the lake at the Elk's Club had been my only misfortune resulting from her weird disposition. However, there were a few touchy moments on Saturday night following the rodeo.

We had been treated to several drinks at the hotel bar before we walked over to a large hall where the rodeo dance was in progress.

Someone called out to Jeri and she turned back just as I entered the building. It was so dark outside that at first I could not adjust my vision to the bright lights in the anteway, but as soon as I could see, I discovered I was one of the very few white persons in the room! I think the entire Fort Peck Indian Reservation was sardined into that small space.

As I eased politely toward the dance area, I thought about Jeri. In accordance with her usual routine, I predicted her first move would be to give someone a shove, with the intention of starting a fight and with just one look at the misleading stoic expressions around me I was assured that she would get her wish.

The outside door slammed open. Jeri stepped in, elbowed laughingly past a broad, frowning squaw, and squinted against the brightness.

I stopped breathing.

In all the time I knew her, that was the only time I ever saw fear in Jeri's eyes. She glanced quickly from blanket to blanket, then gasped weakly to the squaw beside her, "Excuse me, ma'am. It was all my fault!"

I breathed again. Jeri had heard about Custer, too.

On day two as I climbed the chute to mount my eighth (and last) bronc, Jeri called out to me. "Ride him, Jane. I'll take your picture!"

She was perched on the arena fence near the chutes, waving my new Brownie camera in the air (while focusing the attention on herself in the process). Recently I had begun carrying the camera with me with the idea in mind that photos of my rides might help promote some bronc-riding jobs in the future. Earlier that day I suggested Jeri try to get a picture of one of my rides and I stressed the fact that it was imperative that she snap the picture the instant the chute gate opened. That way the photo would show that I was still mounted.

I crawled down on a big black chute-fighting bronc that had his ears laid back, waiting for me. His powerful muscles were quivering so much that it was almost impossible for me to grip the surcingle. Or maybe it was not the horse that was shaking. After all, why in hell would he be afraid?

Just before I nodded to the gate-man I winked bravely to Jeri. I saw her bring the camera up to eye-level. The gate flew open. It was immediately evident that the black horse was not scared, even one little bit. He tossed me what felt like eighty-two feet, six-and-three-eighths inches into the air. The ground jumped up and caught me with a loud thud. I did not care much whether I got up or not.

I lay there, aching all over, wishing bronc riders were allowed to cry. An idea came to me slowly. Maybe if I pretended to be knocked out, the cowboys would make a fuss over me, anyway, the day would not be a total loss.

I waited. And waited. Finally I took a chance and peeked out of one eye to see where all the cowboys were, and the scene I witnessed hurt worse than my fall. At the exact moment I was thrown, Jeri had tumbled from the fence and every single one of the cowboys was hovering over her, offering their sympathy.

I trudged back to the chutes and made my way toward the rodeo office to await the secretary's arrival. I collected my other four dollars.

Later, when I stepped out into the street counting my money, Jeri pushed her way toward me with a friendly smile on her face. I stuffed the money into the pocket of my skin-tight Levi's where it would be safe temporarily.

While I contemplated our next move, Jeri mentioned that a couple of cowboys she had been talking to that afternoon were on their way to a rodeo in Sheridan, Wyoming, that was to begin in four days.

"They said we could ride with them and all it would cost us was our share of the gasoline. What do you think?"

At this point I really wanted to just get back to traveling alone but I knew this offer of free transportation hinged on Jeri's good looks so I nodded in agreement and we packed to travel. On occasion it is possible to get a refund on bus fares immediately, which happened in this case. I gave Jeri her share and quickly stuffed the balance deep into the old Levi pockets.

On our way through Billings, Jeri insisted on calling her home from a phone booth on the outskirts of town. When I could not talk her out of it, I dialed her home number and said, “Lewis-tow-wan, I am ray-eddy with your cay-all,” and handed her the phone.

Jeri learned from her mother that Clint had left Billings the day before and would be gone for several days. Also, she said that my mother was to join him in two or three days but she did not know exactly where they were to meet. I could only hope they had not gone to Lewistown where they would learn of my deception but decided to avoid such negative thoughts and we continued on our way south.

# Chapter Five

We arrived in Sheridan late at night and checked into a boarding-house just as though we had money. The next morning I had coffee and headed for the rodeo office. Jeri wasn't too interested in the preliminaries—just the payoff. She stayed in bed.

The rodeo promoter, a thin-faced man with high cheekbones and bright blue eyes, told me, "Sorry, little lady. We don't hire no women bronc-riders. But I've got a job fer you if you can ride relay."

"You bet!" I interrupted without thinking. "Just so I can try out the horses first."

I hoped he would give me a clue as to what was expected of me. Even though racing was included at most of the county fairs, my sole interest was in the actual rodeo events so I paid very little attention to anything outside of the arena.

At home, I only needed a horse that could outrun a cow.

"Come with me, little lady. We'll bring the horses out on the track right away."

My new boss, whose name was Barney, explained, "You don't need to change saddles, like they do in the men's relay—but then you know all that."

"Yeah," I nodded weakly. "I know all that."

"Well, these old broncs of mine. . ."

I flinched at the word broncs. I hoped it was a figure of speech.

"They been trained to pull over for your change once you start gettin' down," Barney continued.

We were in front of the grandstand, and three cowboys led Barney's relay string over to their stations.

I was just getting ready to admit to Barney that I could never mount those tall horses in a hurry, when he spoke again.

"Come on, little lady. I'll give you a leg up—then when you've gone around once, I'll holler to let you know when it's time to start gettin' off. The horse'll pull into the next station by hisself and I'll be there to catch him and give you a leg up on the next one. Okay?"

I nodded again. My mouth was too dry for me to speak. Up I went.

Barney shouted, "GO!"

We WENT! It was fortunate that I was riding a regular stock-saddle and not a standard racing rig or I would have been lost on that first sprint.

The wind, and fear, made my eyes water. My hair was streaming behind me. I kept praying the horse knew what we were doing because I was numb. In what seemed like a fraction of a second, we had completed our first lap and I heard Barney shouting.

"Start gettin' down!" he hollered. "Right there."

I looked over the point of that big bay's shoulder and saw the ground flying past. No way in hell was I about to start dismounting!

"Get down! Get down! Get down!" Barney sounded frantic.

Barney, the remaining two horses of the team, and the grandstand blurred passed on my right, as I began another loop of the track. Even as lacking in knowledge as I was, I assumed this would cost me the job. On the other hand, no racehorse man was going to get me off of that horse until we slowed to a stop.

We approached the stands for the second time.

Barney's voice squeaked with anger.

"You get down off'n that horse right now, or so help me I'll shoot you off!"

His last words came out loud and clear. By now the horse was panting, and slowing slightly. Maybe Barney did have a gun. Maybe not.

I closed my eyes, gripped the saddlehorn with both hands and "made like I was dismounting." With my left foot still in the stirrup as per Barney's instruction, I swung my right leg over and squatted on the horse's side and the bay began to pull over. For the first time, I felt some confidence. This was what the horse was trained to do.

Then my foot slipped out of the left stirrup!

I don't know how I managed to keep a grip on the horn with my feet dragging beneath the horse, but I did not let go until Barney caught the reins. I dropped to the ground and covered my head with my arms. I guess I still expected to be shot or beaten. Barney stood over me, snorting with rage.

"Get away from here! GET OUT!"

I scrambled out of reach.

"Guess this means I'm fired?"

I did not wait for his reply as I scrambled to my feet and limped away.

It took a while to get back into town. I had twisted my ankle during my sloppy dismount so I waited out on the street until I caught a ride. I limped to our room, more worried what Jeri would say than I was about my ankle.

A note and an empty room greeted me: *Heard you messed up. I'm going home. This isn't fun any more. Jeri.*

Even my throbbing foot and nearly empty pockets could not dispel the feeling of relief. That is, until I discovered that my black hat and camera had disappeared with Jeri.

A hot bath and a good night's sleep did help me partially recover from all of my buck-offs in Wolf Point and my relay race audition but there was still a problem of getting back to Billings.

I had enough money in my cache to pay for the room the next morning but I did not want to spend any of it for bus fare if I could find a motorist heading north. My first stop was at the Palace Bar because I knew Clint had worked there at different times and maybe one of his friends could help me get back home. I did not recognize any of his gambling friends but three cowboys who were recovering from hangovers convinced me that a couple of drinks would make my traveling problems seem less important. Without having had breakfast, the drinks hit me pretty hard and I was feeling real giggly when a cowboy and his wife invited me to go down the street with them where they'd treat me to a meal. On the way we were laughing and acting silly, each of us betting who could spit the furthest as we counted the squares of the sidewalk. Everything was fun until a very cranky policeman pulled us aside and announced that it was against the law to spit on the street! Even then, everything would have been all right if I had just kept my mouth shut but I had consumed just enough drinks and spent just enough miserable days with Jeri, that I proceeded to tell him off. Before I knew it, I was being hauled off to jail with my feet never touching the ground all the way to the station! The cowboy and his wife had been smart enough to keep quiet so they were allowed to go on their way.

There was no such thing as messing with photos, fingerprints, interviews or any such nonsense when the only problem was that the policeman was furious with me for giving him a bad time.

My cell was in the basement and the upper four feet of the wall was actually a row of windows that showed pedestrians from the waist down as they walked past the jail. Out of sheer boredom, I was watching the legs go by when all of a sudden I saw a familiar pair of boots. They had been designed at the Tony Lama boot factory as per instruction from Clint Burnett! It couldn't be. But it was!

In about five minutes, an officer led Clint down the aisle to my cell where he pulled up a chair and sat down to talk to me.

I was so excited that questions came pouring out of me. I wanted to know why he was in Sheridan. How did he know I was in jail? When was he going to get me out?

Answers: 1) Dealing blackjack during the rodeo. 2) The cowboy and his wife told him of my arrest. And his reply to my last question. 3) "I didn't come to get you out! I just came to visit you!"

With this last statement, he got up out of his chair and walked away.

I stared after him. I could not believe he was actually going to leave me in jail. Was it to teach me a lesson? Surely there was a better way.

I slumped down on a cot in the corner, and I was still mumbling to myself about twenty minutes later when one of the officers came to let me out of the cell. He said Clint had paid my $5 fine before leaving the building.

*(Almost thirty years later when I was living in Scottsdale, Arizona, my parents were visiting me for the winter. Clint and I often played pool at a small local bar called the Scottsdale Tavern and one evening when he was to meet me there, I saw his car pull around to the parking lot. When he did not come*

*inside in a minute or so, I went out to see what had happened. At the side of the building, there was an old cistern that had been used for water storage at one time and was now empty. It was always covered with loose boards that were not nailed down. When I rounded the corner I realized right away that Clint had accidentally bumped these boards aside and had fallen into the hole. It was only about three foot square so he was in no real danger. I turned to leave.*

*"Aren't you going to get me out of here?" he sounded panicky.*

*I replied, just before walking away, "I didn't come to get you out, I just came to visit you!"*

*After a few minutes I asked a couple of the pool players to go and help him out of the cistern and they all thought I was pretty cold-blooded until I explained to them that I was just getting even for what he did to me in Sheridan!*

*When Clint finally came inside, brushing the dirt off of his clothes, he asked me why I acted the way I did. He had forgotten about Sheridan. I had not.)*

After I got out of jail I caught up with Clint at the Palace. He said Mother was on her way to Sheridan from Billings but he said if I would actually go to the ranch, and not run off to any rodeos for awhile, he would pay my bus fare to Lewistown. This was only if he went to the bus station and put me on the bus himself. They were instructed not to give me a refund for my ticket if I tried to stop off any place other than my final destination as it was displayed on the ticket. I was not sure if they actually had that much control, but I was ready to go to Lewistown, anyway, so I agreed.

I arrived at the ranch in time to help with the second branding and to trail cattle to a new summer pasture Grandpa had leased. As long as our daylight-to-dark riding sessions lasted, I was exhausted but happy. When there was nothing left except routine ranch work, I began to get antsy again.

I heard rumors of a small one-day rodeo to be held in a small arena in the foothills near Lewistown. I thought it was about time for me to try for a bronc-riding job once more so I caught a ride into town with the last of the cowboys who had been helping us drive cattle to the summer range and would no longer be needed until next spring. When I located the rodeo promoter, he was handling all pertinent business in a back booth at the Montana Tavern.

"What are my chances of getting a job riding broncs?" I asked when I finally had a chance to talk to him.

In my mind I was already contemplating a rebuttal whenever he tossed one of the usual rejections in my face. In the past couple of years I had developed a fairly long list of arguments to counteract rejections and it was just a matter of which one I should use first.

"Sure," he replied without looking up from some papers he was sorting. "But you'll have to ride saddle-broncs. I don't like to see you little gals trying to ride barebacks and steers."

"But you don't understand, I've been riding quite a few. . ." I began with one of my standard arguments and then his words registered and I realized what he said.

"You—you mean ride a saddle-bronc?"

"Sure," he grinned. "That's what you want, ain't it?"

"Right! That's exactly what I want."

I rushed out of the Tavern without even asking how much he would pay me.

I drifted up and down Main Street telling anyone who would listen that I was going to ride a saddle-bronc the following afternoon. The indifference in some of their expressions should have deflated my ego but an equal number seemed impressed with the news and this allowed me to maintain an "ego high" until I ran out of people.

Clint had an open account at the Fergus Hotel so I rented a room there for the night. I was so excited that I could not sleep for very long at any one stretch, and in fact it did not occur to me that I would need any special equipment now that I was graduating to saddle-bronc riding. Early the next morning I made the rounds of the bars in search of a ride out to the rodeo grounds so I could take a look at what was about to be the scene of my very first saddle-bronc ride.

I might find a cowboy or two at one of the restaurants but the odds were in favor of finding someone at a saloon. At the third bar, I was approached by a tall red-haired cowboy. I heard someone call him Bert, and I remembered hearing that he worked for the rodeo promoter.

"You're Jane Burnett, ain't you?" he asked. A nice smile and bright blue eyes overshadowed an ugly scar on his right jaw.

"Yes." I nodded. Before I had a chance to ask about a ride to the rodeo grounds, he interrupted me.

"Somebody told the boss you never rode a saddle-bronc before."

"Who told him that?" I bristled.

Bert leaned closer and spoke confidentially, "It don't make no difference, no-how. It's jest that we was wonderin' if you had hobbles and reins."

"Hobbles?" I attempted to avoid sounding stupid, but there is only so much you can do with a one-word sentence.

"Yeah. Fer your bronc ride."

"The only hobbles I own are the ones I put on my saddlehorse when I let him graze."

If anyone else had laughed at me that way, I would have been really upset, but Bert seemed to be sharing the joke with me so I laughed, too.

"Come on, kid," he took me by the hand and led me out onto the sidewalk. "Let's go find a saddle shop and I'll tell 'em what ya' need. They can build it all fer you in an hour or so."

I was familiar with the store because we bought most of our riding supplies from them, but I just stood back and let Bert take over. He selected two wide straps of good latigo leather and instructed the saddle-maker to cut them to three-foot lengths, then stitch them together so the double thickness would give added strength. Two buckles were to be sewn onto the strap in a way that each of them would be about eight inches from either end. Holes were punched in the loose ends making it possible to fold them back and fasten the end into its respective buckle.

Bert took a look at my feet and said I'd better get some smaller stirrups, too, since I had such small feet. The only thing I brought from home that I thought I would need was my spurs. I learned after my very first steer rides that you needed spurs no matter what kind of a ride you were making.

"The last thing you need is to stick a foot through your stirrup and get hung up when the pickup man takes you off."

He left to go to the Montana Tavern and talk to his boss, but I just waited around the shop and watched them work on my hobbles. Several hours later, Bert returned. He did not offer any further explanation about the hobbles until I had charged the bill for the stirrups and hobbles to the Burnett account and we were back outside.

Bert held the hobbles outstretched in his hands and said, "See how there's a loop at each end when they're buckled? Have somebody fasten one end through a stirrup on the far side after your bronc is saddled in the chute, then bring the hobbles under his belly and buckle the other end into the stirrup on your side."

"But why?" I became more confused by the second. "How can you spur a horse with your stirrups tied down?"

"Women bronc-riders don't have to spur, kid. Didn't you know that?"

"But I thought. . ."

"The idea's to make it possible fer you to ride a tougher bronc. And you can, too, 'cause if your stirrups stay down next to his belly, all you gotta do is keep your feet in the stirrups and you got 'er made in the shade!"

"That sounds great!" Thinking about all of the times I had jammed my head into the hard-packed arena dirt after getting bucked off of a steer or bareback bronc, I was in favor of anything that would help me stay aboard for a change.

Bert stopped and turned toward me. He looked serious. "It ain't always as great as it sounds, kid. I used to shack up with a gal who rode saddle-broncs, and she said there was times when she'd be whippin' and poppin' till she thought her back would break, and she'd give anything to jest get loose and fall off."

"But can't you jerk your feet out any time you want?"

"Sure. But it gets to be a habit turnin' your toes out and gougin' your spurs into that cinch to try and stay on. It ain't as easy as you'd think, tellin' yourself to go ahead and buck off." Bert shook his head and shrugged his shoulders. "Don't suppose there's any use tellin' you that hobbles jest about double your chances of hanging-up in a stirrup when you do buck off. You gals all think you got the world by the ass, anyway, the first time you ride a tough bronc."

I listened attentively to the "hobbles story" but like the man said, there was no use telling me about the danger involved. All I could think about was how proud I would be the first time I rode a bronc without being thrown.

I guess Bert felt he had done his duty by warning me because he just grinned again and offered me a ride to the rodeo grounds.

We had to travel slowly over the last couple of miles of winding road that led to Blind Breed Gulch where the arena was located. When we came over the last rise and circled through the pine trees to a grassy clearing, it was hard to believe that the tranquil sheltered valley would soon be a pandemonium of screaming children, homebrew, dandelion wine, guzzling adults, honking carhorns, and frightened livestock.

Pre-rodeo time may seem to drag for those on the spectator side of the fence, but if you have bucking stock to ride and you are nervous anyway, it seems like you barely arrive at the arena before someone rushes over and says, "You're up next!"

My bronc-ride was to follow the calf-roping. Bert was saddling the small red-roan horse for me when I walked over to the chutes. He had braided some reins for me out of soft-twist rope, and explained to me that this was another advantage I had over the men who rode broncs. With two reins, the bronc was less apt to throw his head back and forth and jerk the rein away from me. Men bronc-riders were allowed only one rein.

"Come here, kid," Bert said to me, "an' I'll show you how to measure your hobbles."

He reached under the bronc's belly with a stiff piece of wire and hooked the dangling end of the hobbles. They were already buckled to the stirrup on the "off side." He slipped the strap through the stirrup on our side but did not buckle it until he explained to me about judging the right length.

"See? You grab this stirrup in your left hand and pull the slack out of the hobbles so the stirrup on the other side is tight against the horse." He demonstrated as he talked.

"Understand?"

I nodded.

"Then double up your right fist and stick your thumb straight out. Like this."

He shoved his fist against the cinch, thumb extended. "When the stirrup is out away from the horse about an inch further than the tip of your thumb, you fasten the buckle right there. Little as your hands are, you better make it two inches."

"I sure hope I can remember all this," I mumbled, more to myself than to him. I was beginning to wonder if I was overmatching myself.

Bert looked over his shoulder as he fastened the buckle. "Now if you're looking' for a cowboy to pack your hobbles and reins around the country."

A silly grin came over his face. "Naw. I guess you're still a bit young!"

My name was blaring over the loud speakers, and the announcer said my ride would be next. He was making a speech about me being a well-known lady bronc rider and it sounded great even though a bit over-done. A lot overdone.

I tied my spurs down solid to the heels of my boots, then buckled on a pair of chaps that one of the bronc-riders loaned me to protect my legs when the pickup men crowded in to take me off after the whistle. I started climbing up the outside of the chute and that little roan seemed to grow taller and taller as I got closer to the top.

"Let's see if you can spit, kid." It was Bert. I thought he had heard about my spitting ordeal in Sheridan, so I tried to oblige, but the attempt was pretty feeble.

"That's okay, kid," he laughed. "If your mouth ain't too dry to spit, you ain't really scared!"

A cowboy I did not know stood straddle of the chute and grabbed the belt of my chaps in the back so he could ease me down onto the horse. If I had any trouble, or the bronc started to rear over backwards, this cowboy's job was to jerk me up out of the way.

I squirmed down into the saddle. Bert handed me the reins. As with almost all right-handed riders, I grabbed the reins with my left hand to leave my right arm free so I could raise it in the air for balance. Bert doubled his fist and laid it on the back of the saddle-horn, then pulled the reins snug and told me to grab both of them at the spot right above his hand.

"That's a good average head when you use two reins," he explained. "But you'll learn to judge 'em fer yourself after you do more ridin'."

With my left palm facing upward I pulled the right rein between my little finger and my ring finger, then the left rein between the ring finger and middle finger. Bert twisted the reins about twice and told me to grip them in my hand with the loose ends coming out between my fist and my thumb. The dangling reins were thrown over my left shoulder out of the way.

I tried to wiggle even deeper into the saddle. I shoved both feet into the stirrups and turned my toes outward. I had to get out of there fast. They waited for me to nod. This was the clue to open the gate. They waited. I froze.

"You like rodeoin', kid?" Bert asked.

I nodded. That's what they needed.

The roan lunged into the arena. He bucked fast and kicked high, but lacked enough size to make him rough or powerful. For the first few jumps I flopped from the cantle to the swells of the saddle with no control. Then a kind of rhythm seemed to take over where my body was in kind of a rocking motion as he lunged and kicked. I was no longer flopping. I was actually riding!

Tony La Fountain, who gave me a ride to one of my first rodeos, was the pickup man. Almost as soon as I left the chute Tony rode in next to me and tried to reach one of the reins so he could take a dally around his saddlehorn and help me off of the bronc.

Clint had arrived in town just before the rodeo and on hearing I was to ride a saddle bronc, had told Tony to get me off of the horse as quickly as possible, but I knew nothing about this at the time. Since this was my first experience with any bucking animal where I actually had the feel of being in control, I was not about to allow anyone to take me off before the whistle blew.

Tony kept grabbing for the left rein and I continued to jerk it out of his reach.

"Goddam it, Tony, leave me alone!" I yelled. "I found a horse I can ride, and I'm not gonna get off." I had no idea my voice carried so far, but I guess everyone was laughing, including Tony, and I was allowed to complete my ride.

After the whistle, Tony took the left rein away from me, dallied it around his saddle horn and helped me off of the bronc before I strutted back to the chutes. I waved to the applauding crowd, and grinned at Bert.

Then, for the first time, I noticed Clint. He was sitting on the fender of a car parked near the bucking chutes. I went over to ask how he knew where I was.

"Where else? We stopped at the ranch before coming on into town and Nate was just leaving to come here. He said we'd probably find you here." He spent a few minutes opening a bottle of beer before continuing. "Agnes is in town and we're heading back for Sheridan tomorrow if you want to come along."

I could tell it was difficult for him to show any softening of his attitude toward my rodeoing, but I also suspected he might have been just a little bit proud of my ride even if he would never say so.

"I'll think about it, but there's someone I have to talk to first."

I found Bert by the chutes saddling another bronc.

"Bert." He turned his head toward me but continued tightening the cinch."I just wanted to say 'thanks', because everything was just right. I guess I'd still be sitting in the chute if you hadn't made me nod with that dumb question!"

He smiled. "Yeah, that works every time. But just remember, kid, they won't all be this easy, so don't let anybody stop you if this is what you wanna do. You'll make it."

I muttered, "'Bye," and walked quickly toward the gate. I had trouble working the latch because everything was kind of blurred. I went over to Clint's car again and told him I thought I would just stay at the ranch for awhile but that I would like to see Mother before they headed south again.

"We'll be at the Fergus Hotel until tomorrow if you want to have supper with us, or anything."

"I'll see." I walked away.

I collected my money and then decided to return to the ranch. Even a short visit with Mother usually ended with one or the other of us being a bit teary-eyed and it left me feeling as though I made things more difficult for her. Nate had come into town for the rodeo so I rode back to the ranch with him.

I am not exactly sure what prompted me to take my new hobbles and other gear to the barn when we arrived, but as soon as I started to hang up my new equipment, I noticed something that really set me back on my heels. My new rope was missing! I had spent several weeks "aging" that rope to where it felt just right in my hands. I stretched it, rubbed it with a piece of chamois to make it feel smooth, and in the evenings I practiced roping a make-shift calf that Nate put together for me. This was really a replica of a calf's head nailed on one end of a "saw horse" but it served the purpose.

But my rope was no longer strapped to my saddle! None of the men who helped us that summer would even consider taking my rope without asking. Nor would Nate. If anyone wanted to borrow any equipment, they only to needed to ask. I might have been reluctant because of my fondness for any particular piece of equipment, but I would have agreed.

This left only one person. Clint. But why would he do something like that. When I was in Sheridan I had heard that he and a couple of other gamblers were thinking about buying a night club, with gambling, on the outskirts of town, where they would have calf-roping in a small arena on the weekends. What a coup it would be to swipe my special rope and show it off at the next jackpot event, boasting that he had finally gotten the best of me!

At first I was furious. This was not funny. I took great pride in that rope, to say nothing of the amount of time spent in getting it in exactly the condition I wanted. I had no intention of letting him get away with it.

The keys were in the ranch pickup truck so I grabbed a twenty-foot length of cheap cotton clothes-line rope that was in the blacksmith shop. We often used it to hang tools from the ceiling rafters, and I made a crude honda in one end so the finished product would at first appear to be a regular lariat. Then I headed for town.

My anger gradually subsided the closer I was to town. If I was right, and Clint actually had my good lariat, I imagined how he would feel when he proceeded to display his "loot" in Sheridan and came up with a two-dollar length of cheap cotton rope!

Clint never locked his car. In those years this was not unusual and, in fact, most of the time the keys were not even removed when a person parked their automobile for days at a time. As soon as I reached Lewistown, I was able to find his Studebaker almost immediately. As I suspected, when I opened the trunk, there was my rope. Coiled exactly as it was when tied to my saddle, and not even covered with anything to keep it out of sight. I quickly made the exchange and headed back for the ranch. I must have looked a little silly driving along, by myself, chuckling all the way home.

(The next time I had occasion to talk to one of his gambler friends from Sheridan it was confirmed that Clint made a really big issue of telling them about the joke he played on me and then he pulled out the cheap cotton rope to display it to his friends and all of the calf ropers were almost hysterical in their delight at seeing that I had gotten the best of him after all!)

Bert had left a message for me at the Montana Tavern with the address of a man named Joe Henderson who would be putting on his annual rodeo in Regina, Montana, in about three weeks from that date. Bert's note said there was a good chance that Henderson would hire me to ride saddle-broncs for their two-day event, but that I should contact him as soon as possible. He said I could give his name as a reference if I wanted to because they were good friends.

Bert's note had been there for several days before I went back into town so I wrote a letter immediately and mailed it before returning to the ranch. After a week of riding to Gilt Edge every day to pick up the mail, my letter of acceptance from Henderson finally arrived with only three days remaining before the rodeo would begin.

I immediately put my gear and a change of clothes together and asked Nate to take me into Lewistown where I would stay while arranging transportation. I had no idea where Regina was located and everyone I talked to said it was in Canada. This only added to my problems.

With only twenty-four hours remaining until the rodeo began, I had no alternative but to annoy the people at the bus stop until I saw some evidence that they were trying to get me to Regina. Even at the Gem Café, which was the local bus terminal, no-one seemed able to help me even though I displayed the envelope with Henderson's name and address attached.

With time running out, I did finally hit pay dirt from an unexpected source. Several cowboys were in a booth at the Gem and overheard me nagging the manager to sell me a ticket to a town no-one could find.

"I know there is such a place," I insisted. I pointed toward the north and added, "It's right out that way."

"Ya goin' to Regina, Montana, ma'am?" a timid-sounding voice said at my elbow. It was one of the young cowboys from the nearby table.

"I'm sure trying to."

He smiled uncertainly, and twirled his hat in his hands for a minute before speaking again. "Well, we're from Billings and we're waitin' for a buddy of ours to come in on the bus from Great Falls. We'll be drivin' straight through to the Regina rodeo whenever he gets here and you're sure welcome."

One of his companions interrupted, "Always room for one more."

"But when you friend gets here, that'll be two more."

"We'll manage somehow. That is, if you're interested."

"You bet!" The suspense of waiting for him to finish was too much for me. "I'll get my gear."

I grabbed a small suitcase with my clothes and a worn zipper-bag that held my reins, hobbles, spurs and the small stirrups. When I approached the table I noticed that three of the group looked about my age. The older man with them made me feel like my levis were too tight when he looked at me, but I was reassured by the soft brown eyes of the boy who talked to me in the first place.

Not knowing how long it would be until we saw civilization again, I put my things next to their booth and headed for the counter to order a meal while we waited. They invited me to join them but I wanted it understood that I would pay my own way.

While we waited, I learned that "Brown Eyes" was Larry, and "Bold Eyes" was Ted, but the other two were names like Butch and Slick and I never could remember which was which. The bus from Great Falls was late, and when it finally did arrive, their friend was not on it so everyone paid for their food and we were on our way.

Larry understandingly opened one of the back doors of the old sedan and arranged a place for me in a corner by myself with space for one more person in the other corner with riding gear in between. Ted looked displeased but he made no comment.

East out of Lewistown, I looked off to my left and did a sort of mini-salute when we passed the southern border of Burnett land. It was getting dark by the time we headed north out of Grass Range and I no longer looked for familiar territory because this was all new to me.

At first I paid little attention to the conversation until I heard bits and pieces of an on-going discussion about the Rodeo Association of America. This information was inserted off and on during their arguments about how far north we had to go before we would reach the turn-off. Not being familiar with that area, I had no idea what turn-off they referred to but I just hoped one of them knew where Regina was.

I began to pay special attention when Ted answered some of their questions about the finer points of the RAA because all I knew about the organization was what little I skimmed over in the *Hoofs & Horns*. It surprised me how well he expressed himself when he went on to explain how it was founded in 1930 in an effort to make the various rodeo events more fair for the contestants.

“In what way?” Larry asked.

“The cowboys were gettin’ screwed, every which way but the right way!” Ted replied. Then he looked over at me. “Sorry ‘bout that, little lady.”

“No problem. But please continue. I’d like to know more about what’s going on with the big shows.”

When he explained some of the problems with the judging, for instance, this was all new to me. My biggest problem was usually just getting paid “mount money” or arranging a “hat collection” for my performances. Ted described how most of the time in the past, the judges were not even qualified to make decisions in the various events because they were selected from the townspeople and might be the town mayor, a local farmer, a saloon keeper, or just a member of the rodeo committee, with no knowledge of the rules or requirements for their particular event.

Larry interrupted, "I've heard they've been known to favor a local contestant or accept a bribe to give extra points to some local cowboy."

"Wow! So is it any better now?" It was Butch. Or Slick.

"They've helped a lot, but still got a long way to go."

Ted explained additional problems that concerned the rodeo promoters and how they mishandled the prize money at many events by promising that a certain "purse" would be added to the entry fees and then only coming up with a portion of that amount.

"Ted! You sure you know where we're going?" Larry interrupted.

"Yeah," he did not really sound too confident. "I used to chase wild horses out in this part of the country, so I know about where it is. We ought'a be coming to the Landusky turnoff before long. It'll be off to your left and then we go another five miles or so and turn right toward Regina." He sounded pleased with himself but that was only temporary.

When we actually did reach the turnoff to Regina, it was easy to see why the bus people thought I was mistaken about there being another town by that name besides the one in Canada. This particular place was so well hidden I wondered how the townspeople ever found their way home.

We had gone less than a mile before it became obvious we would have to wait for daylight before going any further. Larry stopped the car and shut off the engine. There was no need to "pull over" because we were driving along a single set of tracks out in the middle of nowhere.

The others got out to stretch, and I assumed when they went around to the back of the car, one by one, they were taking care of personal business. At first I was too self-conscious to do the same but eventually realized this was not the time to worry about being modest and I took my turn at the outdoor facility.

Each of us walked around the area to stretch our legs after the long ride. When we finally piled back into the car, Ted was now in the front seat on the right side. Larry urged him to tell us more about the RAA and I leaned forward, resting my arms on the seat in front of me.

"Have they been able to do anything about those problems?" I asked. "Is it better for the cowboys, or not?"

"Yeah, most of the time, but the cowboys had to be straightened out, too."

"In what way?"

We were all listening to Ted now, especially since this topic hit closer to home.

He said that from the very beginning, the RAA complained about some of the cowboys' personal habits and appearance. In the early years when the cowboy shifted for himself and felt no-one was interested in his welfare, he showed little interest in his own behalf. Also, he might neglect to appear for his event if a poker game or crap game was progressing to his advantage at the moment. Penalties for such no-shows were now in effect but it was up to the cowboy, himself, to improve his personal appearance.

It was almost daylight now when Larry started the car and we moved on.

"Damn!" he said, chuckling. "And here I thought I already looked pretty damned good!"

At dawn, we began following wagon trails, cow trails, and saddle-horse tracks. I did not know how the others felt, but I was doubtful we would ever find the rodeo, or even Regina, itself.

At last a cloud of dust to the north gave us a new bearing and we made a left turn that brought us over a rise and into full view of the rodeo grounds. The five bucking chutes and the fenced-in arena looked surprisingly well-built. Riders were sorting rodeo stock and a few beer stands were rapidly materializing in various locations.

Once I had located Henderson, I saw very little of my friends from Billings except to thank them for the ride. I wanted to chip in a couple of bucks for gas money, and to assure Ted I did not want to spend the night with him after the dance.

When my saddle-bronc was brought into the first chute, I began systematically getting my hobbles and reins ready while I tried to remember all of Bert's instructions.

On many occasions you lie awake the night before a rodeo and imagine each phase of easing down onto your bronc, taking your rein, and putting your feet into the stirrups. Your mouth gets dry and the fear is so real that the knots in your stomach muscles draw your knees right up under your chin. And yet, oddly enough, when you get to the rodeo and your stock actually comes into the chute, you begin getting ready for your ride and feel more like you were looking through a telescope and watching someone else perform miles away from where you are. I think most riders feel amazingly calm during this period but there is a kind of delayed reaction that does not take over until your ride is complete. Some rider's hands will shake, their lips begin to quiver, and nearly all of them want to talk talk talk—preferably about the ride they just completed, but any subject will do. There are others who don't want anyone to come near them until they have had a chance to return to normal. The physical strain is minor compared to the emotional stress. I was always one of the "chatterers" both before and after a ride.

Several cowboys helped me get my bronc ready. On the Association, the regulation rodeo saddle, we replaced the large stirrups with my small ones. I felt like I made a fairly good ride, at least until after the whistle blew. I had been watching the men broncriders when the pickup men rode toward them, and it looked easy enough the way they handed over their buckrein, then grabbed the saddlehorn and sort of floated with the bronc until they were helped onto the pickup horse or jumped over there without assistance. When I heard the whistle blow that day, I divided the reins and handed the left one to the pickup man, then I let go of the right rein and grabbed the saddlehorn. As soon as I gripped the horn, each jump sent that horse's power straight through me, from my toes on up my spine to my head (which was now snapping like the end of a whip). I took quite a beating for a few seconds until the pickup man could get me loose because I was flopping back and forth so fast he had trouble grabbing hold of me.

When I finally felt solid ground under my feet, I staggered toward the fence and leaned against it. A handsome gray-haired man came over and tapped me on the arm.

It was the trick roper who had performed earlier in the afternoon.

"Come over here where we can talk, child," he said. "I know something that'll help you."

I waited for him to continue.

"Know why you took so much punishment today?"

I shook my head.

"You understand that hobbles keep you pretty tight against your horse? Right?" He did not wait for me to answer. "Well, when you dropped your right rein and grabbed the horn, you were letting go of the last flexible support you had. Your rein."

"But the men. . ."

"The men have their feet free, child. What you have to do is hang on to your right rein, and ride right-handed until somebody can get you off the bronc. Don't ever touch the saddle-horn when your stirrups are hobbled if you can help it. My wife used to. . ."

His long fingers gripped my shoulder with surprising strength, and his eyes opened wide. He whispered hoarsely, "Oh, my God! That's Betty—that's my grand-daughter."

I turned to see what had caused his shock, and realized his granddaughter was on a runaway horse that was racing across the flat with a saddle-bronc and rider right behind her.

We both rushed toward the chutes and I heard someone explain that a small foot-gate had been left open by mistake and the bronc ran through it to open country scaring the girl's horse at the same time.

The pickup men and several other riders chased the runaways over a nearby ridge. Tension made the time seem longer than the actual few minutes it took all of them to return, with no one injured.

This man I had been talking to was so upset I did not have a chance to thank him, but I remembered his suggestion the next two days and many times in the future. After I handed the pickup man my left rein, I continued to ride with the right rein only, until I could dismount. I had learned to stay away from the saddle horn.

Later when I heard the cowboys teasing Larry, I knew it was his bronc that had "pursued" the young girl across the prairie. He looked embarrassed by their questions concerning his intentions if the pickup men had not followed. I tried to think of some way to rescue him, but he accepted the teasing so well, I stayed out of it.

After collecting my $10 for the two bronc-rides, I caught a ride back home and it was easy to see why Regina was not on any bus route.

The *Great Falls Tribune* carried a nice story about the rodeo, and a few Lewistown people who read the article stopped me on the street to comment on my riding in the big Regina rodeo in Alberta, Canada! It was the first time anyone had seemed impressed with me, so I was not about to correct them. After all, when we were following those cow trails, quite possibly we did cross over into Canada a time or two.

# Chapter Six

Two weeks after I returned from Regina, I caught a ride to Stanford again and successfully rode the same red-roan bronc from Blind Breed Gulch. By then it was almost time for the county fair and rodeo in Lewistown. The women's bronc-riding was scheduled to be a contest, so I assumed that sufficient money for my entry fee was the only requirement.

As a matter of fact, with so few women bronc-riders in the Northwest at that time, the word contest was mostly for the benefit of the spectators. The Greenoughs, Alice and Margie, would compete, and occasionally one or two others, but it averaged out so that each rider received approximately the same amount of money for each ride.

There were rumors that a rodeo queen would be chosen for the first time at a local rodeo so I rode my sorrel horse Major all the way from the ranch in order to have him available for the parade. I was not familiar with the narrow trail over the mountains from Gilt Edge to Lewistown so I made one final stop to ask directions from a member of the Dunn family whose ranch house was situated in the foothills on the Gilt Edge side. They pointed me in the right direction, but other than offering water to me and Major, there was very little conversation exchanged. No doubt they had concerns for my sanity because of the decision to make the trip alone.

The narrow road that at times was little more than wagon-widthreally took me through some beautiful country. Once I was through the trees, I entered a valley of tall grass and spring flowers that would have tempted me to dismount and spend time just absorbing the view, but it was late in the afternoon and I was not quite sure how much farther it would be into town. I stabled Major at the fairgrounds and caught a ride into town.

After checking into the Fergus Hotel, I indulged myself by buying a silver satin shirt and a pair of black gabardine pants. I wanted to be sure their queen would look nice while leading the parade. (As a matter of fact, she did look lovely. From my position near the tail-end of the parade, with the other clowns, I occasionally caught a glimpse of Her Royal Highness. She was a pretty young thing with long blond hair whose horse was led by another rider throughout the entire procession.)

After the slight I felt I had received, I consoled myself with the thought that I would make the local gunsels sit up and take notice when I was the only local cowgirl to enter the women's bronc-riding contest. I had already paid my entry fees so I headed for the fairgrounds as soon as the parade ended to prepare for my ride.

Cy Taillon, a former Great Falls radio personality who had just started announcing the Leo Cremer rodeos, came over to speak to me. His high cheek-bones and thin face reminded me of Clint, except that I could not imagine Cy with mussed hair, an unshaven face, or wearing anything but an immaculately pressed western suit.

"You are Jane Burnett, aren't you?" His thin lips scissored each word to separate it from the next, which I assumed was a result of some kind of radio announcing strategy. Although he smiled when he spoke, I almost felt I wanted to deny my identity.

"Yes. Why?"

He sounded less severe when he said, "I wanted to tell you, before I spoke to Mr. Cremer, that I found out you're only sixteen years old."

"So? What difference does that make to you? Or to anyone, for that matter?"

"Simply that you won't be allowed to ride in the womens' bronc-riding contest."

I knew I sounded frantic, but that was exactly how I felt.

"But I've have to! I've told everybody I was going to ride!"

"Sorry." I did not believe he meant it. "You haven't any business riding broncs as tough as these. Not yet, anyway."

I never knew if he said anything more. I climbed on my horse and headed for the outside gate on a dead run. Tears were streaming down my face and all I could think of was that I had to get out of Lewistown. I needed to head for the ranch where I would not have to face all of the people who had heard me brag. This time neither the money nor my bronc-riding experience were my main concerns. After being slighted in the rodeo queen selection, I simply wanted to show off for the home town folks.

And now I was facing further rejection.

It was necessary to go through Lewistown to reach the road leading to the ranch.

I was racing along the edge of the highway, and because of my tears I did not see an old sedan pulling out of a side road. They honked and swerved to keep from hitting me, but it caused Major to shy sideways and he fell on the cement. I was thrown clear, and luckily it was in the direction of the tall grass rather than the highway, so I was not injured.

People poured from the car and rushed to me.

"You okay?"

"Didja get hurt?"

"Can we help you?" They naturally assumed I was in pain. Why else would I lie face down in the grass and pound the earth with my fists?

"Just—just go away," I blubbered. "I don't want to talk to anybody. . ."

The last word was more of a wail.

I shoved a couple of people away. I suppose they concluded if I were capable of such force I was not seriously injured because soon I was alone except for Major who was nibbling grass nearby.

When my tear supply and I were both exhausted, I crawled back onto my horse and started out again. I still had to go through town but everything looked so deserted I decided to stop and have just one drink while everyone was still at the fairgrounds. I tied Major to a telephone pole in the alley behind the Montana Tavern and slipped quietly through the back door and into a dark corner booth.

The month of March had nothing on me. After several hours of solo drinking, and brooding, I stormed out of the back door of the Tavern and went out like the proverbial lion. I was going to the fairgrounds and straighten out a few people. Namely, Cy Taillon.

I crawled on Major unsteadily and reined toward the fairgrounds once more with blood in my eyes and revenge on my mind.

By the time I reached the arena nearly everyone was gone, but a lean square-jawed cowboy was sorting horses in the "catch pens" where the livestock was held after each performance.

I yelled to him, "Where in hell is that son-of-a-bitchin' Cy Taillon?"

"Over at the chutes," he answered without looking up.

I had no definite plans. Only revenge. I stared moodily across the span of the empty arena to where Cy sat perched on a chute gate talking to a heavy-set bull-dogger who was alternately nodding his head, spitting tobacco juice, and whittling on a long stick. I did not know this man's name but any time I had ever seen him between rodeo performances, he was either sharpening his pocket knife or whittling on a new piece of wood.

I make no excuses for what I did then, except to say I sincerely hope all I wanted to do was scare Cy for what he had done. I wanted to get even.

Clint's thievery being the exception, my lariat rope was always strapped onto my saddle. I seldom roped anything except calves' hind legs at our brandings but since all ranch hands carried ropes on their saddles, I figured that custom should include me.

My eyes kept going out of focus, but I unbuckled the rope strap with great deliberation, shook out a loop in one end of the rope, and tied the other end to the saddlehorn. I whipped Major across the rump and stood in the stirrups as I raced toward the chutes swinging the loop over my head. The two men ignored my approach, and this fact in itself would have goaded me on, even if there had been a moment of indecision, which there wasn't. I streaked past the two men, let the loop fly with Cy as the target, and never looked back.

When the rope gave no significant jerk, I slid Major to a stop and sort of wilted. The anger, hurt, resentment, and even drunkenness had drained from me. I slumped forward in the saddle, still facing away from the chutes, and began slowly dragging my rope toward me as I coiled it. My mind was blank. I pulled and coiled, pulled and coiled, until I reached the end. There was no hondo—only a freshly cut end!

I spun my horse around, ready to holler at the two men and ask who in hell had cut my good lariat, and it was then I focused on Cy.

He was standing beside the chutes with the loop from my rope tight around his belly.

The bull-dogger was still whittling.

I spurred toward them and saw that Cy's usually dark complexion was now a sickly grey.

"Oh, my God," I gasped.

Cy nodded weakly.

The bull-dogger wiped tobacco juice from his chin and grinned. He held his pocket-knife up and looked at it lovingly. "I always keep old Bessie razor-sharp—but she never saved nobody's neck before."

I turned and rode away. It was several months before I saw Cy again, and by that time we were able to joke about the incident, but it was definitely not funny the day it happened. Several times in the next few years I would be teased by some cowboy who heard about the near-disaster. I doubt if they really believed the story but it was something neither Cy nor I were likely to forget.

While we were trailing cattle to summer pasture back in my freshman year, a rancher from the Snowy Mountains had approached me about working with several of his two-year-old colts to teach them to "rein." He said he liked my soft hands' approach with my own horse and wondered if I would be interested in the job. At five dollars per colt, so far I had spent a couple of weeks with each one, six in all, and he had been pleased with the results. I was talking to him at the Blind Breed Gulch rodeo and he asked if I had time to take on one more colt, a bay that was a few months older than the others I had worked with earlier. He said this one proved to be more stubborn than the others and he felt I might be able to straighten him out. His colts were always broken to ride before he turned them over to me so I had the easy part.

After the Regina rodeo and my rejections in Lewistown, I took on the job of working with the bay. This proved to be a bit more of a challenge than the others and was requiring at least two hours a day of what I called "get acquainted time" before I could actually get down to the job I was hired to perform. The bay actually threw me against a corral pole and injured my pride and my tailbone, in that order. At one point I had to have Nate saddle him for me before I could get down to business.

One afternoon during the second week of struggling with the bay, I sensed there was someone else nearby and I was surprised to see four youngish cowboys standing in the shade of the horse barn. Those who have handled colts themselves possess one notable trait: they know enough to approach quietly or stand back when someone else is doing it. (On the other hand, there's my mother. I do not recall ever riding a bronc past our house without Mother suddenly appearing on the back porch at that exact moment to shake the dirt out of an armful of huge shaggy rugs.)

I recognized the stocky-built boy who approached. He peered at me between the corral poles, and my first reaction was annoyance at being interrupted. His name was Hank and I had never been able to share his high opinion of himself. For one thing, the straight black hair escaping from his hat to form stringy bangs across his forehead always filled me with the urge to get my hands on a pair of scissors.

It annoyed me to have anyone (uninvited) around when I was working with a colt, even if they remained quiet

I tied the bay to the fence and walked over to confront Hank.

"You want something?" I asked irritably.

I could tell Hank had been drinking enough to give him a newly sunburned look and make him smell like yesterday's beer. His voice was shrill when he spoke.

"We're headin' for the Landusky rodeo and some yokel at the Tavern said you might wanna go. I'm purty sure I can help you get a job ridin' broncs up there."

I could feel a faint stir of interest in spite of myself. Even Hank no longer looked quite so repulsive. Maybe it was not his fault if his hair wouldn't stay combed.

I squinted into the sun at his companions. One of them waved to me.

"Is that Sonny Smith? Let's go talk to him."

I could not understand why Sonny had not been the one to approach me in the first place. He was one of the few local people I felt comfortable with and whether he was working at the ranch or taking part in one of the local rodeos, we always had a good relationship.

(As a matter of fact, at age thirteen I actually over-extended myself in the "drinking department" for the very first time at a Saturday night dance at the Gilt Edge school house. Not knowing how to dance, I assisted Sonny in disposing of a jug of home-made dandelion wine as we sat on the hillside within earshot of the country music audible from inside the building! On my way back to the ranch, on horseback, I actually passed out. When I awoke at daybreak, my horse was grazing near a closed barbed-wire gate that had interrupted my trip and I was still slumped over in the saddle experiencing my very first hangover.)

I considered Sonny to be a good friend and when we approached the barn he stepped forward to shake hands. We exchanged greetings which included confirmation that my folks were still in Sheridan but were moving back to the ranch within a few days due to some political squabbles that had recently caused a shut-down of gambling in most of the Montana and Wyoming towns.

We began a serious discussion regarding the Landusky rodeo.

"I remember about how far it was to Landusky because we went past that turnoff on our way to Regina, but I'd still like some idea how long we'd be gone?" I turned to Sonny. "I really shouldn't leave this colt for more than a couple of days."

"That oughta do it," Sonny said, "just a couple of days."

The third teenager kept poking Sonny in the back.

"Ask her, Sonny," he said in a mock-whisper. "Ask her has she got any money!"

Sonny's face turned red and he glared at his friend.

"Aw, shut up, Jim." He looked really uncomfortable and I sensed this was the real reason he had not approached me in the first place. The others were more interested in any possible contributions I might make to their expense account than they were in having me along for the ride and Sonny wanted no part of their scheme.

"It's just that they. . ." he appeared to be really uncomfortable. "That is, you know how it goes, Jane."

"Sure, I know. I can probably dig up a little cash."

When they headed away from the corral, I led the bay colt over to the barn, watered him, and tied him in a stall. After removing the saddle, I crawled into the loft to throw down some hay and it was not until he spoke that I realized Nate had been in the back section of the barn cleaning some of the stalls.

"If you figure to go with them kids," he called to me over the top of several stalls, "what about this colt? You've got a good start on him so you don't want to start all over again."

"Yeah, I know." I really did know that Nate wanted only the best for me, but this was my own decision to make. "It'll only be a few days so if you'll just water him and toss him a little hay."

There was no response so I rounded up my hobbles and other equipment and headed for the house to pack a few things including a change of clothes.

I left a note for my folks explaining my instructions regarding the bay colt and reiterated that he could be kept in the barn until I returned.

I climbed into the back seat of Jim's old Ford sedan and we headed for Grass Range. From there, we would go north.

I tried not to be annoyed the first time Hank said, "You sure you got enough dough to buy some gas?"

I nodded without admitting I had a ten dollar bill in my left boot. Had I been completely broke, Hank and Jim might have voted to dump me out right there.

Landusky was practically another Regina, only the nothing was fifty miles farther west. Several foolhardy souls had constructed a bar, a restaurant, and a dance hall out there on the prairie, and during the rodeo the proprietor of each of these appeared to be in a state of shock at seeing real live people scrambling in and out of their establishments.

Since Hank actually did know the rodeo promoter as he claimed, he went with me to ask about a job. At first it sounded as though there was no chance for me to ride because of the lack of funds, then Jim spoke up and suggested they give me a saddle-bronc to ride and let the cowboys take up a collection.

"Gosh, I don't know." After having been paid a direct fee for my rides at the last few rodeos, I was more interested in a declared wage ahead of time if possible.

"Why not?" Hank interrupted. "We could make a killing.'"

I flinched. Bad choice of words.

The promoter spoke up then. "If it don't cost us nothin', it's okay by me. I know of a good bronc for you, if we can get 'er."

I doubt that anyone had ever before associated the word "cute" with a bucking bronc, but there is no other way to describe the little white mare called "Snowball" that was brought in for me to ride. She was about three-fourths the size of a grown horse, and had a tiny black colt at her side. In order to adjust the gear to fit, it was necessary to tie knots in the cinch, the flank strap, and the hobbles. When I threw the ends of the buckreins over my shoulder, they still touched the ground.

On my first ride, the gate was thrown open and someone spooked Snowball out into the arena where she just crow-hopped around in a small circle near the chute so she would not get too far away from her colt. No more bucking than she did I felt guilty about the boys taking up a collection from the spectators, but the $17.65 that was dumped into my hat when they finished squelched any feelings of guilt.

Food and drinks for our own group rapidly gobbled up a great deal of the afternoon's profits, but the common opinion that there's another rodeo tomorrow made financial worries seem in bad taste. I did manage to pick up an extra few dollars playing eight-ball at the bar while the rest of them were at the dance. With this new loot tucked carefully into the watch-pocket of my Levis, I slept peacefully in the back seat of the car until dawn.

I hoped I would get a different horse the next day but I found Snowball patiently waiting in the chute. Her owner was there and he assured me she generally "bucked good" as he put it, and had even thrown several of his neighbors, which put her on championship level as far as he was concerned.

We set the saddle on Snowball, then pulled the flank strap tighter than the day before. Just in case this did not make her buck harder,

I left my hobbles loose enough that I could spur her in the shoulders when the gate opened.

What I did not know was that some of the cowboys plotted to release the colt, too, as a joke. It so happened that was the exact gimmick we needed—to take the mare's mind off of her family problems. I nodded for the gate, and reached up and gouged her with my spurs. That little mare just fell apart in mid-air! Had she been big enough to do any real damage, she would have been a terrific bucking horse. I was told later that the black colt was running behind us, whinnying all the way, and playfully kicking up his own heels every few feet as he followed us. I was too busy to know it at the time.

When the pickup man took me off and set me on the ground, I became aware of the crowd. The comedy value of that bizarre performance was certainly not wasted on the audience. They laughed, whistled, honked their car horns, and paid. The hat-in-handers were on duty, and our "take" for that ride was nearly thirty dollars, which was more than the entire purse for the men's bronc-riding.

People were still patting me on the shoulder and chuckling to themselves when they left the arena an hour later.

Hank came over to me with a wide grin on his face.

"Well, Jane," he grinned, "We sure got a bankroll to take home with us, huh?"

I was not without appreciation for the collecting job all of them did for me, but I was disgusted when I learned that Hank had turned out his bronc without even competing for the day-money, just because of the good "haul" resulting from my ride.

"It so happens I'm not going home, Hank." I knew I sounded cool, but when I thought about his reason for inviting me in the first place (and now this *our bankroll* stuff) I really did not care. Besides, his stringy bangs were beginning to annoy me again.

He started sputtering, "But. . .but. . ."

"But nothing. I'll take care of the gas expenses for your trip home, then I'm heading for the White Sulphur Springs rodeo. All three of you guys won money here and I've been paying for all of our meals, so that ought to be fair enough."

At the thought of not going home I felt a momentary twinge while my conscience did battle with my rodeo-urge, but the scuffle was too one-sided to last.

I approached Sonny and told him of my intentions. He nodded, but did not seem surprised.

"By the way," I told him, "if you see Clint when you get back, will you ask him if he'd throw down another forkful of hay to that bay colt? I really will be home right after the next rodeo."

"Sure thing." He looked rather sad. "I only wish I could go with you, but I've gotta get back home."

Hank interrupted, "I think you're crazy."

Apparently sanity was not one of the basic requirements for me to be a "financial donor" because Hank accepted the cash I gave him for gas money. I glared at him until he handed it over to Jim.

With a brief wave of "goodbye" I climbed into an unfamiliar car with a different crew and headed down an unfamiliar trail. A typical finish for a rodeo weekend.

As it turned out, we had to go back through Lewistown and Harlowtown so, actually, I could have gone that far in Jim's car. Truth was, I did not want to be talked out of going on to another rodeo.

The final fifty miles of our trip was on a mountain road that seemed to be crawling cautiously ahead of us on its hands and knees in search of a safe path into open country. The crisp air tinged with the scent of pine, and the impressive beauty of our surroundings turned out to be a misleading prelude to the unkempt buildings, dirty streets, and strong sulphur odors in the town we encountered at the foot of the mountain.

Even though the people of White Sulphur Springs were obviously indifferent to the slovenly appearance of their town at the time, they certainly were all-out enthusiasts on the subject of rodeo. I have seldom seen better treatment bestowed on anyone and everyone wearing the numbered oil-cloth arm-bands of contestants.

The rodeo committee was long on interest and short on cash when I talked to them about riding broncs. I mentioned how well the collection idea worked at Landusky. They agreed to give it a try.

My rides went well, except that the pickup men tried to lift me from my first horse without taking my rein or giving me a chance to kick my feet loose from the stirrups. For either men or women riders, one of the main disadvantages of small rodeos was the lack of experience in the pickup men. Although tougher bucking-stock typified the larger shows, this was more than equalized by pickup men who knew what move to make and when to make it. Also a well-trained pickup horse that would charge right up to a bronc without hesitating was also necessary to the efficiency of the professional pickup man.

While I was getting ready to ride my horse the second day, I watched a young calf-roper named Duffy Crabtree making his bronc-riding debut. The wiry grey horse threw Duffy sideways at just the right angle to jam his foot completely through the stirrup. The bronc circled the arena at least four times dragging Duffy beneath him. The pickup men did not dare get too close or they might turn the grey back over the top of Duffy, to say nothing of the danger of their own horses stepping on him. All anyone could hope to do was slow the bronc enough for several people on foot to ease near him and hang onto the buckrein while they helped Duffy get loose. It began to look as though it was impossible to do anything to help, when Duffy's boot finally came off and he dropped to the ground, free.

Duffy was carried from the arena, dazed but not seriously injured.

Someone standing beside me gasped, "Did'ja see how many trips he made around that arena? I'll bet he made four."

"Yeah." Ever the gambler's daughter, I added, "the hard way."

I was just starting to climb up on the chute to get on my horse when I thought about the time I rode my first saddle-bronc and Bert told me that riding with hobbled stirrups almost doubled a person's chances of "hanging up." My knee caps began to quiver and my arms refused to pull me any farther. I dropped to the ground and squatted on my haunches by the chute.

One of the pickup men rode toward me. He was a burly man with thick lips and black teeth. "What's wrong over here?" he bellowed. "Ya gonna ride today, or ain'cha?"

I stood up, trying to appear indignant. "There's nothing wrong here—and you're damned betcha I'm gonna ride!" Since offense is notably the best form of defense, I attacked him in my most offensive manner. "But you just better by-God do your job today, and when I hand you that rein, take a dally with it. That's what your saddlehorn is for!"

"Okay. Okay." He held his hand in the air in a gesture of defeat. "I only asked."

I tried to overcome the effect Duffy's ride had made on my confidence, but in spite of everything, I made a better ride that day than I had the day before.

The local people donated generously, enabling me to leave town with an extra twenty dollars tucked into the Levi-bank.

A cowboy and his wife were departing for the rodeo in Pocatello, Idaho, and they invited me to travel with them.

"You bet!" I answered eagerly. I think a few extra days in the barn ought to be good for any colt. Make him easier to handle. Right?"

"What?" they asked in unison.

"Never mind. It's a long story."

I climbed into the back seat of their car and we were on our way.

At Pocatello, Idaho, I ran into the usual objection to my request for a job: no money. A friendly man named Doc Sorenson owned the rodeo stock and handled the hiring of contract performers such as trick-riders, trick-ropers, and anyone else whose work did not qualify as competition.

"Sorry, young lady," Sorenson told me. "You should have written to me a few weeks back, and I might've been able to talk the rodeo committee out of some extra loot."

"Yes, sir, I know. But a few weeks ago I didn't know for sure I'd be here—and you wouldn't have known who I was anyway."

"I guess you're right," he grinned. "For that matter, I still don't—except that a couple of the boys said you ride broncs pretty fair. I'd sure help you out if I could."

Sorenson's son, a handsome mild-mannered young man, offered to let me use his saddle-horse for the women's "reining horse" contest. The cash prizes were small but I won enough each day to pay my expenses. Although I pretended to concede defeat in my quest for a bronc-riding job, I was just waiting for the right opportunity to approach Sorenson again.

The last day of the rodeo I received my break—plus a "break" I had not counted on. One of the local cowboys drew a big platter-footed sorrel in the bareback bronc-riding and decided to turn the horse out and not try to ride it. At the time I liked to think he was afraid of the horse and I wasn't, but the truth of the matter was that the sorrel was just rough enough to be miserable to ride, and not showy enough for the cowboy to win any money.

After much wheedling from me, Sorenson finally consented to let me ride the sorrel bareback. By that time I could hardly refuse to accept his terms when he only offered to pay me $2.50. Maybe he thought the low bid would discourage me and I would stop annoying him.

I rode with a two-handhold surcingle, and the bronc barely charged out of the chute before the pickup men rode up on each side to take me off. Their intentions were all right, but the bronc surprised all of us by ducking back and sending me soaring over his head. I took a nose-dive into the dirt and was only partially conscious when I was helped from the arena. For nearly an hour I had no idea where I was, but when my mind did clear I realized there was a terrific pain in my right shoulder. A knob that looked like the jagged end of a bone seemed about to pierce the taut skin covering it.

I had heard rumors of an organization of some kind that was trying to assist the rodeo contestants with their medical expenses, but so far the insurance companies claimed the rodeo events were much too dangerous for them to become involved. I was almost as concerned with what a trip to the doctor might cost me as I was with the injury itself.

Several cowboys drove me to the hospital. I still do not know whether the hospital was just trying out a new doctor to see if he would qualify for medical school, or if they wanted to save money by not using film in the X-Ray machine (in case I was unable to pay my bill). Whatever their reasons, they kept me flattened out on a long black table and various members of the staff "tsk-tsk-ed" over what were supposed to be X-Rays. Two nurses held me down while the doctor (and I use the term loosely) tried to put my dislocated shoulder back in place. They then proceeded to windmill my arm in the air, and despite the crunching sound, the doctor looked sincerely surprised each time they sat me up and the knob reappeared on my shoulder.

I made every effort to be brave about the whole thing because the cowboys were watching. After three of the grinding sessions, when I was about to bite a chunk out of my lower lip, the doctor simply shrugged his shoulders and gave up!

"I can't make it stay in place," he said glumly, "but I'll wrap some elastic bandage around your shoulder while you're lying down, and maybe it'll be okay."

It was such a relief to have him stop, I think I would have agreed to anything short of amputation.

"We'll give you some codeine pills in case you have any discomfort," he told me, as though this were only a vague possibility. "Just pay at the front desk."

"But I can't swallow pills!"

"You will." He looked confident for the first time. "You will."

That same evening, five of us crammed into an ancient three-passenger coupe and headed for Oregon. Two of us at a time took our turn riding in the trunk of the car. The lid was tied in an open position with my buckreins. In all truth I have to admit that the doctor was right on one score: at two-thirty in the morning when the old car quit running and we had no choice but to wait until daylight for help, I not only swallowed the pills, I ate them two and three at a time!

About sun-up a farmer on a tractor appeared and towed us twenty miles to the nearest town. The garage mechanic reminded me of the Pocatello doctor. He banged on the engine with a huge crescent wrench for a few minutes, then gave up.

I bought a bus ticket.

Destination: Lewistown.

The lengthy elastic bandage kept gradually pulling tighter and tighter. When it became too painful, I would have to reach inside my shirt and unhook the tiny metal "claws" before unwrapping my shoulder. When I did this, my shoulder dropped about an inch and the end of the bone would stick up again. Unlike Humpty, I could be put together again, but it was quite a process. At each bus stop I went into the restroom, stripped to the waist, and lay down flat on a table or couch so the bones would fit back into place. Then I would re-bandage the shoulder. Occasionally, one of the other women passengers offered to help but it was something I needed to do on my own.

When I arrived in Lewistown, I immediately headed for the Montana Tavern. If my folks were in town the odds were in favor of my finding them at that location. I dreaded this, in a way, because if I admitted how badly I was injured, I knew I would be reminded about it every time I mentioned going to another rodeo. There was also this thing about the bay colt I had left tied in the barn about three weeks previously.

But home is such a nice place to heal your wounds. I had no other option.

Clint was seated in a booth with his back to the door when I entered. Mother was not with him. I adjusted the bandage, then hooked my right thumb into the front pocket of my Levis in what I hoped was a casual rather than a crippled appearance.

"Hi, Dad!" I called out, trying to sound cheerful. "I'm back!"

He finished his drink, set the glass on the table, wiped his mouth, and ordered another one before answering.

"I turned that bay colt out of the barn."

Conversation over.

I heard later that a cowboy from Billings had stopped at the ranch to see Clint about a job and had actually worked with the colt for a couple of weeks until it could be returned to its owner with "reining" no longer a problem.

I don't know why some folks are so impatient.

The secret of my injured shoulder became public domain the first morning we headed out to pick up a few cows with calves that need-ed to be de-horned. I tried to pull myself up onto my saddlehorse with just my left arm, but my awkwardness spooked him away from me and he lunged, dumping me backwards into a tall pile of manure in the area just outside of the barn window.

I tried to laugh it off but was not very successful

"I guess the old wing isn't working so good. I sort of fell on it the other day."

"I noticed," Clint said. "I'll go catch your horse."

He sounded more suspicious than sympathetic while I brushed myself off. There was an old adage in our family: ask me no questions and I'll tell you no lies, so I just nodded.

Within a week Clint had an accident. Confusing as it may seem, he was angry because a bull calf we had in our "de-horning" chute, kept trying to jump over the gate, so he (Clint) kicked him (the calf) and broke his (Clint's) foot!

In Lewistown, he told the doctor, plus any and all who showed concern, that it was the calf who did the kicking, but I could not permit such untruths to circulate the seven saloons on Main Street and I told everyone what really happened.

With Clint's leg in a cast and my right arm bound to my side with the elastic bandage, gathering cattle became quite a challenge. Each time a critter tried to leave the herd, Clint and I would both stall as long as possible until one of us had to break down and retrieve it.

My shoulder showed no improvement. While flat on my back it seemed normal enough, but all I had to do was sit upright and one section dropped down a notch again. I began to suspect my injury was not a dislocation, but my aversion to "I-told-you-so" prevented my discussing it with anyone.

One day we were all in Lewistown after the cattle had been moved to summer pasture, and I suggested we drive over to Great Falls for the weekend. As an incentive, I knew there were a couple of places where Clint could always find a poker game, and I also felt it would be a treat for Mother to escape cooking and cleaning at the ranch for a few days. I neglected to mention a rumor that the Jockey Club was looking for a singer or that I hoped to get a job there to tide me over while my shoulder healed.

"Might as well," Mother and Clint agreed.

After several "pit stops" on the way, all three of us were in pretty fair shape, alcoholically speaking, by the time we reached Great

Falls. Clint was now carrying his crutches under his arm, and I had removed the yards of annoying bandage an hour before our arrival. His usual poker games did not materialize so he went along with Mother and me to my so-called audition.

The manager of the Jockey Club assured me he needed a vocalist and said he would give me a few minutes at the microphone if we would just wait in the lounge until the band finished their first "set."

There was a cozy atmosphere about the darkened room where the flickering bulbs over the bandstand provided the only light.

"Mother, do you have any cigarettes?" I asked. "I feel kind of nervous."

Actually, I never did learn to inhale so I only smoked on rare occasions when I wanted to appear at least a trifle sophisticated.

"Just a minute, dear. I need to get this bandage of yours out of my purse."

"And now, ladies and gentlemen," the band leader announced, "we have a little lady with us from Lewistown."

Suddenly an enormous spotlight was turned toward our table. I was temporarily blinded by the glare, but I rose to my feet and stood poised to give a casual little wave to my public before approaching the microphone. The audience began tittering, then laughing louder and louder until the place was a bedlam of hysterical patrons. My eyes were adjusting to the light so I looked around to see what was so funny.

There was Mother, completely oblivious to the fact that we were in the center of the only illumination in the room, and she was frantically pawing the bandage out of her purse, hand over hand, yard after yard.

The singing job somehow lost its appeal but I crossed the dance floor as quickly as possible to draw the spot away from our table. I do not think the boss was too impressed with my voice, anyway, although he did write down my address just in case. At least the bandage act had a certain comedic value.

I tried picking up my coke-high with both hands, but my right arm showed signs of growing weaker and I had to accept the truth, regardless.

"Let's go home, Dad. I really think my shoulder is broken."

We stayed overnight in a hotel and headed for home the next morning.

Our family doctor was out of town, so Clint took me along while he had a different physician remove his cast. At first I resisted having him examine me because I recalled rumors that he had been a bit too "hand-y" with his teen-age female patients.

New X-rays definitely confirmed that my shoulder had been broken for the past three or four weeks but had knit just enough that it would be best to put a tape cast on the area rather than re-breaking and resetting the bone.

Clint became restless after his cast removal so he returned to the Tavern to wait for me. Due to their being short-handed that week, the nurse had not yet removed Clint's unwieldy leg-cast from the examining room table before the doctor began wrapping wide strips of adhesive tape from my elbow to my shoulder in a way that it would give me extra support until healing was complete. He worked from the waist upward and was almost through when he got carried away and began making some unnecessary swirl designs on my chest. At this point I smacked him on the head with Clint's cast!

I stormed through the outer office with my hat on sideways, my Levi jacket clutched around my shoulders, and my shirt under my arm, but not before I shouted back at the doctor, "You can just consider yourself lucky there wasn't still a Burnett foot in that thing when it hit you!"

We headed for the ranch to finish our two-person period of recuperation.

# Chapter Seven

As soon as the tape was removed from my shoulder, a severe case of travel-itis was beginning to set in again. Then one Sunday evening when I was with my parents at the Tom Stout family home, my vehicle of escape presented itself with no forewarning whatsoever. A vacationing couple from Hollywood, Charita and Bob, were being introduced to all of the local guests when, as it was relayed to me later, Tom's daughter Barbara added a few words of praise about my rodeo background. I was in the kitchen nibbling on some freshly baked cookies while killing time until the local movie theater opened and Charita came swooping down on me without any warning.

There is no other way to describe her actions. I soon learned that everything she did was pre-planned to make an impression and despite the fact that I shared Clint's aversion to overly dramatic personalities, I was impressed with this woman in spite of myself. No doubt the fact that she wanted to know all about my rodeo experiences did have a lot to do with my lofty opinion of her.

Charita led me into the den and introduced me to her husband, Bob. He was a quiet man, nice looking and obviously very much in love with his wife, but I sensed that he was the head of the family despite her overpowering personality. He had been talking golf with several other men who were seated at an eight-foot bar in the parlor and after acknowledging our introduction, he returned to them.

Clint did not care anything about golf at that time and with two freshly-poured drinks in hand, he wandered into the living room and handed one of the highballs to Mother before seating himself on the sofa beside her. They were waiting to visit with Barbara who was one of their closest friends but they had not counted on Charita's arrival and before they realized it they were involved in a lengthy discussion about their least favorite topic: rodeo.

Tom Stout owned the local newspaper for many years and Barbara had been collecting some of my rodeo pictures and clippings to use in an article later in the year so she displayed a few of them on the coffee table in front of the sofa where my parents were seated. Charita's immediate reaction was that someone with my talent belonged in the movies!

I forgot all about going to the theater. Charita talked about her childhood in Hawaii and, although she denied any islander parentage, her round bronze face, small dark eyes, and hip-wiggling talents suggested the probability of a native in the pineapple fields somewhere along the line. She led us to believe she was extremely active in the movie business and had numerous connections related to that industry. She sounded confident that with her as my sponsor, there would be no problem with my breaking into the movie industry. She said that it would be necessary for me to return to Los Angeles with them on Wednesday, and she would pay all of my expenses.

Even to someone like Clint who was so geared to spotting hustlers in any given situation, this did not appear to be a move that could possibly present a problem for the Burnett family. The only investment on his part would be a monthly check for $20 that would be made out to me and was for my "spending money "only.

I was so excited at the very prospect of meeting, or at the very least mingling with, the many film stars whose names rolled off of her tongue with ease, that I was already composing my acceptance speech for that time in the not to distant future when I would be awarded my very first Oscar. Their entire evening was spent discussing the possibility of my going to California. No doubt the ample supply of booze that lasted into the wee hours of the morning may have helped embellish Charita's proposal but even in the daylight sober hours, the project met with Burnett approval.

We returned to the ranch where Mother packed a suitcase for me with extra Levis and shirts as I requested, a couple of dresses, underwear and one pair of dress shoes. She made sure there was no opportunity for me to smuggle in a set of hobbles or a pair of spurs.

After that, there was little else for me to do in preparation for this new chapter of my life.

Early Wednesday morning I was delivered to Stout's home where I was to meet Bob and Charita. Mother was a bit teary-eyed and Clint actually gave me a quick hug before I climbed into the back seat of the Hudson sedan with California license plates. I did not look back as we drove away.

Throughout the trip I was mesmerized while listening to Charita's vivid word-pictures about life among the movie stars (several of whom she insisted owed their present lofty positions to her ingenuity). They took turns driving so we made the trip without any stop-overs.

My first jolt came on the evening we reached Hollywood and I learned I was not to live in a movie-type home complete with swimming-pool and wall-to-wall celebrities. Instead, they literally dumped me off at a tiny two-room cottage in the back yard of an undertaker's property, and told me I would stay there with "Auntie" for the present.

Auntie turned out to be a native Hawaiian woman who was not really a relative, but had raised Charita from childhood on the island of Oahu. I gathered from their rather heated discussion, in some language I had never been exposed to before, that she was definitely not happy with this situation.

Before her hurried departure, Charita assured me she would return as soon as she and Bob were settled into their estate again. (An estate, which by the way, I never had an opportunity to see).

With Charita gone, the stone-faced, white-haired woman behaved as though I did not exist. She did not speak to me. There was no indication as to where I would sleep. Where I should put my clothes, toiletries, or small suitcase. Or, in fact, how I would go about obtaining any food on a daily basis.

I felt that Auntie's dog, Mey-Lu, might have been friendly had we met under different circumstances, but he was as stiff-necked as Auntie in her presence. I tried to explain to him that I liked dogs, and in fact had once owned a collie named Pal when I lived in Montana, but he had died of pneumonia. After Auntie marched into her bedroom and closed the door without saying a word, I gave in to hunger pangs instead of self-pity and fried a couple of eggs. I settled for eggs mainly because they were the only items in the "Honolulu" kitchen that did not smell like garlic buttons smothered in mustard.

I finally re-crossed the imaginary line that separated the kitchen from the living-room and found Mey-Lu languidly stretched out to occupy the greater part of the only sofa in the room. This was what I assumed was my bed so I approached him feeling confident that the two of us could work out a satisfactory sleeping arrangement and I was right. The minute I curled up on the two bamboo arm-chairs I had shoved together, Mey-Lu stopped growling. His tail made a dull thumping sound against the sofa cushions as he yawned and went to sleep. I tried to explain that it was not my fault that Pal had died, but this did not seem to make a difference.

Three silent days passed before I heard from Charita again. I was usually able to establish some means of communication, even with strangers, so Auntie's indifference to my friendly overtures left me confused and hurt. I ate very little because I did not know what to do with most of the ingredients I found in the refrigerator.

Charita fluttered into the cottage that third night, her shoulder-length black hair and red sequined sarong sparkling like the rowels on a new pair of spurs. Her Hollywoodish beauty was all I needed to convince myself I should have stayed in Gilt Edge. It was obvious I did not belong in Hollywood.

"Hurry and dress, darling!" she exclaimed. "We're going to meet some delightful people tonight—important, too."

"You bet!" I exclaimed right back at her. I knew I was outclassed in every direction, but there is no way to be sure a bronc is too tough if you don't come out of the chute.

"Wait'll I sort through my suitcase."

"Suitcase? Haven't you unpacked yet?"

"No. I didn't know where. . ."

Auntie interrupted then. Her voice was so icy, I expected the words to snap into two-letter groups. "You know I don't have any extra closets."

"She speaks English—I mean, she actually speaks!" I knew this sounded silly, but they were not listening to me, anyway. By then, they were chattering away in their own whatever-it-was language again.

Charita turned to me. "Don't mind Auntie, dar1ing. She's just getting old."

"That's okay." In that morgue, I, too, was aging rapidly. "What dress should I. . . ?"

As though I had more than two to choose from.

"Wear your rodeo clothes, darling. They're so delightfully refreshing. And let's hurry, shall we? I just can't wait to get there."

It was not long before I realized that Charita's eagerness to "prowl" was the real backbone of our project, rather than her professed desire to sponsor a movie career for me. As the evening wore on, and her liquor consumption increased, she admitted to me privately that she had quite often used a series of protegees to override Bob's objection to her hanging around her former Hollywood cronies. I decided this made me sort of an imported shill, and the role did not promise much of a future.

At first I felt slighted when Charita swished through the crowded rooms and left me standing in the doorway rubbing the toes of my boots together, but as the evening crawled forward, I knew I was indeed fortunate to be ignored. Of the some fifty or so talkers at the party, there was not one listener. Even if there had been someone important enough or interested enough to try and help me, how would I go about getting them to shut up long enough for me to ask about a job? I finally hid behind a large potted plant and dozed while I waited for Charita to wiggle around the various rooms drinking with one and all. She located me after two or three hours and we moved on to a different location. Then another.

Three parties later, Charita was in no shape to "hula" and I was tired of helping her from chair to chair so I finally convinced her that we should return to Auntie's house while she was still sober enough to drive. I knew it would be impossible for me to maneuver a car in Hollywood traffic even if I understood the strange gears and gadgets in her Cadillac convertible.

On the way home she began scolding me about being so stuffy.

"Stuffy?" I grumbled. I was already disgusted with this entire situation now that I understood the real reason for my presence in

California. "Just because I don't get wall-eyed with a bunch of jerks who need a job as bad as I do? And for what? So I can tell everybody at the grocery store that I went to a Hollywood party?"

We had arrived in the undertaker's driveway and she was waiting for me to get out of the car so she could leave. Not knowing what kind of a reception I might get from Auntie if I arrived alone, I convinced her to run interference for me until I could at least get through the front door. It so happened Auntie had left it unlocked but I never felt secure about being dropped off at night until Charita talked her into giving me a key of my own. The woman never spoke a single word to me.

A couple of times that first month Charita and I went through the party routine, still under the pretense of meeting the right people. I knew by then that the drunken groups consisted solely of extras, bit-players, and wannabe's, but I still maintained a glimmer of hope that something might develop out of these excursions.

It seems funny that I never questioned the importance of apprenticeship in rodeos, like riding one-dollar mount-money steers and bareback broncs, and yet, like so many people, I naively assumed getting a break was the only requirement for becoming a movie star. Not talent, experience, or training. Just a break.

My one and only enlightening development did actually evolve out of the last time I accompanied Charita on one of her party tours. It occurred when I was seated out on the balcony of our hosts' luxurious apartment and a middle-aged cowboy name Ted came out for some fresh air. He looked as out of place as I felt and really seemed interested in my background when I mentioned rodeos. He said a "bad ticker" had forced him to quit bull-dogging right at the peak of his career so he was able to understand my desire to become a top-notch saddle bronc rider. He did seem puzzled as to why I would hang around with a bunch of phonies like the present group in attendance.

Our conversation was cut short when Charita motioned to let me know we were leaving, but he did whisper to me as I went through the door that there was a rodeo in a few days at Palm Springs.

"Might be worth checking into, kid." He winked at me and turned away.

The next morning I grabbed my suitcase, which was still barely unpacked, and left Auntie's house. When Mey-Lu romped across the lawn beside me, suddenly friendly now that it looked as though I might be leaving, I snarled at him, "One woof out of you, you fuzzy son-of-a-bitch, and you're dead meat!"

I still had most of my first $20 that Clint gave me before I left Montana so I caught a city bus to downtown L.A. and a Greyhound to Palm Springs.

When I entered the rodeo office, it was like attending a family reunion. Even better, if you're as anti-clannish as I am. It may sound far-fetched, but sometimes the sight of a cowboy hat and the smell of horse manure can be the greatest morale builders in the world.

I went from person to person, shaking hands with people I knew and people I did not know. I was grinning like a bull-rider at the "pay-window" (when he's surprised he won some money and even more surprised that he lived long enough to collect it!).

"Hi, Jane" It was Oral Zumwalt, one of the tobacco-chewing bull-doggers from Montana. "Heard you was workin' in a movie. Right?" he asked, juicily.

"Not really. I don't quite fit in with those people."

"I know what you mean. Anyway, it's good to see you."

The rodeo promoter was free for a minute, so I approached him about a job riding saddle-broncs. He said steer-riding was the best he could offer.

"Don't apologize," I told him quickly. "That beats the hell out of what I've been doing."

No explanation was necessary because the drawing began right then, to determine the bucking, roping, or bulldogging stock each cowboy had for the first "go-round."

Everyone crowded around the three rodeo judges. When a number was pulled out of the hat and read aloud, there were the usual accompanying remarks.

One of the cowboys said, "Wouldn't you know I'd get that damned dog? The son-of-a-bitch ain't bucked all year, an' there ain't no way a man can win a nickel on him, even if you was to spur his head plumb off!"

Another bull-rider leafed through a small black notebook. “Number 18? Let me see—I wrote in here that he goes into a left spin after the third jump.”

“You can’t count on it no more,” someone interrupted. “When I rode him at Salinas, he never started spinnin’ fer at least seven or eight jumps.”

Now here were some people actually talking to each other! I leaned against the wall and smiled contentedly.

I don’t think it was just my gay mood that made the rodeo seem exceptionally good. It could also have been because the crowds were more enthusiastic than usual and the applause was just as loud when I bucked off as it was when I rode. They even “Ooooh-ed and aaaah-ed” sympathetically when a glancing blow to my jaw from a steer’s hind leg actually chipped two of my front teeth.

The boy with the spinning bull had a good seat when he came out of the chute. I counted with him and saw him lean toward the inside of the spin he was expecting after the third jump. Instead, the bull continued to buck straight for five extra jumps and the boy was too far off-balance to weather the storm when it finally came. The clowns had the bull under control so even before leaving the arena the cowboy removed the little black book from his hip-pocket, and scribbled something in it. Then he walked back to the chutes shaking his head and talking to himself.

A California rodeo cowboy/promoter named Andy Jauregui was putting a group together for a two-week rodeo on the Hawaiian Islands. He was interested in having me go along to ride saddle-broncs and horseback quadrille and the idea of free passage both ways plus wages of fifty dollars a week sounded as good to me as a movie contract. Even better. I gave him Auntie’s address and phone number and he promised to get in touch with me if the deal went through.

I caught a ride back to L.A. and rode a city bus to Auntie’s house. I was glad to see Charita’s convertible in the driveway because I thought it was quite possible Auntie might have changed the locks over the weekend. She was one strange lady.

I halfway expected Charita to give me a bad time about taking off like I did, but instead she sounded quite excited when she told me about a possible chance for me to get a "walk-on" in a movie being made over at Goldwyn's. She said they needed some extras for scenes in the movie "Hurricane" and I might be able to get hired if I'd go over there that evening while they were making their selections.

I was really excited that she was actually trying to get me a job of some kind, even if only for one or two scenes. She told me I would need to have a swim suit so she took me shopping and we came home with something that I thought exposed more of me than necessary, but I had to take her word for it that the selection was right. After all, she did pay for it out of her own pocket.

That evening Charita took me to the studio and much to my surprise we drove right through the gate without a problem when she waved to the guard. She drove me over to the area where she said the "others" would be waiting, and pointed to the room where I was supposed to go. Then she drove away.

I was starting to feel a bit uneasy because there were only two "street lights" in the area between the buildings and I wondered where I would find the other women who were also there for try-outs. No doubt they were in the room Charita had pointed to, so I knocked on the door and hoped for the best.

A skinny little bald man with horn-rimmed glasses opened the door and although I did not hear any voices behind him, when he motioned for me to enter, I assumed it was all right.

"Come on in, honey," he said. "Let's see what you got!"

I looked past him at what appeared to be an office for several secretaries but there were no other people in the room. And I mean *no other people*!

"So where are they?" I asked, still reluctant to enter any further.

"Where's who?" Just the way he asked this question made me feel there was something seriously wrong.

"The rest of the girls."

By now he was trying to pull me into the room but I backed into the doorway just far enough so that he was unable to close the door behind me.

"Charita said there were others."

I still wanted to give him benefit of the doubt but not at the expense of walking into some kind of a trap.

"That's what she told you?" he laughed, "You're smarter than that, ain't you, kid?"

He grabbed my arm to pull me into the room and for a small guy, he was fairly strong. I was not about to let him close the door behind me if I could help it and I was losing ground fast.

The heel of a cowboy's boot was originally designed for the sole purpose of grasping a stirrup and holding it in place under any condition. However, it should be noted that one good sharp stomping of a boot heel onto someone's instep can be about as painful as anything imaginable. The scream that came out of the little bald man's mouth was evidence of that fact.

The instant he released his hold on my arm I spun away and pulled the door closed behind me. I wanted to run but I was still weak from the fear I had just experienced and I leaned against the outside wall long enough to catch my breath.

I was just turning to leave when another figure appeared behind me. Although he was in street clothes, he was wearing a cowboy hat and for some reason this made me feel a little better.

"Hey, little one. What's your hurry?" He sounded concerned but at that point I was suspicious of everyone, even a man with a Stetson.

When I turned toward him, my first instinct was to run but the fact that he remained a few feet away, hands at his side, made me feel like I could trust him.

Without mentioning Charita's name, in case he knew her, I explained that I had been told I could try out for a job as an extra in a movie they were making, but had been misled about what to expect.

I noticed that the lights were out in the room where the bald man was no doubt nursing a very sore instep but I was sure he was listening to our conversation.

When the man in the Stetson put his hands on my shoulders, I flinched for just a second because I was still upset about the earlier incident.

"Tell you what, little one. You come back tomorrow morning at nine and just tell them at the front gate that Stu said to let you in, and they'll give you directions how to find me. Okay?"

I was still a bit shaken but as he walked me to the front gate, he asked my name and then told me he would take care of the man with the glasses.

"He's pulled this sort of thing before, but I'll put a stop to it."

This man named Stu put me in a taxi and even paid the fare in advance, and although I never actually talked to him again, he had made arrangements ahead of time so that I was able to get my first actual job as a movie extra the next morning as promised. No further mention was made in regard to the Guild, so I assumed this was something he would handle.

When I arrived at Auntie's house I was so upset about Charita that I actually shoved Mey Lu off of the couch and made him sleep on the floor.

Because of the way I felt about Charita at that point I knew I needed to find another place to live right away, but for the present, I just wanted to get some rest and see what developed the next morning.

At nine o'clock sharp I arrived at the studio. Stu left word at the front gate that I was to be admitted and given instructions how to contact the man in charge of scheduling the stunts. I was concerned about not having a Guild card because I had overheard enough at Charita's parties to know they were required for any type of screen work a person might be hired for. Since no-one brought it up that morning, I assumed that Stu had simply by-passed that problem and it was never mentioned.

I learned that a woman named Lila Finn was the regular stunt double for Dorothy Lamour, but on that particular morning she had a cold and preferred not to do a certain scene that would require her to be hanging onto a tree for fifteen or twenty minutes while waves of cold water were being splashed onto her by a huge wind machine. Actually, replacing her did not fall into the "stunt" category because there was nothing dangerous about the scene, so they agreed to consider my job as that of an "extra" which was lower on the pay scale but perfectly agreeable as far as I was concerned. I never did actually get to see Dorothy Lamour, which was a big disappointment for me. However, I collected my $5.00 paycheck and left a thank-you note at the front gate for Stu.

My last thoughts as I headed for the bus stop were about the shopping bag that contained a brand new swimming suit. I wondered if Charita would get a refund.

I arrived back at Auntie's house about noon and I still intended to find a different place to live as soon as possible. What a relief it would be to actually have a bed of my very own, and not have to put up with any more of the weird situations in which Charita continued to involve me.

I never did tell my parents all of the weird things that happened as a result of what we thought would be a golden opportunity for me. I only shared with them the things that went well, and even though these were in the minority, I did have a few good experiences so I guess that made the effort worthwhile.

That afternoon as I walked out of the door for the last time, it suddenly occurred to me that I really needed my first check from Clint because the original twenty given to me in Montana was long gone, and even with what I had picked up in Palm Springs and my one morning of "movie work," I had very little cash to tide me over until I could find a steady job of some kind.

I figured it was almost time for the afternoon mail to be delivered and according to the length of time since I arrived in California, my check from home just might arrive any day. I did not have much faith in the fact that Auntie would save the letter for me, so I decided to hang around and hope for the best. The mail was actually delivered to the mail box of the undertaker who owned Auntie's cabin so I sat on his porch to wait for the postman. I felt somewhat uncomfortable when the owner of the main house came home for lunch. He did not ask why I was sitting on his porch with my suitcase between my legs but he gave me one of those head-to-toe looks sometimes seen on men of his profession (as though estimating my casket size) and I proceeded to move away from the house and wait in the shade of a palm tree until the postman arrived.

Luck was with me. As the saying goes, "The check was in the mail!"

When I moved into my new place which was kind of a "room and board" type setup, I phoned Auntie to give her my forwarding address and phone number. It took four calls before I could get her to listen, and even then I doubted if she wrote down what I said. I had been unable to contact Jauregui about the Hawaii rodeo and I wanted to be sure he could find me.

I worked as a car-hop five days a week but due to the fact that I obtained the job through a type of employment-service, a certain percentage of my paycheck for the first four weeks was paid to them. Anyway, tips were not too bad and having a real bed at night made it all worth while. I ate most of my meals at the drive-in, so the "board" part of my living arrangement did not make much sense, but the landlady was nice so it worked out fine.

The drive-in was just one block from radio station KFI where Stuart Hamblen and his band broadcast five mornings a week. In addition to his radio show and personal appearances, Hamblen was well known for music he composed and performed, and he also appeared in quite a few movies. In later years he wrote "This Ole House" which became a world-wide hit. I was a big fan of his band and during my almost daily visits to the studio, Hamblen occasionally allowed me to sing a song during their broadcast. He even agreed to let me join them at one of their Saturday night "gigs" if I developed an act that would fit in with the theme of that particular dance engagement.

I had seen one of Hamblen's singing guitar players, Sonny Dawson, when he made a tour with a group in Montana two years before, and as a sort of secret admirer, I hung around mostly on the chance that he might ask me for a date. He was friendly enough, but disinterested.

It was during one of my visits that I was introduced to Curtis "Cactus Mack" McPeters who had been part of the Arizona Wranglers and other musical groups, and worked in well over one hundred westerns during his lifetime. We often discussed my rodeo background but I did not think in terms of asking him for help. I was simply happy to find someone who appeared interested.

At no time had I mentioned to Cactus my reason for coming to Hollywood in the first place so it surprised me one day when he asked if I wanted to ride along while he made the rounds of a few movie studios.

This sounded really exciting but I told him that I had to go to work in about an hour.

"Just call in sick, Young-un!" he said in an exaggerated drawl. "In Hollywood, nobody works when there's a cattle call!"

He went on to explain that he was referring to auditions where everyone on the so-called grape-vine manages to get the word about scheduled auditions as soon as it is released. I knew he had been in enough westerns already that he no doubt worked through an agent, but just getting an invitation to ride along was exciting for me.

I developed a really convincing sneeze when I called my boss. I am not sure he believed me, but it was an opportunity to test my acting ability.

Cactus knew which studios were casting for westerns and we stopped at several where he spent a few minutes chatting with the various directors or cast members while I watched from the sidelines. I was fascinated.

Several busy-busy people would go bustling through the crowd, snapping their fingers and pointing at first one actor and then another until they had their quota. Then a quick about-face indicated that the rest of them were extra-extras.

Our last stop was at Cameo Pictures, a movie studio on Sunset Drive in a small building just off of Vermont Avenue. We sat together in a large central area that would be called a lobby in any other business, but in the hub of a small western studio this size it was often referred to as the "catch pen" or sometimes even "The OK Corral!"

I was sitting next to Cactus, rolling a Bull-Durham cigarette, when a thin-faced little man with a ten-hair mustache rushed toward us.

"Oooooooo!" he squealed in a high-pitched voice. "I love that western touch! Love it! Love it! Love it!"

Because Cactus had the rugged look of a typical movie outlaw, I had every reason to believe Twitters was addressing him, until I realized the squealing was aimed in my direction.

I named this unknown man Twitters because the title seemed to fit.

"Me?" I was surprised. "You mean my Levis and stuff?"

"Nuuuuu! Of course not! I mean rolling your own cigarettes!" He clasped his hands against his chest melodramatically, and looked as though he might swoon. "That kind of realism simply overwhelms me!"

"Oh, that!" I laughed. "I only. . ."

Cactus jabbed me in the ribs.

"Shore," he said in an exaggerated drawl. "This here little cow-gal is the real thing. Never smokes nothin' but roll-yer-own's."

As a matter of fact, the whole smoking thing was simply a matter of my trying to appear older than I was. I never did learn to inhale so periodic spells of smoking were mostly for show.

A well-dressed man with a brief-case under his arm motioned for Cactus to join him and they disappeared into an office on the far side of the room. Before I had a chance to ask Cactus what was happening, Twitters had pulled me out of my chair and we were hurrying in the opposite direction.

They seated me at the back of the room between two strikingly beautiful blondes who made me realize I should have remained in Gilt Edge. They were both of the California-tan, perfectly-dressed-and-made-up, beauty pageant type and before I could point out to Twitters that he had made some kind of mistake, he was already hustling toward the front of the room. He sat down at a table next to a heavy-set, perspiring man who was obviously trying to look like a cowboy but his wild-looking red shirt with some kind of steer-head design and his imitation felt hat only made him look silly.

The blondes were interviewed briefly one at a time and dismissed. I continued to watch for Cactus, hoping he would get me out of there before I was called to the front of the room for an interview that was obviously a mistake.

Twitters motioned for me to come forward. I was now close enough to read the name plaques in front of each man identifying

Twitters as Lenny and the bogus cowboy as Wilbur. I looked toward the door again. No Cactus.

"Dammit, little cow-mama, come on up here and talk to us!"

The distance to the front desk and the exit looked to be about equal, and just as I decided to make a run for it, the door opened and Cactus walked in.

"C'mon, Janey. I'll explain in a minute."

I could hear Lenny arguing with Wilbur as the door closed behind us.

When we reached the lobby, Cactus put his hand on my elbow and steered me toward the office where I had seen him disappear nearly an hour before.

The man behind the desk identified himself as Cliff Sanforth when he stood up to shake my hand.

"I'll bet you'd like to know what's going on around here," he said, smiling.

"That's an understatement! I began to think I was being kidnapped!"

With preliminaries out of the way, Sanforth began to explain to me why there had been a need for secrecy for the past hour. It seems that Cactus had mentioned me to Mr. Sanforth ten days before when they discussed a new project that Cameo Pictures was trying to put together. There would be a small role as the kid sister of the leading lady, and casting someone who looked the part and was able to do their own horseback riding or "buggy" team driving, would simplify their job of casting.

I looked from one to the other. When some of this began to soak in, I guess my state of shock showed on my face because they both laughed and assured me that this was all in the planning stages and might take some time to gel.

Cactus stood and prepared to leave, but since I was not at all sure where this conversation was headed, I asked him to stay.

"So where does Twitters fit in?"

"Twitters?" Sanforth asked.

"Lenny. I thought of him as Twitters before I knew his name!"

Both men laughed and agreed that this new name was more appropriate. Sanforth explained that Lenny must have heard bits of one of his conversations with Cactus a week or so before, and decided on his own to try and be the first one to actually interview me. In the event that something developed, Lenny would get credit for discovering me.

It sounded silly, but that was Hollywood.

Sanforth explained the situation to me and what it boiled down to was that Cameo Pictures was planning a western "serial" with filming to begin in the fall with one episode per week being shown on the screen at various selected theaters. As of the present time, there was a good possibility that I might be cast in the part he mentioned and although both of the female roles were small, as was standard in westerns of that era, it would still be a very good opportunity for me to "get my feet wet."

At first, I was too stunned to even ask questions so I sat back and listened as the situation was explained further.

First of all, I would need my parent's signatures in order to validate any kind of contract, and I assured them this would not be a problem. Until then, Sanforth explained, they would simply have me sign an "option" indicating that they had 120 days to determine if the project was a "go," as he worded it, and until that time I would be free to work for anyone at any time.

"And then?"

"And then, we would give you a permanent contract signing you to Cameo Pictures for a period of six years with a salary to be determined at that time. It's all pretty standard, and Cactus can confirm all of this for you." He turned to Cactus. "Right?"

I asked if I might talk to Cactus alone for a few minutes and we stepped outside of Sanforth's office. He said that I could hardly go wrong with the offer because I was simply assuring them that I would be available for a real contract if and when the future of the serial was confirmed. Even if it fell through, there was always a chance I might be considered for something else at a later date.

I returned to Sanforth's office, alone, and signed my part of the option. I was given the paper-work to send to Montana, and with hand-shakes all around I walked out of there a member of the movie business!

Almost.

I thanked Cactus for his part in what had just happened but secretly I was glad when we returned to the radio station and I could go back to my room to try and absorb what had taken place that afternoon.

I continued working at the drive-in and spent my off-hours learning a few rope-spinning tricks. When I felt ready, I took Hamblen up on his offer to let me perform on stage at one of the Saturday night dances where they furnished the music. Although I managed the ropes well enough, my accompanying Will-Rogers-type-patter was a complete flop. I guess it was not nearly as cute as I thought it was when I wrote it.

To top that off, I was flattered when Friendly Sonny Dawson offered to drive me home from the dance, and he was so friendly I almost did not escape intact. I came to the sad conclusion that again I was out of my league.

Still no word about the Hawaii trip. Also, my folks were now temporarily out of touch, somewhere between the ranch and Sheridan, so I placed a collect call to Georgia Woodworth at the Montana Tavern and told her to let them know I had changed addresses and would contact them in a week or so.

Strange things seem to happen whenever I hear about an upcoming rodeo event. At a news' stand near the drive-in, I picked up an issue of *Hoofs & Horns* that included an article about a rodeo that next weekend in Oceanside, California. That was all I needed to get me on the first southbound bus after I finished my shift on Friday. I did not work on weekends, anyway, and my rent was paid for another ten days, so I was free to travel. For a change I actually had enough traveling money for a bus ticket to Oceanside.

I rode two steers that weekend, and even though I made it to the whistle both times, I was kicked in the thigh when I jumped off of the second one. I had a huge purple bruise from just below my hip to about eight inches above my knee, and evidence of the injury did not disappear completely for several months.

My grandmother, Elsie Burnett, and my aunt Gladys lived near El Cajon and because I had only visited with them once since my arrival in California, I decided to spend some time with them while awaiting confirmation of a job at the Lakeside rodeo in ten days. Also, I really needed to share with someone the news of my deal with Cameo Pictures. I asked that they not mention it to my parents although they rarely were in contact anyway. Mimi was happy for me. Gladys was skeptical. A Burnett trait.

As soon as I decided I definitely would not be returning to my job in Hollywood, I called to inform them and to request that they hold my final check until I returned in a week or so. I was not sure about Lakeside.

"Mimi," as I called my grandmother, was an amazingly vital little woman with a round happy face and twinkling eyes. She was twenty-five years younger than my grandfather, and after their stormy marriage ended in a separation, she made her living telling fortunes, teaching music, and selling her own home-made cosmetics door-to-door. I always enjoyed a short visit with Mimi but Gladys' and my own dispositions were too much alike for us to stay together for any length of time.

As soon as it was confirmed that I had a bronc-riding job at Lakeside, Gladys drove me to a saddle-shop in San Diego where I bought a pair of small stirrups and had some hobbles made. While I waited for the leather work to be completed, I braided my own cotton-rope buckreins with the help of one of their salesmen and Gladys did some shopping while all of this was going on. The salesman asked why I needed all this new equipment so I explained that my rodeo gear was still in Montana where Mother held onto it to keep me from rodeoing. He grinned, and nodded. I guess he understood.

On the first day of the Lakeside show I won several reining contests with a borrowed horse, and made a pretty fair ride on my bronc. The only near mishap occurred at the pavilion-dance that night when some gunsel jerked my hat down over my eyes. I took a few wild swings at everyone within reach but fortunately did not connect. Don't ever mess with my hat!

The following afternoon my bronc was saddled and ready to go as soon as the calf-roping was over. Just as the last roper raised his hands in the air to signify completion of his "tie," I turned and saw my bronc rear up and fall backwards in the chute. Someone quickly handed the ends of the buckreins to a pickup man who dallied around his saddlehorn and pulled the bronc to his feet when the gate was opened. No other event was ready to go so everybody was running around in circles. Before they led my bronc back into the chute, I saw that one of my new stirrups had been shattered.

I told the arena director that another small stirrup was an absolute necessity and I needed time to borrow one. There were several young people from the parade and the grand entry who I felt sure would be glad to help.

I realized you should never hire a prune-picker for an arena director when he wheezed nervously, "We ain't got time to borrow nothing. You gotta ride him now. Jest use a big stirrup, and shorten the stirrup leather another notch on that side."

"It's not the length I'm worried about. My foot'll go right through one of those big stirrups."

"You gotta ride him now. Get ready!"

"Okay. If you say so." I tried not to think about Duffy Crabtree being dragged all over the arena in White Sulphur Springs. Maybe if I kept most of my weight on the large stirrup, my foot would not slip through but I was not completely convinced.

"C'mon, Jane. Your bronc's ready."

They did not need to replace the stirrup that fast. I eased down onto the big crop-eared sorrel. Riding with my left hand as I always did, I automatically leaned to the right. This would put the pressure where I wanted it, anyway—on the right stirrup.

I can not speak for the mice or the men, but I know that first jump out of the chute sure raised hell with my well-laid plans! My right foot shot out from under me as if I had stepped on a patch of ice and even without the sharp edge of the top of the stirrup cutting into the calf of my leg, I knew my boot had gone all the way through. Fear hit me like a hard punch in the stomach. I was sure of one thing. I did not dare buck off of that horse!

I remember gouging the right spur into the cinch to give me some kind of leverage on that side, then I was whipped over the saddlehorn and back against the cantle. I somehow managed to stay frozen to the saddle from the waist down, in spite of the beating my upper body was taking. I could not float with each jump like I would ordinarily do.

A pickup man finally rode in beside me and started to take me off without even stopping the bronc. He had me part-way out of the saddle when my head cleared.

"For chrissakes, stop the horse," I yelled at him, "and let go of me!!"

The final calf-roper from the previous event was still in the arena, on his horse, and when he heard me yell at the pickup man he realized what was happening. He charged in on my right side, grabbed one of my reins, dallied, and jerked the bronc to a stop before the pickup man could do any more damage.

"Thanks, fella," I gasped, then slumped over the saddlehorn and fought to keep from throwing up.

When the pickup man saw how long it took them to undo the stirrup leather and get me loose, even with the bronc standing still, he looked as sick as I felt.

I staggered back to the chutes and the arena director trotted along beside me.

"See?" he chuckled. "I knew you could ride him okay with that big stirrup!"

My first impulse was to punch him in the nose.

Instead, I just sighed,"Yeah, I rode him. I damned near had to."

At Mimi's house the following morning, I could barely get out of bed. I took a few experimental steps around the room and when my back made weird cracking sounds, Gladys suggested taking me to the local bone-crusher. I survived that experience but was still very uncomfortable for a few days.

Because of the four-month term of my option with Cameo, I decided I might as well go home for awhile and discuss the studio deal with my parents at that time. When I'd had several days of rest, I could tell cabin fever was getting the best of us with three women in a small two-bedroom cabin. Mimi and Gladys left the house one morning to do some grocery shopping and to wash their clothes at a nearby laundromat. I thought it was sweet of them to include mine in this process. At first it did not occur to me that they might be helping me prepare to "hit the road" so to speak, but I began to catch on when they returned later in the day and each of them called me aside to slip me a copy of the new *Hoofs & Horns* (complete with rodeo dates.)

They did not go so far as to give me a Greyhound Bus schedule but it turned out that a northbound bus would depart from San Diego at 10:55 a.m. Rodeo Standard Time the next morning. I was on it.

During the last minute rush of boarding the bus in San Diego, I did not bother to check my small carry-on and also neglected to inquire about schedules north out of Los Angeles. I figured I would need at least three hours to pick up my clothes and my final check at the drive-in and to see if Auntie might possibly have saved any of my mail that arrived at her house. I was still hoping the Hawaii trip might develop and I did not want to leave the area until I knew something one way or the other.

Since the sign above the bus driver's head stated that he was "safe, reliable and courteous," I felt sure I could get the information from him later on. (This was before I realized he had not read the sign.) Chew-muscles bulged in his square jaw when he snatched the tickets from late-boarding passengers, slammed the door, flipped on the ignition and scooped the gearshift knob into his huge fist with one last dramatic sweep of his arm.

I sat directly behind this safe, reliable, courteous man. When he removed his cap after we were on our way, I noticed his close-cropped sun bleached hair formed white bristles on the back of his neck like the clipped mane on a rope-horse. I preferred horses.

I waited for about thirty minutes, then cautiously tapped the driver on the shoulder.

"Would you please tell me. . ."

"Yeah?" he growled.

"Never mind." It was impossible to burrow out of sight in my hard-cushioned seat but I tried. It was going to be a long ride to Los Angeles.

Even to a ranch-lubber like myself (as opposed to a plain landlubber), the immensity of the ocean was overwhelming. I was glad to be sitting on the driver's side, even if he was such a jerk, because most of the time I had a good view of the Pacific.

The uncluttered vastness had the same power as Montana's wide open spaces to make me realize my own insignificance. I considered the possibility of a worldwide "draft" wherein everyone would be compelled to spend a certain length of time by the sea or on the prairie. How could self-importance and dog-eat-dog mentalities survive in either the individual or their country after that?

I was so deeply impressed that I might have deserted the rodeo arena right then to spend the rest of my life within reach of the cool ocean spray. If only the fish didn't have such a fishy odor. . .

On the other hand, if sailors felt the same way about the smell of horses, where in hell was this "twain" everyone talked about?

The driver wheeled into an alley and slammed to a stop.

"Oceanside! Ten minute rest-stop."

I was about to suggest that he should not have hired out for his job if he hated it so much, but just then he turned to me and snapped, "Now what'd you want?"

He startled me so much that I forgot what it was I wanted to ask. I just stammered, "I, that is, I'm not mad at you!"

A young soldier who was just leaving the bus started chuckling which did not improve the situation.

I was afraid to go to the restroom after this length of time because I had no doubt that Smiling Sam the safe-reliable-courteous driver would leave without me, so I was still on the bus when a Mexican family swarmed through the doorway, assisting a small dark-complexioned woman with leathery cheeks and soft brown eyes. As soon as the señora was settled into the empty front seat next to the door, the one recently vacated by the soldier, a series of tearful "Adios-es" followed and the group departed.

The woman tenderly caressed a bright-colored shawl that covered her head and it made me wonder which of her grandchildren had presented it to her as a "going-away" gift. A cumbersome cardboard box tied with cotton rope was her only luggage, and she seemed to be trying to arrange in under her feet.

The aged have a certain sameness about them that always made me think of my own grandparents.

"Could I help you, Ma'am?"

For a second the dark eyes looked frightened. Then she smiled and said, "No gracias, señorita. 'Sta Bueno. Ees all righ'. I don't go far."

The driver returned just then, so further conversation was squelched. After one final glare at one and all, he started the engine and we were on our way.

We were on the outskirts of Compton when the señora leaned toward the driver and spoke shyly, "Señor, I wander eef you would . . ."

"What!" he yelled. "You gotta talk louder than that if you expect me to hear you."

I felt like hitting him over the head.

The woman sat back as though she had been slapped. Tears came to her eyes but she pulled the shawl tighter under her chin and began again louder.

"I wandered, señor, eef you could let me off at this next cross-road? I won' have so far to walk."

"No can do, lady. Everybody gets off at the bus depot. I'd never make my schedule if I starting making house-to-house deliveries."

I bit my tongue so hard it was almost bleeding. I knew I had to stay out of it or I would only make matters worse. My expression must have disclosed my feelings because she gestured for me to not speak, and smiled.

I knew we were not far from a rodeo arena where the local cowboys gathered on occasion to put on what was known as a "Jackpot" rodeo. Each one paid a certain amount into the jackpot for each round and the first place winner was awarded that money. I estimated that the next cross-road would not be far from this arena so I decided on a plan.

I pulled a few strands of hair over my face and puffed out my cheeks before leaning over the driver's shoulder and motioning wildly for him to stop the bus. His pompous attitude quickly disappeared when he apparently believed I was about to vomit. Maybe even on him. He struggled to wheel to the outside lane and screech to a halt. I grabbed my small bag with my left hand and lunged toward the door that was now folding back to allow me to exit, but from the bottom step I turned and winked at the señora.

I stalled for a few seconds until I saw that she understood, and by the time I was on the ground she had picked up her cardboard box and followed me.

I removed my hand from in front of my face and brushed the stray "bangs" in place under my hat before turning to grin at the driver.

"But. . .but. . ." he sputtered. "I thought you were sick!"

I stepped away from the door and grinned. "Just of you, fella. Just of you. . ."

I walked the next quarter of a mile with the señora where we parted. She gave me a quick kiss on the cheek and whispered, "Gracias!" before we departed in opposite directions. I felt good.

I was not very far from the jackpot arena but I by-passed it on arrival and headed straight for a small adobe building whose paint-chipped "Beer and Mixed Drinks" sign was as welcome as a money order from home. Well, almost.

Just as I reached the bar, a wild herd of giggling gunsels stampeded over the top of me and buried me face-down in the dirt. The jolt stunned me for a minute, especially when I wiped my eyes enough to focus on the culprits and saw rolled up jeans, concha belts, and $1.98 Woolworth's cowboy hats, to say nothing of the Brownie cameras hanging around the necks of nearly every one of them.

"I s'y ol'girl, we're frightf'ly sorry!"

I was being helped to my feet by a white-haired man who was dressed similarly to the others except in a more expensive way. As soon as I was upright, I was seeing red. Not only had I been trampled, my suitcase was knocked out of my hand, my clothes were covered with dirt and worst of all, the ones who trampled me were standing at the bar where I felt I should be. I was out for blood.

I was seeking revenge and when one straggler from the dude group walked by I took a wild swing at him. I missed. Out of nowhere, two cowboys appeared and literally swooped me off of the ground and headed for the rodeo arena carrying me backwards, feet bicycling in the air. They set me down in front of the bucking chutes.

"What'd you do that for?" I yelled. "Didn't you see what they did? I mean besides taking my place at the bar."

"Slow down, kid," one of them interrupted my tirade. "You'll bust a flank strap if ya' ain't careful. Besides we didn't want you killing off the Golden Goose."

He turned to his friend, "Or is it Golden Geese when they come in bunches?"

Just then came the warning, "Heads up! Bronc coming out!"

I climbed the fence just in time to catch a glimpse of a tall rangy cowboy rearing back to spur a pinto bronc in the shoulders when the gate flew open. I recognized Larry Finley's raw-boned good looks when he and the pinto cycloned past. Larry was spurring wildly but riding the bronc with ease.

I knew Larry's rodeo traveling companion, a powerful little red-head named Jimmy "Slugger" Sloan, would not be far away. I was looking around for him when Larry returned to the chutes after his ride.

"Larry! I'm up next. Hurry up."

Problem solved. It was Slugger.

Larry arrived just in time to belt him down on his bronc. When the gate flew open, Larry yelled, "Remember what I said, you little juke-box-son-of-a-bitch. You buck off of this dog and I'll kill you!"

Then, addressing no-one in particular, he muttered, "That little bastard put our last two-bits in a jukebox last night, and we didn't even have breakfast money."

Slugger came strutting back to the chutes just then after completing his ride. His freckled face glowed with pleasure at the applause from the audience and the nod of approval from Larry.

"Hi, Janie!" Slugger said when he reached us. "Riding broncs today?"

"Hey, that's right!" Larry looked surprised. "You rode at Lakeside, didn't you? Tough bronc, too."

"You'd better believe it," Slugger interrupted. "You don't know what a little dandy this girl is." He put his arm around my shoulder and it seemed nice to find myself on a face-to-face level with someone for a change instead of the face-to-belt-buckle ratio with the big cowboys.

"You ride barebacks?" Larry asked. "This is strictly a jackpot outfit. We each ante up two bucks and after a go-round is over the one with the best score takes it all. You want in?"

"I'll have to think about it."

Just then a pretty blonde approached and handed Slugger his loot as winner of this last round. He grabbed the money, and the blonde, and headed in the direction of the Adobe Bar.

A long arm reached out, collared Slugger and lifted him straight into the air.

"Ain't you forgettin' something, Shorty?"

"Oh, yeah! Heh! Heh!" Slugger chuckled. "What say we all have a drink? Now how's about puttin' me down, good buddy?"

"Soon as we get to the bar and you loosen your grip on that cash."

The blonde escaped in the confusion but Slugger was still begging to be put back on the ground. By the time we reached the bar, the other bareback riders were getting impatient. They were yelling for Slugger to come up with the loot so they could pay for the first round of drinks. It seems the winnings were dumped onto the bar after each go-round and when it was gone they retreated to the arena and started over. I was glad to finally get a cold one, and to have it paid for out of the jackpot money.

"Where do you keep getting entry fees? Didn't I hear you say you were broke?"

"Sure!" He flashed that wide grin again. "But we get some of those rodeo-happy gunsels to sponsor us and they're happy just to have their very own cowboys to cheer for!"

Larry paused to finish his drink, and then continued. "You know that Aussie that was following you around to apologize for his guys knocking you down?"

I nodded.

"Well, he's been financing us all afternoon."

"And what does he get out of it? A fourth—a third—or what?"

A wink accompanied the grin this time. "Are you kidding? He's happy just playing rodeo, so why spoil him? Why don't you tap him for three bucks? He can sure afford it."

"I'll see."

"Hell, I'll ask him for you. He sure owes you something for his crew running over you."

"That reminds me, I've got a suitcase around here someplace. I'll see you back at the arena as soon as I can locate it."

I considered leaving without having to explain that I was headed for Montana, but I felt I should at least tell Larry and Slugger goodbye. They were in the middle of one of their usual arguments when Larry picked Slugger up and held him at arms' length over his head. I gathered that Slugger had been arguing with one of the Aussie "bankers" and Larry did not want him to jeopardize their financial status.

"Dammit, Larry, why don't you let me hit him? Just once?"

"You're not in any shape."

"Shape?" Slugger yipped. "Just set me down and I'll show you who's in shape!"

Larry set him on the ground, then ordered, "Okay. Twenty times."

I did not know what to expect, but it was soon obvious that this was something they did on occasion. Larry held his right arm straight out from his body. Slugger jumped, grabbed hold of the arm and began chinning himself twenty times! At least, I assumed he completed the chore but I was laughing so hard by that time that tears blinded my vision and I lost count.

The announcer voice boomed over the loud speaker, "Let's rodeo!"

Everyone suddenly became serious and stopped clowning, and I decided it was a good time for me to just disappear quietly. I would see them again somewhere down the line.

# Chapter Eight

I caught a city bus to my rooming house and, although my prepaid rent had expired a couple of days before, my landlady had left all of my belongings intact. I planned to try and head for Montana as soon as I took care of a few loose ends but I was still more or less recovering from the Lakeside rodeo and after a hot bath I crawled into bed and slept for fourteen hours.

The next morning I took care of the rent I owed, packed the few things that remained in the dresser, closet and bathroom, and headed for the drive-in to pick up my final paycheck. My luggage consisted of my original suitcase plus the small carry-on packed with a change of clothes and my new hobbles. There was no point in bothering with the single remaining small stirrup or the buck-rein so there was room for any of my new clothes.

The bank where I cashed my final paycheck was only two blocks from the radio station so I decided to stop in for a quick "Goodbye" to Hamblen and his crew. I was glad that Cactus happened to be there for their early broadcast and when I told him of my plans he agreed that I might be making a smart move. He mentioned that Cliff Sanforth was busy directing a new movie for Imperial Pictures and was scheduled for two more when this one was completed, so it was possible the serial would be put on a back burner for an indefinite period of time. There were also rumors that Cameo Pictures was having a problem getting financed and he suggested I keep in touch with Sanforth by phone before my option ran out so I would know where I stood with them. I think Cactus knew I was a little homesick, so I thanked him for his efforts and said I would write.

I had saved enough money for a ticket all the way to Lewistown and even had twenty dollars left over. A baby-faced sailor sat beside me as far as Idaho Falls, and began to tell me a sad tale about having been robbed of all of his cash in Los Angeles. With tears of sympathy in my eyes I was able to force a ten dollar bill into his reluctant palm. In a choked voice he asked for my address and promised to send this amount back to me when he reached his home in Iowa.

I still think he will.

When my bus reached Bozeman, Montana, I saw several groups of cowboys walking around in the center of town so this looked like a chance to pick up a few extra bucks on my way home. By the time I located the rodeo headquarters in the banquet room of one of the down-town hotels and learned that the rodeo was over, my bus had already gone on its way. They explained that all of the go-rounds had been completed early and due to problems with the arena lighting they had condensed the last two shows into one.

In front of the hotel I was seated on the curb in an empty parking space, trying to decide what to do. I would have to rent a room if I waited for another bus the following day when a cowboy I met at Palm springs came by .

"Howdy, Jane! Whatcha doin' in this part of the country?"

"Actually, I live here. Well, in Lewistown, anyway. I just stayed over to see about a job riding broncs and found out I was too late. So what's new with you?"

"Nothin' new. We been in Hawaii with Jauregui."

I jumped to my feet. That statement got my immediate attention.

"Did he really go? He was supposed to let me know."

"I guess he tried. I heard him say he couldn't get an answer at the number you gave him. He even went so far as to go to that address and some old gal with a big collie dog ran him off. Wouldn't tell him nothin'." He frowned and put his hands on my shoulders.

"What's the matter? You sick?"

"Like Slugger would say, you better believe it!" I sat back down on the curb. "I guess this just isn't my year."

My luck did change to the extent that I was able to catch a ride with several bronc riders who were going through Lewistown on their way to a rodeo in Malta. They tried to convince me to go all the way north with them. One of them was sure I could get a job riding at least one or two broncs, but right then I just wanted to go home.

One of his friends looked at me and laughed. "Ain't you the little gal that tried to rope and hog-tie Cy Taillon? A bunch of guys was talking about it yesterday and they thought it was the funniest thing they'd heard all year!"

I felt embarrassed but just waved it off as I grabbed my luggage and headed for the car that would take me home.

I asked to be dropped off at the Montana Tavern on their way through Lewistown. Georgia said my parents were in Havre but were scheduled to return in one or two days so I headed for the Fergus Hotel and after a bath and a good night's sleep, I was not feeling so depressed. I preferred the Fergus for a couple of reasons. Number one, we had a charge account there, and second, in those days the Burke Hotel had a reputation for having problems with their water system. I remember hearing a rumor that a traveling salesman send them a telegram from Great Falls, forty-five miles away: SAVE ME A ROOM WITH A BATH. START FILLING THE TUB NOW!

The next day at the Tavern when I asked if my folks had come back yet, a gambler who often traveled with my parents began telling a story about one of my trips when I was trying to catch up with the two couples because I was lonesome at the ranch.

My collie dog had just died and when I reached Lewistown in pursuit of the group, I latched onto a stray hound of questionable lineage and with a long heavy-duty rope tied around his neck, headed north on a "milk train" called the Galloping Goose. It was a horrible trip with stops every few miles to drop off twenty-five-gallon empty milk cans and pick up full ones to deliver to a butter-and-cheese plant in Great Falls. It chugged along at what I imagine was no faster than fifteen miles an hour and then I still had to hitch-hike from Great Falls to Havre.

He implied that both couples wondered how they were going to make room for me and the dog when they moved on to the next poker game in Malta, in the next two or three days. Their hotel had a large NO PETS sign in the lobby so I crawled up four flights of the outside fire escape carrying the dog. When I reached the fourth floor and pried the window open, a maid who was walking in the hall screamed so loudly that the manager heard her, joined us and made me take the dog back outside. I marched right through the lobby with the dog at the end of the huge rope. I was not about to retreat back down the fire-escape. I tied the dog to a lamp-post near the hotel and the next morning the rope was still there, but no dog. I always suspected that one of our group was responsible but none of them would ever admit it.

They were all drinking in their room the next day when they ran out of booze. To make me feel better over the loss of my dog, Clint agreed to let me go to a western movie that was showing that afternoon in the center of town. A liquor store was next to the theater and when Clint ordered a bottle of whiskey, he suddenly realized he had forgotten to bring any money with him, so his solution was to leave me there, in hock, until he returned with enough cash to pay for the booze and to buy a theater ticket for me.

He forgot me!

I tried to convince the liquor store owner that Clint would surely come back, and if he would just lend me enough for the theater ticket, only twenty-five cents, he would be reimbursed when my father returned. He refused. By the time they ran out of scotch, and someone remembered where Clint had left me, the matinee was over and I was forced to go on to Malta with them, but never felt like I was really all that welcome. After three days I hitch-hiked back to Lewistown, and to the ranch.

By the time this gambler finished his story the Tavern was in an uproar. People were leaning against the bar, doubled over with laughter, and even as bad as it had been for me at the time, I could at last see the humor in my disastrous trip.

My parents returned the next day and after expressing their surprise at my return from Hollywood, we headed for the ranch with me trying to figure how much of my California story I would actually reveal. Parts of it they were never told.

They managed to keep me captive long enough to get several weeks' work out of me during haying. I did not believe driving a buck-rake was particularly good training for riding broncs, especially when my team was startled by a coyote and ran off, dragging me for nearly a quarter of a mile with a dislocated knee. No rodeoing for awhile.

I hired out as a rodeo announcer that summer at several small shows and I was actually allowed to use our car a couple of times because they knew I was in no condition to take off in search of any rodeos. Actually my accident worked in their favor because help was hard to find that summer.

When a member of the Lewistown Chamber of Commerce sent me a letter that I had been selected as their rodeo queen for their July Fourth celebration and rodeo, I was especially excited because Grandpa Burnett was to be the Grand Marshall of the parade and grand entries and I would be riding beside him on those occasions.

I was hurt when a few mean-minded teens called out to me during the parade such things as questions about why I wasn't riding broncs during the rodeo. Several of them shouted out that I must be afraid! It is difficult to understand what prompts people to do things like that and it was particularly frustrating to not have an opportunity to explain. The nay-sayers did not know or care that Leo Cremer, who was producing the rodeo, had decided against women's bronc-riding that year, or that a knee injury would have prevented me from competing even if that event had been included.

I enjoyed my reign as queen, especially the events that included Grandpa Burnett, but I still felt cheated at not being allowed to have a more important role in the whole production of the rodeo. Instead of appreciating my various personal appearances, I was more or less pouting about what I viewed as a series of bad breaks that kept me "out of the loop" for all four days of the rodeo.

On the afternoon of the final day, I spent several hours playing pool at the City Billiards with some friends. We were playing to see who would buy the beer, and due to this agreement, I did not realize how late it was until someone reminded me I was supposed to be at the fairgrounds. As the rodeo queen, I was to ride into the arena and make one final circle in front of the grandstand and bleachers, waving a farewell to the crowd until next year.

I caught a cab to the fairgrounds and realized right away that it was too late to get my horse from the stables because the rodeo was almost over. There was one bull left in the chutes and that was the final performance except for my personal appearance. I slipped through the back gate and tried to decide how I should handle the situation.

I finally decided to crawl through the fence so when Cy gave his usual spiel about their "little rodeo queen coming to tell them all good night," I would simply step into the arena and wave to the crowd as a farewell gesture.

As per my plan, I crawled through the poles near the catch-pens, and was slinking along the arena fence when the one final bull-rider came out of the chute and was thrown right outside of the gate after three jumps. With two pickup men trying to chase the bull out of the arena and two clowns taunting him to follow them to the exit, it was just my luck that it was a long-haired gal in a bright gold suit that caught his eye.

I looked up just in time to see the snorting animal bearing down on me. There was no chance for me to crawl over the fence when every available inch was occupied by spectators, so I started to run. Even as awkward as I am, I did a pretty fair job of dodging back and forth just out of reach of the horns swiping at me, when one of the pickup men roped the bull's horns and began dragging him away.

I sat down in the middle of the arena, exhausted.

I started to giggle.

The only thing I could hear above the shouting and laughter was Cy Taillon's droll voice saying, "And there, ladies and gentlemen, is your rodeo queen. Let's give her a big hand!"

I spent more time than usual at the ranch for the rest of that summer. My parents were gone most of the time and I made a couple of trips to Billings with Grandpa when he attended two different stockmen's meetings. He actually let me drive part of the time which was unusual for him as he rarely allowed anyone to take the wheel when they were in his Buick.

After one such trip, when we were back at the ranch, he called me into his room and presented me with a gift that he said was my birthday present, even though that was a couple of months early. He handed me a solitaire diamond ring! I immediately recognized the stone. It was the 1.57 carat Tiffany diamond that he won years before in a poker game. On special occasions, he wore it as a tie pin but now the stone was mounted in a ring. The gift came as a complete surprise to me.

He never let his guard down enough to show any emotion but as I grew older, I would occasionally give him a quick kiss on his cheek, maybe on his birthday or simply as a "goodnight kiss" after one of our rare conversations about one thing or another. He always uttered kind of a grumpy noise that was meant to show displeasure but was not very convincing.

I have always treasured that beautiful ring, not only because it was a gift from him but in all the years that I have worn it, day in and day out, the monetary value never really occurred to me whether I was broke or had money in my pockets.

To hide his own feelings when he handed me the ring, Grandpa said, "I thought you ought'a have this 'cause you're the only one in the family that might amount to something!" He paused, then added in a grumpy voice, "And I'm not too damned sure about you!"

As soon as I felt "rodeo-ready" again, I began checking *Hoofs & Horns* to see if anything looked promising. For some reason I noticed how the spelling of bronc varied from one story to another. In one case it would be spelled as bronk and in others it even varied to the point that it was spelled bronko!

The first article that caught my eye pertained to the Pendleton Roundup. I figured it was out of my league but due to the impressive history of that event I felt it was my duty to take a shot at them at least once. The Montana Tavern would seem like the most unlikely place to hook up with someone heading for that particular rodeo but that is exactly where I made my next connection.

I overheard a man at the bar discussing the fact that his wife was doing some last-minute shopping (or as he put it: last-day shopping) before they were to leave for Portland, Oregon, to visit relatives. The Barklays planned to leave the next morning, and by taking turns driving, they would go straight through without any stop-overs at night.

When his wife returned, I struck up a conversation with them and they asked me to join them for lunch. I managed to bring up the possibility of my traveling with them to Oregon and I was excited when they returned with a verdict in my favor. They agreed to let me go with them provided I did not have too much luggage but when I assured them my "gear-bag" and a couple of changes of clothes would take up very little room, our deal was confirmed.

My parents were living at the ranch at that time and I was driving Clint's car. I had been sent into town for groceries so I made a quick job of this chore and headed home. What ensued was much different from the my usual middle-of-the-night departures. This time there were no objections to my leaving and Clint even drove me into town the next morning to connect with my ride. Mother looked a bit sad but by now she had come to accept the fact that this was bound to happen sooner or later. Because I was not actually paid for my ranch work, nor did I expect to be, Clint gave me three folded twenties for traveling money. I did not even have to blackmail him this time.

Much like my earlier trip to California, I sat in the back seat of the Barklay sedan, surrounded by their multiple pieces of luggage and my one small suitcase. After the first hour or so when they inquired about my reason for making this trip, we carried on very little conversation. I paid for my own meals and even offered to pay for their's once or twice but they would not accept.

We did stop over one night in Spokane to visit Mrs. Barklay's sister but were on our way early the next morning. I planned to get a room nearby but there was a spare room over their garage and they gave me a key so I could sleep there. I was invited to have supper with them but declined. I felt I was already intruding enough so I walked to a drive-in several blocks away and then returned to my room with a bag of food. And a large container of Coca-Cola.

Next, we went south through Pasco to Umatilla where they were to turn west toward Portland. Mister Barklay was familiar with the area and said this would be my best chance to hitch a ride south to Pendleton.

I thanked them for the transportation and offered to help pay for gasoline. Again they would not accept my money so I decided to splurge and ride a Greyhound the rest of the way. I hoped for a nicer driver than the one out of San Diego, but in any case it was better than always catching a ride with strangers. Rumors of various crimes involving hitch-hikers were becoming more common-place and I no longer felt as comfortable with this means of transportation as I did a year or so before.

During my years of traveling, my one regret is that I did not take time to do any "sight-seeing." Our view of a town was somewhat like an occasional glimpse of the entertainer on stage where you saw only the painted, smiling face and temporary vivacity with none of the drab backstage existence showing through. A person could walk right past that same unadorned actor on the street without recognition and this is the way we cruised through various towns, large and small, never being aware of them except at rodeo time. What we saw was the glitz and none of the drab.

On arrival in Pendleton, I was waiting in line at the information desk to ask directions to the rodeo arena when I happened to pick up a small brochure that was so fascinating I stepped aside and sat down nearby while I read it cover to cover. This booklet described various points of interest concerning the city's background but one item, in particular, was different from anything I had ever read before.

It seems that Pendleton's underground tunnels that were dug by the Chinese between 1870 and 1930 covered nearly seventy miles underneath Pendleton's historic district. Reputed to have been active in the tunnels during those years were such businesses as ice plants, butcher shops, and Chinese laundries, as well as illegal saloons, bordellos and opium dens.

When I realized the information line was depleted, the first thing I inquired about, even before rodeo information, was whether it was possible to see any of those tunnels. I was informed that there were several proposals being considered that would allow such tours, but at that time it was not possible.

On my way to the rodeo headquarters, all I could think about was how exciting it would be to have access to the tunnel area. The one time I really wanted to take a tour in a rodeo town and it was not allowed.

At the rodeo headquarters I could see that it would be some time before I had an opportunity to talk to anyone about a job. I was aware that Bonnie McCarroll had been killed in Pendleton in 1926 while riding a saddle-bronc that was to have been her last exhibition before she and her husband retired to a life of cattle ranching. There was no mention of this event in any of the brochures and I assumed this was a sensitive area as far as the rodeo committee was concerned. Even so, I hardly expected to be treated so rudely. They not only rejected my request for a job, but did everything short of having me thrown out of the rodeo office.

The Pendleton Roundup is such a huge event each year that housing is booked months in advance, and even if it wasn't, I assumed the rates were out of my reach, especially since I had no income "incoming."

It would be a week until the next rodeo began but I felt it made more sense for me to move on and try to wangle a job at the new location. Also, with the extra time, I might find housing I could afford. Even without any income from Pendleton, I still felt more secure traveling by bus and with luck, I could earn it back with one or two rides.

I arrived in Colfax, Washington, shortly after noon. It was just another rodeo town; greener, perhaps, and more freshly painted and flower-decked than some, but the pattern was the same. At the time I arrived there, I was suffering from an acute attack of joblessness, brought on by the cold-shoulder I received in Pendleton, Oregon. I did not need a CPA to tell me the Levi-bank was nearing the insufficient-funds stage, so I immediately began looking for a room that I could afford. On a back street, I saw a dimly lit sign over one of the doorways that said, "OOMS." A mental inspection of my vocabulary convinced me the odds were in favor of an "R" as the missing letter until I began climbing the creaky stairs and it occurred to me there might have been two absentee characters, such as "GL."

The musty odor in the narrow passageway replaced the clean-green smell of the town. A yellow 10-watt bulb at the head of the stairs beckoned timidly to any possible customers on the ground-floor and I was still puffing from the climb when I reached a home-made paint-spattered desk against one wall. The yellow glow disclosed a writing tablet with several pages flipped back, a three-inch pencil tied to the desk leg with a piece of twine, and a crudely printed note: SIGN HERE. TAKE ENY ROOM THETS EMPTY. THERE AINT NO KEYS. PAY IN THE MORNING.

Part of the tablet was covered with scribbling that appeared to be parimutuel odds, and the rest of the space was filled with names and addresses. I managed to squeeze my signature in between Lady Moonbeam at 5 to 3 and Cliffie's Little Dandy at 20 to 1. Thinking of my short bankroll, I added a postscript after my name: 100 to 1 on Gilt Edge, if there's a muddy track tomorrow.

I felt my way along the dark hall until I came to an open doorway. I reached in and found the light switch. Nothing. My only match flickered and went out, but not before I saw that the room was vacant and there was a tiny bulb in a pull-chain socket tied to the head of the bed with some more twine. I stumbled over a chair and it went crashing across the bare wooden floor.

"Dod dammit, tut out dat wacket!" someone yelled.

The queer-sounding words penetrated the cardboard-thin wall as I scrambled to turn on the light. The voice had been so loud I actually expected to find someone standing right next to me but when a quick look proved me wrong, I lost no time in shoving an old-fashioned commode against the door to keep it closed.

One glance at the bedding convinced me the linen was changed at the end of the week instead of after the departure of each customer. I spread my spare Levis and shirt on top of the bed and lay across them, fully clothed except for my boots which were tucked under my head as a makeshift pillow. I finally went to sleep.

Even though the first performance was still one week away, I caught a ride to the rodeo headquarters the following morning to begin working on the rodeo committee about a job. The two members who were present gave me very little encouragement.

My first break came as a weird twist of fate when one of the women hired as a "time keeper," called that morning to report that she had chicken pox! Before they had a chance to select a replacement, I talked them into giving the job to me. The wages would cover room rent, such as it was, and in fact, I thought "OOMS" should have paid me to stay there.

During the days prior to the actual rodeo, I tried to make myself useful. I ran errands for the rodeo committee members, answered phones, hand delivered their "goodies" from the nearest coffee shop, while slipping in a word now and then about why they should give me a job riding broncs. The Bonnie McCarroll incident had pretty much put the kibosh on any womens' bronc riding throughout the entire northwest but another strange turn of events gave me an opportunity that I had not previously considered.

To date, the livestock for many steer riding events consisted of local range steers, Texas long-horns, Hereford or Black Angus steers or cross-breeds of any combination of those types. A local rancher had imported several young Brahma bulls to breed to his Hereford cows and a committee member suggested they hire someone to make an exhibition ride on one of the "long yearling"animals (not yet two years old) to see how they would buck. The idea was to save this performance for the final day of the rodeo to give them time to publicize the act.

I had been listening as they discussed the special event and before they went any further, I suggested they give me the opportunity to perform this specialty act. I emphasized the fact that the bull was only a few months past his first birthday and having a woman rider would make the act more exciting for the audience than it would if a seasoned steer rider were to do it.

As always, a committee meeting was required before they made a decision but they said I would be notified the following day.

It actually took them almost three days to decide, but they finally agreed that I would be the one to make the exhibition ride.

I worked some long hours that day and I intended to head for the hotel without even stopping anyplace for dinner. When I passed the never-ending crap game behind the chutes, I heard several outbursts of laughter and noticed a tall, gangling cowboy kneeling on the ground with his back toward me. He was the object of everyone's attention.

"Shoot again, Jebo," one of the players said to him. (*Not his real name*).

"Dod dammit, boys, I dotta make my point. If I dough back home bwoke, my ode lady's gonna till me! Tum on, dice—little Doe fwum Tocomo."

This cowboy was obviously the one who hollered at me the first night when I tipped over the chair at "OOMS." I was curious to see what he looked like, so I moved closer. He was making a joke out of the reason he came to Colfax one week early, and said it had something to do with a car wreck that prevented him from arriving in Pendleton in time to enter. He rolled the dice across the saddle-blanket, and as he reached to retrieve them he glanced up at me.

Jebo's twisted hare-lip did not surprise me because the way he talked had led me to expect it, but something about his pale grey eyes made me feel like a cold wind was suddenly blowing down the back of my neck. I sensed something inside of Jebo that the others did not appear to see. Despite his joking, I felt as though he blamed the world for the deformity of his mouth.

I hurried away to be sure and reach "OOMS" before he did.

All through the week, while working at the rodeo headquarters, I kept hearing bits and pieces of conversation pertaining to the formation of the Cowboys Turtle Association. I was anxious to learn more about how this new organization compared to the Rodeo Association of America as it had been explained to me on the trip to Regina, but I did not know any of the cowboys well enough to ask questions. I did manage to learn that this new group was called "Turtles" and I heard two versions of why that name had been selected.

One cowboy attributed it to the statement from Everett Bowman who said, "Cowboys should be called turtles since it's taken them so long to form an organization." The first slate of directors claim it was so named because, "like the turtle, a cowboy might be slow to start but he's sure to finish."

There had been strikes at several mainstream rodeos such as Tucson and Boston, and there was a great deal of conflict between the Turtles and the RAA but the ones who took the time to answer my questions gave me the impression that both organizations were striving to improve every phase of the rodeo business. They said, as yet, women had not been accepted as members but felt that would change in the near future. One cowboy mentioned that there was already some discussion among members suggesting that if and when we were allowed to join, there would be a minimum amount stated that we could receive for each bronc ride. This sounded good to me, except for the fact that it was already difficult enough to get hired to ride and such a ruling might be a detriment to someone at my level.

Meanwhile, I had my bull-ride to worry about.

Brahma bull riders are a jittery group. The term "stall walking" was coined to describe their nervous pacing back and forth in front of the chutes before the bull-riding event. I had often joined in the laughter when someone slipped up behind these boys and rattled a cow-bell, or hollered, "Heads up! Bull loose!" just to see them run. I now sympathized with their feelings, and even stall-walked right along with them, and I had not even been on one yet, or been gored and trampled as had some of the cowboys at shows where Brahmas were already being used.

It took six or seven people to get me ready to ride. As I walked back and forth, different ones furnished me with advice and riding equipment.

"Got a loose-rope? And a bell?" one of them asked.

"Nope."

"Spurs?" Someone else inquired.

"I've got bronc-riding spurs."

"You can't use those," he muttered with disgust. "You gotta have small rowels that'll dig into these babies. This ain't like tryin' to spur some ol' bronc or a yearling steer. This is grabbin' hold and fightin' fer your life."

"Burnett! Your bull's in!"

About then, all I wanted was "out," but I'd hired out as a tough hand, as Clint once said.

Someone gave me a small soft glove. Although the fingers were cut out of it, it would protect my left hand from the braided rope. A kerchief around my wrist held the glove in place and a durham sack of resin slapped against my palm gave the glove an added stickiness that was supposed to help me hang onto the rope.

"Don't I need two gloves?" I asked. "I always ride steers with both hands."

"You don't ride a Brahma with two hands, gal," a slim nervous boy replied after he'd shifted a wad of tobacco to the other side of his mouth. "You gotta be able to rear back and stay away from that hump or it'll beat you plumb to death."

By that time I was being belted down onto what looked like forty acres of dun-colored hair and muscle. My mouth was so dry I could not ask any more questions, but a cold numbness had temporarily replaced the fear. I knew the big cowbell fastened to the rope was hanging under the bull's belly. Its clanging served as a warning to anyone standing around in the arena and the weight of the bell pulled the rope loose from the bull as soon as the rider was off.

With my legs braced on the inside poles of the chute, I slipped my left hand into the handhold that was braided into the rope. A cowboy above me pulled on the loose end until my hand was drawn down against the bull, then that end was laid across my palm. I knew they couldn't tighten it as much as they would on other types of bucking stock because the expansion of that powerful mass of muscles would mash my hand on the first jump. One wrap was taken around my hand with the loose end, then it was pulled through my palm once more, and I gripped it as tightly as I could.

I eased down and my legs were spread so far apart it seemed there was no way to get a grip with my spurs, but I managed to turn my toes out and gouge the rowels as deep as possible.

With every bit of will power I had, I tried to force a nod for the gate—but nothing happened.

"Don't you wisht you was home?" the slim boy asked from the top of the chute.

"You bet!" I nodded. This scheme worked on my first saddle-bronc ride, and I fell for it again. My "nod" was the clue for the gate to be thrown open.

No one in the eye of a hurricane would be expected to describe where the wind hit him first. I can only say my sole sensation before being slammed onto the hard ground, was the feeling that, one by one, each joint in my body was jerked completely out of its socket, ending with my neck. Then I was lying in the arena.

I was too dazed to move for a second or two. When my vision cleared, I raised my head cautiously and stared straight into the snorting nostrils of the dun colored animal himself.

"Stay down! Don't move!" Cowboys were screaming from the sidelines.

They had no way of knowing it, but I was not about to get up. The big dun rolled me over several times with his nose and his stubby not-yet-two-year-old horns, and someone said later that the bull and I looked like we were snorting at each other, but I was simply gasping for breath.

Then it was over. Almost. The bull-fighting clowns ran past several times, slapping the dun across the face with their jackets, until they managed to lure him away from me.

With the aid of several brave souls, I crawled to my feet and headed for safety when the deadly call of "Heads up!" rang out, and I was alone again.

I was further away from the chutes that I realized and I knew this time the shouting was not one of their malicious jokes when I caught sight of the snorting dun making a return attack from the rear. I started to run toward the nearest haven in sight which happened to be the six-foot high wall that served as the front of the grandstand. It is an accepted fact that fear furnishes us with extreme powers. Even using that as an explanation for what happened next, it is difficult to believe I could actually scale that wall and fall headlong into the lap of His Honor the Mayor of Colfax!

Confusion reigned briefly while Mr. Mayor and I untangled ourselves and crawled upright from our positions on the floor of his private box.

Mrs. Mayor leaned over us and squealed, "Oooh! My goodness, are you all right?"

I nodded, mostly because it took less effort than shaking my head sideways.

The mayor smiled. "Well, well. I guess we'd better take you to dinner this evening so we can show our friends the prize we won at the rodeo!" He chuckled, "If you catch a baseball, you get to keep it. Right?"

The invitation took me by surprise but in the midst of the confusion, all I could think about was my meager wardrobe and whether I should accept, when Mrs. Mayor interrupted. She was staring at the bull-riding spurs. Caught in the small rowels were several tufts of dun-colored hair, slightly tinged with blood.

"Look at that!" she was almost shrieking at her husband. "I insist you look at the dreadful weapons these people use on those poor frightened animals. I'm going to call a special meeting of the SPCA tonight and do something about it!"

I could hardly believe this hysterical woman was serious. The mayor looked flustered, and uncomfortable, as he tried to calm her down. His eyes apologized to me, and I knew the dinner invitation had been cancelled. I crawled back down into the arena that was now cleared of livestock, and was as proud of my restraint in not replying to Mrs. Mayor's remarks as I was of my attempted Brahma ride.

Applause from the crowd made me feel a little better even if my dive into the mayor's box was actually the highlight of my ride. Someone returned my hat that was lost during my brief ride, and I waved it in the air when I left the arena.

I waited around the rodeo office with the real cowboys so I could get paid for my work as a time-keeper and errand-girl plus what ever I would receive for my ride. Every muscle in my body was complaining about the futility of such a profession until they handed me the grand total of twenty-five dollars and I felt much better. I thanked them for the opportunity and suggested I would do better "next time," but there was no response to my open-ended suggestion that I would like to return.

More than anything else, I wanted a hot bath and a good night's sleep, and neither one seemed likely in that weird establishment named "OOMS."

A bronc-rider and his wife gave me a ride to my hotel on their way out of town. The trip to the top of the stairs was a slow painful one and I hobbled toward my room with nothing on my mind but getting my poor old body stretched out for the night. As I side-stepped the chair and leaned over the bed to switch on the light, I heard a noise behind me. I jerked the chain and turned just in time to see Jebo lumbering toward me. He smelled of booze and was kind of slobbering out of the twisted side of his mouth. Before I had a chance to react, he threw himself on top of me.

Jebo was sitting straddle of me and had my arms pinned to my sides with his knees. The way his bloodshot eyes rolled back into his head, his eye-balls seemed to be all one color—red. He reached over and pulled the light chain with one hand, and at the same time he stuck his other hand inside the front of my shirt and jerked it open. The long stiff hairs on the back of his hand sent chills all the way through me. I was wearing my first snap-button shirt, so one flip of his hand and I was bare to the waist except for my brassiere.

He was stupid drunk. I had realized that when he charged across the room and maybe that was why I felt I could still get away even while he tore at my clothes and shoved his body against mine. I was sobbing and begging him to stop while I tried to squirm out from under him, but it was impossible to move because his weight had pushed me deep into the cheap lumpy mattress.

When you have always played down your fears, and minimized them so much that you don't admit them even to yourself, it is almost impossible to start yelling for help, no matter how terrified you are. You try to scream but nothing happens.

Jebo's hands felt wet and clammy when he tugged at my Levis. I tried to push his hands away but I was getting weak from crying and fighting. My sore muscles from the bull ride made the situation even worse and I must have been on the verge of hysteria because I can remember the ridiculous things that were going through my mind. I thought of the Levi-Strauss ads where they promised a new pair of their jeans if any of their products tore under normal conditions. I wondered if they would consider this a normal situation.

"Wath the matter, bitch? I taw da way you look at them udder cowboyth—they all been thcrewin' you. You don' need to fight me 'tause a my lookth! I tan give you ath good a thcrew ath any of dem." Jebo bent over with his face close to mine but he was still sitting on top of me. I had the awful feeling he was going to kiss me and at that moment, this was what terrified me the most.

"All right, Jebo," I sobbed, "but get off of me—you're hurting me. I'll do anything you say."

I hardly dared hope he would believe me but I had to stall for time. After a few more seconds of fumbling with the top button on my Levis, he twisted away from me and kind of gasped for breath as he pawed at the front of his own clothes and started undoing them. That was all the time I needed.

I rolled off of the bed and onto my feet and stumbled through the half-open door. Then I began to run. It was like a nightmare, with the narrow hallway seeming to close in on me, shutting off the exit at the other end. I could hear Jebo cussing and falling around in my room. I became more and more panicky and instead of going straight down the hall, I frantically tried first one door and then another. Each of them were propped closed with furniture except one, and when I jerked that door open, a naked man and woman rolled over on the bed and glared at me.

"Get the hell out of here!" they both screamed, with no loss of motion.

I ran on without closing their door. I was still sobbing when I came to the lobby and stumbled and fell most of the way down the stairs. My shirt-tail was out, and I ran into the street carrying my brassier and holding my shirt closed with both hands. There was no one in sight on that back street, so I just ran and ran and ran.

I have no idea where I went but I ended up in a kind of park, hidden in a clump of bushes. My shirt was still open and I threw myself face down on the ground where I felt the tall wet grass and the clean earth on my skin. At that moment I felt nothing could remove the memory of those hairy hands, that crooked slobbering mouth, and the wild look in the eyes of the man who had attacked me. Finally, toward dawn I cried myself to sleep.

When I awoke I was cold and terribly sore and stiff. With my eyes still closed, I lay there smelling the soil and the grass and the trees. I wanted to go home. I stepped behind some bushes to put my bra and shirt back on and tied my shirt-tail in a square-knot instead of taking time to tuck it into my Levis

To avoid any explanations, I remained in the park while I decided what to do. When I had braided my long hair, I felt I looked presentable enough to appear on the street—at least until I could buy a comb and some lipstick. My intentions were to pick up my riding gear from my room and then head for home, but as soon as I reached the hotel entrance I panicked. It was an emotional as well as a physical impossibility for me to climb that stairway one more time.

I finally approached a cab driver several blocks away, and talked him into retrieving my things and paying for my room with some of my earnings. He had a knowing gleam in his eye when he returned from seeing the kind of hotel I had been staying in, but he was reasonably civil after I bluntly refused to accompany him to his own hotel for awhile.

The taxi-cab office also served as sort of a travel agency and I overheard several men inquiring about prospective passengers, either on a share-the-expenses or a part-time-driving basis. Two days before that I would not have hesitated taking the first east-bound ride offered to me, but now I had the uneasy feeling that each of the men was “leering” at me. I kept creating excuses for not going with any of them.

At last a grey-haired lady with timid blue eyes asked for a woman companion to help her drive to Spokane. She looked as frightened as I felt, so I knew we’d make a good pair and in a few minutes we were on our way.

This woman, whose name was Elvira, was such a terrible driver, I was unable to relax long enough to sleep so I drove most of the way. Elvira insisted on paying for my food, and she took me to a truck stop on the outskirts of Spokane before she let me out. With a fluttery wave of farewell, she ran a red light and took a wrong left turn which headed her north toward Canada instead of south toward her destination.

I was still worrying about Elvira when an elderly farmer stopped to get gas for his pickup truck. He agreed to give me a ride as far as Coeur d’Alene, Idaho, and in spite of his age, I kept a watchful eye on him while we traveled. Apparently he was just as leery of me because he actually made me get out and walk across the state line, even though we were miles from any town.

At the next sign of civilization, the farmer pulled up in front of a hotel coffee shop.

"What say we stop here an' get some grub?" he asked. "You must be gettin' mighty gaunt by now, ain't you?"

"No, not very," I lied. "But I would like to find a room while we're here." I was sorely in need of some sleep but he must have misinterpreted my meaning because his already ruddy complexion turned even redder.

When I stepped into the hotel lobby, I saw an OUT OF ORDER notice on the restroom door. There was a LADIES' sign and an arrow pointed toward the stairway so I followed a series of arrows that led to a vacant hotel room where three or four women were standing in line, chattering inanely. I eased past them and sat on the edge of a small hard bed in a darkened alcove. In those few minutes while I awaited my turn, all of the tension and anxiety of the past forty-eight hours seemed to dissolve, and so did my resistance. I fell back on the bed and went to sleep.

It was the following morning before I awoke. My boots were hurting my feet and my Levis felt like they were cutting me in two. I squirmed for several seconds, trying to get comfortable until I suddenly realized what had happened. I jumped to my feet and smoothed the bed covers before I made a dive toward the bathroom and jerked the door closed behind me. If anyone saw me and demanded I pay room rent, I might have enough cash to handle it, but I preferred to hang on to what money I had.

I managed to avoid the hotel maids, and escaped to the coffee shop. Naturally the farmer had departed hours before, but he did leave my gear with a tall red-haired waitress. When she returned it to me, she giggled, "Are you with the rodeo, too?" She took time out to chew her gum. Then added, "Goll—eeeee."

I was about to order when I realized she had implied that there were other rodeo people in the area, so I forgot about food and probed for information.

"There was four of 'em in here." More gum chewing.

"Yes?"

"—about ten minutes ago."

I grabbed my gear and ran through the front door. It was easy to locate the two cars with their horse trailers parked outside of a tavern at the end of the street. I was still lame from my bull-ride and I nearly fell down when I attempted to run but I finally reached the tavern, and stumbled through the front door.

"Well! Hi there, Janie! Where'd you come from?" It was little Jim Patch, better known as Scrap Iron. "We thought you'd gone to. . ."

I grabbed his hand and pumped it excitedly. "Hi, yourself, you little cigarette-moochin' bastard, you never looked so good!"

Scrappy and the others started to laugh.

"That's quite a greeting, huh?" Jimmy Hazen said. "Things must be really tough if that little Wop looks good to you!"

"As Slugger would say, you'd better believe it." I climbed onto a bar stool. "But right now, I need a cup of coffee more than I need sympathy."

"Order up, gal," someone else said. "We're movin' on after this drink."

I learned that Hazen and his wife Betty were on their way to Chicago. Scrappy and another bull-rider named Whirligig were going with them.

"Why don't you come along?" Betty Hazen invited. "With this crew, I'm going to need a female on my side! We can always make room in our old convertible for one more."

For an instant I was tempted to accept, until I remembered my experience in Colfax, and the way I'd felt about going home.

"What's the matter, Janie?" Scrappy asked. "You've got a funny look on your face."

"Nothing. Really. But I'm going to quit rodeoing."

You would have thought I'd just told the biggest joke of the season. There were ten or twelve rodeo hands in the tavern and every one of them practically rolled on the floor they were laughing so hard.

"Did I say something funny?" I turned to Hazen.

"You sure did! In case nobody ever told you, it's as tough to quit this business as it would be to get off of whiskey, cigarettes, or dope. We've all tried to stop rodeoing—at least once a year—an' the first thing you know, we're right back in there."

"Well, not me. I really mean it."

"Sure you do." Hazen's voice sounded ridiculously soothing as he winked at the others and added, "We believe her, don't we fellas?"

"That's right!" they chorused. "She'll never rodeo again."

"I think we'd better hit the road," Hazen interrupted. "I'd like to drive straight through to Miles City before we stop to sleep, and it's a long old stretch of country."

I rode as far as Billings in Hazen's car. When I said goodbye, Scrappy whispered to me that I could catch up with them in Miles City any time in the next ten days if I changed my mind.

"Not a chance," I told him just before they drove away.

When I arrived in Lewistown I had every intention of going straight to the ranch. Then I saw the rodeo banners hanging across Main Street, and found out that a rodeo that should have been over several days before, had been postponed and there was still one go-round to be held that night.

I was heading for the Montana Tavern when I happened to be crossing the street at the same time as a local young man who I recognized as one of the star athletes in high school at the same time as I was enrolled there. He was quite the big shot in those days and I was surprised that he knew my name.

"Hi, Jane!" he said, as he walked along beside me. "Haven't seen you for awhile. You been out at the ranch all this time?"

I stopped right in the middle of the street and stared at him for a minute. I could hardly keep from laughing.

"Yeah. That's right," I said. "We don't get to town very often."

In the next block near the bus station, I saw Cy Taillon chatting with two local businessmen that I recognized. He grabbed my arm as I walked past and after we exchanged greetings, he said, "You picked a good time to come home."

"How's that?"

"They held this show over so long on account of all the rain that Alice Greenough had to leave for Shelby today. Her sister Margie is still riding broncs here, but I think Leo'll give you a job, too, if you want to take Alice's place."

"But I. . ."

"You do want the job, don't you?" His deep-set eyes opened wide. No doubt he was also thinking about our first meeting when he had kept me from riding.

"Sure. It's just that—oh, nothing." I could quit after this rodeo as well as before. "Do you really think he'll hire me?"

"You might as well ask. He's paying $15 a mount. I'm going to the fairgrounds now, if you want a ride."

As soon as I was sure of a job, I caught a ride back into town. It was easier to locate my parents this time, because they had been promoted from the third booth at the Montana Tavern, to the first table by the front door. They not only deserved this honor, but it was more convenient for the barmaid because their orders were more frequent than the ones from any other booth.

I made no mention of the fact that I was through rodeoing. I thought it best to surprise everyone after my ride that night. They did not attend the rodeo and I always suspected they did not have a lot of confidence in my first attempt to ride a Cremer bronc, but they used the excuse that they were leaving for Shelby in an hour or so. This excuse may have been legitimate because it was possible that gambling was open during the rodeo where Alice Greenough was to perform.

Even if Cremer had allowed me to choose the bronc for my only "hometown" ride, it would have been impossible to pick anything better than the shaggy white horse he gave me. Compliments on a bronc ride do not mean much, because the people who know if it really was good are not the complimenting kind. The gushing gunsels think a ride is good if the horse is a pretty color, or if the rider wears a flashy outfit or happens to be a woman. When the pickup man lifted me off of the bronc after the whistle, I needed nothing more than the warm glow inside of me to tell me I made a good ride. I threw my small chest out as far as my sore ribs and Mother Nature would allow, and strutted back to the chutes. Although we were not actually in competition, it was announced that I was the winner of the women's bronc riding event that evening.

Who is to say what might have happened if I had bucked off on my head again? Or if my folks had still been in Lewistown when the rodeo was over that night? Maybe it would have been THE END. Just maybe.

But the way it did happen, I caught a ride to Miles City and stayed with Scrappy's family for two days until the Hazens were ready to leave for Chicago.

Just before we headed east, I located a copy of the Lewistown Sunday paper at one of the news-stands. On page one there was a large picture of two girls on rearing horses. (They were the ones who led the parade.) I flipped through the paper, eagerly seeking the picture of another cowgirl who was near and dear to my heart. No picture. However, one thoughtful reporter had added a brief sentence to the end of his rodeo story.

On page four: "The only local woman to ride broncs was Jane Burnett."

# Chapter Nine

My first futile attempt to stop rodeoing was by no means the last, but the import of the resolution, along with the Colfax incident that provoked it, was magnified out of proportion in my mind.

During the early stages of our trip to Chicago, I felt warmly grateful to Scrappy, Whirligig, and the Hazens for not razzing me about my short-lived "retirement." I sensed, later, that the silence I had interpreted as understanding was actually indifference.

The Hazens took turns driving. This meant there was nothing for the rest of us to do but sleep, think, and argue over who got to sit in the front seat with the Hazens. Since this was not actually a cabin, I guess it might be said that we had a touch of "convertible fever" with Scrappy and Whirly constantly squabbling about one thing or another. Hazen had to stop the car at least once a day to let them battle it out at the side of the road.

When it was time for Betty to drive, she made it clear that she would tolerate no such foolishness (referring to the numerous "battle stops") while she was at the wheel. She went on to belittle Hazen, and nag him because he had only covered sixty miles in the past two hours.

"Just shut up and drive," he grumbled, "and quit being such a damned know-it-all."

A few times it looked like they might even pull over to the side of the road and duke it out!

Somewhere in Iowa, Hazen finally built a barricade of gear in the center of the back seat. He put Scrappy and Whirly on each side of it. He and Betty still weren't speaking. I was sulking.

We continued eastward, silently.

I was brooding about the preceding week, and began to wonder if Hazen had been right that day in Idaho, when he said it was impossible to stop rodeoing once you had it in your blood. Other thoughts drifted into my mind like the cowboy with the scar who first explained to me about riding broncs with hobbled stirrups. He said there would be times when I was taking such a beating that I would give almost anything just to get loose and fall off, but couldn't make myself do it deliberately.

Was he not right? With a bronc snapping my neck, slamming me forward and back in the saddle, I instinctively tried harder to ride him. I had never attempted to let go and escape. I always thought maybe he would level off after the next jump, and everything would be smooth from then on.

Now I was doing exactly the same thing as far as rodeos were concerned. No matter how broke I was, or what experiences I had in or out of the arena, I held on even tighter just hoping the next rodeo would be the good one—where I'd ride a tough bronc, make a lot of money, and finally be accepted as a "top hand."

But how do you get loose? Wait until Gabriel blew the whistle, and the pickup men carried you away on a shiny white horse that had flapping wings in place of a saddle-blanket? Surely senility would bring about some kind of enforced retirement before that happened.

I thought about the many old cowboys who were no longer able to compete in rodeos, who settled for opening chute gates, unsaddling broncs, or working rodeo stock. They would do just about anything to convince themselves that their lives had not changed. What would my choice be? Rodeo time-keeper, book-keeper, announcer? Or would I someday have guts enough to kick my feet loose from the hobbled stirrups, step off, and walk away without looking back? Hazen had compared rodeoing to drinking or taking dope, and I felt, as with those other habits, the only sure cure would be complete isolation from any form of our profession. Make a clean break. Form a "Rodeo Riders Anonymous" where you could phone a fellow-member to come and lock you in your room every time you heard Grand Entry music on the radio, or saw a carload of cowboys heading out of town.

If I were to ever get loose from the "hobbled stirrups" of the rodeo business, it would have to be a clean break. I decided I would quit forever, right after Chicago.

While I still could.

We arrived in the Windy City on a chilly, smelly morning. The far-reaching stockyards aroma practically knocked me over when I stepped out of the car. Herding cattle on the open range in no way prepares you for the stench of thousands of cattle captive in an enclosed area like a stockyard.

"Whooosh!" I whoooshed—not daring to inhale. "Cows never smelled like that at home."

"You just had more room for them to spread out," Hazen grumbled, still in a sour mood.

"Thank goodness! Our friendly cows would commit suicide if they ever caught themselves stinking like that."

Scrappy chuckled, "Maybe these do, too. That way they avoid being slaughtered!"

Now that the trip was over, there were signs of a gradual improvement in dispositions all the way around. Betty was especially cheerful because her parents lived in a suburb of Chicago and she was headed home as soon as Hazen signed up for the riding events and paid his entry fees.

"Aren't you going to see about a job, Janie?" Scrappy asked when I turned away from the stadium.

"As cruddy as I feel right now, I wouldn't even apply for a job cleaning stalls until I bathed and changed clothes."

"Okay!" he called out. I was already half-way across the street. "See you later."

I noticed a sign indicating there was a small hotel upstairs from a bar called The Billy Goat Inn. The old brown building looked like a square chocolate cake baked by someone who was short of cocoa. Right where a slice of the cake had been whacked off of one corner, there was a narrow doorway. That was the hotel entrance.

There were only about a dozen rooms in the entire building. I saw the "no vacancy" sign as soon as I entered, but I kept urging the manager to try to work out something for me because I had no transportation to search for another place. Actually, I figured this might be one of the few that I could afford.

"Besides," I added for effect, "I have to be close to the stadium during the rodeo."

"Vell, dot's difference," he grinned broadly. "If you're vit das vodeo, ve find you somet'ings."

*Somet'ings* turned out to be a tiny room at the end of a narrow dark hallway. He explained that this room was normally occupied by the maid, who at the present time was spending her nights with her ill sister. Because the manager assumed I was an employee of the rodeo organization, he did not ask me to pay my for my room in advance. Maybe something I said.

Eleven-hundred miles without an overnight stop was almost too much for me. However, one thing can be said for that kind of traveling, the expenses were at a minimum. I still had "eating-money", but I was happy not to pay for my room until I found out about a job. This was one time Clint would not be standing behind the nearest blackjack table.

I needed a hot bath, a "stretch-out" sleep, and a chance to wash my clothes. At the time I left Lewistown, my only gabardine pants were in the cleaners, so one extra pair of Levis and two shirts were the extent of my wardrobe. I knew the Levis I was wearing would take all day to get dry if I washed them by hand so I needed to find an alternative. On our trip, a couple of changes of underwear had been the topic of quite a few jokes due to my sequence of washing them in restrooms along the way and dangling them out of the window to dry.

After a short nap, the substitute maid led me to a large sink in the supply room and loaned me an iron, so before long I felt presentable enough to head for the arena and inquire about a job. Had I known that was my last chance to lie down on the narrow cot, I would certainly have slept longer.

I decided to stop downstairs at Billy Goat's before crossing over to the stadium. When I entered the dark little bar it took a few minutes for my eyes to adjust to the lack of light. As things came into focus, I noticed a bunch of cowboys at one end of the bar, huddled together. There was something about their attitudes, the tension and anxiety to please, that told me a woman must be in the center of the huddle. A herd of bulls surrounding and fighting over one lone heifer react the same way.

I watched the group with mild curiosity. It was no surprise to hear a woman's shrill giggle above the cowboy sounds but it was somewhat unusual to learn it was a cowgirl. As I have mentioned before, the rodeo boys were more inclined to seek out the local girls in each town because there were no entanglements when the rodeo ended. Shotguns are famous for their short range. A cowboy's little black book was never filled with girls' names and addresses, but the names and actions of the different bucking-stock he had observed or ridden. The main difference was that they expected to see the same bucking stock again sometime.

An old cowboy at the bar nudged me and whispered, "She's really ready, ain't she?"

Without turning around, I knew he was old. Really old. He was not in the huddle.

The cowgirl stepped out onto the dance floor with a broad, awkward cowboy who looked awfully drunk and at this point I was able to get a better look at her. She was a thin girl, almost too thin, with frizzy blonde hair showing under the brim of her wide black hat. Even from a few feet away I could see that she wore too much makeup on her high-cheekboned face. Her eyelashes, thick with mascara, surrounded grey eyes that were glassy with what appeared to be a forced gaiety. When I saw the way her long legs looked in the skin-tight rodeo pants, from her crotch to the floor reminded me of the bottom half of a capital "H" and it made me wonder if she ordered her saddles made with a special square-topped seat.

"Who is she?" I inquired of the old cowboy.

"Who? You mean Sally?" (*As with Jebo, I prefer to give her this alias.*)

"Yeah. If that's her name. I've never seen her in my part of the country."

"Sally's a trick rider. Rides broncs once in a while. I think she and her brothers are from Indiana or someplace like that." He looked longingly toward the bull-bunch, no doubt regretting his age. "She's been married to a mighty good man, but he got fed up with her chippyin' and run her off a month or so ago."

"She working at this show?"

"Trick ridin'—and quadrille. They don't have no women bronc ridin' here no more. Why'd you ask?"

"I thought maybe she could help me get a job. I don't know anybody."

"Job?" The wrinkled face screwed up into a mass of tighter folds and his voice kind of squeaked. "What can a little gal like you do? Ride quadrille?"

"Quadrille? Never heard of it. Do you ride four horses at once?"

He laughed. "Nope. It's just like square-dancing, only it's on horseback." He pronounced it skwar-dancin', and it was a second or so before I figured out what he meant. "But you don't wanna get mixed up with Sally, little lady. You'd be better off goin' over thar alone."

"Why? What's wrong with her as far as the rodeo is concerned?"

"Nothin' really. It's jest that she—er—that is—she drinks too much, fer one thing."

"Don't we all?" I asked innocently. It was mean of me to egg him on, because he was sincere in his intentions, but I thought it was cute the way this old cowboy was so flustered, yet protective. In his time, he probably had been one of the wildest of the wild bunch.

"You know what I mean, don't you?" he seemed painfully embarrassed.

"Sure. I know." I patted him on the arm. "And thanks, anyway. All I want is some information—then I'll be on my way. Okay?"

He shrugged his shoulders and turned back to his drink, rather sadly.

When the music stopped, I elbowed my way through to Sally.

I introduced myself and inquired, "Did you try to get a job riding broncs here? I thought I might."

"Broncs?" Sally's wink covered one eye that was glassy from booze and gave her thin face a lop-sided look when she replied, "Nope, just trick-riding, and Slim here can tell you I'm pretty goddamned good at tricks. Tell her, Slim, you no-good bastard! She laughed shrilly and nudged a tall cowboy at her side.

"Best there is," Slim agreed, patting the back of the "H" with approval.

I don't know why the cuss words sounded so rank to me, just because they were coming out of Sally's mouth. I had learned a few of the standard cuss words at a very young age, but now I wondered if those expressions categorized me in the same way, when others met me for the first time.

Just then the bartender came out of a back room leading the billy-goat that was their mascot, and I forgot about Sally for the moment. The goat made the rounds of the tables eating peanuts, potato chips, cigarette butts, or anything that was fed to him.

It seemed to bother Sally that she was being ignored, especially because of a goat, and she began talking to me again in her high-pitched voice.

"How come you're asking about the rodeo?" she asked. "You need a free pass or something?"

"No. I'm going over in a few minutes to see about riding broncs."

"You are?" Sally sobered slightly and squinted her eyes as she stepped away from Slim and looked me over from Stetson to Justins. "Don't tell me you ride broncs? You look more like a kindergarten teacher."

"That's what my mother was, before she married my dad." This conversation sounded out of place to me, but I guess without knowing it, I was lonely for a woman friend. Betty hadn't been much company on the trip, once the fighting began between our two male passengers and then the Hazens against each other.

"Your old lady taught school, too?" Sally laughed that shrill, raucous laugh again.

I flinched when she used the term "old lady" when it applied to my mother, but when she continued, I realized it was just her way.

"I suppose you had to go through the *whom-who* and *I-me* gig every time you opened your mouth?" She nudged me with a bony elbow, and giggled, "I know what it's like. My old lady was a school teacher in Kansas and I used to devil her all the time by sayin' ain't just for the hell of it. She got so she'd slap me real hard whenever she knew I was talking wrong on purpose."

Sally paused long enough to take a drink, and glance around at the hovering group of men. I think she was checking to be sure she was still the center of attraction. Then she continued, "I remember once I fell off an old bronc my brothers put me on. I came into the house and my old lady wanted to know what happened to me. When I told her I'd been *throwed*, she hauled off and slapped me for not saying *thrown*. She didn't even ask if I was hurt!"

I smiled, but the term "the old lady" still bothered me. It sounded crude. I guess my expression did not show how I felt because she continued.

"But that slap wouldn't have been so bad, if it had been the last one. The very next Saturday when I stayed out all night after a dance, I sneaked through the kitchen so she wouldn't catch me." Sally threw back her head and cackled, "Slim, are you listening? You'll get a bang out of this."

She gulped some more whiskey. "Well, when my old lady caught me sneaking in, she said, 'What happened to you this time?' and I thought I'd better watch my grammar, so I said, 'I was screwn by Georgie, the neighbor boy.' You know what? She slapped me anyway! Boy, that old lady of mine's a corker, I'll tell you."

When the laughter subsided, I tried to get Sally back to the subject of my getting a bronc-riding job. She looked at me again, briefly, and said, "First of all, you gotta put on rodeo clothes. They won't even talk to a gal in Levis at a show like this."

The cowboy called Slim whisked her away to the bandana-sized dance floor to jitterbug to an orchestra that sounded like a washing-machine full of tin cups.

I returned to sit by the old cowboy.

"What's the matter?" he asked, "Thet Sally say somethin' to hurt your feelin's?"

"No. But she told me I'd need some regular rodeo clothes if I expected to work here—and I don't have anything but Levis."

"Why don't you see Ben? He. . ."

"Ben who?"

"Ben's the only name I know. He sells all them bright colored clothes the gals wear, you know, them bell-bottomed pants and stuff.

He's got a camper full of them and you oughta be able to find him around the rodeo headquarters."

"Maybe I'll give it a try. Thanks."

I started to leave but Sally caught up with me and grabbed my arm. She had a powerful grip in those long thin fingers.

"Say, Jean," she began. "If you're alone, why don't we share a room? It'd be cheaper for both of us."

"I'm sorry, Sally, but I already have one. Upstairs."

"Good!" she giggled, "I don't have one so we can share your room!"

Before I could object, she had returned to the bull herd, so I left.

I located Ben, the rodeo tailor, at a hamburger stand inside the stadium and he brought several outfits from his camper for me to try on in one of the restrooms. I finally bought a beautiful red and blue suit with a white satin blouse that fit like it had been tailor-made for me. Ben assumed I was one of the contract riders with a standard contract so he extended credit to me without question.

I always wore expensive boots and a good-looking hat so when I donned my new clothes, and tied a red silk scarf around my neck, I strutted over to the headquarters feeling for the first time as though I actually belonged.

At the rodeo headquarters I was told in no uncertain terms that women's bronc-riding was out of the question.

"What about quadrille?" I asked Fred Kressman, the man in charge. "Couldn't you work me into that someway?"

"We have all the riders we need—but we'll keep you in mind."

How many times had I heard that "brush-off"?

The arena director stepped up just then and whispered to Kressman, before turning to me. "Let us know where we can reach you. There's one of the riders we're not too sure about. Might go on a binge any time. We're kind of worried about her."

"You won't have any trouble finding me," I promised. "I'll be under your feet every time you turn around."

They both smiled at what they assumed was an exaggerated statement. They did not know about the $20 worth of rodeo clothes and $2 per day room rent that had to come out of my non-existent wages.

I think they closed the rodeo office that night just to get rid of me. Kressman finally told me there could not possibly be any changes in the quadrille group until the rodeo started the next day.

I returned to the Billy Goat Bar, and while I was having a couple of beers with Scrappy, I saw Sally leaving with her friend, Slim. I assumed she had found a room for the night and I felt much better.

Before long I decided to go to bed so Scrappy offered to walk me to my room because there were a lot of drunks in the area. We kind of giggled about it when I told him my room was just upstairs from the bar. When we reached my room, I told him good-night, and when I inserted my key I was surprised to find the door was already unlocked. I pushed it open.

There, on my narrow little cot were Sally and Slim, completely nude! I was so surprised, I just stood there and stared at Slim's active backside. It was not only a shock to find the two of them in my bed, but it was their nonchalance at what should have been an embarrassing situation, that stunned me. However, giving him credit for a modicum of modesty, Slim did reach back and pull a sheet part way over the two of them, but when he said, over his shoulder, "Hi, kids! Somebody light me a cigarette?" that was a bit much.

I heard Sally giggle when Scrappy pulled me out into the hallway.

"You know they were here?" he asked, stunned. He looked as wide-eyed as I felt.

"Hell, no! She mentioned sharing my room, but I thought she meant with me."

"What'll you do about her? I mean, *them*."

"Damned if I know." I slumped against the wall and slid down to sit on the floor. "Suppose if I wait out here long enough, they'll go away?"

Scrappy shrugged. "Your guess is as good as mine, but I wouldn't count on it. I'll wait here with you till we find out."

We sat and visited for awhile. Cy Taillon came up the narrow stairs and sat on the floor with us. That was the first I realized he was announcing the show that year and I was equally as surprised to see him staying at such a small hotel. Guess money was a factor to everyone that fall, and besides, we were right across the street from the arena. While Cy was there with me, Scrappy went downstairs and brought back some beer for all of us. Cy did not asked any questions so we did not volunteer any information.

After Cy went to his room, I asked Scrappy if he would mind asking Slim and Sally when they might be leaving.

He stuck his head in the doorway then came back to report.

"Them bastards are asleep!" he told me. "Now what're you gonna do?"

"Damned if I know."

"I'd ask you over to where I'm staying, but there's already six of us in Davis' apartment!"

I thought for a minute, then suggested, "Let's go in and see if we can't fix me a bed on the floor or something. Okay?"

"Sure! But I ain't leavin' you with a mess like this."

I took my levis and shirt to the bathroom down the hall, and changed into them to protect my new red suit, then I came back and tried lying on the floor and covering myself with the blankets that had been kicked off of the bed. It was much too cold.

Meantime, Scrappy examined the only piece of furniture in the room besides the narrow cot and it was a long old-fashioned dresser, with two drawers of about five feet in length.

"I know!" he grinned. "Remember the kid in the comics that was always sleeping in dresser drawers? If he can do it, we can do it. He began pulling the drawers out and setting them side by side on the floor.

"We?"

"Sure. I ain't gonna leave you alone with these jerks." His eyes wrinkled at the corners, and he grinned. "You won't mind if I share your twin-drawers with you?"

I bowed dramatically. "I assure you, Mister Patch, sir, it would be a pleasure! We seem to be a bit short of linen for the spare beds, but you're more than welcome to join me. That is, if you don't mind a rather hard mattress."

He bowed in return, dramatically, and took the fingertips of my right hand as he led me to my drawer. "And so, madam, I bid thee good-night!"

At that point, each of us climbed into our own bed. Draping hand towels over the end of each drawer as pillows, and hanging our feet out of the other end, we went to sleep.

My faith in humanity took an upward swing.

In the morning, Sally and Slim thought it was funny to find Scrappy and me asleep in the dresser drawers so I tolerated their witty remarks until Sally giggled about Scrappy sleeping in "Jean's drawers," and I abruptly switched the conversation to other topics.

I told them about my job search and how it might depend on one of the women not showing up for work. I had a feeling that person might be Sally, but she didn't seem offended so I decided I was probably wrong.

"All of which reminds me," I said, jumping out of my drawer, "I've got to get over there, in case there's some news."

I rushed to the bathroom again to change back into my new suit. When I returned, the room was empty. Sally had already left with no explanations, no apologizes, and no "thank you" note. Also no share of the room rent.

I headed for the rodeo office to begin my daily vigil, underfoot. At least they had some doughnuts and coffee on hand.

The rodeo began that day. Although I was still unemployed, I watched every move of the quadrille riders just in case I had an opportunity to replace one of them. I tried to make as many inquiries as possible without disclosing my complete ignorance of this program. I learned from one cowboy that the horses used in the quadrille had been ridden so many times in that one event that they seldom needed to be reined by the rider and they performed each of the turns automatically.

As the cowboy put it, "With them big old paint horses, all you gotta do is hang on, and protect your knees in the turns!"

"Knees? Why?"

"When they skid to a stop and make them Alaman Lefts, them paint horses cut 'er so short they'll tear a leg plumb off'n you if you ain't careful."

I had square-danced at a couple of after-rodeo events and understood the basic principles of a quadrille, but as I watched, I could see what the cowboy meant about those horses crowding each other during the turns. The entire ride was executed with the horses at a dead run, from beginning to end. If I ever did get the job, I'd be lucky to stay on, let alone worrying about reining the horse. Financially speaking, I'd manage some way, if given the opportunity.

For the next two nights I continued to sleep in the dresser drawer while Sally entertained an assortment of cowboys in my bed. She somehow always got to the room before I did.

"Why don't you run her off, Janie?" Scrappy asked one afternoon in the rodeo office. I had just told him how tired I was after sitting in the hall most of the night waiting for the cot springs to stop squeaking so I could go in and get some sleep.

"You know she's nothing but trouble," he added.

"Yeah, I know," I yawned, "but she's the first woman rodeo hand who's ever been friendly to me and that ought to be worth something."

"From what I saw the other night, I'd say she's pretty damned friendly with just about everybody."

Just then the arena director charged into the office.

"Where's that girl?" he blurted. "Can you find that girl to ride quadrille today? Ruby's on a bender."

Kressman answered wryly, "Did you look under your left foot? She's bound to be under one of them."

"Here I am!" I jumped up from where I was seated on the floor reading a magazine. "Over here behind the desk. You mean me, right? To work? Riding quadrille?"

He looked over the desktop and frowned. "Yeah. That's right, but it might be just this one performance. It'll depend on Ruby."

"That's okay!" I crawled to my feet. "Where's my horse? Who's my partner?"

"For Chrissakes, kid, slow down a minute!" he grinned. "Soon as you sign a release form, you just go on down the ramp to the horse stalls and ask for Ruby's horse. They'll get you mounted up and tell you who to ride with."

"Do I sign a release just to ride quadrille?"

"Sure," he answered over his shoulder as he hurried toward the arena. "We can't be responsible in case anything happens."

Nothing did happen. Nothing bad, that is. I managed surprisingly well, but the credit really goes to the black and white pinto horse I rode, and the man who was my partner. Luckily he was aware of my ignorance and with quiet rapid instructions each time his horse circled mine, he prepared me for the next move.

I was notified after the show that I would ride in every performance the rest of the week.

"The hotel man, the tailor, and I thank you," I thought to myself, but only uttered the "thank you" part out loud.

Once my quadrille job was certain, I began pestering Kressman to let me ride one or two saddle-broncs. I think he considered it some sort of a joke to string me along because his "no's" were generally interwoven with enough kind words that I kept trying.

Buck Jones, the movie actor, was making a personal appearance at the stadium and was one of the judges in the riding events. He had hired Joe Venus, a jockey and bareback bronc rider, to help care for his famous white horse, Silver.

When Joe first hit Chicago, he was so broke that the task of babysitting Silver appealed to him, but after winning some day-money in the bull-riding and bareback riding, the extra work was a drag. One evening following the rodeo, Scrappy asked him if he would be coming over to Billy Goat's Bar with us.

"Naw," Joe replied dejectedly, "I gotta put the baby to bed. I think Jones'd keep Silver in his own hotel room if they'd let him. He's sure nuts about that horse!"

"Okay, we'll see you!" Scrappy told the sad-faced Joe. "Someday you'll smarten up and quit asking for work."

When we had a bite to eat and headed back to Billy Goat's, we saw Joe riding Silver, bareback, across the street from the stadium, right through the heavy traffic.

"Good God!" I gasped. "He'll get killed!"

Scrappy shook his head. "Even worse, he'll get that horse crippled up."

We hurried over to Joe and it was easy to see he had been drinking since we left him. He was so tiny, he looked like a monkey on a circus elephant.

"What're you doin' here?" I scolded him. "Don't you know you'll get fired?"

"Yeah," he grinned, "I bet I will at that!"

"After you put Silver away, why not come back and have a drink?" I suggested. Joe squinted over his shoulder at the speeding cars. "Me ride through that mess? You think I'm crazy? If Jones wants his baby, he can come over here and get him."

By that time we were entering Billy Goat's, and Joe rode through the door right behind us. He caused quite a commotion at first until everyone saw how well-behaved Silver was, then they began buying whiskey for Joe as fast as he could drink it.

As the novelty wore off, the free drinks stopped coming and Joe reined Silver toward the door.

"Where you goin', Pal?" Scrappy asked.

"To find a new bar."

Scrappy and I looked at each other.

We had been drinking just enough of Joe's leftovers that it seemed like a good idea to join him. If it worked for Joe, it just might work for all three of us.

"We're with you!" we both hollered above the bar noises. Scrappy motioned toward the end of the bar. "Pull your trusty steed over to a bar stool so us little people can get on. You got yourself a couple-a passengers."

Because all of us were small, we must have looked like three little monkeys on the back of Buck Jones' pride and joy.

At the next three bars, we had more free drinks than we could handle.

"Let's go back to Billy Goat's," I begged. "I wanna be closer to home when I fall off of here." Even though I was seated between Joe and Scrappy, I did not feel very secure, the way they were both weaving back and forth.

At Billy Goat's we climbed down and led the horse onto the tiny dance floor. The pitiful band was trying to play some Spanish music and I managed to pry Silver's mouth open far enough to put the end of a maraca into it. When the horse shook his head to dislodge it, his rhythm was not all that bad.

"Listen to that!" I announced proudly. "He's better'n any of them."

A shadow fell over us and the music faded. The ominous hush did not register because my brain was too fuzzy but I wanted to know what was between me and the back bar lighting so I turned around. I found myself staring at the fanciest belt buckle I'd ever seen. I looked upward, one pearl snap-button at a time, until I met the glaring eyes of Buck Jones himself.

"Oh, hi!" I began weakly. "Didja hear. . . ?"

With cold deliberation, Jones removed the maraca from Silver's mouth and led the horse from the bar. He fired Joe with one look.

"Whew!" Scrappy said. "We're lucky he didn't have us thrown in the pokey."

I had more important worries. "If you ask me," I grumbled, "he's got a lotta guts abducting the only good musician in the place!"

People were crowding around Joe to offer their sympathy because he had lost his job, but as soon as they saw the contented smile on his face, they cleared away.

I might have tried to hold one more drink if I had not seen Sally dancing up a storm with her latest "friend." This looked like a good time to sneak to my room and lock the door so I could sleep in the cot at least once. I figured I might need to hang my feet over the end of the bed from force of habit, but at least I'd have a pillow.

The night clerk probably thought someone was chasing me when I came stumbling up the stairs as fast as I could travel. He started to say something but I charged on past him to my room. I did not stop to wonder why the door was not locked but immediately saw the reason. There was Slim, sitting on the edge of my bed, smoking a cigarette!

"Well, Helloooo!" he laughed, jumping to his feet. "I didn't figger Sally to send in a sub, but that's okay. Com'ere, little one."

Slim made a grab for me and I ducked out of his reach. I felt so angry that my scheme had been thwarted that it tended to slow my reflexes. However, I snapped out of it in time to escape and run down the hall toward the bathroom with Slim stumbling after me, giggling like a teenager. His attitude was playful, rather than insane as Jebo's recent attack had been, but he was no less determined. I barely reached the bathroom in time to slam the door and lock it before he smashed into it right behind me. I was surprised that the feeble lock held, but it did.

The walls of the bathroom were actually eight-foot partitions, and there was a three-foot gap between the top of them and the high ceiling. The bathroom itself was directly over the stairway and I could hear Slim climbing onto the bannister in an attempt to scale the wall on that side, but he must have come close to falling because the chuckling ceased abruptly and a few not-too-mild oaths followed. He returned to pound on the door again.

Once I was confident the lock would hold, I gave up my dream of having a bed to myself and crawled into the bathtub. In a surprisingly short time I fell asleep.

Someone knocked on the door, and I heard Cy Taillon say, "Open up! You going to stay in there all day?"

I unlocked the door and stepped into the hall, rubbing my eyes. I mumbled something like, "Is it morning already?"

Cy just shook his head and pushed past me.

I felt groggy most of the day. I was sore and stiff from spending the night in that hard bath-tub and I had also managed to catch a cold. Otherwise, I felt fine.

In the midst of the other concessions at the stadium, there was a thirty-foot bar. I really wanted a drink as soon as the quadrille was over that evening. I had just passed the popcorn stand that was directly across from one of the arena exits when I glanced at the sexy-looking blonde who was handing several bags of popcorn to a fat man in a baggy suit. During the brief period while she looked down to make change out of a drawer beneath the counter, the arena door flew open and a Brahma bull charged through. Someone had left the gate unlatched and the bull ran out, hitting the marble floor in the hall and skidding straight across until he slammed into the popcorn stand with his chest. When the bull came to a stop, his nose was resting on the top 38 of the 38-27-38 blonde.

The girl's eyes kept getting bigger and bigger. She gasped for breath, then started screaming. She was still screaming after the bull had backed away and skated down the hall. The fat man just stood there, hanging onto the counter for support, a yellow puddle gradually forming between his legs.

I moved on toward the bar. The bull might come back and I sure did not want to be killed feeling as bad as I did. I wanted to die happy. I figured one beer might help prepare me for the worst, but by then we had word that the bull had been roped by a pickup man who had followed up the ramp to the seating area. A few of the spectators must have thought this was part of the show because they began to clap at the unexpected thrill they received for the regular price of admission. No one was hurt.

The blonde stopped screaming. The fat man relaxed his grip on the counter and shook his legs one at a time before stepping away from the counter and heading toward the restroom. He left the popcorn and his change on the counter.

I ordered another beer.

"Wasn't that just too thrilling? A warm, soft voice came from my right but I was unable to see who it was until I dropped my elbow back to my side and set the empty glass on the bar.

What I saw was a sleek brunette wearing more fur than a Yellowstone Park bear in the wintertime, and from her left wrist dangled the first diamond charm bracelet I had ever seen.

In a minute I closed my mouth.

"I said, wasn't that thrilling?" she repeated.

"You bet." I replied. Clever dialogue. I blinked against the glare of the bracelet. "I always get a big charge out of those Brahmas. No pun intended."

"Charge—out of the Brahmas! Oooooh! That's clever," she squealed. "Some of you rodeo people have the cutest sense of humor."

She stepped up to the bar. " I was just buying a drink—won't you join me?"

"You bet." It would have been silly to mention that the charging-bull pun was unintentional. If she bought drinks for funny people, then I would try very hard to be one of the funny people.

It turned out that this furry sparkling gal's name was Alicia and she had just discovered cowboys. Scrappy, Joe and several others had now joined us and no-one else was allowed to buy a drink. This, of course, was fine with us, and when she invited the entire group to a party at her home there was a chorus of "You damn betcha!" replies all along the bar.

During the course of the evening I wandered around the mansion and was introduced to a newsman from the *Times*. His name was Al something or other, who happened to be a left-over from Alicia's be-kind-to-reporters phase. We talked about the forthcoming rodeo performance when all of the *Times*' newsboys would be given free passes to the rodeo. Joe Louis was also scheduled to make a personal appearance that day, especially for the boys. I told Al how disappointed I felt at not being allowed to ride any saddle-broncs after coming "all the way from Montana for that very reason." The more we talked, the more excited he became at the prospect of my riding a bronc for the newsboys' show.

How clever of him to think of it all by himself!!

The next thing I knew, Al disappeared. I figured my scheme was a flop, so I forgot about him. Maybe I overplayed my hand.

As the last of the guests straggled out the door I guess I must have appeared exhausted because Alicia invited me to spend the rest of the night at her house

"You mean sleep in a bed? You bet!"

Apparently she thought I was being funny because she clapped her hands so hard I thought the diamond bracelet was going to fall apart. I cupped my hands under it but no such luck.

"Ooooh!" she squealed. "You say the funniest things!"

"Yeah. Where else would a person sleep? Heh! Heh!"

Alicia beckoned to one of the maids and told her to take me to my room. I was tempted to sleep on the floor or in the tub so I would not get spoiled, but it was impossible to resist the fifteen-acre bed.

"We've got hay meadows at home smaller than that bed," I told the maid. She made a quick exit, giggling. Maybe I should think about putting together a standup comedy act.

After a hot bath in a lavender sunken tub (prepared by a different maid), I crawled between the lavender sheets and collapsed. I did not awaken until Alicia called me on the house phone at noon the following day to say her driver would take me back to the arena whenever I was ready.

As soon as I arrived, I rushed into the rodeo office to make my daily plea. Kressman was on his way out when I stopped him and began my daily routine. "Mister Kressman, don't you think it would be a good idea for me to ride just one bronc during the show tomorrow afternoon while the newsboys are here?"

"I. . ."

"I know you haven't had any women bronc-riders here for two years, but that's all the more reason for me to do this. For the kids. They might never get another chance to see a woman ride a bucking horse. There aren't too many of us, you know."

"I. . ."

"You shouldn't refuse me until you've given it a great deal of thought, Mister Kressman. If you'd let me ride one bronc tomorrow, I'd stop pestering you. That in itself should make it worth while."

I had not noticed the man seated with his back to me until he rose and turned toward me. It was Al, the reporter.

"I think Mr. Kressman's been trying to tell you he's already agreed to let you ride. Isn't that right, Fred?"

Kressman sounded exhausted when he replied, "That's right. But the promise she just made is worth a great deal. Maybe I should get it down on paper."

And so it was that I had a chance to ride a saddle-bronc in the Chicago Stadium. The horse bucked enough to make my ride look good and the newsboys provided a wonderful audience. Al took pictures of me with some of the boys for the next edition of the Times and with them, at least, I rated as much applause as Buck Jones and Joe Louis.

I was getting spoiled with Al taking so many pictures and when I had an opportunity to sit behind the saddle on a horse Joe Louis was riding around the arena, I put on my best smile for the camera man. Problem was, when I browsed through the *Times* the next morning I discovered that Louis was so huge I was not visible in any of the pictures!

Even without the extra money for my bronc ride, I still would have been one very happy cowgirl.

When the rodeo was over, I collected my wages and began paying bills. I paid for my room (my room?) And then I located Ben. I splurged for one more *pants-and-vest* outfit plus two blouses. Little did Ben know he was lucky I finally had enough cash to pay my bill in full.

"How'd you gettings along vit da voom?" the manager asked when I counted out the cash. "Vas da bed goot enuffs?"

"I think it must have been," I assured him. He continued to look puzzled when I waved goodbye and walked away.

Scrappy and Sally's friend Slim were standing on the sidewalk when I came back downstairs. We were discussing where each of us would go from there. Scrappy to some rodeo in Texas and Slim to Nevada. When I admitted I was undecided, Scrappy asked if I had already checked out.

"Yup. Just got through."

"Sally pay you anything for the room?"

"Nope, but that's okay."

Slim interrupted, "It's none of my business, but there's something you maybe ought'a know." He looked ill-at-ease at the thought of divulging a secret. "You know when you first told Sally your job depended on one of the riders getting drunk and not showing up? Well, she spent twenty bucks of her own money getting Ruby too drunk to show up for the quadrille!"

Scrappy and I looked at each other and started to laugh.

"Well, I'll be damned! What d'ya know."

# Chapter Ten

When the Chicago show was over, I was somewhat less vehement about dropping out of the rodeo business, but I was still seeking an alternate career. My first obligation was to call Cameo Pictures Corporation in Hollywood and double check on the status of my option with them. The last time I talked to Cactus Mack when I was on my way home from Hollywood, he had more or less prepared me for what was taking place at that time. It sounded as though money problems had stalled the progress of the western serial we had previously discussed and with Sanforth busy directing two movies in a row, he was not likely to devote much time to their financial roadblock. I decided to forget the whole thing for the present.

So what next? I had paid for my room and as I stepped out of the front door, I ran into Scrappy. He was on his way to find the Hazens to see about going to New Mexico with them and he asked if I wanted to go along.

I told him I had about decided to hang around Chicago for awhile, at least until February when the Florida rodeos would begin. I thanked him but said I had to decline. "No Whirligig this time." he said, grinning.

"That's not it. This is my first time in Chicago and I'd kind of like to check out the night life in a big city. So where's Whirligig going next?"

"Damned if I know. Let him hassle somebody else for awhile." He grinned, no doubt thinking, as I was, about all of their squabbling on our trip from Montana.

I asked him to tell the Hazens "thanks" for me, again, because I had rarely seen them during the rodeo. Then we both agreed they were no doubt happy to be free of us after our strange trip from Montana.

Before we parted, I let him know how much I appreciated his help during the rodeo and we had a good laugh about the dresser-drawer sleeping arrangements. I gave him a goodbye hug and as he turned to leave, I realized I had no idea what I was going to do next.

I returned to the Billy Goat Hotel and checked in again. This time I would sleep on a bed, and I insisted they give me one that was at least three-quarter size. Actually, their beds were not a noticeable improvement over their dresser drawers and the bath tub!

At the front desk, I bought a copy of the *Times*, which was now my favorite newspaper, so I could check rooms for rent. I had no idea why I was remaining in Chicago, but with no other plans for the immediate future, one place was as good as another. Quoting from an article in the paper: "Chicago is a prosperous, wide-open city. It is a city without a price and those who know their way around, can buy anything from women to dope to politicians. The hundreds of night-clubs from the famous Chez Paree to the many little bars on Rush Street, cater to every taste."

Riding city buses throughout my first day as a Chicagoan, I actually did locate, and rent, for one month, a dark high-ceilinged room in a dirty high-roofed brownstone within walking distance of The Loop. I put my two new suits and my four new blouses on hangers in the closet, put my recently acquired changes of underwear and socks in a dresser drawer, put my toothbrush, comb, and lipstick on a two-inch shelf above the sink, and I was unpacked. My hobbles, buck-rein and spurs were in their own little satchel as a reminder that I would not remain unemployed forever, regardless of what happened in Chicago. There would always be a rodeo someplace, sometime.

It took one entire day for me to build up enough courage to go job-hunting. As a rule, my quests for employment took place at one rodeo headquarters or another so I was generally surrounded by friends—or at least acquaintances. Now it was pretty scary for me to challenge a city of strangers to move over and make room for one solitary cowgirl.

Even if I found a job, I had a feeling that the loneliness and strangeness of Chicago would bother me the most, to say nothing of the damned wind. I swear, that damp icy air blowing across the Michigan Avenue bridge, never stops. twenty-four hours a day!

During our few hours with Alicia, she of the diamonds and furs, I did remember being introduced to several different bar owners. One of them, a short pudgy man, was more friendly than the others. That much I remembered. He described his place as more of a night-club and said it was actually below ground level. He made quite a fuss over my rodeo performance and what he referred to as my "costume." He said when the rodeo ended I should see him about a job if I decided to stay in Chicago. At the time, I could not imagine any job in a big city night club that I could possibly be qualified to do so I assumed that the free-flowing booze at Alicia's house had prompted his offer.

For the first three days, I had no intention of checking the validity of this man's offer, but the more I wandered around, answering one type of ad after another, the more I became convinced I should slip in, unannounced, and see exactly what kind of a place this man owned.

I had the address on a business card he gave me and at seven o'clock on my third evening, I put on one of my new rodeo outfits and caught a cab to the aforementioned down-stairs nightclub called Ye Olde Cellar.

The hostess seated me in a small two-person booth where I tried to adjust to the dimly lit surroundings. As everything gradually came into focus I discovered several items of interest. First and foremost, scattered throughout the club there were individual mini-crap tables which were really just one-person booths with the dealers rolling dice out of a cup in some sort of dice game I had never seen before.

It was while I was taking in all areas of the place that I spotted Alicia with four husky male companions at the bar. Someone I knew! I was so glad to see a familiar face that I practically ran over to where they were.

"Hi, there!" I said, extending my hand eagerly. I sensed her reluctance to shake hands and I decided maybe she did not recognize me. After all, we had been drinking quite a bit the evening we were in her home so this was a possibility. Although my wardrobe should have been a clue, I was just about to remind her where we met when she turned away from me to speak to one of her companions.

To cover my embarrassment, I said, "How about I buy you a drink?"

"Sorry," she replied, without looking at me "We're just leaving."

I was totally confused. Her manufactured excuse did not hold up under the evidence of full glasses in front of each of them.

So who needs a brick wall to fall on them?

"Sorry." I bowed from the waist and headed for the door, leaving my own drink at my booth. Untouched. Unpaid for. . .

My friend Al, the *Times* reporter, almost knocked me down as he barged through the front door, stumbling on the bottom step.

"Hello, there, bronc-rider!" he exclaimed. He pumped my hand vigorously.

"Hello, yourself," I told him. "You arrived just in time, d'ya know that? I have recently been led to believe that hand-shaking was an ancient rite, performed during certain primitive ceremonies like the 'Drunken Cowboys Convention' and such."

"What?" Al looked puzzled, then glanced over my shoulder. "Oh. *Her*."

His eyes looked sad for a second—but only a second. "The rodeo's over, y'know. Alicia's playing International Hockey this week."

"Good for her." I tried not to sound bitter but I was still embarrassed. I was leery of making another mistake, and I am sure I sounded downright timid when I asked, "Could I buy you a drink, Al?"

"You sure can," he answered, "right after I buy you one!"

Before long the boss, Pudgy, arrived. In my own mind, this was always his name.

With Al as an enthusiastic supporter, I inquired about a job. I did not remind Pudgy that it was because of his invitation that I was there, because if he had forgotten the incident, he would think I was lying.

"You know anything about dealing a twenty-six game?" Pudgy asked.

I had been observing the five girls at their individual dice tables and I replied honestly, "I've never even seen one before—but I cut my teeth on a pair of dice, and I can count to twenty-six. Does that qualify?"

"Okay. You're hired!" His chins slapped against his red polka-dot tie when he laughed.

One thing bothered me. "What about wardrobe? I noticed that the other dealers are wearing formals."

Al interrupted before Pudgy could reply.

"She'll wear her rodeo clothes, won't she? That'd be the biggest attraction you've had in here for a long time. Right?"

Pudgy rubbed his chins reflectively, then nodded, "Why, sure! That's what I figured all along. . ."

I wondered if Al knew how right he was when he said I had to wear rodeo clothes!

They put me to work immediately, with only a few minutes of instruction as to how the game was handled. There was barely time to thank Al before he received a message about a story assignment and had to leave. Except for a phone call a week later saying he was going to New York, I never talked to him again.

With my two new suits and blouses, and half-a-dozen bright colored neckerchiefs, I managed to get by for a week or so. Then, one day I was chatting with Mrs. Ellerby, an elderly woman who lived down the hall from me, and when I mentioned that I was going to need more blouses to add variety to my wardrobe, she asked why I did not make some of my own. She said she would be glad to help me if I wanted to rent a sewing machine! This would never have occurred to me because Mother did not sew and consequently neither did I, but with Mrs. Ellerby's help, maybe I could do it.

I had nothing else to keep me occupied during the daytime hours so Mrs. Ellerby and I picked out enough bright-colored material for three blouses, thread to match, and a pattern with instructions that she promised would be easy to follow. We also decided to take a chance on a package of the "pearl snap buttons" that were popular on most sportswear at that time. With the do-it-yourself instructions, I thought it was worth a try.

I used Mrs. Ellerby's sewing machine that was activated by pumping on a foot pedal, and with her giving me directions, I actually made three very attractive new blouses to add to my wardrobe. Snap buttons, and all.

At work, the novelty of my western garb attracted a great deal of attention, which in turn meant more customers at my dice table. We received a percentage of winnings over and above our wages so the fact that I was making more money than the other dealers did not endear me to them. To be honest about it, they were openly hostile, especially the svelte gal with orange-colored hair who talked to mirrors. One night when she and I were seated at the bar after work, her mouth talked to me but she never took her eyes away from her image in the mirror.

Finally I said, "Dammit, pay attention!" If it is possible to slither indignantly, that is exactly how she departed.

One of my steady customers was a wealthy middle-aged man I knew only as Mister Sanderson. Each night he played one $5 game at my table. If he lost, he was satisfied and if he won, he tipped me his winnings. For personal, as well as financial reasons, I always enjoyed talking to him. He inquired about my family, the ranch, and different phases of my rodeo life. One evening he explained that his only living relative was a daughter, a girl about my own age, who was spending a year in Europe. He seemed to miss her terribly.

I eventually learned that Mr. Sanderson's first name was Warren, although I never called him by that name. He was a handsome man and his girl friend, Fifi, was a dancer at the Chez Paree. In age, she was only a few years older than me. The first time he invited me to go out to dinner with them, I invented an excuse to explain why I was unable to go. He looked at me with a knowing smile, and immediately departed in a taxi to bring Fifi back, between shows, so she could extend the invitation to me herself.

After that I went to dinner with the two of them once a week. Mister Sanderson picked me up after work and we caught the last show at the Chez Paree, then the three of us had a bite to eat and they took me home. Sometimes we dined in his penthouse in the early evening, and we all became good friends. Fifi showed no signs of jealousy, but the way she was built, why would she? After all, we Burnett women are so un-endowed that only our fingers are in danger of getting caught in the wringer, as the saying goes.

One night Mr. Sanderson told us, “If you girls want to meet me at my wholesale store tomorrow you can each choose a set of new airplane luggage that just came in.”

I needed luggage like I needed a lifetime supply of chopsticks, but the prospect of buying it wholesale appealed to my wee bit of Scotch ancestry.

It had never occurred to me that Mr. Sanderson might mean the luggage as a gift until I selected a three-piece set of my preference the next day, and handed him some money.

“What’s this for?” he asked.

“Isn’t that the right amount?”

“Hell, no. This was supposed to be a gift for each of you.”

It was my turn to look surprised. “Gosh, I didn’t know that. I was just glad to get it wholesale. In fact, I’d much rather pay you. Okay?”

He accepted the money, reluctantly, yet somehow pleased that I was not trying to get somthing for nothing.

I returned to work, happy.

At Ye Olde Cellar I had not been trying to force my friendship on any of the girls but I did attempt to be as congenial as possible. Orange-head with the “mirror complex” needled me constantly. Everyone knew she was shacking up with Pudgy when his wife was not around, yet I was in no way concerned with their private lives. I doubt that any of this would have come to a boiling point had it not been for our Christmas party when the entire crew drank more than they should after the bar closed for the night. During the late-late hours, I was in the ladies’ room where I had stretched out on the couch for a few minutes to keep from passing out on my feet.

“You’d better stay awake, honey,” the Orange-head smirked. “It’s about time for Sanderson to come and take you beddie-bye, ain’t it?”

We exchanged insults for a few minutes and she became progressively more insulting. When it reached the point where she said, “You try to make everyone think you’re so damned innocent, you make me sick.” She glanced at the others in the room as though to receive their approval, then added, “We know Sanderson didn’t give you fifty bucks worth of luggage for nothing!” She stood back, looking pleased with herself.

I struggled to prop myself on one elbow for a counter-attack.

"Well," I mumbled, just before passing out for good, "At least I don't hafta shack-up with the boss to keep my job!"

When I awoke, Orange-head was still employed and I was not. I was sure this had been her goal from the very beginning, no doubt because I had been doing quite well with the dice game. I also knew my rodeo garb had a lot to do with my success and that the novelty would soon wear off so it had not occurred to me that there was so much resentment among the other dealers. Now I knew.

I could tell Pudgy was not happy about the situation but Orange-head had him over a barrel.

I phoned Mister Sanderson and told him what happened. I was more upset about the things they said about my friendship with him than I was about losing my job. After all, I was often out of work, by choice, but had rarely ever been fired! I was seeking sympathy.

Mister Sanderson said all the right things to make me feel better and assured me that no-one really believed what they said about his and my friendship, so I felt better. Especially after he told me he and Fifi would find me another job as soon as they had a chance to think it over.

True to his word, within a week I went to work at Kitty Davis', a noisy collegiate hangout whose owner was a good friend of Fifi. Kitty hired each member of her staff with the understanding that they hold down two jobs: catering and entertaining. Again I was allowed to wear my rodeo clothes and because of the novelty, my job of selling corsages to the customers was a great success.

On occasion, when I felt the noise was sufficient to cover any errors I made in the unfamiliar lyrics, I fulfilled the other role required of me as an employee. The flower selling turned out to be a great racket. Quite a few of my male customers would buy a corsage and pin it to my shirt if they happened to be at Kitty's without a companion. Then, as soon as they departed, I removed the corsage, sprinkled a little water on it, and returned it to the cooler to resell later! Since my deal was on an inventory basis, I was able to keep all of the extra money. I was never sure how the boss of the flower concession would feel about such goings-on but since he received the required amount for his original inventory I did not worry about it.

The first few evenings I attempted to walk to work but when the wind blew me back across the bridge a couple of times, I hailed a cab to finish the trip. I soon realized it would be cheaper to move to a small hotel near Kitty's bar but I would miss Mrs. Ellerby.

On my days off, I sometimes returned to take her to lunch or just visit with her for a couple of hours.

I had a terrific crush on a handsome dark-haired bartender named Jacques. He worked at the upstairs bar of Kitty's two-story establishment, so I spent much of my time "stalking" him. Jacques paid no attention to me, which was natural enough, considering all of the well-dressed, beautiful young college students who surrounded him every night. However, I kept hoping and convinced myself he was just playing hard to get.

I still wore rodeo clothes every night that I worked, and since I was making good money for a change, I placed a call to Terre Haute, Indiana, to tell Ben (the rodeo tailor) that I needed another suit. He was gone but his wife took the message and even though my first purchases from him had been two outfits he had in stock, he had taken my measurements for future reference. I gave my order regarding color schemes and designs to Ben's wife and asked that they mail the clothes to me, C.O.D. in care of Kitty Davis' Bar.

One night after work several of us from Kitty's went to a Chinese place to eat. Jacques asked if he could take me home. I was flattered to have him finally paying attention to me until we reached the door of my room and when I told him "Good night!" he began wrestling me around the hallway. I could see why he was such a good bartender. He had eight hands.

Out of sheer disgust, Jacques said, "What's the matter with you, anyway? You been chasing after me ever since you came to work at Kitty's. What'd you expect?"

I tried to think of something sophisticated to say but all that came out of me was, "At least the cowboys I know can be friendly without acting like this." I neglected to mention Jebo.

"Cowboys!" he sneered. "I can show you things that'd make you throw wine bottles at those yokels!" He added, knowingly, "I'm French, you know."

"Yeah?" I sneered right back at him. "So was Joan of Arc, and look what happened to her."

"C'est plus qu'un crime! It's worse than a crime to be so damned stupid."

His face was filled with rage for having wasted precious time with me. He no longer looked quite as handsome when he stomped away and disappeared down the stairs.

I let myself into my room, mumbling, "A man is a man is a man."

The next day around noon, I was awakened by a neighbor and told that I had a phone call. There was one telephone in the hallway of each floor of the building and I draped a blanket around my shoulders to answer the one near my doorway.

"Come on down and have coffee with us?" a male voice invited. "We're on our way to Florida."

"Who is this?" I grumbled. I was still half asleep and my first thought was about the incident with Jacques.

"It's Ben. I'm downstairs at your rooming house. My wife had me call the Kitty Davis bar and they told me how to find you."

A friendly voice!

"Oh, hi! Did you bring my clothes?"

"I've got a car full of them. This way you can see what you're getting."

I dressed hurriedly and when I reached the lobby, I saw Ben with two cowboys and a short, round girl whose face might have been pretty had it not been completely devoid of expression.

Ben and I shook hands and he introduced the other two men. "This is Jerry. And this is Harm."

After the cowboys and I exchanged greetings, Ben turned to the girl, "And this is Ann. She's—er, that is, she's Jerry's wife."

Once we were seated in a booth, Ben said, "I heard you mention that you might take in some Florida shows, so I thought I'd see if you'd like to ride down there with us. We've got room for one more."

I knew Ben's camper was generally full of rodeo clothes, so I asked, "All of you going?"

"Yeah! I've got a bigger rig now. We've got room for five of us besides the clothes."

I thought it over for at least thirty seconds before I said, "You bet! As of yesterday, I've had my fill of city life. When we leaving?"

"Soon as you finish your coffee."

I asked if they could give me one day to take care of a couple of obligations. At first I was afraid they might go on without me but they all agreed that a good night's sleep might be a smart move before starting the long trek south. They planned to take turns driving with no stop-overs. This sounded too familiar. Thinking about the trip from Montana, I did not really look forward to the next few days but I was eager to rodeo.

They said they would pick me up at dawn the following morning.

I explained the situation to Kitty Davis when she arrived at the bar around four o'clock that afternoon. She was very understanding and even gave me whatever money I had coming so there would not be a problem of having my mail try to catch up with me.

I had a cab wait for me for a few minutes while I thanked Mrs. Ellerby for her kindness when we were living in the same building, and then my next stop was to say "Goodbye" to Mister Sanderson. I thanked him for everything and asked that he pass that same message on to Fifi. He gave me his address and told me to drop him a line once in a while so he would know I was okay. He was truly a good friend.

I rushed upstairs to "pack." All of my belongings, including hobbles, reins and spurs, fit into the medium-sized case and I filled the other two with old newspapers I found on a table down the hall from my room. I hoped the weight would be similar to an equal amount of clothing because I did not want anyone to think I was crazy enough to haul around a set of empty luggage.

At every opportunity, Harm would tease me about one thing or another and since he did not mention my suitcases, I assumed my secret was safe. Still, I wanted to get even with him if an opportunity presented itself.

At one of our gasoline stops somewhere in Kentucky, Ben and Harm were having coffee and sandwiches at the lunch counter inside the station when my chance at revenge presented itself. Jerry and Ann were looking at road maps over in a corner and I had not ordered anything, so the check for the coffee was only fifty cents.

Harm paid the waitress with a silver dollar and was waiting for his change so he could give her a tip before we left.

When she did not return to the table, he finally called out, "Say there, girlie, how's about my change?"

"Them two coffees was fifty cents," the waitress explained.

"I know that. But I gave you a dollar and I've got change coming."

"Dollar?" she echoed. "You gave me a half-dollar."

I realized this girl had probably never seen a silver dollar, so immediately a tiny elf named "Sweet Revenge" prodded me into action.

"Now, Gunner," I began reprovingly, "You shouldn't pull that kinda caper down here in Kentucky. Them con tricks was okay in Chicago, but this li'l gal will hafta make up the diff outa her own pocket if she gives you change you don't deserve!"

I nodded toward the startled waitress. "Ain't that right, honey?"

"It sure is," she said, backing toward the kitchen. "So don't you try nothing funny."

"Janie," Harm pleaded, "tell her the truth."

"I am. And I think it's a damned shame to try and cheat this little gal outa fifty cents. In fact, I don't even wanna be seen with you. Come on, gang. Let's blow."

The others followed me outside just as the owner of the diner nabbed Harm and threatened to call the police. We watched from the sidewalk in case it might become necessary to rescue Harm, but he came out in about fifteen minutes looking slightly pale. The rest of us exploded into laughter at the expression on his face.

After a few seconds, Harm joined in the hilarity.

"Jane!" he said, shaking my hand. "What say we call a truce. Okay?"

"No more teasing?"

"Nary a word."

"Okay!"

"How'd you get out of there?" Ben asked.

"It wasn't easy. I had a hell of a time gettin' that boss to look in the cash register. I guess he was afraid I'd rob him if he did! Must not be many silver dollars in this part of the country."

When we stopped laughing, we headed south again. There was room for three of us in the front and two in "jump seats" on either side with a row of clothes in between. Jerry and his wife were always pawing at each other when they were in the front with whoever was driving so Ben tried to split them up by assigning them to the jump-seats whenever possible.

By the time we reached Pensacola, Florida, they nearly had me convinced that sex was here to stay. I barely had time to get out of the car before they headed for the nearest hotel—and I never saw either of them again.

In all the rush, I left my luggage with Ben and did not pick up my new suit until the next day. Considering the fact that my bankroll was slightly depleted after I paid Ben for my new clothes and my share of gas for the trip, it came as kind of a blow to learn from the rodeo officials that they were not interested in having a woman bronc-rider in their show. Not that this was anything new, it was just that several cowboys recalled seeing women bronc-riders in various Florida shows in the past. I wandered around town, then finally went out onto one of the grassy boulevards and leaned against a palm tree while I planned my next method of attack.

With more money than usual in my Levi-bank, I was not pushing as vehemently as usual for a job. I noticed a policeman eyeing me from across the street and since there were no other people loitering in that area, I walked away with no particular destination in mind.

Once I knew I was not being followed, I slowed to a window-shopping pace. A tray of costume jewelry attracted my attention and I was lured into a novelty store by a large purple and gold ring priced at $1.50, including tax. The only jewelry I wore was the ever-present diamond ring and since I was not accustomed to frivolously spending money on myself, I resisted the urge and continued walking down the street.

My next stop was at a pool hall. Although the sign said "25-cents an hour" the rack-man agreed to let me practice on one of the tables for an hour for nothing. I finally challenged one of the players to a few games of eight-ball at fifty-cents per game, but I had overmatched myself and after losing four games in a row, I decided it was time to tackle the rodeo promoter again before my spare time depleted my bankroll even further.

I was a different person this time when I strode purposefully out of the pool hall and went straight to the rodeo office to begin my pitch. I named a list of the shows where I had performed and even displayed some of the newspaper clippings from Chicago.

By the time I left the rodeo headquarters that afternoon, I had a job riding saddle-broncs and quadrille, keeping books at the rodeo office, and making spot announcements on the local radio to advertise the show!

There was a single vacant room where Ben and Harm were staying so I moved in and Harm carried my luggage in from the car. Just before he set the large one inside the door, he hoisted it up and down a couple of times.

"What the hell you got in there?" he asked. "A bunch of rocks?"

Maybe I over-did it with the newspapers. Anyway, I did not answer and I was grateful that he did not comment further.

The rodeo was great. I rode three saddle-broncs and the only time I was thrown was when one of the pickup men took me from my bronc and set me behind the saddle on his horse. Something spooked the pickup horse, and we were both dumped into the middle of the arena.

When the show ended, I made a deal to ride in several Florida shows to be put on by Buddy Medford, a contestant and promoter.

Next was Kissimmee, Florida. I arrived there with some small change and a single $50 bill. My very first. Having a bill that size for the first time in my life, and having a bronc-riding job waiting for me, gave me a feeling of security I had not experienced before. In fact, I felt so secure I was probably a trifle obnoxious about the whole thing.

I did not realize it at the time, but it was not unusual for some of the rodeo people to carry large bills, especially the top professionals. They might win $100 to $1,500 at a single show, then compete in various events for several months before they had any income at all. Non-rodeo people do not realize that rodeo is the only professional sport where the contestant pays all of his own expenses, so they are often less than sympathetic when a cowboy's bankroll reaches the zero mark.

In the rodeo office, I was lipping off about my $50 bill, as though Grant had autographed it personally, and a hulk of a man named Norman Pearson better known as "Muscles," stepped up to me and said, "Where's that big money you keep talking about? I ain't never seen a bill that size."

Old Gullible herself fished it out of her Levi pocket and handed it to him.

"Well, well," Muscles said with mock seriousness, "I can tell you sure ain't used to handlin' that much loot so I figger there's only one way to be sure you don't leave here broke. With a quick flick of his wrists, he tore my precious money right through the middle of President Grant's nose.

"Hey! What the hell you doin'?" I shrieked, trying to grab the money away from him.

Muscles calmly handed me one half of the bill and said as he walked away, "See you after the rodeo. You can have the rest of your money then."

I was not only unfamiliar with $50 bills, but I also had never seen Muscles Pearson before. Although I already had a job for the Kissimmee rodeo, I did not know Medford well enough to ask for an advance on my wages. I not only felt sick, I felt stupid.

A nervous bull-rider with a twitching right eye, patted me on the shoulder. "Might as well face it, ma'am," he whispered, "you cain't whup the big bastard, so jest do laik he says."

I headed for the door and bumped into someone who was entering. I shoved past without looking to see who it was.

"You bettuh watts where you goin' dal," the man said.

A chill went through me. I did not need a second look to know the man was Jebo. When I started to run toward my hotel, I could hear his laughter following me all the way down the street.

*Author's photo*

First ride. Age 4. Gilt Edge, Montana

*Author's photo*

Burnett Ranch

*Author's collection*

Oceanside, California, 1937

*Author's collection*

Hollywood, California, 1937

JANE BURNETT LANDS FILM JOB IN HOLLYWOOD



NATIVE FERGUS GIRL AND GRADUATE OF LOCAL HIGH-SCHOOL TO WORK IN PICTURE SERIES FOR AL WAGER PRODUCTION CO.

The many friends of Miss Jane Burnett, daughter of Mr. and Mrs. Clint Burnett of the Gilt Edge section, and a graduate of Fergus High, will be interested to learn that this popular native Fergus County girl has just recently been signed up to appear in a series of short film subjects being made by the Al Wager Productions Co. in Hollywood.

Miss Burnett, who has the reputation of being one of Montana's cleverest women bronc riders, has been in Hollywood for several weeks looking over the picture field and is considered particularly fortunate in getting a break as soon as she did. After several weeks work on the Al Wager Productions series, it is understood she will do "doubling" and extra work with the Republic and Universal studios in the cinema metropolis.

Miss Burnett, who is one of, if not the youngest to graduate from Fergus High, and who attended the state university at Missoula for one year, writes that she attended the recent Montana picnic in Los Angeles and met a number of people from this section of the state.

*Lewistown* News-Argus

*Used with permission of Gene Autry Entertainment*

Posing with Gene Autry.

*Author's collection*

Kissimmee, Florida, 1940

*Author's collection*

Mexico City, 1940

# GREAT FALLS TRIBUNE

Great Falls, Montana, Sunday Morning, February 1, 1942

## Montana Girl One of U.S. Top Rodeo Riders

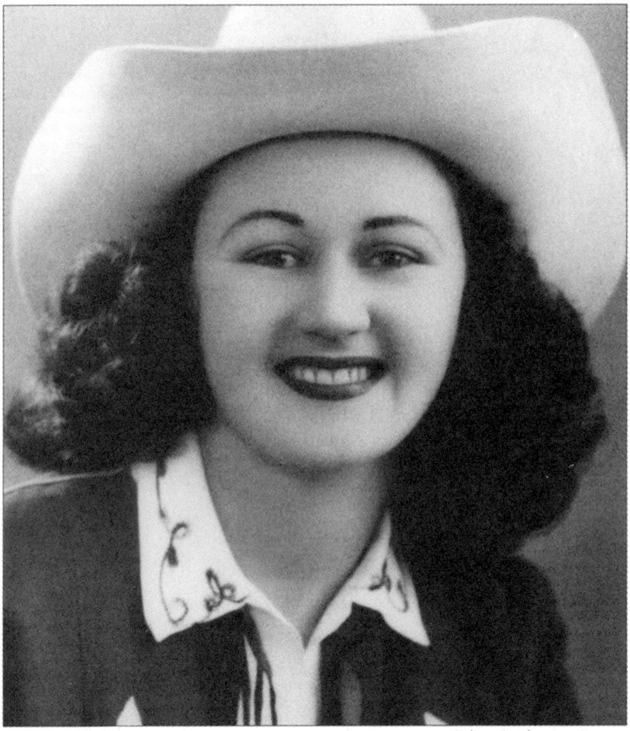

Culver Studio, Lewistown

This is Jane Burnett (Mrs. Rufus Morris), a Montana girl who is one of the nation's outstanding rodeo riders. Lewistown is her home. She is the daughter of Mr. and Mrs. Clint Burnett of the Gilt Edge area and granddaughter of William Burnett, pioneer cattleman. Jane has ridden in rodeos all over the United States. Recently she and two other Montana girls – Margie and Alice Greenough – were chosen to perform in the Madison Square Garden rodeo in New York City. In April and May this year, Miss Burnett has a contract to work for Gene Autry in a series of rodeo shows. He now has his own rodeo outfit. Jane rode with Autry and other performers last year at Palm Springs, Calif. She will soon be starting with the Autry outfit at Ardmore, Okla. She and her husband have been in major circuits the last two years. He is from Beaumont, Tex., and has returned there to work in the shipyards. For pictures showing Jane in a Lewistown celebration three years ago, see pages 8 and 9 of this issue.

**Fans Will Throng City**

**Famous Wyoming Cowgirl**
**Will Perform In Parade**
**And Shows This Week-End**

**Getting onto a bucking horse is almost as ticklish a job as staying on him, but Jane Burnett, girl rider from Lewiston, Mont., has proved her skill at both operations.**

*Author's collection*

Minneapolis, Minnesota, 1940

*Author's collection*

Palm Springs, California, 1941

*Author's collection*

New York City Hall. Posing for the press, 1941.

*Author's collection*

Cowboys' Turtle Association membership card.

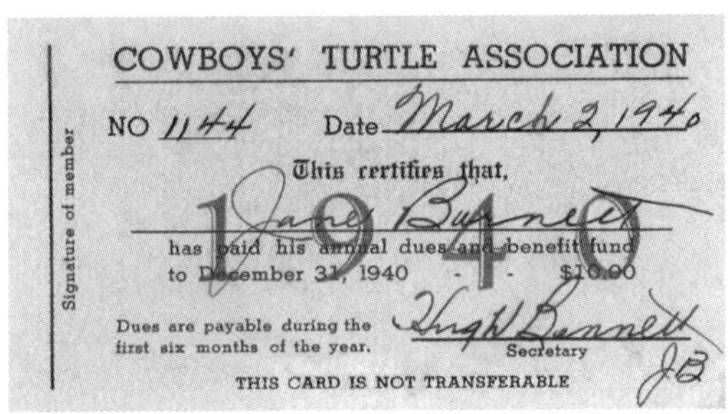

COWBOYS' TURTLE ASSOCIATION

NO 1144 Date March 2, 1940

This certifies that,

Jane Burnett

has paid his annual dues and benefit fund to December 31, 1940 - - $10.00

Dues are payable during the first six months of the year.

Hugh Bennett
Secretary

THIS CARD IS NOT TRANSFERABLE

Signature of member

**Original Papoose Shirt**

Hand made, sleeveless Scalp Shirt of white corduroy. Bright felt appliqued flowers embroidered in wool yarn. White fringe front and back yoke. It's new and different! This is another JB-Original, designed and tailored by Jane Burnett Smith. No catalog. Send chest, waist, hip measurements. Specify colors to be predominant in yoke. Shirt comes in white only. $19.95. Send cash, check, M.O. No C.O.D.'s to Papoose, Care of Bar-87, Windham, Montana.

*Western Horseman Magazine,*
August 1952

*San Antonio* Express News

Kelly Field, San Antonio, Texas, 1943

*Author's collection*

Reno, 1974

# Chapter Eleven

The day I rushed away from the rodeo headquarters in Kissimmee, Florida, I gradually slowed to a walk and began looking for a place to stay. The only available rooms were in private homes, so I approached a small white cottage that had pale lavender shutters, and a ROOM FOR RENT sign on the porch. I was greeted at the door by a nervous little woman whose white hair and pale lavender complexion were a perfect match for the house.

"Do you still have a vacancy, ma'am?" I asked.

"Yes. Yes, I do." She sounded apologetic when she continued, "But Cousin Sarah (pronounced Ser-ee) told me I ought to get the rent in advance. I never had a room to let before."

"I'm sorry." I withdrew the remaining half of the $50 bill from my pocket. "This is all the cash I have."

Before I had a chance to explain why I would not have immediate access to the money, she interrupted.

"Fifty dollars!" She made kind of a wheezing sound. "I don't have change for that much money—but I guess it shows that you carnival people aren't moochers like Ser-ee said you'd be!"

She grabbed my arm and practically dragged me across the hall. I hurried to keep up with her because I wanted to complete an agreement of some kind before she decided to take another look at the money. I had not intentionally deceived her, but when I realized the folded bill had given her the wrong impression, I wanted to rent the room and get out of there as quickly as possible. I even allowed the "carnival people" comment to go uncontested.

She showed me a small lavender and white room at the front of the house, facing a public park across the street.

"Is this room all right? You might think it's too noisy from traffic and everything, but we really don't have any problem except on holidays."

She told me her her name was Alma Benning and this seemed to be my cue to introduce myself so I gave her my name and assured her I would like to rent the room until the rodeo was over.

"Do you want to get your luggage out of your car so you can unpack? Your things must get terribly wrinkled with you carrying them in suitcases all the time."

I explained that I had traveled with some other people and needed to get my luggage from their motel. Just the thought of unpacking and hanging the newspapers side by side in the closet struck me funny and I could barely keep from laughing out loud. I guess I was grinning although I did not realize it.

"Yes?" she asked, puzzled. "What is it?"

"Nothing." I was afraid I might develop a case of high-school giggles so I tried to sound more serious. "Just tired, I guess, and I need to get something to eat."

Alma offered to make a sandwich for me but I declined and assured her I would be back in an hour or so.

The folded-bill hoax also worked at the small local coffee-shop, but this time it was intentional. It was surprising how much credit I accumulated on the strength of half a bill. Everyone seemed short of change over the weekend and surprising as it might seem they allowed me to sign for things. Nothing beats having an honest face.

While I sat in the coffee-shop, a woman entered wearing rodeo clothes. Her hair was blonde, obviously bleached, and was pulled back into a large figure-eight type bun at the back of her neck. Although her plain black suit was severe according to rodeo standards, that same severity made her so uniquely attractive that everyone in the restaurant turned to stare as she walked by.

This woman was a stranger to me, but I nodded. In her brief answering nod, I sensed a reaching out, almost a look of gratitude for my unsolicited greeting. Then a veil of something I interpreted as indifference shut me out, and she turned away to take the only available table.

George Yardley and Dale Adams, two cowboys I met that afternoon, walked in and headed toward my table. The blonde was forgotten temporarily.

"Care if we sit with you, Janie?" George inquired.

When we met earlier, I wondered how the Hollywood talent scouts could have overlooked this unusually handsome, broad-shouldered man with the friendly smile.

"You bet! I guess their loss is my gain."

"What?" George asked. He was already settling himself into the booth facing me. "What're you mumbling about?"

"Oh, I was just talking to myself."

His slightly crooked grin assured me he thought I was okay, even if I did not make much sense.

George and Dale discussed Medford's bucking horses, and the stock each of them had drawn for the opening performance the next day. When I had an opportunity, I inquired about the blonde in the black suit.

"You mean Terry?" It was Dale who spoke. "She and her husband, Jock, are trick-riders. She also rides for his horse-catches in the trick-roping. Why?"

"Nothing special. I just wondered."

A look I did not understand passed between the two men, then George continued, "That big bay has a miserable head on him—a man's got to take a long rein."

Although I still had enough pocket change to pay for my lunch, George took care of the tab. I wanted to pay for my own food but he said they owed me for sharing my booth with them. Besides, he was too big to argue with.

Later in the evening someone suggested going to a dance at a road-house about ten miles from town. It was a huge barn of a place with a good orchestra and a crowd packed in there like sardines, well-oiled. I sang a couple of songs with the band, much to George's delight, but when he insisted on too many encores, the band leader, (who was more sober, more objective, and a better judge of music) vetoed the idea.

From there we went to Orlando, about twenty-five miles down the road. It was getting late so we decided to settle down in one night club and stay until closing time. The place we chose had a tiny crowded dance floor, but was really not crowded enough to warrant people dancing as closely as the couple I spotted when my eyes became adjusted to the darkness.

I was about to make some kind of clever pun about Siamese twins when I recognized the woman who was cemented to her dancing partner. It was Terry. She still wore black, but this time it was an unadorned tight-fitting silk dress. Her blonde hair now touched her shoulders where the soft waves swayed like pendulums in time to the music.

"Hey, look!" I grabbed George's arm. "There, on the dance floor. It's Terry and her husband. I never would have figured him for a trick-rider—he looks more like an insurance salesman."

"What'll you have to drink, Janie?" George asked, ignoring my comments. "You want the same, Dale?"

"Yeah."

In the few hours since I was first introduced to George, I had been impressed with his good manners and I felt reasonably sure he was not ignoring me on purpose. I had to assume there was a reason for his odd behavior so I tried to pretend I was not aware of Terry and Jock. Other than an occasional furtive glance, I really did manage fairly well.

George soon made his way to the stage and asked the band leader if I might sing a song or two. I was flattered by his enthusiasm and sang three songs before I stopped. The only light in the place was the spotlight shining on my face, so I was stunned when I stepped from the bandstand to discover the entire room was completely deserted except for George, Dale, two waitresses and the bartender.

"Hey! Where'd everybody go?" Even Terry and Jock were gone.

George looked sincerely sympathetic. "Sorry, Janie, but your singing ran 'em off."

"You're kidding. Right?"

Dale frowned and shook his head. "No. Honest. And I didn't think it sounded that bad, did you, George?"

Each of them shook their head and patted me on the shoulder sympathetically.

As the bartender let us out through the side door, he whispered to me, "Don't let 'em kid you, girlie. It was closin' time, and I quit servin' fifteen minutes ago."

"Thanks!" I whispered back. "Have a good night."

At the rodeo the following day, George and Dale told all of the cowboys that I could empty any bar in the country in just ten minutes, armed with only two choruses and a verse. I never let on that I knew what really happened.

I rode a black and white pinto saddle-bronc the first day, and borrowed Billy Keene's one-eyed trick-riding mare to use in the flag race. When they first explained the rules to me, I was worried about the way the event had been set up. I would have to ride along the fence on the right side, grab a flag from a bucket of sand that was fastened to one of the fence posts, then cross the arena, place that flag in the same type of bucket before racing to the finish line. This entire race was not only performed at a dead run, but on each approach to a target, the bucket would be on the mare's blind side.

"Won't she run into the fence?" I asked Billy.

"Don't worry about that," he winked. "I been trick-riding and clowning for this outfit long enough to have some pull. You just be ready when they call your name."

That was all he told me, but I soon understood what he meant when a last-minute announcement was made before the race: "The committee has decided to have the riders in this event reverse their directions. First, they will approach the bucket on the left side of the arena and then cross over to the right side before making the final run back to the starting gate. This will give us an opportunity to see if the horses work just as well while racing in a different pattern than usual."

Because of these changes that Billy managed to bring about, my mount would now be approaching the buckets on the side of her one good eye!

I won two of the three go-rounds in the flag race, and at the end of the rodeo I gave Billy one-third of the purse as we had agreed upon. Then I suggested a cash bonus for "actions above and beyond the call of duty." He assumed an innocent pose and said, "I don't know what you're talking about. It was just pure luck that they changed the rules."

The rodeo grounds was several miles from town and George gave me a ride to Alma's house. I stopped by to bathe and clean up, and by the time I reached the coffee-shop all of the cowboys were gone.

I saw Terry sitting in a corner booth. I am not sure what prompted me to do it, but I walked over to her and said, "Mind if I sit with you? I'm really tired of eating alone."

When she first glanced up, she was frowning. I added quickly, "That is, if you're not expecting anyone."

"Oh, no," her face relaxed and a shy smile appeared. "Please do! I know how you feel."

For awhile we chatted in the usual strained manner of two people who do not know enough about each other to make easy conversation, and then she invited me to ride out to the arena with her and I accepted.

On the way, she suggested stopping at a little roadside tavern for a drink. I was not anxious to go, mainly because we were outside of my folded-bill credit zone and I had spent the last of my small change at the coffee shop. I did not realize it at the time, but I was entitled to pick up the money I had already earned in the flag race. At the rodeos where I rode for mount money, I generally would not be paid until the entire rodeo ended.

"I just don't want to go home yet," she insisted. Her voice sounded more desperate than the explanation warranted.

"Okay, but I won't be able to buy any drinks."

"Don't be silly." She actually snapped at me when she spoke. "I'm not worried about that."

We entered the small roadside tavern and Terry took a seat in a booth where she had a full view of the bar. I watched her eyes as she sipped the first highball. They kept flitting from place to place nervously until her gaze finally settled on one area of the bar and held there until it was almost impossible for me to resist turning around to see what she found so fascinating. She began taking short, quick breaths.

"Excuse me," she said, crawling out of the booth, "I'll be right back."

I was disappointed when I looked behind me and saw nothing of interest in that direction, either. In fact, there were only three people at that end of the bar. One of them, a man in a brown pin-stripe suit, was sitting alone.

In a few minutes, Terry returned. Now I was the one who stared, but it was in amazement. She was a different person entirely.

I saw the transformation, felt it, and yet did not quite comprehend what was happening. Terry's long hair had been loosened to fall to her shoulders as it had that night in Orlando. She walked slowly, with a sensual swing of her hips, and her satin rodeo blouse looked too tight across the front. She did not glance toward the pin-stripe man but there was no doubt that this change was associated with him. The bartender delivered our second drink just as Terry sat down in the booth.

"Jane," she whispered hoarsely, "I just remembered, I have to help Jock with the horses. Can I just take you back into town?"

"Sure."

"1'm sorry, really." She headed for the door without touching her drink.

I was confused, but not so much so that I was going to leave a full drink that was already paid for. As I gulped my coke-high, I saw Terry pause briefly, and glance toward the bar. Just one look, then she was gone.

The pin-stripe man stared at the closing door.

When the ice hit my teeth, I followed Terry outside. She had the motor running and once she dumped me off in town, I did not not see her again until after she finished her trick-riding act the next day. She performed well but with an air of indifference as she started to ride past me at the arena gate.

"Hi, Terry!" I called out.

For a second I saw that same frown—a kind of freezing up—and I thought she was not going to stop, but instead she pulled her horse around in front of me.

"Hello, Jane." She sounded like a small child who expected to be reprimanded, then she smiled, cautiously, and inquired, "How you doin' today?"

She put a peculiar emphasis on the word "today"as though yesterday had never happened. It was almost impossible to associate her with the scene at the tavern. Right now she had the demeanor of a virginal lady-librarian.

"I'm fine." I tried to put her at ease but somehow I felt that anything I said would be wrong, so I steered conversation away from her.

"I'm a bit sore and stiff, but that's nothing new. If we'd ever have some of that famous Florida sunshine you hear about, I don't think I'd stay so stove-up after each bronc ride."

"That's right. I noticed the cowboys built a bonfire behind the chutes."

"Yeah. I never thought I'd see them bundled up in winter clothes in Florida. A couple of the boys even had trouble switching dice with those heavy gloves on! It'd be too bad if they had to keep that crap game honest until the weather warms up!"

Terry laughed one of her rare throaty laughs, then reined away. "I have to change horses to ride for Jock's rope act. How about a cup of coffee later on? At my trailer?"

"You bet!"

"See you."

Terry's tiny trailer was parked near the rodeo grounds. It was spotlessly clean. She set out two dainty china cups and saucers. The damask table-cloth looked out of place in the midst of spinning-ropes and riding gear.

Before she sat down, she glanced nervously out of the window, then asked softly, "Would you like something in your coffee?"

"No thanks, just black."

I had not realized what she meant until she reached behind a pink and white bread-box and brought out a bottle of brandy. The slug she poured into her own cup left little room for coffee.

"Just a nip before Jock gets here," Terry explained, barely above a whisper. She gulped the Coffee Royal like a starving person gobbles food. Then, before she had a chance to reach for a refill, Jock stepped into the trailer.

This was my first face-to-face view of Terry's husband, and as I had already guessed, he was not the man she was dancing with in Orlando. Jock was a medium-sized, moderately handsome man who had a clean farm-boy look about him.

"Jock, you know Jane, don't you?" Terry's voice kind of quivered and she stepped over to her husband without awaiting his answer. She pressed herself against him for an instant and he seemed completely unaware of the gesture.

"Howdy!" he said to me, congenially. He picked up a couple of halters and went back outside.

Terry's face was flushed when she returned to the table. She poured herself another drink, but this time she did not bother with the coffee. After several such slugs, I became uncomfortable about being there.

"Terry, if I'm going to catch a ride back into town, I'd better. . ."

"Don't go," she pleaded. "I need someone to talk to."

With trembling fingers she pulled the pins from her hair, one by one, until her long hair lay in soft waves. The pathetic way she tossed her hair back from her face and held her shoulders erect made me feel sorry for her, without really knowing why.

"You'll stay?"she persisted. "Please? I'll take you in later."

"Well, okay." I had a feeling I was going to need a little bracer myself, so I added, "Better pour me a nip of that stuff, too."

As the brandy level got lower and she got higher, Terry became more talkative.

"You kind of like Big George, don't you?" she asked.

"Yes, I do. Who wouldn't? He's been awfully nice."

"Nice? Ha!" Her words were beginning to slur. "Who wants a man to be nice?"

"You know what I mean. He treats me with respect, and he's a lot of fun to be with. I know he thinks I'm just a kid, but I'm happy just to hang around."

Terry shook her head and began a long mumbled monologue. At times I had to lean forward to catch what she said.

"Ain't that amazing?" she asked herself. "Anyone wanting respect?"

She took another drink, then looked at me with a puzzled expression on her face. "Of course, maybe you're just one of them slow starters. You'll be different one of these days. That is, if you don't wait too long."

Terry brought out another bottle from under the sink. "You know, there's only two kinds of people in this whole world: the pure and the passionate. You can't be both, I don't care what anybody says. You gotta be one or the other. But you'll know what I mean one of these days—an' heaven help you if you marry a cold fish like I did."

At this point she paused to take a drink, and check my reaction. I assume she did not see how uncomfortable she was making me, or maybe she didn't care, because she continued, anyway.

"Don't think I'm not in love with Jock—I am. It's just that sometimes I even get up and sneak out in the middle of the night to find someone else.

"What about Jock?"

"He knows. So does everyone else. But cowboys are good people—mind their own business, even if their wives don't. I never go out with cowboys. They're all Jock's friends."

"Terry, I. . ."

"Don' interrupt! I wanna talk, an' I want you to listen. Maybe you'd get that strained expression off your face if you learned to relax a little. You're scared of yourself, you know that? And you're lonely—that's what's wrong with you."

She leaned forward, put her head on the table, and went to sleep.

I hurriedly placed an extra chair so it would keep her from toppling over, then I tip-toed out of the trailer and caught a ride into town.

It was a relief to escape, but I could not help thinking about some of the things she said, and applying it to people I knew. It had been embarrassing, at first, to hear such intimate facts about her married life, yet pathetic as she was, I wondered if some of her strange philosophies might not be true. Given the same set of circumstances, and the same group of restless hormones, was it not possible that many of the holier-than-thou types might react exactly as she does?

So what about that strained expression of mine she mentioned? Maybe she had the insight to sense the basis of much of my restlessness when even I did not understand it yet. Would marriage be the answer? At nineteen, many girls my age were married. Some even had families. Naturally I was tired of being snubbed by cowboys' wives, and being left out of things because I had no "man of my own" but that hardly seemed sufficient reason for me to go husband hunting.

I was still mulling the situation over in my mind when I caught a ride back into town. At the coffee-shop, I saw George Yardley in the center of a group of cowboys and I headed toward him.

"Where you been, Janie?" he asked. "You look kinda cross-eyed—and the show only ended about an hour ago."

"I had a few drinks with Terry." Even if I were unable to make any definite decisions in her case, I still was not about to listen to any snide remarks about her, especially from people who could not possibly know the whole story. I glared defiantly from face to face and grumbled, "So what about it?"

"Hey, now!" George laughed. "Don't get yourself in a big old drunken tizzy and come in here trying to pick a fight. You're too little to be very mean."

"It's just that. . ."

"Speaking of Terry," Dale interrupted.

"Yes?" I bristled defensively, expecting the worst. "Did you see the way she handled that horse today when the loose end of Jock's rope made a half-hitch around his foot? She pulled that palomino up with just inches to spare, and nobody else even realized Jock was in trouble."

"Yeah!" another cowboy agreed. "An' she was a dude not too long ago!"

I caught George staring at me. "What're you grinning about?" he asked. "A minute ago you had a chip on your shoulder the size of a saddle-blanket, and now you're sitting there looking down-right smug."

"Just thinking. You know what? I kinda like you guys."

He shook his head. "Poor little gal. Finally popped her neck one too many times on those broncs."

"And she used to be fairly bright, too," Dale added.

Terry was right about one thing: the cowboys really did mind their own business and they did not even understand why I was so proud of them.

While we stood around and talked, I began acting differently toward George Yardley than I had before. For some reason I no longer felt like "one of the boys," and I wanted him to know it, too.

Finally he pulled me aside and asked me, confidentially, "What's with you today, Janie? I never saw a 'motel look' in your eyes before. Just what kind of hootch did Terry pour into you? Gin?"

"Nope. What Terry poured into me was some heart-to-heart conversation that's beginning to make a hell of a lot of sense."

"Is that right?" He smiled wisely and tapped me on the wrist with his forefinger like a teacher scolding an unruly child. "Well, speaking as a brother, a much older brother, I'd say you best forget any advice she gave you. At least for now."

"Oh, really?"

"Yup!" His eyes were no longer teasing me when he added, softly, "But from where I sit, you don't even remotely resemble any member of the Yardley clan, so who am I to tell you what to do?"

Just then Dale called out, "Hey, George! Come over here a minute, will you? Hinkle wants to know about that steer he drawed in the doggin' tonight. It's the same one you had in the last go-round a week ago."

"Sure thing," Yardley replied. Then he turned back to me. "Don't go away, Janie. We've got some more talking to do."

"I'm not about to leave," I assured him. "In fact, I'll just go with you. Okay?"

"Yeah, sure." He grinned, taking me by the arm. "Probably wouldn't hurt to keep an eye on you for awhile, anyway."

We reached their booth and Yardley motioned for me to take the place next to George Hinkle, then he sat beside Dale, facing us. They ordered some beer and began talking rodeo. I sat back, silently sipping my drink and watched the changing expressions on Yardley's face. I mentally dissected every sentence in search of a hidden clue that would prove he had not forgotten about me, but the endless conversation was purely impersonal. No doubt my next actions were a result of too much beer and too little attention, because I had no other reason for standing on tip-toe and pulling the string to turn off the light above our booth. The waitress charged over and switched it back on, reprimanding me briefly as she did so. As soon as she left, I repeated the stunt for no reason other than a juvenile ploy for attention.

Hinkle, who was a huge bull-dogger about Yardley's size, shoved me back against the booth and told me to behave myself. Admittedly, I was acting silly, but I thought Hinkle was being overly domineering.

"Stop that, you big son-of-a-bitch," I snapped.

Wham! He back-handed me so hard my head slammed against the wall, and for a few seconds I actually blacked out.

Yardley jumped up. "Take it easy, George!" he snapped. "There's no call for being so rough."

"Take it easy, yourself, George," Hinkle snapped back, emphasizing the duplication of their names. "Nobody calls me a son-of-a-bitch and gets by with it. I don't give a damn who it is."

My ears stopped ringing long enough for me to comprehend the situation. "Skip it, you two Georges. That expression is just part of my everyday vocabulary. I shouldn't have said it—and I'm sorry. Okay?"

Yardley settled back, and it appeared that everything would be all right. They ordered another round of beer.

When the drinks arrived, I lifted my bottle to Hinkle, with a grin, and said, "No hard feelings, huh? Even if you did kinda act like a son-of-a-bit. . ."

Wham! This time I did not even finish the sentence!

Yardley stood up, wearily, and sighed, "George, I'm just gonna have to whip your ass. I told you not to do that."

Hinkle got to his feet. He replied in the same unemotional tone, "Yeah, we were bound to get around to this sooner or later, anyway. And you're sure welcome to try."

Outside of the flat place on the side of my head where I kept hitting the wall, and the ringing in my ears, I felt okay.

"You know, Hinkle," I said, covering my head with my arms, "you really don't have much of a sense of humor—at all. If any."

He just glared at me.

"If somebody'll shut off that damned alarm clock, I'll go with you guys." I assumed that ringing in my ears came from an outside source.

As the Georges headed for the door, Dale called out, "Where you fellas going? Out in the street?"

The two men looked at each other and Yardley said, calmly, "Let's take some beer and go out to the horse barns. One of those big stalls ought to be as good a place as any."

"Okay with me," Hinkle agreed. "It shouldn't take us long, anyway."

So it was that three carloads of us headed for the horse barns, complete with a couple of cases of beer. On arrival, the combatants located a fairly clean stall and the rest of us found places to sit where we would have a good view. The battle was carried on very matter-of-factly, with the Georges stopping occasionally to drink a beer.

At one point, a local merchant came through the barn pointing out various race horses to his out-of-town friends. When he noticed the fight in progress, he charged into the stall importantly, and commanded, "Here now! We'll have none of that. You ruffians stop fighting this instant!"

They stopped. They looked at each other.

"Can I have him?" Hinkle asked.

"Be my guest," Yardley replied, as he sat down to have a beer.

With one uppercut, Hinkle knocked the gunsel right over the top of the partition, into the next stall.

"Dammit, George," Yardley complained, "I didn't even get my beer open. Sit down and have one yourself."

"Okay. Don't mind if I do."

The "out-of-towners" were hauling the victim to his car. As they passed the stall, he observed that the Georges had stopped fighting.

"See?" he told his friends, proudly. "At least I stopped the fight!"

Then he collapsed completely.

"Ready?" Yardley asked, when he had gulped his last gulp.

"Any time."

Yardley struck the first blow. As far as delivery was concerned, it seemed no different than any other blow, but he caught Hinkle on the point of his jaw, hurling him backwards where he hit his head on the manger.

It was a few seconds before anyone realized that Hinkle was hurt. When he did not get to his feet, we all rushed to him, but Yardley was there first. Hinkle's eyes rolled back in his head, and the way he lay there looking so limp, I guess we all came to the same conclusion.

"My God!" Yardley gasped. "I've killed him. Somebody call an ambulance!"

I was thankful he avoided the word "hearse," even though it would have seemed more appropriate under the circumstances.

The ambulance arrived in a surprisingly short time. Yardley was thoughtful enough to take a moment to reassure me that a fight between them would have happened sometime, anyway, and I was not to blame myself. Then he climbed into the ambulance just as it drove away.

Dale also came over to me and explained, "Jane, he's right. With two men as big as him and Hinkle, they were bound to test each other's air eventually. Don't feel too bad."

I had not realized my self-reproach was showing, but I guess it was.

It was nearly time for the night show, and as much as we hated to, the rest of us had to go to work without awaiting the final news about Hinkle. It was a sad group that dispersed to different spots around the chutes. No one had much to say. It was generally accepted than an injury received during a rodeo event was just part of the job, but not when it occurred needlessly.

That's where I came in. The needless part. I was miserable.

I chatted with Billy Keene's wife for a few minutes. She was one of the few cowboy's wives who acted civil toward me. The others had their own little clique which definitely did not include the women riders—especially single ones.

While we were talking, I was approached by a retarded teenage boy named "Dilly." A day or so before, I had felt sorry for him and asked the cowboys to stop teasing him. Now he sidled up to me and grinned.

"Jane," he kind of gurgled when he talked, "Do you really love me, like them fellas said you do?"

"I think you're a nice boy, Dilly," I told him, "but don't pay too much attention to those cowboys. Okay?"

Tears came into Dilly's eyes and I was afraid he might get too carried away so I hastily retreated toward the chutes.

As soon as my bronc ride was over, I heard Yardley's voice near the arena gate. Even as anxious as I was to get an update on Hinkle's condition, I could not force myself to go over there. I did not need to. Just then, two bull-riders walked past.

"How's Hinkle?" one of them asked. "Did'ja hear?"

"Yeah. He broke his neck."

To me, a broken neck meant certain death. I wanted to die, too. I slipped away and headed down the road toward town. It was beginning to rain and I was walking along in the darkness with tears streaming down my cheeks, when a pickup truck pulled up beside me, and the door opened. There were no dash lights to illuminate the driver's face but I saw a cowboy hat so I climbed in. Just as the pickup roared into motion, the man beside me spoke.

"I tott you might not dough wiff me—aftow dat udder time."

It was Jebo! I'd heard his name announced in one or two events but had managed to avoid being anywhere near him.

"Oh, Dear God! No!" I felt like I had screamed the words but I only made a kind of whimpering sound. I grabbed for the door handle but Jebo was too fast. He had his hand on my left wrist and twisted that arm behind me.

"Don't det scared," he spoke in a low tone of voice but it was still terrifying. "I was dwunk dat time in Tolfax."

"Okay, Jebo. If you say so." I thought maybe if I stopped acting afraid, he would just take me into town and let me go. Like he said, he had been drunk that night in Colfax. I huddled in my corner of the front seat, but he never relaxed his hold on my arm.

In a couple of minutes we hit the highway, and Jebo turned in the opposite direction from town.

"I have to go into Kissimmee, Jebo. They're expecting me at rodeo headquarters. Something about me being a 'time keeper' in the roping tomorrow." I tried not to sound as scared as I felt. I had an idea he was turned on by my fear of his dominance and since that seemed to be the truth, the "play acting" was not easy.

"We'll dust have a dwink at the tavern, fust."

When he sped on past the sparkling lights of the roadhouse, I knew I was wrong to think his attitude had changed. He drove about two more miles, then turned to the right onto a cutoff, and stopped.

He did not say a word, but just grabbed me and tore my shirt completely off of me. I thought I had almost gotten over my previous experience with him but it all came back to me now. If anything, this was worse. He was sober, now, and there was no room to escape. He clawed at the pants of my new rodeo suit and ripped them all the way down the left side. The close quarters in the pickup cab were a disadvantage as far as he was concerned, but they also made it tougher for me to squirm out from under him. For one terrible moment, I was so scared I actually thought I was going to faint—then I remembered hearing about the damage someone could do with a blow to a man's groin area, and as a last desperate attempt to get away, I brought my right knee up between his legs with as much force as I could.

Jebo let out a scream like a wounded animal, and fell away from me, groaning with pain. The way he sounded, I believe he would have killed me if he could, but in just seconds I was out of the pickup and stumbling through the darkness. I could not run out onto the highway because there was very little traffic, and I knew within minutes Jebo would be after me again. I was crying when I made a dive into the underbrush along the side of the road and found myself waist deep in icy swamp water. I kept floundering around and trying to drag myself out onto dry ground, but just then I heard the roar of the motor and saw Jebo's pickup turn around and drive back and forth within a few feet of where I stood, shivering from the cold water and from fear. I knew then, for sure, I would have to stay off of the highway until I was positive he had gone.

I managed to get back on solid ground and walked through the trees in the general direction of town. I passed several farmhouses in the dark, but with no blouse, and part of my riding pants torn away, I felt safer alone. I stayed about twenty yards from the road and walked all the way into town. Much of the time I was in water and underbrush and by the time I reached the lavender and white cottage I was numb with cold and exhaustion. Fortunately, there was a private entrance to my room and I was able to slip in and go to bed without disturbing anyone. I cried most of the night.

At one time, I heard a rustling outside my window. When I peered out into the darkness, I could see someone standing by a tree just a few feet from me. I felt like I was on the verge of hysteria, but I kept telling myself I was safe as long as I stayed in my room. It would do no good to tell the little lavender and white landlady because she would be as scared as I was, and would no doubt blame it all on the "carnival people," so I crawled back into bed and covered my head with the pillows and the bed-covers. I could hardly breathe but I managed to overcome my fear enough to doze off and on for the rest of the night.

Just at dawn I crept to the window on my hands and knees to peek over the sill, unobserved. There was the person, all right, but it was not Jebo. It was Dilly! I began to laugh. The idea of my being a magnet for all the misfits was almost too much for me to consider in my near-hysterical condition. I went to bed again.

I slept most of that entire day. Alma brought me some soup sometime during that time period but I have no idea exactly when, and I drank very little of it. She said I was delirious for awhile and I let her believe it was due to the cold I had caught "at the rodeo," I knew I could never explain to her what really happened.

When I finally felt well enough to dress and go down town, I discovered that most of the cowboys had already left. At first I was glad, because I did not want to see any of them for awhile. As much as I liked Yardley, I still was not ready to talk to him. Or Terry. Her "world of sex" was impossible for me to understand, especially at that point.

Medford had left my money at the coffee-shop, along with the half-a-bill Muscles was returning to me. I paid my various charge accounts and returned to my room to pack and decide on my next move. Through the window, I saw several bull-riders standing around a car across the street. Before I had a chance to think twice, I ran out onto the porch and called out to them.

"Hey! Where you guys headed?"

"Texas!" one of them replied. "We done had enough-a the state of Florida!"

"Me too! Got room for one more?"

"Y'all jest git your gear an' come on."

"There's just me!" When they looked at me, puzzled at my response, that was my initiation into "Texas talk" where *y-all* can mean one person or a hundred!

With more enthusiasm than I would have thought possible, I ran back to my room for my luggage. I paid Alma what I owed her plus a few extra bucks for taking care of me, and even gave her a "good-bye" kiss on the cheek.

Then we headed for Texas.

# Chapter Twelve

During the first part of our trip from Florida to Texas I was not permitted to drive, so it was a long dreary period for me. It was not until the others were completely played out that they put me behind the wheel for a test run. Apparently they were satisfied, because I drove more than my share from then on. The lengthy sessions of driving were tiresome and yet it was a welcome relief to be too preoccupied to dwell on my Florida experiences.

When the cowboys were not sleeping, they were talking about past rodeo events. I overheard someone in the back seat saying, "Ol' Hinkle's gonna have to judge for a few of them shows 'till he gets his neck out-a the cast." Then he yelled, "Hey, Jane. Watch what you're doin'. You damned near ran us off-a the road!"

"I. . . I. . ."

"You what? You gonna have a stroke or something? You sure look sick."

"Yeah. I guess I misunderstood you—what you said about George Hinkle."

"Oh, that." He sounded as though it were nothing. "Didn't you know Hinkle busted his neck? But don't worry none about him—he'll be rodeoin' again before ya know it."

"With a broken neck?" I still thought this must be some kind of a grisly joke.

"Sure 'nuff! When Kid Fletcher busted his neck, he never even quit ridin' bulls. He had some kind of steel brace on his neck. 'Course, his wife rode saddle-broncs right up to the day she had her baby, too, so the two of them are just a little bit ranker than average."

"Then you mean Hinkle's really going to be okay?"

"Well," there was a short pause, "I reckon he's been in better shape—but he'll make it, if that's what you mean."

I took a deep breath and let the air out of my lungs slowly. "That's what I mean, all right. That's exactly what I mean."

As I began to relax somewhat, I forgot my own troubles and paid more attention to the others. Although I had long been aware of the fact that the rodeo world was divided into four definite "cliques," I did not know until then that bull-riders were really a breed of their own.

Contract performers, such as trick-riders, trick-ropers, horse-trainers and such, were more theatrical than western. They were a hard-working, determined group who devoted every spare moment to perfecting their acts, and they rarely mingled with the cowboys.

Then there were the calf-ropers and bull-doggers. They also spent a great deal of time practicing and/or training their horses. Possibly because so many of them were older than the general run of rodeo cowboys, they took themselves seriously enough to seem downright stuffy to the rest of us. Members of this clique were not above getting on a good binge, but it would be in a night-club instead of a saloon and they were more apt to have their own wives with them than were some of the other cowboys.

The next classification included strictly saddle-bronc riders and/or bareback-bronc riders who sometimes rode saddle-broncs. They were not so easily segregated into a certain area. Some of them were single, liked to party, and hooked up with one or more of the young gals that hung around the rodeo headquarters looking for a cowboy "all their own."

That is not to say a few of the married bronc riders would not stray on occasion, but the single ones were not hampered with family responsibilities.

The combination bull-rider and bareback-bronc rider group were mainly considered to be the "wild bunch." The majority of them were young, single, out for a good time, and lucky if they made enough money to get them to the next rodeo. Of course, the really serious ones did not take their profession so lightly and married or single, they were more apt to steer away from the fun and night life of their counterparts.

The majority of bucking-horse riders, like ropers, had been raised on cattle ranches, and their profession was a natural outgrowth of their background. However, that is where the similarity ended. The age level dropped here again, and since the riders had less responsibility, with no practice required between shows, and no horses to haul or take care of, they had more of a happy-go-lucky outlook and could spend more time just having fun.

There were only two things that groups one, two, and three had in common: (1) rodeoing, and (2) a feeling of superiority (and/or resentment) toward group 4: the bull-riders.

Women bronc-riders never actually had a classification of their own. There were only a few in the United States at any one time and each of them made a place for herself in whatever group her husband or boyfriend belonged. And of course, those of us who were single never belonged anywhere special. The rodeo clowns and announcers were also kind of freelancers who might be a combination of any one or two of the other types.

And so, that day in early spring when we rolled along the highway between New Orleans (N'awlins to my new friends) and the Texas border, I had absorbed enough information to piece together a life-size jigsaw picture of "Any Bull-rider, U.S.A." The discovery that was most amazing to me was the fact that, almost without exception, bull-riders came from southern towns and cities, and did not even know how to ride a saddle-horse! They were further individualized by being only thirteen to nineteen years old. In the days when high-school rodeos barely came into being, this was considered young for rodeoing. It was apparently not a passion for fame or handsome monetary rewards that prompted their choice of career, but rather a craving for excitement plus a general dislike of attending school or working for wages.

It was only natural that the more serious-minded members of the rodeo world frowned upon, and maybe envied a little, these carefree teenagers who went happily on their way with their only goals being (1) to have fun; (2) to earn enough cash for a few beers and a few bowls of chili; and (3) transportation to the next show. In that order. As with all generalizations, there were exceptions to the different categories, such as the alcoholic trick-rider, the affable roper, the sedate bull-rider, and the non-gambling, non-drinking, non-chippying bronc-rider, but they were rare specimens.

I was attempting to be a little more stingy with my money on that trip, because I had no idea when or where I might get the opportunity to add to my meager cash-in-hand savings. I left Florida with more money in my pocket than I generally would have, but there was no way to estimate when I might be able to earn more. I did pay my own way, as far as food was concerned, and when it seemed appropriate, I helped pay for gas. This was not the same as my old hitch-hiking days in Montana where I traveled with a few local boys. Even then I was aware of it when one or more of them tried to take advantage of the fact that I made money at that particular show and they did not.

Unlike Clint, whose habit of paying for every round of drinks was too much like buying friendships, most of the time I restricted my donations to what I thought was my share. Nothing more—most of the time. I inherited his aversion to being "hustled," and I was becoming a lot more careful with my meager bankroll.

On our arrival in Beaumont, Texas, one of the cowboys, Beau Chesson, invited me to stay with his parents until I had rested and decided on my next move. Beau came awfully close to being one of the rare specimens. He was a quiet, sincere boy who had the bull-riding ability to go on to greater heights, and yet his primary concern was helping his father provide a living for the family. Unlike most of his companions, Beau went rodeoing only when there were no conflicting obligations at home.

I enjoyed staying with the Chessons. The fact that Beau's sister, "Poodle" and I looked enough alike to be twins, added to my feeling of belonging somewhere, which was a treat for me after the many weeks since I left Montana.

Almost immediately I realized I had one huge problem when it came to getting a job with the Texas rodeo promoters. Without a single "y'all" in my entire vocabulary, it became necessary for Beau and his friends to make any and all contacts for me. They arranged a couple of bronc-riding jobs for me, and promoted horses for me to ride in the barrel-races and flag-races. The regular contestants accepted me at face value, despite the handicap of my being a Yankee, but the general civilian populace appeared unaware that the Civil War had ended. Apparently, Texas schools used different history books than we did in Montana.

I had been in Beaumont nearly a month when I became aware of the name Rufus Morris cropping up in nearly every conversation. At first I said nothing. Somehow the name "Rufus" did not depict a particularly romantic figure to me, and anyway, at that point I was only mildly interested in the male species in general. However, being a normal, red-blooded, female-type human, I was eventually compelled to inquire about this boy who was described by such contradictory adjectives as "comical, quick-tempered, flippant, reckless, fussy, rebellious, arrogant, modest and tender-hearted." That was a combination I wanted to observe firsthand.

"So where is this Rufus person I keep hearing about?" I asked one afternoon.

"He's been riding in some shows over in west Texas," Beau replied, "but I hear he got back last night. If you want to, we can go over to JoJo's house later—that's where the whole bunch hangs out."

It happened that Beau spent the rest of the day helping his dad, so Poodle and I caught a ride to JoJo's with a friend of hers named "R. Lee." Texas history again, I presume. When we pulled up to an unkempt two-story house that was surrounded by a full acre of sandy earth and a few stems of dried-up grass, Poodle said "Here it is!"

"It is?" I could not keep the surprise out of my voice because I really thought we were approaching a vacant house.

"Sure! But the boys'll be around on the back porch—they always are."

Because there was no lawn to worry about, we drove straight across the yard to the rear of the building. We were forced to stop a time or two in order to avoid running over about a dozen sluggish, mangy-looking chickens, and an almost equal number of ragged, dirty-faced children who simply stood and stared at us. Two more little girls and a woman stared out at us through uncurtained windows.

Poodle and I remained next to the car when R. Lee climbed out and headed toward the back porch. Still no one moved. There were two bull-riders I recognized from a California rodeo who sat on their haunches and leaned against the side of the house. A stocky, apple-cheeked boy, who was also vaguely familiar, sprawled across a homemade hammock that was actually a urine-stained baby mattress tied to a couple of posts with a clothes-line rope. It was impossible to miss seeing the fourth cowboy because he stood spraddle-legged at the foot of the narrow steps, leaning against the stair-railing. With his arms crossed and his large-brimmed hat pulled down so far it caused the tops of his ears to lop over, this belligerent-looking boy held his ground, making it necessary for R. Lee to crawl over his legs in order to get to the porch. This was the only complete stranger to me, so I figured we had drawn a blank. None of these characters could possibly be the one we came to see. Anyway, the stench of sour milk and wet chicken feathers could discourage anyone's curiosity.

"Let's go back to your house, Poodle," I whispered. "We can come over some time later when Rufus is here. There's really no big hurry."

"Don't be silly," Poodle laughed. "He is here!"

With that depressing announcement, she took me by the hand and led me toward the house. In the confusion, I tripped over two chickens, and what I assumed was one small boy. The closer we were to the porch, the more I was convinced of the frowning character's identity, but I kept hoping a gay, devil-may-care youth would spring out from under the porch and surprise me.

When Poodle stopped beside the boy on the steps and exclaimed, "Hi'ya, Rufus!" I was surprised, all right, but not by any previously unseen cowboy jumping at me. The change that came over him instantly made it easier for me to understand the contradictory descriptions I had heard. Rufus pushed the brim of his hat back from his forehead to disclose a thick crop of blond hair (allowing his nice ears to flip back into place) and a wide boyish grin that caused deep dimples in his square-jawed face. Even his squinting, long-lashed blue eyes took on a mischievous gleam of their own.

"Hi yourself, girl!" he said to Poodle in a husky voice. "How y'all been?"

"Just fine," she replied. "Beau's helping Dad."

I cleared my throat and nudged Poodle with my elbow.

"Oh, yes—I almost forgot," she turned to me. "You know Johnny and Bubba, don't you, Jane?"

The two cowboys on the porch nodded, and so did I.

"And JoJo?"

By way of greeting, the chubby boy in the hammock raised a limp hand about an eighth of an inch off of his chest.

As though deliberately needling me, Poodle hesitated several moments before continuing, "And this is Rufus Morris."

Rufus looked at me in such a direct, searching way, I found myself actually stammering when I acknowledged the introduction. I felt ridiculous.

"Hi, girl," he said simply. He did not unfold his arms or alter his spraddle-legged stance in any way. He now looked relaxed and not at all antagonistic as he had seemed at first. "I done heard-tell that Beau brought home a 'Poodle twin' all the way from Florida and it sure looks like he did!"

It seemed as though we had interrupted a rodeo conversation, because it was resumed immediately and I felt more at ease. Jojo's only contribution was an occasional, "I know what you mean," as we all discussed the prospect of attending the Fort Worth rodeo the following week. Plans were shaping up satisfactorily about the time R. Lee remembered he had to be home in a few minutes.

As we headed for the car, Rufus asked, "See you tomorrow? We can figger out how to handle this Fort Worth thing. Right? And don't y'all take no wooden Indians!"

"Okay!" Poodle answered, laughing. She turned to me after we pulled out of the yard. "That boy's got a 'saying' for every situation, but he mangles them so bad you'd never recognize them. Guess you'll get used to it, though."

I was thinking how I had reacted when Rufus stared straight into my eyes. I replied quietly, "Could be."

Within a week, I joined Rufus, Jojo, and five other cowboys on our way to the Fort Worth rodeo. I had paid more than my share of the expenses from Florida to Texas, and I decided it might be wise to leave at least $30 at Poodle's house, along with most of my rodeo clothes and the Chicago luggage. The others in our group did not seem at all embarrassed at the idea of me paying more than my share so I was glad that I was being smart for a change.

Due to the restricted seating room, the only baggage I took with me was one small case with a change of underwear, one of my new outfits, and my bronc-riding equipment. It seemed a shame to leave the new outfits behind but there was no room for anything more. Beau had other obligations at the time and since Poodle was never actively into the rodeo profession except to occasionally ride in a barrel race, neither of them went with us. Most of the time four of us squeezed into the front seat and three others jammed into the trunk with the turtle-back propped open, but we kept changing around so it would not be too tough on any one person. Because of tire-trouble (no spare) and engine trouble (a sieve-type radiator), we finally had to abandon the old Chevy about fifty miles from Fort Worth and hitch-hike the rest of the way. At least, all of us did except the poor guy that owned the car. Thoroughly disgusted, he caught a ride in the opposite direction and returned to Beaumont.

Due to our unexpected delay, we arrived at the rodeo too late for the boys to enter, or for me to get a job. They could have wired their entry fees ahead if they had been in a financial position to do so, but since it was always necessary for them to convince someone to pay these fees, it would require more time for the transaction. I helped pay for a couple of meals and then decided to back off and see how they planned to return to Beaumont. It was an education in itself to see how they operated. I was not accustomed to being around people who promoted every nickel of their expenses and had no qualms about admitting it.

We soon realized it would be several days before another rodeo began anyplace in Texas, so one of them suggested we get passes from some of the contestants and attend at least one performance before they went back home. By the second day, their bar-to-mouth existence was made possible only by their out-right cash loans or repayment of old loans they received from Beaumont friends who were there as spectators.

I thought seriously about using my last few dollars to take a bus back to Beaumont but I was fascinated by Rufus and the way he manipulated people, including me.

Another of their hometown friends who drove to Fort Worth in a pickup truck with a camper shell said we could sleep there for a couple of nights as long as they earned enough money in the rodeo to warrant their hanging around. I soon learned that saddles and other gear do not make for comfortable accommodations, but with three of our group in the front seat we were able to survive.

One of the friends furnished tickets for us to see the matinee on the third day and although I had been to several really large rodeos, I could not help being impressed with this show entitled Fort Worth Southwestern Exposition and Fat Stock Show! It was also the first time I attended a rodeo where the livestock for the bull riding consisted entirely of Brahma bulls. Most of the shows at that time had a mixture of cross-bred animals that were only part Brahma and to see these magnificent animals perform made our trip worthwhile as far as I was concerned.

That evening, we were all in a bar on Exchange Avenue near the stadium. There were several booths, a dance floor, and a small bandstand at the rear of the room. No matter what tactics I tried, I could not get Rufus away from the bar to dance with me. He was kind of a Texan in the manger as far as I was concerned, anyway. He led the others to believe he considered me "his girl," but he did not put himself out in any way to prove it to me. Psychologically I was still not completely healed from my go-round with Jebo in Florida, and yet I was woman enough that I did not want to be ignored.

I walked to the back of the room and leaned against the wall, enviously watching the dancers. When I remembered how enthusiastic George Yardley was in regard to my singing, I decided that ploy might work on Rufus so I approached the master of ceremonies a couple of times (using that term loosely to describe him) and asked if I might join the band for just one song.

"I suppose so," he agreed. "What do you wanna do?"

I thought he seemed unduly nervous about something.

I always started out with one of my favorites. "How about *After You've Gone*?"

He was looking past my shoulder and he suddenly turned pale. "That might be a right good idea! Here comes my wife."

I turned to see a tiny little woman approaching who weighed about ninety pounds. Even in anger she could hardly be considered a threat.

"Why y'all talkin' to my husband?" she demanded.

"Now, Tessie." he tried to interrupt.

I was feeling irritable about then, anyway, because of Rufus' attitude, so I mentally weighed her in and asked, "What difference does it make to y'all why I'm talking to him?"

I winked at Rufus, pleased with my sarcastic reply. He and the others were watching from their ring-side seats at the bar.

When I turned around to face my opponent, it was evident that I still had a problem with that damned "y'all" expression. I thought I had challenged just that one little woman and instead, I came face-to-face with a 200-pounder who looked capable of bench-pressing someone my size, and maybe even a second one with the other hand. Sometime in the past few seconds the Fort Worth Texans had brought in their first team.

Before I realized what was happening, I was swooped off of the floor and carried out through the swinging door where I was unceremoniously dumped onto the sidewalk!

I sat on the curb for awhile, mulling over what had just happened. I felt sure I had made an impression on Rufus, but not in the way I planned. Only one of the Beaumont cowboys bothered to check on me.

"You okay, Janie?" I recognized the voice. It was Buck, which really surprised me because most of the time he went along with whatever Rufus did. He made this move strictly on his own.

He sat down beside me. "Kind of overmatched yourself, didn't you?"

I nodded.

"I know why you did it."

"Oh?"

"Yup. An' I think it was pretty stupid."

He pronounced it like *purty* and it was a second before I understood.

"You really want his attention," Buck continued, "there's gotta be an easier way."

"Such as.?"

"Damned if I know. Just think of something." He disappeared back through the swinging doors.

In a few minutes the others came out, one by one, to be sure I was all right. There were no cars parked in the spot where I sat on the curb so as each cowboy came outside he sat beside the end person in our group. Noticeably absent. Rufus.

"Janie gal," Buck finally spoke again, "Why don't you just give up? The rest of us are headin' down the street to a basement bar, and you're welcome to tag along."

One by one they stood and started to walk away.

Someone said, "Rufus can catch up with us later."

I don't know how long I sat there alone with my head down, trying to decide what I should do. Again, someone sat down beside me.

"How you doin' girl?" Rufus asked, softly. He put his arm around my shoulder.

It was such a pleasant surprise, all I could do was nod my head.

"You got a lot of guts, girl! Y'know that?"

I nodded.

We sat there quietly for awhile and he finally said, "A couple of bareback riders from Beaumont are leaving tonight. They're the ones who gave us passes for the show today but they're out of the competition and said they might as well go home."

I waited to find out where this conversation was headed but I was afraid to interrupt the only decent conversation we had up to this point.

He seemed unsure of how to continue. He finally said, "They had a hotel room that's paid for and we could sleep there tonight."

I guess I looked startled because he put his arm around my shoulder.

"I don't mean. . ." He pulled his hat down, almost covering his eyes. "What I mean, is, all of us—not just you and me! I figured you might be tired of sleeping in that truck."

"Oh." I relaxed a little. "That sounds great, if the rest of them are in favor of it."

We stopped to relay our news and they agreed to meet at the hotel as soon as they finished the round of drinks someone just paid for.

On arrival at the room, I was surprised to see that there was only one bed, three-quarter-size at that, and realized that the only way all six of us could share the bed was to sleep crossways!

I took a quick shower before the others arrived and put on some clean underwear from my small hobbles carry-on that I retrieved from the pickup on our way to the hotel.

The others arrived and before long we were asleep, fully dressed. I lay across the foot of the bed with Rufus next to me and the others beside him one by one all the way to the headboard. We must have made quite a picture, with twelve stockinged-feet (sans footwear) hanging over one side of the bed, and five unwashed faces plus one that was reasonably clean on the opposite side.

Everyone slept late the next morning. One by one, they crawled out of bed and took turns in the bathroom. It surprised me that I was the only one to take a shower.

At last Buck said, "What now? There ain't no shows startin' for a couple-a days, and we done run out-a guys to borrow from."

"Maybe we oughta just go home. . ." someone said.

After some discussion, two of the boys agreed to return to Beaumont, thereby taking their share of our meager funds along with them. Only Rufus, JoJo, Buck and a young cowboy named Willie remained. Up to that point I do not recall hearing Willie speak a single word.

I felt a tinge of guilt about the twenty-dollar bill tucked away in my boot, but was beginning to realize more and more that I needed to keep a small "cache" for myself until I saw where all of this was headed. I nearly slipped up while removing my boots the night before, but no-one was looking when the bill dropped out onto the carpet. I was able to retrieve it immediately.

The four of us who remained sat around in the room for awhile trying to decide if we should follow suit and return to Beaumont. I was in favor of it, but the knowledge that we had a free room for one more night made decisions even more difficult. We decided to go for a walk and carry on the discussions outside in the fresh air.

Several ideas were mentioned, and rejected.

Willie spoke for the first time. "Too bad we don't know nobody in this town we can borrow from."

JoJo interrupted, "Say, Rufe! What about that old gal from Corpus? I seen her here the other day. She's al'ays good for a touch, even if she is a beast."

"You mean Mattie?" Rufus grinned. "The one with legs like a jaybird?"

"Yeah. That's the one."

"Man, if you ain't tried it, don't knock it. For a gal her age, she can do more drinking—or anything else—than anybody you ever saw!"

JoJo's pink cheeks flushed to a deep red. He was almost panting when he continued. "If them widder-women went for me like they do for you, Rufe, I'd never do a day's work the rest-a my life!"

"Who says I'm going to?" Rufus grinned.

A hard knot of injured pride, and embarrassment, formed in the middle of my stomach.

"So it's Mattie to the rescue!" Rufus continued. "Let's go find her."

Even though I hated to be ignored completely, it seemed better to tag along than to stand on a street corner by myself. Besides, it was downright fascinating the systematic way they stalked their prey.

Rufus strode purposefully down the street, wearing the confident smile of a born hunter. The other cowboys bird-dogged the saloons on either side of the street, and although they flushed out two blondes and a red-head, I sensed the real quarry had not been sighted until we rounded a corner and saw Buck standing in a doorway, waving his arms over his head. The others stopped their search and rushed toward him.

Everyone except me. That particular bar was built on a hillside street, so I was several steps behind the others after making my way up the steep incline. However, I did arrive inside just in time to see what I considered an old, old woman (at least forty!) throwing her arms around Rufus and squealing, "Well-l-l-l, if it ain't my li'l ol' dimpled cowboy! Rufie Baby, where y'all been for so long?"

Rufie Baby! I almost gagged. And yet I felt encouraged as I waited for him to turn toward me. I wanted to observe, first-hand, his look of disgust and embarrassment. When he did maneuver around to glance from one of us to the other, I was completely bowled over to see the wide grin of pride that spread from hat brim to hat brim. He winked. The big ham was actually enjoying himself!

Only one thing kept me from storming out of the place. Two men at the bar were already eyeing the untouched drink that had been placed in front of me. They seemed to be hoping I would do just that so I defiantly stood my ground and reached for the drink.

When Rufie Baby grabbed one of Mattie's bony elbows to guide her out onto the dance floor, I felt my face getting hot.

"Janie gal," Buck whispered, "you're turning purple agin!"

It was difficult to talk with my teeth grinding, so I simply replied, "I know."

I gave the knife another twist with my very own hand and watched the cavorting couple on the dance floor. Although Rufus was not a good dancer, Mattie followed every little show off step he threw at her. The tinny music stopped, and the beaming pair moved back toward the bar.

Rufus chuckled and flexed his dimples at Mattie before he announced (louder than I thought necessary), "Man, she shore does rein good!"

I was still choking on the last of my drink when I reached the sidewalk.

Nearly two blocks later I realized I had company. It was Buck.

"Janie gal," he began, "y'all don't wanna think too harshly of Rufus. Life is one big game to that boy—and he thinks it's being played just for him!"

As though to further convince me, he added, "But he's good-hearted as hell—not a selfish bone in his body."

"I know. But this generosity kick can be overdone, you know. Like maybe spreading himself around too freely."

"Sure—sure. I see your point. But your first mistake is falling for a guy who won't never settle down with any one woman."

"Hey, you've got it all wrong. Why in hell would I fall for a man I don't even like? He's nothing but a. . ."

Buck tugged at my shirt sleeve and pleaded, "Hey, Janie gal, cain't you be mad just as good at a walk as you can at a trot? You're wearin' me plumb out!"

I stopped and looked at him. I started to laugh.

"It is kind of silly at that. I've got some change left over from breakfast. Let's go have a beer someplace."

"Now you're talkin' *Texan*, girl. That's my language."

Before we reached the nearest bar, I told him, "You realize I meant what I said about not liking Rufus? The way he acted with that Mattie person."

"Sure. Sure. But you just watch yourself with him. Every time he throws out a few crumbs you're gonna grab 'em up. I've seen it happen before."

"Not with me, you haven't."

Just then a voice behind us called out, "Wait up, girl. I might even let you buy me a drink." It was Rufus, of course.

Without even demanding an explanation, I'll be damned if I didn't actually "wait up—and buy him a drink." Just like he said! I refused one myself because I did not want to bring out the twenty until it was absolutely necessary.

"Say, Rufus," Buck sounded puzzled, "what happened to Mattie?"

"0h, her?" Rufus grinned. "She wouldn't come up with nothing but her bony old body an' I couldn't see playin' her for two or three days when we got another rodeo to go to. Even then she might not hand over any loot!" He held up a bottle of Bud. "I did get me a free beer, anyway."

My face felt hot. I really was stupid.

"You didn't get no cash out of her at all?" Buck looked at Rufus' clay feet with amazement.

"Nope. I guess you can lead a horse to drink, but you can't make him water. . ."

"Rufus," Buck announced solemnly, "you're losin' your touch! Never thought I'd see the day."

Rufus put his arm around my shoulder. "Mattie thought there was something going on between me and this silly girl here," he said, giving me a quick hug, "so I told her she might just be right. An' that's when I walked out. Man, right now I don't really care if school keeps or not."

As per Buck's predictions, I scooped up the crumbs with both hands. Not once did I allow myself to think what the outcome might have been if Mattie had made her customary cash donation. Instead,

I leaned against Rufus and purred as though I had personally accomplished something special.

We had no plans for the immediate future so the boys took turns sipping Buck's drink while they discussed entry fees for the next rodeo. Rufus shared his beer with me but I refused to wonder whose money really paid for it.

An unexpected turn of events kept us in drinks all evening. Another cowboy from Beaumont, a curly-haired bull-rider with the amazingly original nickname of Curly, arrived at the bar with Mattie in tow. It was soon apparent he considered a few free beers to be sufficient stud-fees despite the "bony body," and Mattie proved she had resigned herself to accepting the substitute when she included the rest of us in the next round of drinks.

I often caught Mattie's glassy stare following Rufus as he and I danced, but I kept him turned away from her until she and Curly departed for the "breeding corral," as Buck so aptly put it. I was relieved when they left even though it meant an end to our free drinks. Even with my secreted $20, I felt I could not withstand much competition, bony or not.

The next afternoon, we were standing in front of a shop that displayed Justin Boots in the window. When Curly joined us, I was proudly showing off a pair of red and gray boots in the window that I had special-ordered when I was in Kissimmee. One of their reps took my order, and my measurements, with only a $3 deposit, and I was allowed to send them one or two dollars every few weeks until they were paid in full. I had no idea when I might be able to get them out of hock, so to speak, but the waiting was worthwhile because they were specially designed according to my instructions.

I kept showing the boots to anyone who would take the time to look in the store window but no-one seemed particularly interested.

The others in our group soon forgot about my boots as they listened to Curly's colorful summary of his experiences with Mattie. The fact that he had escaped with breakfast money for all of us (taken while Mattie slept) was enough to evoke cheers of "Good man!" and "That's the old fight" The others were not openly envious, though, until Curly pulled up his shirt-tail and exposed deep finger-nail scratches across his back.

I had been trying to appear preoccupied with various items in the shop window, but I was unable to keep up the pretense when Curly and Rufus started to compare notes. I spun on one boot heel and charged across the street, right through the oncoming traffic.

I reached the other side safely and a glittering array of jewelry in one of the windows gave me an excuse to pause while I determined my next move. It was while I was staring through my reflection to try and make out the price of one of the wedding rings, that the pain hit me. There was a burning sensation in my chest, and at the same time it felt like someone behind me had shoved a long dull knife under my shoulder blade. I was barely able to breathe.

I have no idea how long I stood there, gripping the narrow metal ledge along the bottom of the window, but the short, painful gasps I managed were not supplying my lungs with enough air, and I started to sag to the sidewalk.

Rufus' voice sounded like he was calling to me through a mile-long culvert when he and Buck grabbed my arms and prevented me from falling.

"Good Lord, girl," he said hoarsely, "what's wrong?"

"I. . . I. . ." It was impossible to answer. Even if I had been able to speak, I could not explain something I did not understand.

All four of the boys were there. I could tell by their voices they were frightened, too, and yet each one did what had to be done with the same calm deliberation he might employ to control his natural fear of bucking bulls. Three doors away there was a stairway leading to a small hotel. Rufus and Buck carried me while two of the others rushed ahead to get a room ready.

"Be right back," Curly called out. "The druggist on the corner across the street might be able to help us."

The next few hours are not quite clear in my mind. I remember Curly saying something about a pleurisy attack, and the druggist telling him they should bind my chest as tightly as they could. Buck gave me several pills. JoJo tore the bed sheets into eight-inch strips while Rufus removed my shirt and with Curly's help, wrapped me like a mummy from neck to waist. I was too weak to protest when the binding was pulled so tight I thought my ribs would cave in, but it is probably just as well. A woozy feeling replaced the pain gradually, and I finally drifted off to sleep with four cowboys taking turns bathing my forehead with cold towels. (This bit of information was relayed to me later on.)

Almost eighteen hours later I awoke and the pain was gone but I could barely move with all the binding around my body. When I managed to struggle to a sitting position, I saw my friends sleeping in a circle around the bed. Sort of a South Texas Vigil. It was ironic, in a way. Six of us slept crossways on a small bed for two nights because we could not afford a room and now that they had somehow managed to rent a place with a large double bed, four of them spent the night on the floor rather than disturb me!

Where the pain had been, there was now a nice warm glow. I felt really good, and it was not just a matter of health.

"Hey, you guys!" I said loudly. "How the hell do you expect me to ride broncs in this strait-jacket?"

All of them jumped to their feet. Except JoJo of course. He had to be prodded awake.

"How are you, girl?" Rufus asked softly. He sat beside me and began carefully removing the binding. "Feeling' better?"

"Sure am. But how are we going to get out of this hotel, and get to that rodeo you were talking about?"

"Never fret," Curly replied, proudly. "It's done settled. After y'all went to sleep last night, I promoted ol' Mattie out of payment in advance for a return bout in Houston in a month or so. Now we even got enough dough to have breakfast before we leave."

I was standing, facing the corner of the room, while Rufus helped me into my shirt.

"God damn!" he snorted. "If I'd known ol' Jaybird Legs was going to come through like that, I never would've let her go."

"Why you. . ." I whipped around to face him with one hand holding my shirt closed and the other doubled into a fist.

His face was expressionless, but his blue eyes were so shiny with mischief, I could almost see my own reflection.

"Whoa, now, girl," he chided, "or I'll hafta wrap you up again."

With that announcement, Rufus stepped over to me and methodically kissed me on the mouth—playfully, at first, and then tender, more determined.

In a moment or two, the sound of cowboy boots scuffing the rug nervously on the opposite side of the room brought that brief scene to an end.

My convalescence was complete.

# Chapter Thirteen

Several of the rodeos where we performed in the weeks following Fort Worth were in towns named Something-Springs, Wells, Creek and rarely was there evidence of the body of water suggested by their title. Maybe their reasoning was that these names on a map of Texas might lure unsuspecting outsiders to the arid sagebrush flats to set up new businesses and build new homes, but they should have advised, "Bring your own water!" Other than the towns along the Gulf of Mexico, most of the rodeo sites reminded me of our Montana prairies.

I fell into a routine for a few months that in no way resembled that of someone who was trying to become a champion bronc-rider. With Rufus and various other local cowboys, depending on who wanted to go with us on that particular weekend, we hit town and began promoting. I was seldom hired to ride broncs but most of the time I made a few bucks in barrel races or other such events. If I did get a job riding or time-keeping, it was generally with the understanding that my only payment would be entry fees for the three or four bull-riders in our group.

Before long I woke up to the fact that I was the only one with serious goals. When it became evident that every cent I earned quickly evaporated to pay expenses for the ones who were along for the ride, I knew it was time to do some serious thinking about my future. Even the cash I brought with me from Florida had dwindled to almost nothing.

Rufus and I frequently drifted in and out of Beaumont but when we hit town, he always headed straight for home with no suggestion that I meet his family. The cowboys warned me that Rufus' Mama would be my toughest competition, in case our relationship ever became too serious. They said he was the baby of the family and took advantage of it

"So what?" I tried to sound as cheerful as possible. "I'm the baby in the Burnett family, so it's about a toss-up."

The truth was, I felt unsure of my relationship with Rufus and it bothered me that everyone seemed to know it.

I still stayed with the Chessons when I was in Beaumont. They would never accept any money from me but I tried to help out around the place whenever I was between rodeos. Also, Poodle was scheduled to attend some sort of a musical thing in Houston for a week and I gave her the largest of my set of three suitcases that I still hauled with me since Chicago. At least now it would have something in it besides newspapers.

I liked Beau a lot, but I guess he was just too nice to me. Maybe a woman who rides broncs for a living, requires a man who fights back. I don't really know. That's the way it was with me, anyway.

At one of the shows we attended, I was approached by a man who was lining up rodeo hands to go to Venezuela for two months and he wanted to hire me to ride saddle-broncs. I was excited about the proposal until I learned there was no opening for Rufus, and I was just serious enough about our budding relationship that I declined. I still might have accepted if we had not heard about a different group going to Mexico and then Venezuela. The latter deal was being promoted by a man named Milt Hinkle (no relation to the cowboy with the broken neck). This man was strictly a promoter and several of the older cowboys warned us against doing business with him because he had been putting on wild-west shows for years, and had a history of running away with the gate receipts and leaving the rodeo hands broke and stranded.

Wild-west shows differed from contest rodeos in that the cowboys and cowgirls were hired by the week, like employees in a circus or carnival, and were paid regardless of their riding or roping results. Money-making possibilities were limited in wild-west shows, but ordinarily the people who hired out to them were seeking security, no matter how small the paycheck might be.

Rufus and I discussed the Mexico job with his friend Johnny Kersh from Beaumont. He had gone to a couple of rodeos with us, and although he seemed to resent my friendship with Rufus, the three of us got along fairly well. We finally agreed that Hinkle would be compelled to pay everyone on the Mexico tour in order to hold the crew together for Venezuela, therefore it should be perfectly safe to sign up with him. After Mexico, we could either demand our Venezuela wages in advance, or quit, so what did we have to lose?

After several long-distance calls, five of us, feeling smug and secure, headed for Laredo, Texas, to obtain our visas and our instructions. We hitched a ride as far as San Antonio where we stayed all night. Our intentions were to catch a bus to Laredo the following morning, but we spent all of our money on beer except for $1.25. The only reason we salvaged that much was because the honky-tonk closed for the night. Hard benches, chilly winds, and a grouchy policeman discouraged our attempts to sleep in the city park, so we walked briskly up and down the street to keep warm.

Johnny spotted a small round sign over a dark doorway that said "BEDS—15 cents & 25 cents."

"Hey, let's give it a try," he said. "I'm dead on my feet!"

"How about it, girl?" Rufus asked. "If we each take a fifteen-center, we'll still have enough for a short beer in the morning."

"I really have to lie down someplace," I told him. I was nearly exhausted by that time. "Let's see what it looks like."

We practically had to feel our way up the narrow pitch-black stairway. When we arrived at the top, the grotesque scene that was exposed by the light from two small yellow bulbs made me wonder why they had not left the entire place in darkness. It would have been an improvement. The room, besides smelling of stale beer, sweat, and stinking feet, was filled with four rows of cots occupied by what appeared to be drunks, bums and hop-heads. One man acted like he had the DT's and several others were snoring loudly or talking in their sleep.

"Keerist!" Johnny moaned. His eyes looked enormous in his small hollow-cheeked face. "Ain't this a mess?"

Just then a dirty, unshaven man crawled out of the nearest cot and staggered toward us. He hugged part of a bottle of wine as though he thought we had come there to take it away from him.

"Yeah? Wha-dya want?" he mumbled, falling against an apple-crate that served as a hotel desk."

"These the only cots you have?" I asked. "We really need someplace to sleep."

"S'all we got. S'all we got. 'Less you wanna pay two-bits each."

"And then what would we get?" I interrupted.

Johnny whispered, "Besides lice, you mean?"

The "wino" overheard the last remark and tried to look insulted.

"There's not a louse in the place, I'll have you know!" Almost under his breath he added, "At least not in the two-bit beds."

By this time he had turned on a tiny bulb at the end of a short hallway to the right, and we saw ten or twelve empty cots. Each of these had an army blanket tucked tightly over the mattress, and even had a pillow with a fairly clean cover.

"Don't get many calls for the high-priced beds, so you got the room all to yourselves. If you want it."

"What d'you think, girl?" Rufus wanted to know. "It's up to you."

It was an easy decision. "No choice. As for me, I'm exhausted. Out of that many beds, we ought to be able to find five that are clean enough to sleep on."

In trying to appear indignant, the wino nearly toppled when he straightened to his full five-foot-five. I was afraid he'd collapse completely if I did not stop belittling his precious high-priced beds, so I apologized, and we paid him our last $1.25.

Still hugging his bottle, he left. No doubt to put the money into a cigar-box "cash register" before returning to shut off our light.

"Can't you leave that bulb on?" I asked.

"Nope. Gotta cut expenses. Overhead's too high in this place already."

He did relent and allow us to have some light until we selected our cots and lay down on top of them. Rufus pushed his bed close enough to mine to hang onto my hand all night. We were soon asleep.

I was the first to awaken in the morning and I hurriedly called the others. Though I had slept comfortably enough, I somehow cringed at the idea of filing out of that place in broad daylight along with the occupants of the 15-cent beds. We departed ahead of all of them except one scroungy character who went ahead of us down the stairs, scratching himself vigorously.

I muttered to myself, “There, but for an extra dime, go I.”

“What?” Rufus asked.

“Nothing. Just quoting somebody or other.” Now he had me doing it!

“Hey, let’s head for the highway,” Johnny suggested. “We got quite a ways to hitch-hike before we get to Laredo.”

“You bet!” I agreed. “Maybe Hinkle’s already there, and we can get some cash for food. Let’s go!”

Two of the cowboys decided against the Mexico thing, so only three of us headed south.

Johnny and I had the only suitcases. I was still traveling light but with my mid-size case I had room enough for two of my hand-made suits from Chicago, one new pair of Levis, changes of underwear and socks plus, of course, my bronc-riding gear.

Johnny’s was a well-worn metal suitcase, of sorts, with his and Rufus’ change of clothes that he guarded as though it were filled with gold. When we arrived in Laredo, I headed for the post-office to mail my monthly letter to Mother and while I was there, Hinkle showed up just long enough to tell Rufus and Johnny where we were to get our meals, and said he had to leave town for a few days but would pay the café bill when he returned. Knowing his reputation, I was skeptical but the manager of the café did not seem worried, so I saw no reason for me to be.

On our way to check into a small motel, Johnny loaded some rocks into his suitcase along with the clothes.

“What the hell you doing that for?” I asked.

“You’ll see. Especially if we get into a bind when it comes time to get out of here.”

I still did not understand, but the three of us checked in on the strength of just one suitcase each, and I had no desire to break a winning streak by asking questions.

It took nearly ten days to get our visas squared away. In the meantime, the boys borrowed a few dollars from the restaurant owner and had him charge it to our bill; this way we were able to get on a couple of cervesa binges across the river in Nuevo Laredo, Mexico, while we waited.

I won some small change playing pool but with my cohorts drinking up the profits, the only thing I got out of the games was the joy of winning once in awhile.

On one of our excursions when we walked across the border, we were invited to join a cute American couple who owned a novelty store on the Mexican side. As we awaited our drinks, Harvey, the American, motioned all of us to hover nearer.

He whispered, "See that old Mexican woman over in the corner? I'll show you something funny."

We all settled back in our chairs, and I glanced around. Huddled behind an unpainted round table was a tiny shriveled old crone with stringy grey hair. Her bony fingers caressed the glass of beer in front of her, and I wondered what could possibly be funny about a pathetic little creature like that.

By way of explanation, Harvey said, "These people are extremely radical when it comes to politics. They're wholeheartedly for someone, or against them. No in-betweens. Like Avila Comacho, the presidential candidate. Well, I'll let you see for yourself what I mean."

Harvey's wife began snickering with anticipation, even before her husband made his next move.

Harvey turned his head away from us, toward the wall, and cupped his hands over his mouth in a way that it disguised the origin of the sound as he shouted, "Viva! Avila Comacho!"

The "pathetic little creature" came to life over in the corner and turned into a tigress! Her beady black eyes shot sparks of hate as her gaze flew from one face to another in search of the villain. The beer glass she had been handling so reverently was sent flying across the floor just as the tiny woman jumped to her feet, climbed onto her table, and began screaming and waving her arms hysterically. I had never seen a display of emotion quite like that, and although I laughed with the crowd, the incident did not really belong in the category of humor as far as I was concerned.

Harvey provoked several repeat performances whenever the fanatic old woman calmed down for awhile, but I was relieved when it was almost time for us to go. While these antics were going on, I asked Harvey's wife about a ladies' restroom. She and her husband exchanged knowing grins and pointed toward a swinging door at the back of the saloon.

I was in for another surprise when I pushed through the doors and found myself in a vacant lot! In deference to the mostly male customers, there were what appeared to be drainage troughs along each side of the adjoining buildings. I could not picture myself squatting over one of these troughs so I made a hasty retreat and dragged Rufus and Johnny with me as I headed out the door to return to good old U.S. soil.

The following morning Hinkle returned to Laredo.

He was a dark-complexioned, heavy-set man with an oversized nose and an under-developed conscience. He limped noticeably but I never knew if he really did have a wooden leg like some people said, or if this was part of an act to throw his "prey" off guard, as others said. Anyway, his cowboy hat and boots looked out of place when combined with his wrinkled gunsel-suit, especially when he tried to tuck the baggy pant-legs into the tops of his boots.

Hinkle approached me in the café shortly after noon. As soon as he began talking in a whiny voice that indicated he wanted a favor, I tried to think of a fast exit.

"I have to go," was not fast enough.

"Jeanie," he wheedled, "you're the only person I know that can do this job for me. Surely you wouldn't turn old Milt down when his whole show depends on you."

"Please, Mr. Hinkle," I interrupted, "get to the point. What is it you want—I'm afraid?"

"Now, Jeanie, you know I wouldn't ask anything of you that I wouldn't ask of my own daughter."

"Please. The favor. Just ask. Okay?"

"Well, we need somebody to go on ahead to Mexico City to handle the advance publicity. You know, interviews on the radio—stories to the papers—that sort of thing."

He was smart enough to play on my ego. I immediately pictured myself posing for front page photos and attending radio interviews.

"Why didn't you say so? I'd love to." I turned to Rufus. "Wouldn't we?"

Hinkle cleared his throat and stepped over to pat me on the arm. I swear his limp was suddenly worse. "Well, it's not exactly like that, Jeanie. I only bought one bus ticket, and your visa is the only one that's ready."

"You mean you want me to go alone?"

Rufus was nudging me and clearing his throat, but I pretended not to notice.

"That's right," Hinkle said, "but the rest of us will be there in two or three days at the latest. And it really is necessary." He pulled a dirty white handkerchief out of his breast pocket and dabbed at his eyes, bravely, as he added, "Of course, if you won't do it, I'll just have to suffer the losses. Maybe even cancel the show."

"Okay. Okay. So stop crying on my feet—I hate soggy spur-straps!"

"Fine! That's fine, Jeanie." He perked up immediately and strode away, hardly limping at all. He stopped at the door. "Meet me back here at bus time tonight. Nine-fifteen. I'll have your visa and your ticket—and of course, I suppose you'll need money." A pained expression crossed his face. "You'll need a little money, anyway. . ."

Although I hated to leave Rufus for even two or three days, I was excited about the trip. I collected my suitcase from the hotel and told the clerk my room would be paid for when the boys checked out of the other rooms. Everything seemed to be working out fine.

At exactly nine-fifteen, Hinkle stopped for me in front of the café in his ancient black Cadillac. He said it was necessary to accompany me to the customs office, and I could catch the bus on the Mexican side of the border. The explanation sounded reasonable enough so I gave Rufus a quick goodbye kiss and climbed into the car. He barely acknowledged my kiss.

It only took a few minutes to acquire my work-visa. Hinkle kept glancing nervously at his large gold pocket watch, and each time he flipped it open, or closed it, the cover made a clicking sound. I assumed he was worried that I might miss the bus.

"I guess that's everything," I said when the customs official handed me my papers. "Should we go, Mr. Hinkle?"

"No!" he answered sharply. Then he visibly controlled himself and spoke in a normal tone of voice. "There's no big rush, and you can just call me Milt."

Smooth.

He looked at his wrist-watch. "It's still ten minutes 'til bus time."

"Ten minutes? Well, for Chrissakes, let's go!"

Reluctantly, Hinkle limped back out to his car and I was now more confused than ever. He flooded the car once, deliberately, then after looking at his watch again, he had no problem starting the car and we drove away.

I was the nervous one by that time because I saw the Mexico City bus preparing to leave. In fact, we pulled up beside it and I had to run all the way around the front end to get inside before the door closed. I heard Hinkle's car spin its wheels as he drove away.

The driver reached for my ticket without a word, tore part of it off, and handed the rest to me. I headed for a vacant seat midway to the rear just as the bus got underway, and then I decided to make one inquiry before I sat down. I returned to the front of the bus and asked, "Say mister, what time is our first stop? In case I want to get a sandwich."

The round face turned toward me with an aggravating grin and he replied, "No comprendo Engles, Señorita. No comprendo!"

Suddenly the fog lifted. I spun around and glared at the happy smiling faces. All Mexicans. I was the only American on the bus!

"That phoney old son-of-a-bitch!" I exploded.

It was obvious why he did not want me to get there too soon. He knew after one look at the bus, I would insist on a first-class bus ride. I suppose he saved six or eight dollars at the most.

I had reached what I thought was a vacant seat, and fumbled around in the semi-darkness to sit down. A sound like "Brrrrt! Brrrrt!" came from beneath me. I jumped to my feet and discovered I had just planted myself on top of the biggest turkey gobbler in Old Mexico.

"Ooooooh!" I shuddered, both in fear and surprise, to say nothing of anger. "I'll murder that miserable old bastard. So help me, I'll murder him!"

Anger, like love, can be communicated in any language, but the woman who owned Old Tom must have misinterpreted the cause of my frustration. I think she decided I was planning an early Thanksgiving the way she gathered the gobbler into her arms protectively and kept him next to the window all night. That was okay with me.

At the first opportunity, I moved to another seat. This proved to be a stroke of sheer stupidity. The woman in front of me put her baby over her shoulder to burp him, and he threw-up in my lap.

I was positive I could not stand one more mile of that horrible bus when we pulled into a roadside café on the outskirts of Monterey. The way my luck was running, I halfway expected someone to direct me to the nearest race track when I made use of my only Spanish expression and kept repeating, "Agua caliente?" in request of hot water. The best I could get was warm drinking water but several glasses of it rinsed the debris off of my pants fairly well, anyway.

I found an empty table in a corner next to some kind of an indoor irrigation-ditch, so I sat down. Although I had never been an avid fan of ham and eggs, I decided that was one thing that should taste the same in any language. I tried to explain to three waitresses, and finally the manager, what it was I wanted. I cackled and flapped my "wings" to indicate that I wanted eggs, and even squealed like a pig so I might have ham or bacon. After watching my truly great performance, the manager inquired, in almost Bostonian English, "And what was it you wanted, ma'am?"

I had to decide whether to kiss him or hang one on him, but to play it safe, I still ordered ham and eggs.

My plate arrived at the table and the food looked positively delicious. I cut off a big chunk of ham and had it almost to my mouth when someone bumped my elbow and I glanced around to see who it was. I never learned the identity of the man, but I quickly discovered the purpose of the irrigation ditch. The elbow-bumper was peeing right next to my table!

My breakfast plans ended when I made a dive for the front door and rushed out to lean over the front fender of the bus and throw up. I did not attempt any more food until I reached Mexico City.

Except for the the time a farmer handed me two baby pigs to hold while he fished a bus ticket out of his pocket, the rest of the trip was fairly uneventful. The way I smelled by that time, it was the pigs who turned up their noses, anyway.

To my surprise, Hinkle had reserved a nice room for me in Mexico City at the Coliseo Hotel. The first thing I did was order food sent to my room, and I told the bellboy to go out and buy me some clean clothes, all of which I charged to the room, including tips. I had other clothing with me but I was determined to teach that sneaking old baboon a thing or two.

The only garb the bellboy could find that even remotely resembled my rodeo clothes was a pair of mens' bull-fighting black toreador pants with a flowered vest and a ruffly white shirt. He even bought a size that fit me, and being flat-chested was a point in my favor for a change.

I took four hot baths before I felt clean enough to go to bed, and it was nearly sixteen hours later when I finally awoke and went to work. A few phone calls, with the help of the hotel clerk, started the ball rolling. I was informed that the reporters would come over at once, because they would be terribly busy after the election the following day. That was fine with me. The sooner I finished with them, the sooner I could take another bath and return to bed.

Most of my interviews were handled right there in the lobby but I did appear on two radio shows. What with talking through interpreters all of the time, it was confusing, to say the least.

The third morning I decided to eat my breakfast someplace other than in my room. I went down to the front desk and asked the clerk where I could find a good café nearby.

"We have a coffee-shop right here in the hotel, Señorita" he replied. "An' the food ees veree goot."

"Yes, I know. But I want to go out this morning."

"I beg your pardon, Señorita, but I theenk you had better eat here. Eet's on account of the election, you know."

"Election? Is that what all the fireworks is about? That doesn't mean anything to me. I'm no politician and I don't even vote in my own country!" I started toward the front door, then turned, to add,

"Besides, I don't like the idea of you trying to steer me to your own café!"

"Steer? I don' understan', Señorita." He looked confused and sort of helpless when I drew closer to the front door. "Whatever you say."

By the time I pushed on the wide swinging door, I was actually eager to get outside. There were no windows in the lobby, only tapestry-lined walls and solid wooden door, so I knew I would have to get out and mingle with the crowd in order to really observe the celebration. I put one foot on the sidewalk, and I still held the door open with my right hand. Zing! The sound meant nothing to me for a second because of the confusion in the street, until I saw the splintered wood on the door just above my head. I stumbled backwards through the doorway and landed flat on my rear-end in the lobby.

"Holy Keerist!" I shrieked. "They're shooting real bu-bu-bullets out there!"

The clerk approached me timidly. "Are you hurt, Señorita? Can I help you?"

"You damn sure can!" I snapped. "Just tell me what kind of celebration's going on out there."

"Celebration?" he asked, frowning. "No lo comprendo! This ees no celebration—this ees a revolution! Any time we have the election, we have the revolution for at least five or six days!"

"Okay," I said weakly. "I believe you. So where is this coffee-shop of yours? I'm convinced."

"Righ' through that door by the stairway, Señorita." He helped me to my feet and smiled. "Now eef you would permeet me, I weel—how did you call it—steer you to our coffee-shop!"

"You bet, Señor," I agreed. "You just do that."

Rufus and the others did not reach Mexico City until almost a week after I did. The "election" kept me isolated in the hotel most of the time, but everything had calmed down about twelve hours before they arrived. I was so glad to see my friends, I did not hit Hinkle on the end of his bulbous nose as I had planned. Instead, the first thing I did was tell all of them about my close call with the stray bullet. It was apparent that no-one believed me. Even the splintered door did not convince them of the hand-to-hand fighting I had witnessed in the streets, so I dropped the subject. However, it should be noted that at no time was I the first one to go through that door for the rest of my stay at the Coliseo.

Our rodeo was held in the bull-ring, where four bucking chutes had been constructed. Although it was common knowledge among rodeo people that the biggest and stoutest bucking-horses were raised in Canada and the Northwestern United States, I had no idea they continued diminishing in size all the way south to Mexico City. The small seven-hundred-pound broncs they had for us to ride looked so puny as to be laughable. For me, riding with hobbled-stirrups, it was the easiest job I ever had, but for the long-legged cowboys, those wiry little horses presented a definite problem. Many of the bronc-riders spurred right over the top of their mount and sailed through the air. Since they were under contract and not competing, the only thing that bothered them was the idea that they looked and felt pretty foolish.

The Mexicans were almost childlike in their extremes of emotion. If someone were thrown from a bronc, or missed a loop in the roping, the entire crowd booed loudly. On the other hand, if all went well and they were pleased with the performance, they rose to their feet and cheered until it was almost deafening. There were several reasons why I rated higher than I should have on their "cheer meter." For one, the only woman any of them had seen performing in a dangerous event was the country's lone lady bull-fighter, and she was practically a national institution. Another reason was my not being bucked off of my bronc. Hobbled stirrups meant nothing to them and as far as they were concerned, the important issue was that I completed each ride without being thrown. When the pickup man, who by the way was part of our crew, took me from my bronc, he always set me down in the center of the arena, and the cheering began. The first time the spectators threw their hats and bouquets of flowers at me, I was not too sure of their intentions. The election was still fresh in my mind. Then, as soon as twenty or more of them jumped into the arena where two of them lifted me to their shoulders and carried me in a complete circle of the bull-ring, I decided I was in!

I returned to the chutes after one such display, and Johnny said to Rufus, in a deliberately loud whisper, “Don’t you know she’s gonna be a bitch to get along with for a few days?”

“Yes, siree,” Rufus replied with a grin. “After all that fuss, she’s just liable to outgrow them bull-fighting clothes of hers!”

“The word is breeches,” I corrected with mock severity. “If you insist on exchanging mixed quotations about me, I’d like them to at least be recognizable.”

Our little mock-squabble was interrupted by the arrival of a dozen Mexican Charros (cowboys), who were to perform next. Hinkle had agreed to include several Mexican events to make the show more interesting, but the things those Charros did were so wild, we looked like kindergarten classes by comparison.

One of their first events slightly resembled our bull-dogging, except that the contestant rode his own saddle-horse bareback, and the critter that was turned out of the chute was not a horned steer, but a wild bronc! The rider was allowed one hazer, just as in our bull-dogging. Their “hazer” was another gaucho who rode along on the opposite side of the pursued animal, trying to force it closer to the contestant. In this case, the hazer drove the bronc close enough for the contestant to jump from the back of his own horse and straddle the loose bronc. Then he’d try to stay aboard until the whistle blew, with nothing to hang on to but the mane! I guess we sounded as excitable as the Mexicans when we watched a few of these wild rides.

And then came the really tough event! With people who handle wild horses all of the time, it is the accepted practice in a corral to rope a colt by his front feet, jerk the loop tight, and somersault the bronc. This gives the roper’s helpers a chance to jump on the colt while he is down, and either tie his legs together, or just hold him down. It all depended on the end purpose of their job, which may be to get a saddle and/or a halter on them, or both.

When the second Charro event began, it appeared to be simply a contest of who could “front-foot” a colt and flip him the fastest. A closer observation disclosed a lot more to it than that.

“Look at that!” Johnny gasped. “That Mex has got a rope tied around his own neck. What the hell’s he doin’?”

"Damned if I know," Rufus answered. "I guess everybody can pick their own event, but whatever he's gonna do, I sure as hell wouldn't try it!"

The roper had a loop around his neck, all right, and it was knotted in a way that the noose would not tighten, but still it was terrifying to see his actions after catching the front feet of a running colt. The instant the roper jerked the slack out of his rope to tighten the loop on the colt's front feet, he held both hands above his head, stiffened his neck muscles and leaned back to brace himself against the jolt. Without touching the rope again with his hands, the roper then somersaulted the colt by using only the strength of his neck and back muscles!

It made me weak-kneed just to watch him. I slumped to the ground and leaned against the chutes while one after another of the charros performed. Some of them were only able to catch one front foot, so consequently they could not flip the colt, and were disqualified. In such a case, they just removed the loop from their own neck, and flicked the rope until it fell from the colt's leg.

"Goddam!" Rufus gasped. "Looks to me like they're playin' Mexican Roulette!"

"Look, Rufus." I tugged at his pant leg to get him to sit beside me. I pointed to the next contestant. "That big red-headed Charro is next. I'm surprised to see so many Irish-looking Mexicans."

"Red" threw his loop before I finished. It was traveling in too wide an arc, and too high, with the result that it sailed right over the colt's head for a perfect head catch! The other Charros knew what this meant, and even though it took the American cowboys a few seconds to realize the danger, they were close on the heels of the Mexicans who rushed to Red's aid.

What happened was that the instant the loop settled over the colt's neck, he hit the end of the rope at a dead run and up-ended Red. The bronc then dragged Red around the bullring and no one was able to stop him. Two or three men tried to front-foot the colt, and several others attempted to grab onto Red's rope to slow the colt enough to get Red's neck out of the noose.

Red was holding onto the rope just above his head to maintain enough slack that he would not be choked to death or have his neck broken, but we all knew he had to be rescued immediately as he could not hang on in that manner for very long. All of the Mexican contestants were so excited they just seemed to get in each other's way. The bronc circled the bull-ring no less than three times, and maybe even more, before one of our boys front-footed him and with the help of Rufus and Johnny, they jerked him down.

One of the Charros quickly cut Red's rope.

"He can't be alive," I moaned. "He just can't."

"You think not?" Johnny laughed. "Look at him!"

Red was climbing to his feet slowly with the help of several of his friends. His red hair and long red mustache were caked with arena dirt, and yet he took time to turn around and wave to the cheering crowd.

I stopped one of the Charros who spoke a little English and asked if they were taking Red to the hospital.

"No, no, no!" he laughed. "Not the red-haired one. He weel rest un momento then he'll show off his famous gaited show-horse! You will watch heem, yes?"

"I guess I could handle something like that, and maybe Red can go on with the show, but I'm afraid I'd come unraveled if I watched any more events like that last one. You guys are too tough."

I joined Rufus, Johnny, and two other cowboys when they headed for the exit to catch a cab to the hotel. We left Pancho mumbling to himself, "What ees this kind of talk? Yo no comprendo *un-ravel*."

A short time later we climbed from the taxi and Rufus suggested we find a bar.

"Okay," I agreed, "but no more of that black stuff we drank yesterday. I thought because Cerveza Negra only cost a nickel a glass, American, I couldn't get looped on twenty cents but I sure was wrong."

Johnny chuckled, "What's wrong with getting drunk on twenty cents? I might just decide to stay down here!"

We almost ran over the well-dressed, smiling young man who approached, hand extended. He spoke in amazingly good English.

"Ah! What a pleasure it is to meet the rodeoing Americanos! I would like to shake your hand, each of you. My name is Juan

Sanchez. It is a great honor to have such brave ones visiting our city."

"Why, thank you," I answered, since it was my hand he shook first. "It's nice of you to say so."

"Not only that," he continued as he moved from one to the other, "but I would be very proud if you would grant me the pleasure of taking all of you to dinner. Any time you say, of course."

The boys appeared to be as pleased and flattered as I was, so I accepted for all of us. "I'm sure right now would be fine. We were on our way to get something to eat, anyway."

"Wonderful, wonderful," Juan said with relish, "I know just the place. It's only three blocks from here."

I should have remembered Clint's theory that the world's biggest suckers are those who are trying to get something for nothing. Although we had not actually been looking for a free meal, that was the determining factor in our decision to accept the invitation.

Over and above our vanity, of course.

Juan was a slight man, not much taller than I, but when he swaggered into the elaborate restaurant ahead of us a few minutes later and led us to a secluded table amid tropical greenery, he appeared to be eight feet tall. A mere snap of his fingers brought waitresses from every direction.

It was exhilarating to order food from the left side of the menu for a change, instead of running my finger down the list of prices until I found something I could afford. The boys kind of went berserk, too, except that their their idea of a feast was not Prime rib or Sirloin steak like I ordered, but rice, black-eyed peas, and slices of raw onion. After living on hamburgers for a couple of months, to me this was paradise.

As soon as we ordered, Juan suggested we have something to drink while we waited. Naturally, everyone agreed. At the time the drinks were delivered, Juan happened to be in the restroom, but we were glad to have the opportunity to buy him a drink anyway.

Then there was the second round of drinks, and the third. We were conveniently given the opportunity to pay for those, also. By that time we were almost through eating, except for dessert, and I whispered to the boys before Juan returned to the table for the third time, "I think we're getting something."

"Besides free food? Whatdya mean?" Rufus whispered back.

"Either that little Mex bastard has awfully bad kidneys, or we've been steered. And it's not too difficult to guess which is the case."

"What'll we do, girl?"

"Here he comes now," I hissed. "You guys just take off—right now! Let me handle Señor Bigshot."

"Okay." They scrambled to their feet and ducked out through the front door.

Juan hurried to the table. "Los otros—the other ones," he said nervously. "Where have they gone?"

"Oh, they'll be right back. They went to the corner to buy some American cigarettes."

"Are you sure?" he asked, chewing on his upper lip.

I smiled. "You bet! Now you just sit down and enjoy your drink."

I nibbled at my dessert, and chatted about our visit to the Floating Gardens the day before, and about the rodeo. I am quite sure Juan did not hear a word I said. His gallantry had flown with the cowboys.

I gave Rufus and Johnny sufficient time to escape, then I rose to my feet, dabbed at my lips daintily with a white linen napkin, and extended my hand to a grey-colored Juan.

"Well, I guess the boys decided to meet me later. But on behalf of all of us, I do want to thank you for a lovely dinner." Rather confidentially, I added, "I would leave a tip, but the truth is, I don't have any money!"

"Wha–what?" he squeaked, jumping to his feet so fast that his chair tipped over with a loud crash. "You can't do this to me!" Then he pounded on the table and yelled angrily in Spanish.

It made me uncomfortable to not understand for sure what he said, so that seemed like a good time for me to leave. To soothe his injured pride, I did say, in his native tongue, "Adios, Señor," just before I headed for the exit.

As soon as I reached the sidewalk, I felt good. I begun whistling and I strolled along, gazing into various shop windows.

"Psssst!" I heard the sound coming from around the corner. It was Rufus and Johnny. "How'd it go?" they asked.

"Great! But it's sure a good thing we figured out his scam in time! There's no way we could have paid a bill that size. Down here, if they put an American in jail, they just throw away the key."

"I wonder if Juan can even pay it," Rufus asked.

"I doubt it," I replied, grinning in spite of myself.

Johnny chuckled, "So how do you say tuffshit in Spanish?"

I'm sure the three of us were looking pretty smug as we sauntered down the street, arm in arm. It was a beautiful evening in Mexico City. That is, it was until a large cloud blotted out the street lights behind us, and two ape-like arms swooped all three of us off of the sidewalk. We were hauled toward a "Mexican paddy-wagon" at a terrifying pace. Despite our squirming and kicking, (and I don't know about my partners, but I was also biting!), our captor never weakened an inch. The only thing I was aware of besides anger, was that Juan was running beside us, pointing an accusing finger at me and rattling off a bunch of Spanish that I felt sure was not complimentary.

When we reached the paddy-wagon, a uniformed policeman stepped from behind the wheel to help the giant who held us. As though he needed help! We were roughly set down with our backs to the police van and only then was I able to crane my neck to look up at the face of the man who had abducted us. He was not only a large man with ape-like features, he was one damned irate human being.

"Now just what's the meaning of this?" I looked up at his face two feet or more above me, and demanded as indignantly as was possible with my head tipped back at such an angle.

"If it's about that café. . ."

Gorilla Boy glared at me, and said, "No hablo Engles." Then he poked me on the wishbone with his huge forefinger and ordered, "Usted hable en Español!"

I massaged the welt that was also forming and glared at Juan.

"Come on, you tourist-robbin' little Jessie James! What the hell did you tell this guy? If he can't speak English, and I can't speak Spanish, how'll I know what's going on?"

"Yeah," Rufus growled, and made a dive for Juan.

A palm the size of a ham grabbed him by the seat of his pants and suspended him mid-air.

"No hablo Engles, tambien," Juan replied innocently, before he continued giving the policeman what I imagined was his own version of events. This was done in Spanish, of course, so I could only guess at what was said.

All this time the three of us were being shoved into the back end of the paddy-wagon, and the door was closing when a man's dignified, authoritative voice demanded, "What's going on here? Stop it at once!"

People can say what they want about French, Italian, and Spanish being musical languages, but those last four English words out-Beethovened them all.

I pressed my face against the woven wire and saw a round face, blue eyes, and red hair.

"Mister!" I called out. "If you speak Spanish at all, you just might be able to save our lives."

Juan whirled around as though to leave, and the red-haired man snatched him back to his side. Then the Spanish really flew. It was easy to see the English-speaking newcomer had a certain amount of authority because even the gorilla spoke to him with respect, but all the yelling and arguing was just so much jibberish to us.

Finally our benefactor pointed to the door and commanded the gorilla, "Abra lo! Open it!"

"Man, I'm with you," Rufus sighed as we scrambled out onto the sidewalk.

Unwillingly, the gorilla put Juan in the paddy-wagon in our place, and drove away.

Rufus and Johnny were pumping the hand of our new friend so I had to wait my turn. When we had introduced ourselves, he said, "My name is Don Carlos."

"It's what?" Johnny interrupted. "We thought. . ."

"Yes, I know. Many people think I am an American. My father was Mexican, my mother was Irish, and I am a native of Mexico. But I was educated in the United States. Confusing, isn't it?" He smiled. "Right now I am an official in this city and that's why it is so important for me to put a stop to the kind of things Juan and others like him are doing to the tourists. It gives our lovely Ciudad a bad name."

"Then you know what happened?" Rufus asked .

"I can only guess. Juan has been fleecing unsuspecting visitors for several years, but we were unable to catch him—how do you say it—red-handed?"

"Well, Señor," I said. "You couldn't have picked a better time. And by the way, what did Juan tell that big gor—I mean, that policeman?"

Don Carlos shook his head, and replied with disgust, "He said you had stolen his wallet."

"Who, me?" I asked.

"Yes. And when he insisted it was you, and not either of your friends, we knew we had him."

"How could you know I hadn't?"

"I just—er, that is. . ." he looked painfully embarrassed all of a sudden. "I was sitting in my car and saw you before you reached your friends a few minutes ago."

"So?"

With a wave of his hand he indicated my pocketless, skin-tight pants and sheer blouse. "After all," he smiled, "where could you possibly hide it?"

# Chapter Fourteen

In the next ten days we saw Señor Carlos frequently. He played the role of Latin romanticist all the way, and constantly teased us, suggesting that Rufus marry me in Mexico and turn our trip into a honeymoon. I nodded during each of these discussions, but was getting nothing for my trouble but a sore neck so I finally quit. Then one evening when the Señor took us out to a delightful place for dinner, we were given our first champagne, and somehow a decision was made that Rufus and I would get married. In Mexico.

I am not quite sure whether Señor Carlos decided it or I did, but the happy event was to take place the following day. We had a gala all-night celebration and promised to meet at the city hall the following morning.

There were several reasons why the wedding did not take place as scheduled. (1) Don Carlos was summoned to Guadalajara on urgent business. (2) We were informed we had to leave for the Puebla, Mexico rodeo immediately, which was one week ahead of schedule. And (3) which was the most important of all: Rufus was a coward.

Two days before the Puebla rodeo ended, Milt Hinkle preceded the rest of us back to Mexico City. He said he was going to line up one final week of events for us, and collect the money still due from the local sponsors. Other than expenses, we had received nothing up to that point. Everyone was having such a great time, we were all caught off guard, and did not object.

On the day we returned to the Coliseo Hotel in Mexico City, we asked them to please ring Mr. Hinkle's room.

Even the clerk's puzzled expression meant nothing until he splashed us in the face with these cold words, "Didn' you know? Señor Heenkle, he ees gone."

"Gone?" I asked, weakly. "You mean gone to eat. Right? Or maybe gone for a walk?"

"No, Señorita. I am sorry. I mean he ees gone. Back to the United States."

Reactions to Hinkle's untimely departure were varied. Most of the cowboys headed for the nearest bar, I banged my head against the tapestry-covered wall in the lobby, and Rufus shook the hotel clerk by the shoulders until his curly black toupee fell to the floor.

"Leave him alone, Rufus," I pleaded, straightening my hat. "He's already coming apart and besides, it's not his fault."

"Yeah. I guess you're right," he conceded unwillingly. "My handle just flew off for a minute."

"Let's find Johnny and go have a beer while we decide what to do."

"Okay," Rufus agreed. "He's probably already at the bar."

We found some of the cowboys and their wives gathered around a long table in the tavern. Other than the ones who had hauled their own horses to Mexico for roping, bulldogging, or trick-riding, no one had any transportation. All together these people only had room for half-a-dozen extras, which left the rest of us stranded. By eavesdropping, we learned that Hinkle had paid all of the hotel bills, at least. On a previous trip he apparently had advertised that someone would bulldog a steer from a motorcycle, and the Mexicans made Hinkle do it himself when he was unable to produce any such act. I guess this left him a bit leery of chiseling on the Mexicans. Too bad he was not that concerned about his employees.

Johnny was not there when we arrived, but he appeared a few minutes later. He looked pleased with himself.

"Guess what?" he grinned, "That dirty crook, Johnny Kersh, ran out on his hotel bill in Laredo, and the law's after him!"

"Law? Looking for you?" I gasped.

"Shhhh." Johnny jabbed me with his elbow. "One of the cowboys called a friend of his in Laredo this morning to tell him what happened down here, and the guy asked if he knew about Kersh. We can worry about that later. Right now we need to get the hell out of here."

"Didn't anybody settle up for those rooms in Laredo?" I asked.

"Hell, no." It was Rufus who replied. "Hinkle said he couldn't pay us nothing till we got down here, so we just wore all our clothes out of the place and left Johnny's cardboard suitcase full of rocks for security."

Johnny laughed, "I told you them rocks'd come in handy. I was in a fix like that once before."

"Then you must be full of ideas about how to get out of this country with very little money?" I prodded.

Johnny's levity was replaced by a grim expression when we finished telling him our sad news. We held our own separate "board meeting" in a corner booth, to decide what we should do. It was agreed that each of us would be be assigned to one phase of the operation, such as contacting Don Carlos, phoning the U.S. Embassy, and /or promoting free bus tickets. Rufus dumped all three jobs into my lap so smoothly I did not realize it until the tasks were complete. Don Carlos was still out of town, and the embassy people were properly sympathetic but said too many Americans were stranded and they would be unable to help us.

On my way to the bus depot, I stopped off to send a telegram to Montana. There was no way I could reach my parents but a wire to Georgia at the Montana Tavern was always a last resort.

After I paid cash for the telegram, I was informed that the money order from Montana would only come as far as the U.S. border at Laredo. The laws at that time prohibited wiring money to anyone across the border.

What remained was the small obstacle of 750 miles between us and the cash.

Fortunately, the manager of the bus-line was an American. My tale of woe about how urgently my two "brothers" and I needed to reach Texas because of an illness in the family, brought even better results than I hoped. I offered to pay our fares when we reached Laredo, but instead the American gave us free passes.

I hurriedly phoned the boys at the hotel and had them pick up my small bag and meet me at the bus depot.

Typically, they used part of their remaining cash for a taxi. Four blocks.

They stepped out of the cab, their hats tipped rakishly and puffing on big black cigars. Our benefactor eyed them with suspicion but did not renege on the passes. Considering the totally different appearance of each of my brothers and me, I imagine he decided "Ma" must have been quite a girl in her day. Family trees notwithstanding, we were on our way to the States within an hour.

On arrival in Laredo, the boys offered to accompany me to the Western Union office. I pointed them in the general direction of a combination bar and café and told them to wait there for me while I went to collect the money. On return, I did not disclose how much Montana-money I had received. For a change I was playing it smart.

I was surprised to see two more cowboys who had been fortunate enough to catch a ride north from Mexico City with a calf roper and his wife. I gathered from their conversation that one of them was waiting to be picked up by his cousin and they were heading for a rodeo in Shreveport, Louisiana. Both Rufus and Johnny were looking forward to spending some time at their respective homes in Beaumont, but the more they heard about Shreveport, the more they became excited about making the trip and agreed to go. The cowboy they talked to said his cousin would be driving what he called a "five-seater" and he would be glad to have us go along if we shared expenses.

"We're interested, ain't we, girl?" Rufus took it for granted I would agree, but in fact I was growing a little tired of being expected to take care of our finances all of the time.

Being stupid enough to misjudge the Mexico thing was not a real morale booster. I had been so sure that Hinkle's plans for Venezuela would force him to pay those of us on the Mexico trip, that I felt worse about falling into a sucker-trap than I did about not getting paid. I had been broke before. Often.

But to be *had*. . .

"I don't know, Rufus."

"Well, I'm going," Johnny sounded defiant. He seemed to be drawing a line in the sand to see which side Rufus would choose.

From the very beginning, any time the three of us traveled together, Johnny seemed to think I was a threat to his and Rufus' relationship. I thought it was a bit childish but did not consider it a serious problem. No doubt the marriage discussions in Mexico made a bad situation worse. I wondered what he planned to use for cash.

"Rufus?" Johnny looked at Rufus and then at me. He waited.

I thought about how I would feel if the two of them took off for Louisiana and left me in Laredo and I was too exhausted to take a chance.

"Guess we could give it a try, but we couldn't help much as far as expenses are concerned." I spoke before Rufus could say anything. I often wondered what might have happened between Rufus and me if I had refused to go. Just as well that I never found out.

I slipped away to mail sufficient cash to the Laredo Motel to cover my own overdue room-rent. They would simply be stuck with a rock-filled suitcase for Johnny's bill but that was no longer my problem.

I did not know it, but Johnny had made arrangements to get some money from an uncle when we went through Houston, so that helped to explain how self-assured he sounded during the discussions.

The cousins took turns driving and because they had obviously been broke a time or two themselves, they never asked us for gas money but accepted a few dollars from me and from Johnny after our stop-over in Houston.

Rufus and Johnny still had enough of their Mexico "daily fare" to pay for their own meals, and for a change, I did not offer them any of my cash. As a matter of fact, I never disclosed to them how much money had been sent to me from Montana.

We were actually dropped off about twenty miles out of Shreveport when the cousins detoured to see one of their relatives who lived on a ranch nearby.

We were extremely fortunate to catch a ride the rest of the way. In fact, we were picked up by a farmer who not only bought each of us a steak dinner, but also furnished Rufus with enough money to pay his entry fees in the bull-riding at Shreveport. He had ridden in a few local rodeos when he was younger, and was anxious to have even a small role in the upcoming event.

On arrival in Shreveport, we used the rancher's money for food and drinks, and when I told Rufus he needed to save that cash to pay his entrance fees, he just laughed at the idea.

"Remember, a beer in the hand is worth two in the bush."

I ran into the usual objections when I applied for a job, but it did appear our luck was changing when Johnny easily promoted his own entry fees in the bull-riding.

At first I was skeptical about Rufus' apparent endless supply of cash, but he slyly refused to talk about it except to say, "Don't fret yourself, girl. We've got 'er made in the shade. You'll never see another poor day!"

The rodeo was rained out for three consecutive days and we all became restless sitting around the hotel. One afternoon, in my room, I jokingly suggested, "Rufus, why don't we just get married today?"

He frowned for a moment or so, then replied nonchalantly, "I suppose we might as well. There ain't nothing else to do 'till it quits raining." How romantic!

I was too surprised, and delighted, to feel any irritation at his attitude. The real shocker came with Johnny's first words.

"You ain't serious about marryin' a Yankee, are you, Rufus?" he asked. "You must be nuts or somethin'."

He spun on one heel and stomped out of the room.

Rufus stared at the closed door for a moment before I put my arms around him.

"Don't mind him, honey. He'll be okay as soon as he sees I'm not trying to convert you into a Yankee. Besides, it's your life."

"That's right. I don't haf'ta answer to him." Rufus straightened his shoulders and smiled down at me. "Let's go find us a preacher—or whatever it is we have to do."

"I'd like to at least put on my red and blue suit. I'd hate to get married in Levis."

"All right. But don't get too fancied up. I don't have nothin' but Levis to wear."

He gave me one real pre-wedding kiss, then released me and headed for the door. "I'll go to my room and comb my hair, then I'll locate Johnny. He ought'a go with us." He paused, looking down and kind of scuffing one boot against the other. "If he will."

As soon as he left, I hauled out my small folding iron, and pressed my clothes on an inverted dresser drawer as always. Then I unplugged the iron and took it to the boys' room to see if I could do their shirts. I completed Rufus' shirt and thought I would do the same for Johnny, since he had returned to their room. He was obviously sulking and before I had a chance to reach for his shirt or realize what was happening, he grabbed my right hand (the one holding the hot iron) and twisted my wrist far enough to shove the iron against my left upper arm! When he finally released me, I pulled the hot metal away and it brought a three-inch triangle of skin with it. I was in a lot of pain but I walked out of the room without a word. I found a maid down the hall who put some kind of salve on the burn and covered it with a crude sort of bandage. Neither Rufus nor Johnny ever mentioned the incident but it was the first time I was aware of how much Johnny resented me and what he considered to be an intrusion on their friendship.

As often as Rufus lost his temper, he did so only for reasons of his own. At such times as the "iron" incident when a tantrum might be expected, he did nothing. I was hurt by his lack of concern, but I was also determined to get married, and a woman in such a mood is anything but logical.

So it was, on a rainy May afternoon in 1940, I was married for the first time in a dingy little chapel someplace in Shreveport, Louisiana. The wheezing minister rattled off the ceremony more like an auctioneer than a man of God. His wife coughed and blew her nose at two-minute intervals. Johnny pouted and shifted from one leg to the other uncomfortably. Rufus awaited his execution with a kind of deliberate patience. That is the picture I see as I look back, but at the time the minister stood straight and tall, and his words sounded distinct and heavenly. The woman's sniffling was a mother crying at the lovely wedding of her only daughter. Johnny was not a frustrated Rebel, but a well-meaning friend anxious for his companions to be happy. And as for Rufus, I held his hand reassuringly to let him know we were doing the right thing. Neither of us was perfect, by any means, but now each of us had that one important thing: someone to love.

Too quickly it was my turn to say "I do," and the ceremony ended. I stepped out into the rain, a married woman. Now that I was no longer alone, the rain felt warm and comfortable, not cold and damp as it had been when we came to the chapel an hour before.

Johnny continued to sulk. He defiantly refused to trade rooms, so Rufus moved into my tiny room with the single bed, and Johnny occupied the larger room with the double bed by himself.

The next day after our wedding, the weather cleared enough for the rodeo to begin. I felt my new marital status gave me the right to inquire further about the sudden bankroll Rufus had acquired, but it was only a few minutes prior to the bull-riding event that he revealed his "secret."

"Remember the rancher that gave me money for entry fees?" he asked, boastfully. "Well, I found some more people that wanted to enter me on a percentage, and they just handed over the cash instead of taking it to the rodeo office."

"And that's what we've been spending?" I was almost afraid to ask. "But you can't do that!"

He grinned disarmingly, "Sure I can, girl. All I had to do was offer each of them one-fourth of my winnings in the bull-riding. If I win, I'll pay 'em. If I buck off, we've still got all the money left except for what I really entered with!"

"Rufus," Johnny called from the chutes, "your bull's in!"

"Gotta go now," Rufus said over his shoulder. "See you later."

As I watched Rufus pulling on his bull-riding glove, I tried to reconstruct his calculations on the entry fee business, so it would be more clear to me. I figured for a minute, then it occurred to me that four people giving him twenty dollars each added up to eighty dollars. This accounted for all of our spending money. Since he naturally only entered once, he'd have sixty dollars clear whether he bucked off or not. Good thinking, except for one thing: the four donors would divide the entire purse if he did win something. That wasn't so good but it was senseless to stand around worrying when all I had to do was ask him. Maybe only three men had entered him . . .

I hated to bother Rufus again, but I had to know. I rushed over behind the chute as he was being belted down onto his bull, and I asked anxiously, "Just how many people did enter you in this event?"

Even with his hat pulled down on top of his ears, and his mouth twitching nervously, he still sounded proud when he whispered, with a wink, "There's eight of 'em, girl. How's that for promoting?"

"But you can't. . ."

I tried to be heard above the call of "Heads up!" but the gate flew open and Rufus' bull charged out into the arena.

Johnny and I just looked at each other. We moved over to the arena gate and both of us leaned against it, with our backs to the arena, afraid to watch.

An excited old man, wearing a grocer's apron, clawed his way to the top of the fence.

"Look at that boy ride!" he chirped. Then he poked Johnny on the shoulder with his finger and said, "I've got him entered in this event, you know!"

"You ain't alone, mister," Johnny sighed. "You shore ain't alone."

"Ride 'em cowboy!" the grocer shouted.

"Don't you dare!" Johnny and I pleaded in a whisper. Rufus was making a beautiful ride.

Too beautiful, as a matter of fact as we could see when we finally were compelled to watch him.

"If that jerk wins this bull-riding," I told Johnny, "we're dead. For every hundred he wins, he's got to pay eight people twenty-five dollars each!"

"I know," Johnny muttered. "Let's just hope Rufus knows it."

As anyone whose livelihood is based on the number of seconds you are able to stay on an animal, or rope and tie a calf or perform in any of the other rodeo events for any length of time, you get so you can feel when it is almost time for the whistle. I felt it right then. The sight of Rufus still "fitting a ride" scared me silly. I stood there, holding my breath, when suddenly Rufus jerked his hand out of the loose-rope and threw himself backwards off of his bull.

"Well, finally," I sighed.

The grocer looked around, confused, and asked, "Wasn't it strange how that bull tossed him just before the whistle blew? I certainly did think he was going to make it."

"So did I, mister," Johnny replied. His relief was a little too apparent. "So did I."

Rufus made his way back toward the chutes in a daze. Even when the announcer warned him that another bull was coming out, he still kind of staggered along the fence, talking to himself. When he finally reached us, he pushed his hat off of his ears and just stood there, staring at his boots.

"Well?" I asked, still puzzled. .

"I guess I don't figger too good, huh?" he asked, looking extremely young and very foolish.

I slipped my hand into his and whispered, "You just keep riding bulls like you did today, and let me take care of the arithmetic!"

He grinned, "An' we'll never see another poor day. Right?" Any feeling of guilt had already passed.

Now that the emergency was over, Johnny began acting as distant toward me as before. He won a little money in the bareback riding and since the rain had resumed, he informed Rufus he was leaving for Beaumont the next morning. He did not share his winnings but I never mentioned it. We never saw him again for a year or so.

Two days after Johnny's departure the weather still had not cleared and the rodeo was postponed indefinitely. We heard about a rodeo in Southern Oklahoma that we could make if we caught a bus out of town right away. Since Rufus had no option in Shreveport but to deliberately fall off every day, Oklahoma sounded like a logical solution to our problems and the bad weather gave us a legitimate excuse.

As it turned out, we were two weeks early for the Oklahoma rodeo, but Rufus hired out to help build their new arena, and I became sort of an "assistant" to the cook. It was an education in itself to be associated with the couple who were putting on the rodeo at their home ranch. She was one of those rugged gals with hairy arm-pits, and the big part of her legs at the bottom. Her husband, a cattle rancher, might have been a nice friendly guy if given a chance to say anything except, "Yes, dear!"

The "boss lady" did the cooking for the ranch hands when she was not out at the arena giving orders to the men. She seemed to take a liking to me and would have kept me with her around the clock if Rufus had not appeared at the cook-shack one evening to help me finish my work. When he entered the dining room, I stopped clearing dishes from the large, ranch-style table, and rushed over to give him a long newly-wed type kiss. The boss' eyes were blazing when she stormed past me and gathered up the few remaining plates.

It was nearly 9 p.m. by then, and I had been working since 5 a.m. The time span, along with the fact that I was simply working in exchange for our sleeping in a cabin behind the main building, convinced me she was being pretty unreasonable.

This was even more evident when she snapped at us, "If you two are so damned hot for each other, you better get back to your bunkhouse. You sure as hell ain't no use to me here!"

Rufus whirled toward her and I was so afraid of what he might say or do, I did not have time to get angry at her, myself. As I maneuvered him toward the door, I was tempted to steal his Fort Worth quotation, and tell her, "If you ain't tried it, don't knock it!" Instead, we made a quiet exit.

"Why didn't you let me tell that sow what I thought?" Rufus grumbled, "She's got no right."

"Shhhh," I soothed. "Remember, I have a bronc-riding job here and there's only a few more days to go. You're making good money, too, so it'd be silly not to tough it out. Come on, let's just forget her and go to bed."

On that point he was agreeable.

Ordinarily, infuriating your employer would mean extra work, but such was not the case with my gravel-voiced boss. Because she no longer chatted with me, I was able to complete my chores faster and had considerably more spare time each afternoon. I spent every possible minute at the arena. Most of it was already finished except for what would eventually be the "catch-pens" at the far end. I was watching Rufus and the other workers dig post-holes and was particularly fascinated to see them bring out their individual Mason jars of "White Lightning" from the empty holes.

One of the workers explained the procedure involved in drinking from those particular containers.

"You take the jar with one hand, and then before you take a drink you place the other hand on top of your head so the 100-proof-dynamite won't blow it plumb off!"

I was present one afternoon when the boss-lady visited the arena. She slammed her pickup truck to a stop, jumped out, and stomped over to the workers' area.

"It's a damn good thing you men are busy," she roared. "When I come by here, I don't want to see nothing but asses and elbows. Any man that's standing up straight, ain't earnin' his pay!"

As soon as she drove away, everyone started laughing. The reason her crew appeared to be so busy was not because they were hard at work, but because all of them were trying to bury their White Lightning before she saw them!

The days passed quickly and it was rodeo time. I rode a saddle-bronc each day, and although there horses were smaller than those in the northern states, the audience seemed to enjoy the performances. Rufus won some of the bull-riding and bareback riding.

We were having a good time, now that the mundane labor had ended and even the boss-lady was jubilant now that two young women from the east were visiting her for the rest of the summer. In fact, her exuberance was so unusual, I was compelled to ask one of the local cowboys about her change of attitude.

"That's quite a deal, all right," he chuckled. "Fer ten months outta the year, that woman ain't fit to be around. Then, them two females come to see her, and she jest giggles and carries on like a high-school girl on her first date!"

"What about her husband?" Rufus interrupted.

The cowboy's face turned slightly pink, and he said, "When them dude-gals go back home, I guess she jest kinda goes on the wagon and starts sleepin' with him again."

"Jeez, girl," Rufus laughed. "No wonder she kept you working so late at night!"

"Don't worry, honey," I assured him, "I prefer the clean-shaven variety, anyway, like you."

Our next stop was Tulsa, Oklahoma. For the first time we were able to check into the hotel of our choice, and had no worries about whether Rufus could get entered in the rodeo. In fact, the only hitch in our otherwise peaceful existence was my refusal to let Rufus spend our hard-earned cash to enter me in the women's bronc-riding when we heard it was to be a contest.

"Why the hell shouldn't you enter it?" he demanded.

"I can think of several reasons, but the best one is that I don't want to make a damned fool of myself and pay cash to do it. Three or four years ago I'd have been tickled to death to get a chance to compete against the Greenoughs, Vivian White, Tad Lucas, Alice Adams or anyone else, but I've ridden enough broncs now to know I'm not anywheres near ready. Maybe in another year or so."

This discussion took place in our hotel room. After my little speech, Rufus just turned and walked out. I guess I was kind of hoping he would reassure me, and say that I was good enough to compete with those other women, but he said nothing. In fact, I was still feeling sorry for myself the next afternoon when we arrived at the stadium. I felt that everyone else had a reason for being there except me. I had wanted to be a "hand," and yet the first time there was an opportunity to see how my riding stacked up against the older bronc-riders, I backed off like a scared coyote.

When the rodeo bookkeepers type the list of riders and events that make up the daily official programs, they make so many carbon copies it would even shame the army. After distribution of these copies to members of the rodeo committee, judges, chute help, the arena director, and everyone remotely connected with the performance, the remaining lists are tacked on various posts throughout the arena. Participants can read these for any information pertinent to their event, without bothering the announcer or bookkeeper

From force of habit, I paused and thumbed through one such list posted behind the chutes. The stock had been drawn for all three days and I was curious to see how many bulls Rufus would have to ride. In some cases where there were too many entrants in an event for all of them to take part during any one performance, the "go-round" had to be divided into two or more shows. This time it happened that each bull-rider drew two bulls for the three-day rodeo. I noticed that Rufus was to ride on the first day and the last, but I deliberately avoided reading the three or four names listed each day for "Ladies' Saddle-bronc Riding." In this case, a shortage of money made it necessary to keep the event limited to just one go-round for the entire show. These women were members of the Turtle Association by now and it was required that they be paid no less than $20 per mount. This, added to the shortage of female riders, meant that no more than three would perform at each show. On the final page of the program my own name jumped out of the jumble of print, and I had no choice but to read the lineup for the last day.

There it was: Jane Burnett, riding Texas Rose!

"What the hell?"

I did not realize I had spoken out loud until Rufus answered with another question. "What d'ya mean 'what the hell?' You didn't think I'd let you sit this one out, did you?"

"But I told you. . ."

"I know what you told me, girl, but this is not a case of 'rithmetic, so I figgered I could handle it myself!"

"I feel shaky inside already," I told him, "just from reading the program. I wonder what shape I'll be in after three days of stall-walking! I kind of wish I was up today so I could get it over with."

Rufus put his hand on my arm and I noticed he, too, was trembling. "Well, I'm up today, so let's see what that old bugger looks like, should we?"

With several of the other bull-riders, we headed for the pens to "case" the opposition. Rufus had drawn an impossible bull for his first one, but his mount for the final go-round was reputedly a money-maker.

Smoky Snyder, one of the greatest bull-riders and bareback-riders of all times, was standing next to us and he advised Rufus about his second ride.

"You drawed a good one, boy," Smokey said, "but you got to be careful he don't fool you. He's only part Brahma, and looks like a big white-faced longhorn steer. He ain't in the pens yet, but you'll see him soon enough. When the time comes, you'll ride his high, straight jumps easy at first, but that's what'll confuse you. About the time you figure he's rideable, and you loosen up to start spurring him, he'll throw a whing-ding at you that'll toss you plumb out of the stadium!"

"Thanks, Smoke," Rufus replied. "I'll try to remember."

The information was correct about both bulls. The first one threw Rufus so fast I would not have dared to sneeze or I would have missed it entirely.

As we were leaving the arena, a teenage girl in an elaborate leather western outfit told me I was needed at the rodeo headquarters. I had the same feeling you get when you're sent to the principal's office, I wondered what I had done wrong.

They simply wanted to tell me that I would not receive the maximum pay for my ride unless I joined the Turtles first. I was relieved to learn there were no other problems, and I was also excited about being able to join this recently-formed cowboys' union. In 1940 I became a full-fledged member and although this status did not automatically entitle me to the same amount of money each time like it was supposed to, on many occasions my fees were better than average.

Just before time to leave the hotel for the final performance, I began developing imaginary aches and pains that might keep me from riding that night. Rufus ignored me so I trailed along with him, silent and reluctant. I was more afraid of looking like a complete gunsel than I was of being thrown. I guess all of the years as the only woman rider at most of the shows where I worked had spoiled me. When it came to competing against "my own kind," a sort of stage-fright enveloped me. At least that was the way I analyzed my emotions until Texas Rose actually came into the chute and it was time to saddle up. As yet, Rufus had no experience saddling my broncs so a couple of other cowboys helped me get ready. The saddles they had on hand for the women's bronc-riding already had smaller stirrups, so that was not a problem.

The way the arena was graded, there was a definite downward slope out of the chute. This was not too good for the riders because the slant was enough to make it almost like bucking down hill. It was even worse when you approached the chutes on foot, and had to look up at an animal that suddenly appeared to be ten feet tall.

"Rufus!" I looked around and headed over to where he was standing at the end of the last chute, out of the way.

I grabbed his arm. "All day I been telling myself I just had stage-fright, but that's not it at all."

"No?" he grinned. "What ailment you got now?"

"I'm not sick this time," I admitted, "I'm just flat-assed scared!"

All too soon, the trick-roping was over and it was time for our event. Generally I was bored with the long, drawn-out trick-roping and trick-riding events because I had seen them so many times, but that night I honestly believe they did a "capsule" performance in thirty seconds flat.

By the time I was belted down onto the broad-backed grey mare, I was numbly calm. None of the other women ventured one bit of information regarding how long a rein I should take or anything, despite the fact that everyone of them had ridden Texas Rose, or tried to, at least once. Several men bronc-riders gave me advice but it was so different, riding with two reins, that they were unable to offer much help in that department.

"She's got a fair head, Janie," one of them said, "but she'll keep jerking more and more rein away from you as you go along. You got to feed it out."

There was no time to explain to the nice man that I always twisted my reins after drawing them through my fingers, and although I could hang on tighter that way, it was virtually impossible to "feed" any extra rein when necessary like a man could do with a single rein. In fact, there was no time for anything. I nodded and the gate flew open.

The first few jumps were encouraging. Texas Rose jumped high, kicked high, and hit the ground hard, but she bucked fairly straight. Then, about the time I thought I had it made, each jump grew progressively higher and harder, and she slammed her head from one side to the other and I felt myself being pulled further out of the saddle with each jump. I felt sure I was already bucked off when my reins began to slip through my fingers in spite of the way I twisted them in the palm of my hand before the ride. I was as far out of the saddle as my hobbled stirrups could go with my feet still in them, when one of the pickup-men rode by and literally reached into the air and grabbed me. I threw both arms around his neck and kissed him on the cheek.

"Fella," I told him, "I've never been so glad to see anyone in my whole life!"

He was still chuckling when he set me down in front of the chutes. Rufus rushed over to me.

"I'm sorry, honey," I apologized, "she was just too much horse for me."

"Too much horse?" he exclaimed, and gave me a big hug. "Girl, you just made one hell of a ride on that old mare!"

"You mean I made it to the whistle?"

Smokey stepped over to me and answered for him, "You sure did! They blew it just before the pickup-man grabbed you." He tipped his hat forward to rest on the bridge of his nose, and said, teasingly, "As a matter of fact, if your reins and your legs were about three feet longer, you could ride that bronc all day long!"

I figured my ride must have looked pretty fair when several cowboys went out of their way to compliment me, but I was not entirely convinced until a couple of the cowgirls actually went out of their way to avoid comment. Only then was I satisfied with the job I had done.

It would have been nice to stand around and talk about me some more, but bull-riding was the next event, and Rufus had to get ready.

There was no way for Rufus to win first place because Smokey had made the whistle on one of the impossible bulls, but from what the other contestants around me were saying, the "longhorn" would buck hard enough for "second money" if Rufus could ride him.

Just before the gate opened, I peeked through and said to Rufus, "Remember what Smokey told you, now. Just don't get over-confident."

He nodded for the gate just as he asked, "What's over-condiment mean?"

"Too much 'pepper,' I guess," I muttered to myself. Rufus had already gone.

I was mighty proud of the way he sat on that tall red half-Brahma, and the high, picturesque leaps were almost breath-taking. After about six seconds my "southern-cured ham" did just what we all feared he would, he jerked his spurs out of that steer's belly and began chopping at his neck. Again, as per Smokey's predictions, that was just in time for the "whing-ding." Actually, it had not been the spurring that provoked the terrific explosion of bucking just before the whistle, it was simply that particular animal's style.

I guess "somebody up there" was blowing the whistle for the Morris family that evening because Rufus had been as nearly bucked off as you can be, and still qualify, when the shrill "brrrrt" sounded. If I had been less excited about his ride I would have berated him for not listening to Smokey's advice, but how can you stay mad at a man who just won $125?

In spite of the kind remarks about my ride, it still surprised me to learn I had placed first in the women's bronc-riding. The prize money was much smaller than in the men's events, but I was able to add $30 to our growing bankroll. When we reached our hotel room we tossed our money into a pile on the bed and danced around like a couple of little kids.

"Look at that loot!" he grinned. "I told you we'd never see another poor day!"

"I hope you're right. I'm learning to like the feel of twenty-dollar bills."

Rufus tossed his hat in the air, grabbed me around the waist and danced me around the room. "We got 'er made, girl! I feel it in my bones."

After a few minutes of dancing and giggling, we stopped. Rufus stood looking into my eyes soberly. "And now we're heading for Beaumont. We're gonna show them rice farmers that me and my Yankee wife can do something!"

"You bet! Besides, don't you think it's about time I met your family?"

"Yeah, I guess I do." He slumped into a chair and pulled me onto his lap. "I shore want Mama to see what you're really like. There's no telling what she's heard by now."

# Chapter Fifteen

On our way to Beaumont, I kept trying to picture Rufus' mother. The images varied from a clinging-vine to a dominating shrew, but always as a woman who would resent her "baby boy" being married to any woman, especially a Yankee stranger. I was so convinced she was going to hate me, I was tempted to check into a hotel in Beaumont until Rufus went home to break the ice.

Filled with something resembling bull-riders' panic, I struggled to remain calm when we finally arrived at the plain looking frame house where a dissimilar assortment of people were streaming in and out of the front door.

"Here we are, girl," Rufus said. He sounded a bit shaky, too. "Let's get this over with."

That encouraging statement was almost enough to scare me off forever, but I took a deep breath and replied, "You bet!"

The traffic through the barren sunbaked yard came to a halt as men, women, and children eyed our taxi suspiciously until the moment Rufus stepped out. He was practically mobbed by the excited group who crowded around asking, "Home from the rodeos, young fella?"

"Guess you been makin' lotsa money. Hey, Boy? Comin' home in a taxi and all."

"Got yourself a wife, too—that right?"

Big-eyed faces peered at me through the cab windows. Another voice said, "Hey, Rufus. Is that her?"

Rufus tried to reply to the first few questions, then gave up and motioned for me to climb out and we elbowed our way to the porch.

"Is that your family?" I whispered hoarsely. "I mean, are all of them relatives?"

"Hell, no!" he laughed. "Some of 'ems relations, but they's mostly folks my Mama washes clothes for. Sometimes I wonder how she gets her work done at all, with them chargin' in and out all day."

Inside the house it was more of the same, with questions and curious stares. But still no Mama. Then at last a screen door at the back of the house opened and a robust woman came in carrying an enormous basket of clothes. Her face was flushed and her greying hair lay in damp ringlets across her broad forehead. Suddenly the room was quiet.

"Hello, son!" the large-boned woman said in a deep voice. She set the basket on the floor and embraced Rufus.

"Mama," he began hesitantly, "this is. . ."

Before he could finish, she stepped over to me, drying her right hand on her apron. She gripped my hand tightly and sincerely as she shook it.

"Of course," she said. "This has to be Jane." Her smile disclosed fine white teeth and deep dimples. She released my hand and stepped back to take a long look at me. Then, much to my surprise, she pulled me toward her ample body and hugged me so hard I could barely get my breath.

She added softly, "Welcome home, daughter. We been waitin' for y'all every day."

I was so touched by this simple genuine greeting, my throat felt tight and with a burning sensation in my chest I had trouble suppressing the tears. I was unable to reply aloud, but I was certain she understood. Then I stood on tiptoe and kissed her cheek. I had needed a close woman friend for much longer than I had needed a husband, and now I had both.

It was apparent the others had also been dubious of my reception, because the moment the tension passed, bedlam enveloped the small house again. I turned to Rufus' mother for refuge in the confusion, since my new husband was too preoccupied with relating rodeo experiences to pay any attention to me for awhile. I addressed his mother as "Mrs. Morris" until she explained that another husband, a Mr. Treme, had come and gone since Rufus' father. In fact, her children of several different marriages kept me so confused I never did really get them straight.

Because I had been received so graciously, I discounted the occasional remarks about Rufus being a "Mama's boy," but within a few hours I began to understand.

Regardless of her other work, Mrs. Treme waited on Rufus hand and foot. I offered to help in any way I could around the kitchen, but the rest of the clan moved only when they felt it was necessary to give Mrs. Treme more room to work. Daughters and daughters-in-law wandered in and out with sewing and alterations that Mrs. Treme was to do for them. Sons and sons-in-law trailed in behind them to "borrow a few bucks 'til payday." And to top it all, Rufus flopped onto our bed (located at one end of the long narrow kitchen) and wheedled his mother into bringing him coffee and a piece of pie.

For a few days I kept myself occupied sewing some new rodeo blouses, with welcome advice from Mrs. Treme who asked that I please call her "Mom." She also showed me how to iron Rufus' shirts according to his requirements. I was not able to do much else as Mom was a woman who had done her own work for so many years, she did not know how to share it with others. Rufus slept until noon almost every day, and I served him coffee in bed, only because I hated to see his mother saddled with any more work. As soon as he was dressed, he would disappear with friends or relatives to be gone most of the day, while I remained at home.

Our bankroll was rapidly shrinking due to Rufus' many donations to his gunsel "buddies," who constantly fed his ego by making a big issue of the winnings he brought home. They were obviously making a sucker out of him but I was in no position to say so. He did not offer to pay any of the household expenses but I paid for groceries whenever I had a chance.

When I finally realized that Rufus had every intention of remaining in Beaumont indefinitely, I began phoning the promoters of a few shows in South Texas. I rode a few steers and one bareback bronc for "mount-money" but was unable to get a contract to ride saddlebroncs. Mainly I wanted to get Rufus back in gear while we still had a few dollars left from our recent winnings. It was clear almost from the start that we needed to hit the road if my new husband was ever going to grow up.

Rufus did purchase a delapidated jalopy from one of the "relatives" for $25. Water dribbled out of the radiator constantly, and we had to carry waste-oil in five-gallon cans in order to replenish the motor every ten miles or so when it ran out of oil. It was also kind of a non-converting convertible, with no top, and more than once we had to pull into a covered filling-station just to get out of the rain, or to purchase some of their used oil. On one particular occasion when I stepped out of the car under cover of a service-station roof, buckets of rain water that had accumulated, poured out when I opened my door.

However, the tires were pretty fair, and we made it to five or six local rodeos without getting stranded. Besides the jalopy, I made the final payment on my grey and red boots and had them shipped from Fort Worth. Otherwise, we had absolutely nothing to show for our stay in Beaumont. Nothing tangible, that is. Since my friendship with Mom was to eventually outlast my marriage by many years, it should be considered my one treasured possession.

A contract to work in Minneapolis in July was a direct result of a letter I sent to Gene Autry at his ranch in Oklahoma. Had it not been such a good offer, I sometimes wonder if Rufus would have ever left Texas again, but much to my relief, we traded our jalopy in on a late-model used-Ford and headed down the road.

Despite Mom's feeling toward all of her children, and Rufus in particular, she seemed to understand how important it was for us to be on our own again. She showed no signs of displeasure or resentment when we left, even though she knew it was all my doing.

After the car purchase, we had almost nothing left from our previous earnings and consequently it was necessary to wire rodeo headquarters in Minneapolis and have them enter Rufus with part of my contract money. By hauling several cans of cheap Texas gas with us, driving straight through with no stop-overs, and living on baloney sandwiches, we made it from Beaumont to Minneapolis on $11.55. Every time I took a bite of baloney and dry bread, I thought about the money we had donated to Rufus' many unemployed buddies, and it made me more determined to be the Morris family "banker" whenever possible. Rufus had never driven a car in strange territory before, so he slept while I drove, and then kept me awake reading maps and giving directions while he drove. I arrived in Minneapolis in a semi-coma from lack of sleep.

The weather during the Minneapolis Aquatennial and Rodeo was suffocatingly hot, even after Texas. The humidity was high, and what with riding quadrille, grand entry, and broncs in two shows per day—to say nothing of riding in the down-town parades each morning, I earned every cent of the money I received for the ten-day show. With a weight loss of ten pounds during that period, I had sufficient data for an artlcle on "Advice to the Obese," but I doubted this method would catch on.

The third evening, Autry invited me to a radio broadcast where several of us were to be interviewed about rodeo life in general. Rufus became dangerously silent when I told him what I planned to do but I had made my own decisions for so many years, it did not occur to me to consult him ahead of time.

I returned to our room right after the broadcast and found Rufus pacing the floor like a caged tiger. He began raving about my behavior with Autry and demanded a minute-by-minute account of my time while I was gone. His accusations came as such a shock, I hardly knew whether to shout protests at him, plead for understanding, or just keep my mouth shut. I took my cue from his eyes and said nothing. Several times at the peak of his anger, I thought he was going to hit me, but he finally raved himself into kind of a calm, deadly state that was even more frightening.

"There is something going on between you and that singing baboon, ain't there?" he demanded coldly.

"For Christ's sake—no. I only. . ."

"If there hadn't been something, you'd a-told me about it first."

By then he was standing over me, fists doubled and arms held rigidly at his sides. Then suddenly, he sort of wilted and tears came into his eyes. The storm was over.

"I'm sorry," he whispered sincerely. "I know better—it's just that I can't stand to see nobody fussing over you. I won't act like this again. I promise."

"But it's so ridiculous."

"I said I was sorry!" A hint of anger returned to his voice.

"All right," I quickly agreed. "Let's just forget it. Tomorrow I'll draw some of my wages and we can go out and have a few drinks after the show. Okay? Maybe the heat's getting the best of both of us."

"Whatever you say." This new docility was so unlike him, I was more confused than ever. I made it a point, at that time, to be very careful whenever I was around Autry.

Possibly Rufus' anger and resentment were outgrowths of an insecurity he felt at being so far from home for the first time, plus a need to prove himself to be the man of the house. Whatever the original motives, he now became fierce and aggressive for all the wrong reasons. When we made love that night, it was done savagely, and without tenderness. It was so reminiscent of my nightmarish ordeals with Jebo that I began to fight against him and he jerked me out of bed and slammed me across the room where I stumbled against a chair, sobbing. There were no apologies and/or hollow promises this time. I slept where I fell.

The following afternoon Autry asked me if I would accompany him to a Kiwanis meeting that evening for further advertisement of the show. I was ashamed to explain why I had to refuse, but I guess my manufactured alibi was noticeably phoney because he did not invite me again.

I returned to our room immediately after the matinee performance, as per Rufus' instructions, and while I awaited his arrival, I did something that was a carry-over from my childhood: I wrote out my frustrations in a lengthy letter to my parents—a letter that would never be mailed. (I often used this means of "letting off steam" at home, even when my folks were in the next room. The evidence was destroyed at once, but so was my "gripe," insignificant as it might be.) This time, however, I explained to them that I was in love with my husband, but loneliness and discontent may have been partially responsible for my decision to get married. Now, ironically, I was being smothered by my own ingenious plot. With my marriage, the "rodeo wives" had become more friendly, as I had hoped, but now I was becoming ill-at-ease with everyone, male or female, due to Rufus' extreme possessiveness. I needed to be around people, and laugh with them, without fear of the consequences.

"Gcod Lord!" I asked in my letter."What have I done to him? And to myself?"

Without signing the letter, I quickly tore it into shreds, then wrote a short note of the "having a wonderful time, wish you were here" variety and prepared it for mailing. In the postscript I mentioned Deadwood, South Dakota, as our next stop after Minneapolis.

I withdrew as much cash as was allowed that night, and we went on a real bender. We stayed in bed until noon the next day and barely made it to the afternoon show. Neither of us felt up to riding in the morning parade in downtown Minneapolis, which was actually a breach of contract if anyone wanted to make an issue of the offense. Rufus rode a really rank bull that day that won him a second-place for that particular go-round. I teased him about doing better when he was hung over, but he said there had to be an easier way.

On the next-to-last evening of the rodeo, we went to a nearby restaurant and while we were waiting to be seated, a south Texas cowboy who was in line ahead of us asked if we wanted to join them. It was our very first opportunity to be included in a group of rodeo "couples," and I held my breath for the few seconds it took Rufus to answer.

"Sounds like a winner," he replied, grinning.

I began to breathe again and eight of us were seated in a large circular booth with Rufus at one end of the circle and me next to him. Now that I was more aware of Rufus' jealousy I wanted to avoid any problems, especially when this was the first time we were ever included in a couples thing. I was relieved that one of the wives sat next to me. Her name was Sandy and she seemed genuinely glad to have us included in their group.

The evening went extremely well with everyone exchanging humorous anecdotes about previous rodeos. I told about my bronc ride where the cowboys had turned loose the colt of the mare I was riding and how the crowd had reacted. When everyone laughed at my story, Rufus became tense.

From the day of my very first rodeo, I was always treated as just another "hand," and I did not see any reason for this to change just because I was a married woman. I now stayed out of the conversation even though Sandy and the other wives periodically teased their husbands about one thing or another. I no longer felt as comfortable in that group.

When we finished eating, I excused myself and went to the restroom. On my return, when Rufus stepped aside for me to sit down, Sandy also headed for the Ladies' room and this placed me next to her husband while she was gone. I did not think anything about this new arrangement until he leaned his elbow on my shoulder when he reached past me to get some sugar for his coffee, and I felt Rufus' entire body grow tense.

Even though I knew we would go back to the original seating arrangement when Sandy returned, I mentioned that I was expecting a phone call from Montana and we would have to leave. After thanking the group for letting us join them, we left enough cash for our share of the meal and the tip and went back to the hotel.

What should have been a pleasant evening was not the happy occasion I had hoped for. I was glad when we headed west two days later.

The rodeo headquarters in Deadwood, South Dakota was filled with Montana and Canadian cowboys I had not seen for nearly a year. I am sure some of them were puzzled about how I had changed, but I hoped they understood I was not snubbing any one of them personally when I avoided the various groups gathered to relate their rodeo experiences of the past few months.

While Rufus paid his entry fees, I came to an agreement with the promoter about my job. The bookkeeper overheard someone mention my name and asked if I was Jane Morris.

"Yes. Why?"

"There's a message here for you, "she said. "A phone call."

"For me?"

"Yes. You're to come to the Black Hills Bar right away."

"Okay, thanks." I noticed the promoter eyeing me, so I explained, "My name is Jane Morris, now, but I still ride under my maiden-name, Burnett."

As soon as we stepped outside, I realized Rufus was about to start interrogating me so I wanted to head off a tantrum before it got out of hand.

I spoke cautiously, “I suppose we better see who it is, don’t you? Might be somebody who knows my folks.”

He relaxed slightly, so I continued. “We ought to check it out, anyway. Right?”

“Whatever you say,” he relaxed slightly.

Maybe I would eventually learn how to handle this marriage thing.

I just shook my head and climbed into the car. We drove into town and started looking for the Black Hills Bar. Deadwood was so filled with cars we had to park nearly four blocks from our goal and elbow our way through the crowds once we located the right saloon. Otherwise, I might have wasted a lot of time wondering about who had left the message. As it was, I was totally unprepared when I stepped through the front door of that saloon and saw a wonderfully familiar thin face, big ears, and a cowboy hat that was tipped forward to keep the light from shining directly into the eyes of the black-jack dealer (who just happened to be my father).

I shoved through the crowd, fighting back the tears. By the time I reached the blackjack table, I had myself under control. I silently tossed out a nickel.

“Four-bits is the smallest bet,” Clint said in his most business-like manner, without glancing up.

“Wouldn’t settle for a two-headed quarter, would you, fella?”

He snapped to attention. “Well! Hi, Skipper! What d’you know?”

“Not a hell of a lot.” We were both grinning and the blackjack game was temporarily on hold. “Where’s Mother?”

“She’ll be here shortly. And Rufus?”

I turned, expecting to find him at my elbow. He was still standing by the front door and I felt ashamed that I had actually forgotten about him for a few minutes.

“I’ll go get him.”

By the time I rescued Rufus and we returned to the card table, Clint had been relieved by another dealer and we made our way to the bar. Mother arrived just then, and when the greetings and introductions were out of the way, the four of us set out to deplete Deadwood’s liquor supply in a very methodical manner.

Rufus deserves a great deal of credit for being so tolerant that evening. There is nothing more boring than drunken-reminiscing when you are just a spectator. Mother finally bowed out of the competition a couple of hours later and since Clint had reserved a room for us across the hall from their own, Rufus saw this as an opportunity to escape so he offered to escort her to the hotel. Ordinarily I would have felt some concern as to whether Rufus was angry or not, but I was enjoying the hilarious reunion to such an extent I hardly missed him when he left.

The town was operating on a twenty-four-hour schedule and along toward dawn Clint and I staggered to our rooms. He disappeared through their unlocked door, but after finding myself locked out, I curled up in the hallway and went to sleep leaning against the door. Sometime during the night Rufus must have peeked out because I tumbled backwards into the room and he patiently put me to bed. Talk about a man of many moods!

Rufus' first impression of his new in-laws had to have been discouraging, to say the least. I should have been more sympathetic about his situation but he was no more out of place than I had been in Beaumont, so I decided to let him make his own adjustments. He was actually starting to take part in the conversations by the final day of the rodeo.

During each performance of the show, I had been watching with awe three Hungarian girls who did a tight-rope act high above the arena. Without a net! It was terrifying to see those tiny figures doing acrobatics at an altitude higher than most cowboys would go in an elevator. While I awaited time to ride my bronc that last afternoon, these girls approached me at the arena entrance.

"Vwy you do thees dangerous theengg" one of them asked. "Vwe are so frighten' for you, when you ride zee buckeeng bronco!"

"You're afraid for me?" I was shocked. "Ladies, I wouldn't trade jobs with you for all the beer in Milwaukee!"

We chatted for a few minutes about the various interpretations of the word "danger," and then it was time for me to go.

The leggy sorrel they gave me that day kept rearing up and going over backwards in the chute. Only the quick actions of the man who was belting me down saved me from being pinned beneath the bronc when he fell over. About the fourth or fifth time I climbed to the top of the chute to try getting down on my mount, I glanced toward the arena exit and saw the ambulance backing up to the gate with its doors open.

"Those bastards are getting a mite eager, aren't they?" I asked Rufus nervously.

"Don't worry, girl, soon as we get you out-a this chute, you'll be okay."

"You bet," I tried to sound convinced.

In spite of many rodeo superstitions, such as the one I shared with a lot of other rodeo people about bad luck for anyone who tossed their hat on a bed, I had never felt even a twinge of concern that my fate would be decided by anything except sheer ability, or lack of same. However, this ambulance thing was beginning to get to me.

Rufus had slipped a short piece of rope around the neck of the bronc and then wrapped it around the top pole of the chute, on the opposite side from the gate. This kept the sorrel from throwing himself backwards until the gate could be opened, but there was no guarantee what would happen when the rope was released. However, we were delaying the show, and since that was always a major complaint against women bronc-riders, (taking extra time to put hobbles on the saddle, etc.) I knew I had to take a chance and get that bronc out of the chute.

As the gate flew open and the bronc's neckrope was freed, he made a high lunge into the air. I was certain he would fall over, but he hit the ground bucking, and lined out across the arena, whipping his head to each side so far that he hit the toes of my boots with his jaw-bone. It was a relief to be out of the chute. I knew I was making a pretty fair ride, when suddenly I felt something snap loose beneath the horse. A buckle on the hobbles broke with the result that I was catapulted off of the right side of the bronc with such force that during the split-second in which my left foot hung in the stirrup, I dislocated my left hip before I hit the ground.

The pain was almost unbearable when they lifted me to a stretcher and carried me toward the waiting ambulance. From that time on I had a special superstition of my very own. On the way to the hospital I kept telling Rufus I had been jinxed, and I also insisted it was my left hip that was injured, even though I had fallen on my right side. I guess he thought I was delirious, because he just patted me on the head.

My folks reached the hospital almost as soon as we did. They came into the room where I was stretched out on top of a hard black table with two nurses trying to remove my boots. Clint took one look at my face and shoved the nurses away.

"For God's sake, cut the boots off," he commanded. "Can't you see what you're doing to her?"

For just an instant I was relieved that the tugging and twisting had ended. Then I realized I was wearing my grey-and-red boots that were finally paid for, and I struggled to raise up enough to see Clint approach my bed with an open pocket-knife.

"Don't ruin them!" I yelled. "Cut along the seam and I can get a zipper."

Clint looked toward me, the corner of his mouth kind of twitching, and said, "I guess you're not too bad off, if that's all you're worried about!"

During all that time, about forty minutes or so, the doctor still had not arrived. When he finally did get there, he took command immediately, issuing a series of terse, explicit orders.

A nurse approached me from behind and held some kind of a gadget in her hand. "Can you take gas, young lady?"

"You bet," I replied through gritted teeth, "just fill 'er up!"

When I regained consciousness, I was flat on my back in a hospital bed. My folks and Rufus were standing around the bed, peeking at me through the maze of ropes and pulleys that controlled the weights on my legs.

"What the hell's this?" I grumbled. "Some new kind of hay-stacker?"

Their answering titters were strictly hospital variety tension-relievers that did not quite break the hush-hush sound barrier.

"How soon can I get out of this?"

Clint looked down at the Stetson he was rotating in his hands when he replied, "They said you'd be out of here in three or four weeks."

"Three or four? Like this? But I can't even sleep on my back—never could."

Rufus spoke then, with kind of a nervous chuckle, "Bet my—I mean, bet *our* bottom dollar, you'll learn to!"

"This boy has possibilities," Clint grinned. "It's time our family had one member who restricts his betting to cinches."

I was interrupted by the arrival of a horse-faced nurse who held a thermometer in one hand and a hypo in the other. She briskly herded my folks out for the night.

"Anything we can do for you before we leave?" Mother asked.

"You might nail the furniture to that far wall so I'll think I'm sleeping on my side."

On their way out the door, Mother added, "Better watch what you say, honey. If they think you're delirious, they might put your head in traction, too."

The nurse whinnied loudly, and they left.

Both of my parents remained in Deadwood for two weeks, but Clint had to return to the ranch at that time so Mother decided to wait and ride to Lewistown with Rufus and me. She and Rufus took turns trying to find games for us to play so I would not lose my mind completely while I was in traction.

I stayed in bed for another week after we reached the ranch, then walked on crutches for a month. To keep from flipping my Stetson completely, I tried my hand at writing saleable stories for *Liberty Magazine*. I actually struggled with this project over the years because of their lucrative payoffs for short-short stories, but was never able to produce anything that met their standards.

I was surprised that Rufus took such an interest in the ranch, and he and Clint seemed to get along well together. Too well, in fact. It was not long before the two of them began disappearing in the general direction of Lewistown with Mother and me being left at the ranch. One time when they were away most of the night, I decided I was going to put my foot down (the good one) the minute they got home. I was lying in bed, awake and angry, when Rufus entered quietly. I turned on the light so my angry glares would not be wasted.

"Hi!" he said cheerfully. "You still awake?"

Obviously I was, so I continued to glare.

While Rufus slowly undressed, he struggled very hard to appear sober. Even if his eyes had not been glassy, I would have known something was wrong when he put his Levis and shirt on a hanger (unheard of, for him), and patiently draped each sock across the top of a boot. I was determined to withhold comment until I saw just how far this comedy of errors would go. My restraint amazed even me, but when Rufus crawled into bed, told me good-night, and rolled over to go to sleep, I exploded with laughter instead of the outrage I had planned. He was still wearing his cowboy hat!

Although that one incident had a happy ending, it had kindled my suspicions that I might suddenly find myself in the stay-at-home-farm-life category and I thought about how Rufus accepted that existence for his mother as being normal.

That was certainly not my idea of married life.

Rufus was not prepared for a Montana winter. The novelty of ranching had gradually run its course and was being replaced daily by his yearning for a warmer climate and Mom's pampering.

Now that I was completely healed from the Deadwood disaster, I was also ready to head south. I saw no reason for us to remain at the ranch permanently. Clint had taken over the place from Grandpa Burnett just a short time before, and our status would be as "hired hands" for too many years if we decided to stay.

Besides, I had no intention of dropping out of the rodeo business until I had at least one crack at a World's Championship title. I felt I should be ready to try the Garden in two more years.

We drove straight through to Texas, but this time Rufus was able to do his share of driving without requiring my directions every half hour or so. This gave me a chance to sleep part of the time which was a big help. Whenever we stopped to eat or use the restrooms, I checked our maps for highway numbers and wrote down the ones he would need for the next hour or so.

At a service station in one small Wyoming town, I was curious about an extra entrance to the women's restroom. For safety's sake, I locked them both. When Rufus had not returned to the car after about fifteen minutes, I went around to the front entrance and saw him leaning against the far wall, apparently waiting to enter the door marked MEN.

"I guess some gunsel's got hisself locked in there!" he grinned. "I'm about ready to bust down this door."

Due to the size of that small station, I suddenly realized why he had a problem. The door I had locked from the inside of the women's facility was the very same one that was keeping Rufus out!

Before I went back to the side entrance to open the other door, I asked the attendant to explain the reason behind this peculiar arrangement.

He looked kind of sheepish when he explained that there was a new law in Wyoming requiring every service station to have a facility for men and one for women so this was their solution.

Once Rufus had shared the facility, we headed south once more, and kept laughing for the next twenty miles on down the road.

We had planned to drive straight through to Beaumont but banners and flags on both sides of the street indicated the Houston Fat Stock Show and Rodeo was to begin in two days. I could hardly believe we had forgotten it was that time of year again, but without checking *Hoofs & Horns* for several months, this topic had not been open for discussion.

Although we were far from being burdened with income-tax problems, we had wisely managed the money Clint gave us when we left the ranch so we felt secure in checking into a small hotel for at least one night. The first thing on my agenda was a very long hot bath, including shampooing my hair, and then I could consider any discussions about the rodeo.

Actually, I awoke some time later in a tub full of water that was only luke warm. I climbed out and called to Rufus while I toweled off and put on clean underwear. There was no answer.

Rufus arrived shortly after I finished getting dressed. I told him I wanted to go to the rodeo headquarters, but he said he had already inquired about a bronc-riding job for me, and had been turned down. If we decided to stay for the rodeo, he would need to enter before noon the next day.

"There's somebody wants to talk to you, though." He added, "Fred Alvord."

"He's with Colburn, right? Did he say what it's about?

"Nope. Just asked if you was here."

We reached the cafe where quite a few of the cowboys were waiting to be seated, and Rufus pointed to a corner booth.

"There's Fred now. You might as well see what he wants."

I was surprised that Rufus was turning the reins over to me which was a welcome change of attitude he had developed since our stay in Montana. He did not insist on being there during the discussion but I asked him to, anyway.

As soon as we were seated across from Alvord and the usual small talk was out of the way, he looked straight at me and asked, "How'd you like to work at the Garden this fall, Jane?"

"Doing what?" I laughed. "Howing potatoes? I think that's about my speed."

"No. I'm serious. I work for Everett Colburn, you know, and I'm hiring women bronc-riders for New York."

"Hiring? For New York? But it's always been a competition event."

"Before. But not now. There's so few women riders any more, Cobe decided to put them under contract and have four or five exhibition rides every performance, instead of messing around with a contest."

"What about the championship? If New York folds up the women's competition, it means the end of the title, doesn't it?"

He nodded. "It's liable to. That's why we're making this attempt to keep it alive and see if a few more women turn out next year. Are you interested?"

"Gosh, I don't know."

"You don't know?" He and Rufus both stared at me as though I had sprouted an extra head.

"No. It's just that I hadn't figured to try New York for two or three years yet."

"I'll tell you something, Jane," Alvord said gravely, "if you want to ride at the Garden, you'd better do it while you can. The future looks pretty grim for women's bronc-riding if there aren't enough of you who stick with it."

"Rufus, what do you think?"

It was out of character for me to shift the responsibility for such a decision, but I really wanted someone to talk me into believing I should do it. Or if I could.

His wide grin was encouraging when he replied, "The Lord hates a coward, girl. Just take a long rein, a deep seat, and don't never look back."

"Well, I suppose he's right," I nodded to Alvord. I was still not totally convinced I was ready. "Bring on your contract."

"Great! And if you want a job riding quadrille, we can work that in, too. I'll drop it off at your hotel. If it sounds all right, just sign it and mail one copy to my home in Alvord, Texas."

I nodded and started to rise.

"One more thing, Jane," Alvord added. "I saw you win that bronc-riding in Tulsa and you don't need to worry about your ability. I know you can do it and I've told that to Colburn."

"Thanks. I guess I'll see you in New York." Rufus and I both shook his hand and walked away. I was afraid if I remained, I might admit to him that I was riding "way over my head" at the Tulsa show and it was in no way indicative of my usual riding ability. Now that I had agreed to work at the Garden, it made no sense to get myself fired before the contract was even signed.

Rufus was mumbling to himself.

"Anything wrong?" I asked, as soon as we were outside of the restaurant.

"Did you hear what he said? He's got a town that's all his very own! Alvord, Texas. I'll be damned."

He was still shaking his head when we walked back to where our car was parked.

Since I had no job at the Houston rodeo and there was not sufficient time for Rufus to promote entry fees for the bull-riding, we decided to go on to Beaumont the next morning.

In the past, Rufus had never been away from home this long and I watched him become more anxious with each passing mile as we headed for Beaumont the next day.

# Chapter Sixteen

For the first couple of months after our return to Beaumont, it was impossible to pry Rufus away from home. I am sure, to some extent, that returning to "breakfast in bed" territory had a great deal to due with his attitude, but with his old buddies making such an issue over his experiences up north, it was a while before he came back to earth.

By reminding Rufus that we would need to build a bankroll before our trip to New York, we finally began some serious rodeoing by mid-summer. Rufus seemed to feel a little more secure when we were around other people, and although he still showed signs of jealousy, I was learning which situations to avoid so he would not be angry at me quite so often.

He was a man of moods. We were at a country dance in a local gymnasium one evening after the rodeo when I happened to mention that I liked a blouse that one of the rodeo queens was wearing. I did not give this any more thought. Then, later in the evening one of the local cowboys asked me to dance, and because he was a friend of Rufus, I agreed. By the end of the dance, Rufus was nowhere in the building and it made me really nervous because I was never sure how he might react in any given situation.

When the dance ended, I returned to my seat in the bleachers of the gymnasium where the dance was held, and I kept anxiously watching the front door for Rufus' return.

In a few minutes, I was shocked, and then delighted, when he came through the front door and walked straight toward me with that girl's blouse draped over his arm!

Besides being relieved that he was not angry about my dancing with his friend, there were also a few seconds when I panicked, wondering exactly how he managed to be in possession of the blouse.

As he made his way through the crowd to where I was seated, the aforementioned girl waved to me from the doorway, and she was wearing a different blouse than when I saw her earlier.

Rufus had bought the blouse from her as a gift to me.

I rode saddle-broncs in several Texas and Oklahoma rodeos and Rufus was winning enough money in bull-riding to keep us on the move. At the rodeos where I was unable to get a bronc-riding job, I quite often was hired as a time-keeper for the roping or bull-dogging events with my wages being applied toward Rufus' entry fees.

At larger rodeos, the time-keeper whose job it was to blow the whistle for the riding events, would not participate if their spouse or traveling companion was entered. I learned the reason for this regulation the hard way when I was hired for that particular job at a small Texas show.

Two timekeepers are required to handle stop-watches in the events such as roping, bulldogging, and wild-cow milking and certain of the cowboys' wives do this at quite a few of the same rodeos each year. They have their own expensive stop-watches and are quite adept because they often time their husband's practice sessions at home. A third clock-watcher has the responsibility of blowing the whistle in the riding events to indicate the end of each eight or ten second ride, as the case may be. The length of time required for the ride varies according to the event, generally eight seconds for bareback and bull-riding, and ten for saddle-broncs. Local rulings often determine a different riding time for a certain event.

At this particular show, I was assigned to the whistle job, and got along fine until Rufus rode his bull. As soon as the chute gate opened, I punched the button to start the stop-watch, then became so absorbed in his ride that I forgot to check the watch or blow the whistle until he had ridden just over nine seconds instead of eight. Immediately after I came out of my daze and blew the whistle, he was thrown. He placed first in that go-round, but if my trance had caused him to disqualify, instead, he might have threatened to chop off my stop-watch arm just below my chin. Even one or two seconds of civilian time may not seem like much, but in arena time it could seem like twice as long.

When the show ended that day, I rushed down to compliment Rufus on his great ride.

"Thanks, girl," he said proudly. Then he frowned and asked, "But didn't that seem like a helluva long ride to you?"

"Naw, I don't think so," I interrupted. "Probably felt that way because he was such a rank bull."

"I suppose." He still looked puzzled but I did not volunteer any other information.

Now that I was acquainted with more of the contestants, I was frequently given an opportunity to ride one of their horses in the barrel racing event. Our bankroll gradually grew and I was becoming really stingy with our cash as we added to our "Send the Morrises to New York" fund. The final two shows in Texas and one in Oklahoma did the trick.

Shortly before it was time to leave for New York, I was riding a saddle-bronc in Chickasha, Oklahoma. With my toes turned out, I was chopping at the bronc with my spurs when the pickup-man charged in right after the whistle blew. His horse slammed against my left foot when he approached, doubling it back, and I could almost hear the big-toe joint snap. The fear that something might jeopardize my job in New York in less than two weeks was even greater than the actual pain in my foot, so I refused to go to a doctor. In fact, I would not remove my boot for fear I might not be able to get it on again.

People who know nothing about made-to-order western boots generally question the comfort of such footwear, but the truth is, when ordering a pair of boots, the circumference of each foot is measured every half-inch from your toes up past your arch, and ankle, to the calf of your leg. Few civilians can boast of shoes that fit like an outer layer of skin.

I mention the precise fit of made-to-order boots because that is the very quality that made it possible for me to continue rodeoing. I was now wearing a new pair of Justins identical to the original grey and red pair that I had protected so diligently after the Deadwood incident. With the snugness typical of a month-old boot, the left one served as sort of a walking-cast and I did not remove it even once until the New York rodeo was starting its second week. There were minor difficulties involved, however, such as sleeping and bathing with my booted-foot hanging over the side, and it was necessary to put zippers in the leg seams of several pairs of my tight, bell-bottomed pants so I could remove them over the boot, but all in all, my do-it-yourself doctoring did the job.

On our way to New York, Rufus and I had little time for sightseeing. However, we did spend a couple of hours on our way through Washington, D.C., at 3 a.m., viewing the Capitol and the White House.

Several cowboys had given us explicit instructions for locating the Garden once we reached New York City, but we made the error of going through the Holland Tunnel instead of the Lincoln Tunnel and we had to stop along the way for a whole new set of directions. When at last we arrived at the designated spot on 8th Avenue, between 49th and 50th Streets, I still thought we were lost.

"This can't be the place," I told Rufus emphatically. "There's nothing along here but stores and office buildings—and kind of grimy ones at that. We must be on the wrong street."

Just then I saw a theater-type marquee partway down the block, that announced: MADISON SQUARE GARDEN—World's Championship Rodeo.

"I guess that's the entrance," I added dejectedly, "but it sure doesn't look very glamorous from where I sit."

"It sure don't," Rufus agreed. "The arena must be in back of them store buildings." As though he were trying to convince himself, as well as me, he muttered, "Maybe it looks better on the inside."

We circled around until we found the Belvedere Hotel where most of the cowboys stayed. It was near the back entrance to the Garden and we wanted to stay there but no rooms were available so we checked into the Hotel President one block away. On the way to our room, two couples joined us in the elevator.

"Look at what she's wearing!" one of the women said. "How can they walk with those things on their feet?"

"And those tight pants!" the other woman added. "Imagine going out in public dressed like that."

Rufus grabbed my arm and held me in the corner until we reached our floor. I was so tired from our trip I was in no mood to listen to that idiotic conversation and he was wise to hold me back. However, I could not resist a parting statement.

"And guess what? We not only speak English, but we're smart enough to keep our mouths closed when we run into morons like the four of you."

Still not sure I might not react physically, Rufus shoved me out of the elevator ahead of him and I think he was relieved when the door closed behind us.

We were both anxious to get back to the Belvedere Bar because we had been told that was the cowboy hangout regardless of where you were staying. Almost immediately I sensed a difference in the cowboys. Their conversations were more serious than usual, and the overall tension was so real it was almost visible in the air. Whenever someone struck a match, I had an eerie feeling that the entire building might explode. There was the usual amount of drinking, but not the usual relaxed, carefree sort of thing. Laughter was a bit too shrill, and tempers too short.

We made a quick hello-tour of the tables and booths, then headed for the rodeo headquarters to check on Rufus' entries and pick up our numbered arm-bands and passes. Rufus returned to the bar right away, but I wanted to wander around the building for an hour or so by myself. The inside of the Garden was fascinating to me, even though there was a damp, musty chill and a strangely impersonal feeling about the place. Workers were rushing here and there, making last-minute preparations, but their white coveralls and Brooklyn accents drove out any pre-rodeo air that might have slipped through the gate with the arrival of the Brahma bulls.

Colonel John Reed Kilpatrick, who was in charge of the Garden events, patiently answered my barrage of questions. He said it took sixty truck-loads of soil and tanbark, spread to a depth of six inches, to get the arena ready, and there were enough stalls in the basement to handle 600 broncs, steers, calves, bulls, and saddle-horses. Because the arena required so much room, the regular facilities for seating around 18,000 was reduced to a little over 14,000 for the rodeo. Contrary to the impression given by the unimposing entrance on 8th Avenue, this huge building occupied nearly two-thirds of a city block and was as high as the four-story office buildings that fronted it.

All of these statistics, though interesting to me, did not alter the fact that I felt let down. I guess I had expected the site where World's Championships were won and lost, to resemble a marble-and-gold castle, or at least something equally magnificent.

I was not scheduled in the bronc-riding until the third performance but I was so nervous and excited about finally appearing in Madison Square Garden that I rushed over to the arena three hours early on the first night, to get ready for the Grand Entry. Each quadrille rider was "issued" one certain horse to use every day of the three-week rodeo, in both quadrille and Grand Entry, and I found my snow-white gelding saddled and waiting as though he expected me to be ahead of time. When I had adjusted the length of the stirrups, I mounted and rode up the wide, dirt-covered ramp that led to the arena, then I began loping in circles and figure-eights so I could get the feel of the horse.

Quite a few ropers and bull-doggers were already in the arena, limbering up their horses, but I seemed to be the only one who found it necessary to "warm up" for the Grand Entry! After fifteen or twenty minutes, I returned to the basement feeling rather foolish.

Before too long the other cowboys and cowgirls were pouring down the ramp like a sack of gaily-colored Christmas candies being dumped into a bowl. Most contestants preferred a flashy wardrobe, anyway, but New York was one of the few rodeos where even the more conservative were required to "dress up" for the show. Among the new arrivals was Gene Autry, who was making another personal appearance at the Garden. He was surrounded by the "Glamour Gals" (a name given to the assortment of southern rodeo-queens who appeared with him "strictly for pretty").

At the time the arena director loped by and hollered, "Get lined up for Grand Entry," there was so much confusion that I doubted if anyone would be able to organize the group by show time, but actually, it was only a matter of minutes before we were in position.

Immediately outside of the arena gate were the color-bearers, then Autry, the Glamour Gals, and cowgirls. Behind us, all the way down the ramp to the basement, were the hundreds of cowboy-contestants. It was not until the Grand Entry actually began, that I had a chance to see past the gate, and when I loped into the arena behind the other cowgirls, I reined my horse over to one side, and just sat there gaping.

A magical transformation had taken place! With 14,000 eager, cheering spectators surrounding the oval where artificial lights reflected on every satin shirt and silver buckle, Madison Square Garden now emerged as the sparkling, jeweled castle I had dreamed about.

"Hey, move out!" someone behind me hissed impatiently.

I snapped to attention, and realized I had been blocking the gate during the few seconds while I stared. Other riders raced past and I fell back into line. Since I was one of the "pivots" that the other riders circled around when they did the serpentine ride (snake-dance on horseback), it was no simple job to get back into place, but I did manage to drop out and stop my horse in the right location.

The quadrille followed immediately. I was so busy trying to keep everyone from bumping against my sore foot, I had the front end of my horse turned a bit too far to the left, and my quadrille partner spun around me and knocked my old trick-knee partway out of place. Luckily it snapped back and I was able to finish the show, but I was pretty gimpy for a few days. It was necessary for me to wear a wide elastic bandage around my knee for the entire New York show.

During the first two night-performances I watched the other lady-bronc-riders whipping and snapping on rank broncs that were tougher than anything I had ever seen in women's events. I knew if those women, who had so many more years of experience than I, were having trouble, it was a dead mortal cinch I had overmatched myself. For once I wished I had not hired out as a tough hand.

Our bronc-rides were actually "exhibitions" but the regular riding-judges scored each one as though we were in competition against each other, and the winners in every go-round were announced for the benefit of the spectators.

To my surprise, and delight, I managed to complete my first three rides, even to the point of scoring third-place in one go-round on a showy little horse called Humpty Dumpty, that jumped high and kicked high, but bucked straight ahead and was not too tough to ride. My self-confidence, which had now increased until it bordered on conceit, was whittled to the nub when I drew a big powerful bronc aptly named "Separator."

When I climbed down onto Separator's broad back, I could see the muscles ripple along his powerful neck and shoulders. My two reins were braided together for the first two feet from the halter, then at the point where they split, the crotch of the "Y" hit in the vicinity of the horse's lower neck; so I was actually pulling on his neck rather that the halter. This way, a horse had to whip and jerk his head almost to the point of touching your stirrups before it took any slack out of the reins. The cowboys were unable to give me any advice except to say that he was "a tough sonofabitch with a miserable head," so I measured my reins as always, gave them a quick twist, tossed the ends over my shoulder, and nodded for the gate.

The first jump out of the chute, Separator lunged high into the air. I leaned forward in the saddle just in time to be snapped like the ragged end of a bull-whip when he kicked his hind-legs straight in the air and plunged his head down between his front legs, jerking me out over the saddlehorn and slamming me onto the ground in front of him.

Then, as Rufus was to describe it later, "Thet old bronc walked her like a foot-log!"

I took a hard fall, all right, and I guess it appeared worse than it really was, with the bronc charging right over the top of me because even before I had my wits about me, I was loaded onto a stretcher and hauled out of the arena. I kept protesting that I was okay, and I was busy snapping my shirt closed where it had been ripped open on the saddlehorn, but I was not permitted to get off of the stretcher until we reached the first-aid room.

Besides Rufus, Gene Autry and Colonel Kilpatrick were the first ones to reach me. Although I assured them I was fine, they insisted I remain with the nurse until I could be thoroughly checked. As they were leaving the room, I became aware of a great deal of discomfort in my chest and I turned to face the nurse so I could unsnap my shirt and see how badly that area had been skinned. Along with the fact that the entire front of me was scraped and bleeding from my collarbone to my waist, I made another amazing discovery.

The absence of a certain item was confirmed just then by the arrival of Bob Estes, a young cowboy from Texas whose job it was to unsaddle the broncs at the catchpens.

"Say there, Janie," he said, grinning, "I found somethin' hanging on yore saddlehorn that I figgered you might need." In front of Autry, Kilpatrick, Rufus and the other rodeo hands who carried my stretcher to the first-aid room, Bob handed me my brassiere!

Apparently, on the very first jump when I was slammed forward, the front of my new snap-front blouse caught on the saddlehorn and popped open, at which point I was de-brassiered without even knowing it. Several years passed before the cowboys stopped teasing me about that incident.

As soon as the nurse patched me up, and loaned me a needle and thread to complete my own repairs, I returned to watch the rest of the show even though she advised against it.

Rufus and I came through the small foot-gate by the chutes, and I was stopped by Margie Greenough. She wanted to know how I felt.

"Okay, I guess," I replied. "A little sore around the edges."

"I meant to tell you," her sister, Alice, said casually, "that Separator horse takes a real long rein."

Rufus turned and glared at her. I tried to elbow him away before he could say anything, but he still stated loudly, "Now's a hell of a time to tell you! She could'a said somethin' before you rode!"

Good point.

The men's saddle-bronc riding had just started. We walked past the chute where a cowboy named Jesse was being helped down on his horse by another bronc-rider named Willie.

"Take a look at those two," I said, nudging Rufus. "Their faces look like they'd been tromped by Separator, too."

He laughed, "Not them. They tangled last night outside the Belvedere. Something about Willie's wife. And they plan on doin' battle again tonight, soon as the show's over."

"You've got to be kidding! Willie's giving Jesse advice on how to ride that bronc. And belting him down."

"Who could do it better? Willie's the only man that's ever rode that bronc to the whistle—and he's done it twice." Then Rufus frowned at me as though the behavior of the entire female population was my responsibility. "Sure as hell's different from the way the women act, huh?"

Again I had to agree.

It was not long before Rufus had to get ready for the bull riding; this was another reason I had been so insistent about seeing the last part of the show that night. I knew he had drawn a bull that was almost impossible to ride. According to several cowboys with scars to prove their point, it was also a vicious animal to get away from after you were thrown. Even though I could do nothing to help, it was better to stay and watch than to go to the hotel alone and worry about the outcome.

The big black bull was supposed to go into a left-hand spin just outside of the chute, then whip back and spin the other way. On the advice of Dick Griffith, who was the high-man in that go-round, Rufus jabbed his right spur into the bull's neck just as he whipped back to go into the right-hand spin, and the bull lined-out to buck fairly straight. Although the black threw some wicked whips and kicks at Rufus, he rode him to the whistle.

Fulkerson was one of the first rodeo clowns I had ever seen who jumped in and out of a barrel in the arena, when he fought bulls. During Rufus' ride, he stayed inside of the upright barrel, ready to pop up and tease the bull into butting the barrel when the ride ended. No one expected Rufus to ride his bull as far as the barrel, least of all, Rufus, so he had a split-second decision to make when he heard the whistle and knew the bull would spin and charge him the instant he hit the ground. His idea was to jump off beside the barrel and duck behind it. Choosing the exact spot to land was no simple matter, what with unwrapping the loose-rope from his hand and swinging his leg over the bucking bull's back, so Rufus' wild leap did not put him next to the barrel, but right in on top of Jasbo.

There was an immediate hush throughout the stadium, then Jasbo's voice sounded loud and clear, "Get off'n me, you sonofabitch! You're spurring me plumb to death!"

As soon as the arena was cleared, Rufus crawled out of the barrel, cautiously, and then Jasbo appeared, scratching his black, painted-on beard. The crowd went wild. Probably most of the spectators thought the whole thing was an act, but it was no joke to either Rufus or Jasbo at the time.

Rufus said later, "I wasn't about to come outa there till thet black bastard was long-gone."

When the scores were tallied for that go-round, Rufus was in first place (which would make us $300 or $400 richer). For a newcomer to win a first place day-money in the Garden was unique enough to draw praise, even from the stoic, difficult-to-impress veterans.

Dick Griffith was one of the first to congratulate Rufus, and he added, jokingly, "That's the last time I tell somebody how to beat me!"

We had been staying away from the bars pretty much, up to that point, but that night Rufus was elated over his ride and wanted to celebrate. I went along because I was deflated, and hurting all over, after my brief skirmish in the arena.

I returned to our hotel to bathe and change clothes, then joined Rufus later at the Belvedere Lounge. I found him signing a tab for $16 worth of drinks.

He gave me a broad, little-boy grin, and said excitedly, "How about this place, girl? All you gotta do is sign your name, an' you get free drinks, spending money, or anything else you want." He patted his shirt pockets that overflowed with bills. "See? They got a hell of a credit system here."

I hustled him aside and explained that the tab-signing was for the Belvedere residents only!

"Before they send your slips to the front desk and realize you're not registered here, give me all the cash in your pockets and I'll pay as much of the bar tab as I can. I'll have to go draw enough of my wages to pay the rest of it, so you'd best quit spending until I get back."

"Okay, girl," he agreed, with feigned disgust, "but I liked it better before you got here."

In a few minutes, I returned to the Belvedere Lounge with some money, but Rufus was gone. He had left word for me to come up to Loren Fredricks' room as soon as I squared the bar bill, but by then I was ready to have a few drinks by myself. We had not eaten anything since noon and the drinks hit me pretty hard. When I got to

Loren's room, the door was open so I walked in and watched the crap game in the corner for awhile, and after seeing Rufus place a couple of small bets, I poured myself three or four drinks out of a bottle on the dresser. By the time anyone realized I was there, the game had dwindled down to four players. If Rufus was making an occasional bet, it was obvious he had held back part of the Belvedere money that he had "signed" for, so I elbowed my way into the game with the idea that I might be able to win back some of the cash he had already lost. As it turned out, we simply went broke twice as fast!

Rufus finally crawled to his feet. His face was slightly flushed from the drinks, the excitement of the crap game, and annoyance at going broke so soon.

"Let's go back to the bar," he said to me, sharply. "Ain't nothin' here for us."

Downstairs, we borrowed $20 from a Texas cowboy Rufus knew and had several more drinks. I was secretly planning to try and win our money back, so the first time I had an opportunity to steal some of Rufus' change, I slipped away and returned to Loren's room.

The door was unlocked and the game had already ended by the time I arrived. I turned to leave, but I was feeling sick so I headed for the bathroom and spent nearly thirty minutes throwing up before I staggered out and fell across the foot of the bed.

I must have slept for awhile because I did not hear Rufus enter the room. The first I realized he was there was when I awoke to find him standing over me, screaming all kinds of foul accusations about Loren and me, then he dragged me off of the bed and started knocking me around the room. His first blow broke my nose. I tried to protect my face after that but each time he hit me, the blood spurted from my nose even worse. The last thing I can remember was seeing spatters of blood all across one wall, almost to the ceiling.

It was a hell of a time to think about the punch line of an old joke, "And what position were you in when this happened?" I lost consciousness.

I have no idea how Rufus managed to get me to our own hotel room, or if he did, but that is where I awoke the next morning. I rolled my eyes around far enough to see where I was, then lay there staring at the pale blue ceiling, trying to remember what happened.

My face, and every inch of my body throbbed with pain. I could barely move. I slowly made my way to the bathroom and it was there I had my first look at the mangled mess that was supposed to be my face.

It was hard to believe a person's face could be that swollen and distorted. My eyes peered out through two tiny slits in what looked like the top of an enormous, purple rutabaga. When I stared straight ahead, into the mirror, my cheeks and jowls were so swollen, I could not see my own ears. I was too stunned to cry—or even think, for that matter. I picked up the phone to have a bottle of Jim Beam sent to our room, but I hung up before they answered.

By evening my brain began clicking slowly, and the only solution I came up with was for me to head for Montana, immediately. I dressed as fast as I could, considering how agonizing it was for me to move, stuffed everything into my suitcase, and walked out. The only cash I had left was one single $5 bill and some small change, but I planned to drive until our car ran out of gas, and then check into a hotel. I made no plans beyond that point. My fear of leaving clues for Rufus kept me from asking directions at the front desk so as soon as the garage attendant brought the car around, I headed out. In my haste, I did not even glance at the gas gauge.

My plan was to drive until I was out of the city and then locate the right highway to take me home. In the confusion of night-time traffic, one-way streets, and look-alike buildings, I took off in the wrong direction, and by the time the car and I both registered "empty," I discovered I was in the suburbs of Bridgeport, Connecticut!

Had I made even a little headway in my trek to Montana, I might have been brave enough to try and work something out until I could have money wired to me from Montana. Not only had I driven in the wrong direction to start with, I realized I could not even get a job in Bridgeport because of my appearance.

I checked into a small hotel where I paced the floor for several hours.

"I'd rather take a beating than ask Rufus for help!" Salty tears burned the cut on my lip, and I hastened to add to the weird-looking person in the bathroom mirror, "Poor choice of words, Girl. I've already been there, done that!"

I took a hot bath and crawled into bed. Maybe tomorrow would be better.

The next morning I reached for the phone several times to call Montana. When I thought about the fact that I was still obligated to complete my contract at the Garden, I knew I could not renege on my deal regardless of the situation. I was not scheduled to ride another bronc for two more days, and there was always someone available to take my place in the quadrille, so I spent most of the day arguing with that ugly person who stared back at me in the bathroom mirror.

About five o'clock that evening I was able to get ahold of Rufus at our hotel. That was the most difficult phone call I had ever made. There was some satisfaction in how upset he was about my disappearance, but it was impossible for me to feel sorry for him. I gave him directions to the hotel in Bridgeport, as nearly as I could recall, and asked if someone could bring him over there to take me back to New York. He said he would be there as soon as possible.

After I hung up the phone, I lay back on the bed and went to sleep.

I was awakened by a pounding on the door. As I fumbled around in the dark to unlock it, I forgot momentarily where I was. And why.

Rufus stepped into the room, quietly. He was alone. He waited until I found the light switch and turned to face him. The shock reflected in his eyes when he first saw my face, reminded me how I looked. Still silent, his wide mouth began to twitch and his eyes filled with pain, just before he crumpled to the floor, his arms hugging my knees. With his face hidden from me, he sat there and cried.

I wanted to feel something. Anger. Hurt. Sympathy. But nothing happened. It was then I knew for sure my marriage had to end. It might take some time to do it legally but without emotion there was nothing left to build on.

In a few minutes, I pulled Rufus to his feet and suggested we head back to New York. The cowboy named Charlie, who had driven Rufus to Bridgeport, had already left, so we paid for my room, filled the car with gas and after getting explicit directions from the service station attendant, we headed back toward the Garden.

Neither of us spoke during the entire trip.

I stayed away from the stadium for two days. My reluctance to being seen by anyone was only partly responsible for my absence—I also wanted to be away from Rufus. Without looking me in the eye, he hastily agreed to my suggestion that I remain in our hotel room while he went to the Garden and confirmed that they had a permanent substitute for me in the quadrille. His shame was evident, but I was never sure if it was for me or for himself.

On the third day after my beating, everyone was required to appear for a panorama photo. I coated my fat face with several layers of Max Factor's "fight-losers-special" and headed for the Garden, alone. I tried to avoid as many of the cowboys as possible, although I need not have made the effort. Even with the discolored portions fairly well covered, my face was still so swollen that hardly anyone recognized me. The other cowgirls crowded to the front of the mob of contestants, but I eased around to one side, hoping the photographer might miss me entirely. Instead, he conscientiously snapped one extra section of film in order to include my Mardi Gras-type balloon-head.

Right after the photographer dismissed us, Colonel Kilpatrick summoned me to his office. I thought I was healing rapidly enough, until I saw the look of concern on his face.

"Good Lord, Girl!" he gasped, unbelieving. "I had no idea you were bruised like that."

"It's not too bad now," I interrupted, "but I sure want to thank you for letting somebody else ride quadrille for me. I can take over by tonight, though. I think I'm up in the bronc-riding."

He frowned, and squirmed uncomfortably, then said, "That's what I want to talk to you about, Jane. Cobe decided—er, that is, we both decided, maybe you shouldn't ride any more broncs this year. You've just got one more to go, and after seeing your face. . ."

"But my contract. I'm supposed to."

"Now don't worry about your contract," he said hastily. "We'll pay you in full. We just don't want you hurt again."

"It's not the money I'm talking about," I blurted. I was almost in tears. "I hired out to ride broncs, and that's what I figured on doing. Besides, all these bruises on my face aren't. . ."

When I paused, Kilpatrick sat there behind his desk, patiently waiting for me to finish.

Finally he asked, smiling softly, "Aren't what, Jane? Aren't too bad?"

I nodded. I wanted to explain that Separator was not responsible for my visible bruises, but suddenly I was too ashamed to admit it. I knew in my own mind that at least half, and maybe more, of the broncs in the women's string were too tough for me, and yet I couldn't stand the thought of being fired, or backing-out just because of it.

"I did hire out to ride broncs," I argued. Then in a more pleading tone, "Couldn't you give me one more chance? I've ridden some pretty fair broncs before—maybe not as rank as these."

His inscrutable expression stopped me. He stared at me for so long I was afraid he might not answer at all, then he nodded slightly and said, "I'll talk to Cobe. We'll let you know. All right?"

"You bet! And thanks."

With a noticeable twinkle in his eyes, he added, "It's just that I sit up there in my box seat, watching the show, and it scares me to death every time one of you girls come out of the chute."

Just before I walked out of the office, I looked back at him and tried to smile.

"So how the hell do you think I feel?"

I could hear him still chuckling when I closed the door.

In spite of my brief attempt at cheeriness, I felt pretty discouraged when I walked along the dark hallway. I was not yet ready to return to the wild bunch at the Belvedere Lounge, so I wandered back to the stall where my quadrIlle horse stood, munching hay peacefully. Although Colburn's grooms kept the stock in top condition, I spent nearly an hour currying and brushing the gelding, enjoying the old familiar feel and smell of horse-hair. When I finished, I stood for a long time with my arms around his neck and my face buried in the soft, flowing mane. How many years had gone by since I last turned to my own saddle-horses at home for companionship, comfort—yes, even strength? Now here I was, in our largest city, and it appeared my only friend was a snow-white horse with a velvety nose, and a stalwart shoulder to cry on.

"Whassa mattah, missy?" a voice said behind me. I straightened to see one of the grooms peering at me from the next stall. There was kindness and sympathy in his wrinkled black face and watery eyes, as he said, "Y'all don' wanna carry on so, missy. It'll all come out in the wash."

Although he displayed more emotion than the men in my family, there was still something about this trite, rustic expression that made me think about Grandpa Burnett, and I no longer felt quite so alone. Country people were everywhere, not just west of the Mississippi. I was not really such an outsider after all.

I reached inside of my shirt for a handkerchief, since there was no room for pockets in my skin-tight rodeo pants, and blew my nose before I turned to leave.

I said, "Thanks," when I walked away, but the old black man was already busy currying a horse in the next stall.

On my way out of the basement, I noticed the perpetual crap game going on in the aisle between the horse stalls. Ten or twelve cowboys were gathered around a horse-blanket they had spread out on the floor. I stood and watched the game for a few minutes, and I was soon chuckling in spite of myself. Whenever a shooter received the dice, he'd switch dice and throw in his own "loads" or "mis-spots", and then after several passes, he'd switch the originals back in, and hand them to the next shooter. One boy even went so far as to pick up the red dice from the blanket, and when he pulled the switch, out came a set of green dice! Everyone just laughed about it, because each of them was aware that the others were cheating, too.

"What's it take to get into this game?" I asked.

One of them, a raw-boned cowboy named Eddie Taylor, looked up and grinned. "Just a ten-dollar-bill," he said, "and your own dice!"

The boy who had made the red-to-green switch glanced up just then and I saw he was one of the players who won most of our money in Loren Fredricks' room. I doubt if I would have thought any more about it, even then, if he had not begun to blush the minute he saw me standing there. He looked so flustered, I knew for sure why we had lost our money so fast. I guess I had not learned all that much from Clint, after all.

Without looking directly at him, I commented wryly, "The red-faced man with the green dice can stop sweating. I learned from a real gambler, how to be a quiet sucker."

Most of the players were too preoccupied to hear me, but I felt sure the message got through to the right party.

I did not mention to Rufus what I had discovered about our crap game. It so happened I was allowed to fulfill my contract with the provision that I would not have to ride Separator again. I still felt as though I was not carrying out my bargain to ride each bronc when it was again my turn, but I tried to console myself with the fact that I was at least being permitted to ride.

I was actually judged first place in one of the later go-rounds so my ego crawled out from behind the chutes and expanded to almost normal size again, briefly. I continued to ride quadrille at each performance, too, and Rufus won more money from time to time in the bull-riding.

Meanwhile, our relationship was about as exciting as a cold fried egg, and just as impossible to reheat. Those few words muttered by a Louisiana preacher one rainy afternoon no longer seemed to apply to two strangers named Jane and Rufus Morris.

Rufus' attitude reflected everything from being ashamed for what he had done, to blaming me because I could not forgive him. We slept in the same bed but did not touch each other. I did not want there to be any more gossip about us than was necessary and I was always on edge because I never knew what he might say within earshot of the others.

During the short pre-rodeo period one afternoon, while everyone waited on the crowded ramp for the Grand Entry to begin, Autry eased his horse through to the lead position just outside the gate. I was clear over to the right, and because there was so little space between my horse and the wall, it seemed perfectly natural for Autry to put his hand on my leg, pushing me away slightly, so his horse would not run into my bandaged knee. Rufus was behind me, further down the ramp, apparently near enough to observe the little scene first-hand. His outburst of descriptive four-letter-words left no doubt as to his interpretation of the gesture.

I had no way of knowing whether Autry heard the remarks, but the cowboys surrounding Rufus did and their laughter bounced off of the ceiling and walls, stinging me like a shower of cruel, icy hailstones. I had no place to hide, so I simply sat there, praying for the arena gate to open and swallow us all. I was determined not to cry, outwardly at least, but my tears were always so near the surface that I was always afraid I might lose control in front of the people whose respect I hoped to earn eventually.

Then the Grand Entry music started, promising a quick reprieve. In a few seconds I reined my horse into line, and as I did, I glanced at the rider behind me. It was Loren Fredricks. There was no sign of laughter or mockery in the dark-brown eyes that were looking at me so intently. There was sympathy and understanding. I gave him a half-nod of gratitude, then I rode on into the arena.

I did not see Loren again until that evening, prior to the night show. When I stopped on the ramp to talk to him for a few minutes, I discovered this slim, quiet boy with the short-cropped, black curly hair, and sensitive face, was almost as miserly with his conversation as he was with his slow smile. But when he did speak, he had a knack for saying the right thing, without taking sides. The topic of my obvious marital difficulties was never mentioned.

Each day after that, I found myself hurrying to the Garden a few minutes early, and from one performance to the next, I looked forward to my talks with Loren even though I did most of the chatting myself. I did not tell him about Rufus' accusations the night of the crap game. I did not want him to feel self-conscious around me, or shy away from me completely. This possibility worried me. I had never needed a friend as much as I did at that moment, especially one who seemed to understand and not criticize, to feel sympathy without giving advice. I needed someone to give me strength.

Under different circumstances, Loren and I might have become good friends but the "here today, gone tomorrow" pattern of rodeo life in general, plus the "Greetings!" he was soon to receive from Uncle Sam, ended with a nod of his head when we lined up for our final Grand Entry at the 1941 Madison Square Garden rodeo.

When at last it was time to leave New York and go on to Boston, I made one final trip to the arena, alone.

The local workmen were busy again, but this time they were "de-rodeoing" to make way for the next Garden event.

For awhile I stood inside one of the bucking-horse chutes where the gate had already been removed. I rubbed my hand along one of the planks in the chute, feeling the roughness of it. Only three weeks before, that same lumber had been snowy-white, and bright with anticipation of things to come. Now the same boards were covered with dried mud, manure, and slivers like porcupine quills that resulted from the abuse they had received.

"I know just how you feel," I said softly. "I'm a bit bristly myself these days."

A workman came around the corner and eyed me skeptically, so I walked away, but not before I took one more long look at the high ceiling, empty seats, and rodeo-free arena. I wondered how I could ever have thought Madison Square Garden was a cold, impersonal building. It was friend, enemy, glorifier, executioner. People should be so human.

By the time we checked out of our hotel in New York and prepared to leave for Boston, Rufus had already conveniently dismissed our recent skirmish as though it had never happened. This was not the case with me, but I did consider it silly to make a big issue of separating when we had two more eastern rodeos to attend, and most of the U.S. to cross before we reached our own section of the country again. I had not threatened divorce this time, or even mentioned it, for that matter. I felt I had hollered "Wolf" too many times already.

The Boston rodeo turned out to be much the same as New York, except on a smaller scale. This time, however, it was not necessary to leave the building at all when we went from our hotel to the arena. The Manger Hotel was connected to the stadium by a long hallway with stores and other business establishments along each side.

When I first walked through this wide roof-topped street, I felt just like the bull-rider ahead of me, who looked all around and exclaimed, "Holy Keerist! They got more stores ratcheer in this ho-tel, than we got in the whole goddam town where I come from!"

There were no spectacular occurrences at Boston, at least as far as I was concerned. One afternoon I hired a cab to take me on a tour of the city so I could see part of the Harvard campus and just a few of the many historical sights. When I returned, Rufus was so suspicious of my reason for going without him that I decided to skip any future sightseeing entirely. The only other time I was out of the Manger building was the night Turk Greenough and his new bride, Sally Rand, took Rufus and me to the Coconut Grove. For a change, Rufus remained in a good mood all evening.

Rufus won a second day-money for one of his bull-rides and I rode two saddle-broncs and quadrille. There was nothing special about the rodeo except for the fabulous building, and as a couple we were definitely not having fun. We left for Buffalo, New York, as soon as we collected the money each of us had coming. Quite a few of the cowboys returned to the Cow Palace Rodeo in San Francisco instead of going on to Buffalo.

There was no women's bronc-riding at Buffalo, but I did get a job riding quadrille. It was not until we actually arrived there that I knew for sure whether I even had a job or not, since that show was not put on by the same producers as New York and Boston.

The third afternoon some of the rodeo people were having lunch when one of the wives suggested we drive out to see Niagara Falls. Rufus was in a sour mood and declined but since I was going with a carload of women, he did not object.

On leaving Buffalo, we drove straight through to Montana. Once we were away from all of the rodeo people, Rufus seemed to relax and act more like he did when I first met him. We actually were enjoying ourselves by the time we arrived at the ranch, and since I did not want my parents to know about our problems, I tried to act as though we were still getting along. Evidence of my beating in New York had disappeared. The exterior part, that is. Mentally, I was not sure if I would ever get over what had happened.

Our visit to the ranch was not entirely satisfactory. There was a lot of partying, with everyone having fun and this had a tendency to gradually ease whatever tension still remained between Rufus and me. And then along came the greatest of all-time "divorce squelchers," in the form of Christmas. It was impossible to retain my resentment toward Rufus when we actually had a holiday celebration at the ranch, including a real Christmas tree surrounded by more presents that I had ever seen at any one time.

By the middle of January, I knew I had to make a decision one way or another as to whether I was going to stay married. We had been snowed in for over a week and each day after several loads of hay had been scattered to the cattle in our winter pasture, the entire afternoon was devoted to an almost continuous game of pinochle.

Whenever I had an opportunity, I would slip out of the house in the later afternoon to spend an hour or so in the horse barn. Sort of a meditation period. Sometimes I simply curried my sorrel horse, Major, while he munched on the meadow-hay that overflowed his manger. Other times I crawled right into the manger and fed the hay to him by hand. The snow was always falling silently outside of the barn, but Major's munching and my talking broke the quiet-barrier on the inside.

"What can I do, fella'?" I asked him one afternoon. "The way things look now, I'm in worse shape than ever. I want out, and I don't know how to go about it. I keep wondering if I am somehow to blame. Maybe it's partly my own fault. I've always done pretty much anything I wanted to, and I never once realized this would change just because I got married."

Major nodded in agreement. He could be counted on to go along with anything I said, since the simplest way to shake weeds loose from the hay in his mouth was to flip his head up and down.

Encouraged, I continued. "Then, too, there's a problem about the 'where' of this divorce thing, to say nothing of the when, if I decide to go that route. If I go through that ordeal here in Montana, I know damned well I'll end up spending the rest of the winter out here with nothing but a bunch of cows and horses."

Major laid back his ears.

"Sorry, fella. No offense intended." To square myself, I put the conversation on a more personal basis for Major's sake. "But we do have to be fair about this. Right?"

He nodded.

"So just suppose somebody came along and hauled you away when you were still pretty much of a colt and didn't know anything about life outside of your own fence. Then maybe you and this person didn't hit it off like you should. Even if they got sore because you bucked 'em off, or even kicked 'em a few times, they still got no business dumping you out of the trailer some 1500 miles from home. The least they could do is haul you back to your home pasture. Right?"

Major nodded and nodded.

"So that settles it." I scrambled down out of the manger and patted him on the neck. "Thanks, fella. I never could'a figured it out without your help."

I would swear he was shaking his head sideways when I glanced back and waved goodbye.

It would be a simple matter to talk Rufus into going back to Texas. Feeding cattle in sub-zero weather did not appeal to him for all the obvious reasons.

Funny thing about those "Best laid plans."

The storm let up that evening so the four of us headed for Lewistown the next morning. As was the custom during the winter months, there were two scoop-shovels in the trunk of the car. They came in handy when we were stuck in a couple of deep snow drifts and had to shovel our way out. At least, one of the shovels was put to use. Clint remained in the car.

By the time we hit the Tavern, all of us were more than ready for one of Georgia's "hot toddies." I was surprised to see Duffy Crabtree seated at the bar and was about to head toward him to say, "Hello."

Just in time, I realized I was going about this all wrong so I took Rufus' hand and led him across the room so I could introduce him to Duffy. Whew! Another close call.

I returned to our booth and gave the two cowboys a chance to get acquainted.

So far, I had not mentioned my idea about going back to Texas, and it came as a total surprise when Rufus joined us and hour later and announced that we were headed for California! Apparently Duffy had been telling him about all of the winter rodeos up and down the Pacific coast and after shoveling our way into town from the ranch, California sounded like the answer to a prayer.

My folks asked no questions and made no comments when Rufus and I packed to go, but I thought Mother's eyes seemed sadder than usual. I knew she always hated to see me leave, but somehow it was different this time. I learned at a much later date that they were more concerned about Rufus' temper than they ever let on. I guess my puffy face had not healed as completely as I thought.

# Chapter Seventeen

Rufus was in an exceptionally good mood during our journey westward. Again, we took turns driving but he had returned to his old habit of keeping me awake to read maps and give directions. One day, shortly after noon, when we finally reached northern California, I was totally exhausted. I told Rufus I had to have at least one night of real sleep or I might wreck the car when I was at the wheel. Within an hour we checked into a six-cabin motel somewhere on the northern California desert. It looked every bit as beautiful to me as the Belvedere or Boston's Manger Hotel. Rufus headed for their small coffee shop as soon as we registered, but I went straight to our cabin. I stripped down to my bra and underpants and was asleep almost immediately.

Along about three o'clock the next morning, a throbbing headache jarred me out of my stupor and I struggled to get out of bed. When I was awake enough to remember where we were, I tried to clear my head but a strong odor in the room became the center of my attention.

The room was filled with gas that was leaking from a small heater at the foot of our bed! As soon as I realized what was wrong, I staggered toward the door. I should have shut the heater off before doing anything else, but my first thought was to get a breath of uncontaminated air. Just as I reached for the doorknob, I passed out.

Possibly due to the fact that the cabins were poorly constructed, enough outside air seeped through to revive me. I became conscious again just long enough for me to open the door before I passed out again.

It was daylight when I regained consciousness. I was lying in the doorway, still in my underwear, and my head was throbbing so hard that I scooted across the sill and threw up.

Rufus slept through the entire episode, even when I managed to crawl back and shut off the heater. I shook him awake and explained what had happened but I don't think he ever realized how close we had been to a complete disaster because all he could think about was "hitting the road."

He did not even have a headache.

As per one of Duffy's suggestions to Rufus, we drove straight through to Palm Springs. Within forty-eight hours of our arrival, we were both employed as dude wranglers at Rogers' Ranch. (No relation to Roy!) As with many such resorts in the area, mini-rodeos were put on every weekend for the entertainment of the guests, and we were to receive additional pay each time we participated. It was not a competition thing but more like an exhibition for the dudes. This gave us an opportunity to get some practice after our three-month layoff.

Many of the guests were well-known movie stars and Rufus was in what he would call "hog heaven" whenever one of them complimented us in person. We had a great time in spite of our long working-hours and he was thriving in this new environment.

The world had been shaken by news of Pearl Harbor in December, but neither Rufus nor I had ever seen a war, and I am ashamed to say we were not as concerned as we should have been. When Rogers staged a two-day benefit rodeo with all proceeds going to the British War Relief Fund, for the first time I actually thought in terms of the big picture. Even then I was selfishly more concerned with my role in this event than I was with the war itself.

Besides modeling western clothes in the pre-rodeo style-show, I rode one saddle-bronc each day and Rufus rode one steer. Due to our appearances in the rodeo, we were treated more like entertainers than ranch hands so on the final night of the show, during a jam-session with Rudy Vallee as the m.c., I sang two songs on the stage. No doubt an ample supply of free booze made me brave enough to voluntarily follow such performers as Vallee, Judy Garland, and Jerry Colonna, but the spectators had access to the same vast supply so I was not thrown off of the stage.

During that final gala evening, I was approached by a freelance photographer who said he would like to take a series of stills to depict "A Day in the Life of a Lady Bronc-rider" with no real chance to sell it to *LIFE* magazine. He had been unable to attend the benefit show, and wondered if I might reride one of my broncs for him the next morning. I was just publicity-happy enough to agree. The one thing I did not consider was the terrific hangover that was inevitable after such a party.

As if it were not bad enough having to pose on top of chute gates, and at various points in the arena with the sun boiling down on my head, the also-hungover photographer ruined the first set of action pictures and I had to ride the bronc twice. The irony of it all: *LIFE* was not even mildly interested in how lady bronc-riders spent their days and the photo spread was never used. At least the resulting pix looked great in my scrapbook.

One thing wrong with meeting movie stars is that you discover they are just people, after all, and not god-and-goddess descendants of the Muses. This leads many uninformed individuals, like myself, to believe, "If they can do it, I certainly can."

Once the big benefit show ended, our status as entertainers did a quick flip-flop back to the dude-wrangler level. With rodeos throughout Southern California now in full swing and the novelty of Palm Springs having worn off for both of us, we agreed on the need for a home base where we could rest and/or heal up after each weekend of rodeoing.

It was easy to let Rufus believe it was his own idea to give Rogers two weeks to find our replacements, and then we would head for Los Angeles. Not that they would have a problem finding someone to handle the dude-wrangling part of our jobs, but many of the prospective employees were unable to perform in the Sunday rodeos.

At the end of the allotted two weeks, we drove into Los Angeles and located a cute little two-room apartment in Compton.

Granted, I had misled Rufus on my reasons for wanting to live in that part of California. Although I was as serious about the weekly rodeos as he was, I once again wondered if I might have a future in western movies.

Three weekends in a row we both made a little money in small rodeos within a forty-mile radius of our apartment. We did manage to earn enough money to make the effort worthwhile, but decided to skip the next one in the northern part of the state. This was our first Sunday at home and we planned to do some sightseeing around Los Angeles and Hollywood. I was especially concerned that Rufus might hear about that crazy jackpot rodeo in the Compton area, where I ran into Larry Finley and Slugger Sloan two years before. I knew there was no money to be made in those Sunday events, and it could quickly deplete our bankroll if he were to become involved with them.

Disaster struck one Sunday morning when I was shopping for groceries and Rufus went to a service station across the street to gas up our car. He ran into two Texas cowboys who told him about a jackpot event not far from there, and suggested he join them. As soon as he picked me up at the Safeway store, I tried to discourage him from going but he was determined.

They followed us to the apartment and I met Robbie, the driver, while they waited for Rufus to unload my groceries. I held back as much of our money as possible before he drove away following the Texas car. I hoped this would be a one-time thing.

After I put the groceries away, I wandered out to the grassy area behind the apartment where I saw a picnic table and several well-worn folding chairs. Just as I was settling into one of the chairs, Mrs. Moody, the woman who rented the apartment next to ours, came around the corner followed by two Pomeranian dogs. One of them was the mother of a six-month-old pup that I immediately fell in love with. Part of the money that I was hoarding so Rufus would not spend it foolishly went for the purchase of that small bundle of fur that I immediately named "PeeWee."

I did not know it at the time, but that pup would have his own five minutes of fame in the very near future.

Through an item in the Sunday edition of the *Los Angeles Times*, I noticed that Gene Autry was filming a picture at Republic Studios. I thought about the last time I saw him at the end of the rodeo in Minneapolis. He was saying "Goodbye" to some of us at the rodeo headquarters, and he added that we should be sure to contact him if we were ever in the Hollywood area. At the time I assumed this was a standard Hollywood invitation and I had no intention of actually taking him up on it.

Late that afternoon while I was trying to wade through the huge Sunday paper, a series of unexpected events completely disrupted our plans for the next few months. I was surprised when someone knocked on our door.

It was the Texas cowboy, Robbie. He seemed really uncomfortable, and it took him a minute or so before he could finally explain why he was there.

"Ma'am, I don't know how to tell you this."

Several things flashed through my mind, and because of his approach, I naturally expected the worst.

"Is it Rufus? Has something happened to him?"

He immediately tried to put my mind at ease.

"Nothing really bad, Ma'am, but Rufus did dislocate his shoulder about an hour ago when a bronc went over backwards in the chute." He reached out to put his hand on my arm. "He's gonna be okay, but he needs for you to pick him up at a little medical clinic a couple of blocks from the arena."

I was relieved that it was no more serious than that, but for a second or so I was also furious at him for going to that stupid jackpot rodeo after I asked him not to.

I hurried to the cowboy's car with my purse under one arm and PeeWee under the other. It only took us about ten minutes to reach the clinic, and without even remembering to thank Robbie for the ride, I rushed through the front door. Rufus was seated in the waiting room when I arrived, and as soon as I was convinced he was going to be okay, I intended to try and make some kind of arrangements to pay his bill. I almost forgot about PeeWee until Rufus yelled at me.

"What the hell's that thing?"

"Shhh! It's my new dog. They'll make me leave him outside if they see him, so you just hold him while I see what to do about your bill."

"Me, hold that thing? No goddam way!"

I glared at him, and placed PeeWee in his lap and headed for the front desk without giving him a choice. Neither of them appeared to be happy with the arrangement but since there was very little I could do about the bill except to pay a few dollars on the account, I returned in a very short time and we were on our way.

By the time we reached our apartment, Rufus was in a really foul mood. I do not think it was due to his discomfort because he assured me he had enough pain pills to get him through the next few days, but the idea that he would not be able to ride for several weeks was his main concern.

I was glad his medication was strong enough to put him to sleep as soon as we reached the apartment, and in the meantime I wondered what we were going to do for money while we waited for him to heal. We had signed a three-month lease on our apartment and I knew Rufus well enough by then to know he would not allow me to go to any rodeos by myself, and he would be just as adamant about not going with me. It made no sense, but to him it would be degrading if I were to appear as the only "bread-winner" in the family.

By Wednesday, I had already decided to get some kind of a job to take care of our bills. At least, for the present. There was a small drug store just two blocks from our apartment and I was able to get a job behind the soda fountain four days a week, noon to six. Rufus did not object to my working but was upset that I worked the late afternoon shift. When I pointed out to him that we had no choice, he gradually quit complaining and accepted it as fact. He was even beginning to warm up to PeeWee and they were company for each other when I was away.

Man and dog came to the drug store one evening to walk home with me, and Rufus did not even seem embarrassed to have that little fur ball trotting along ahead of him on a leash. While he waited for me to get off shift, he struck up a conversation with a customer at the soda fountain who mentioned that they were really short of help at the welding shop where he worked. He said a lot of their welders had quit to go to more lucrative jobs at the shipyards.

Rufus' arm was still in a sling but the doctor had said he could remove it in about a week. He shared this information with the welder and they agreed that Rufus would check back with him about working at their shop. It would take a certain length of time for him to learn to weld on his own, but there were other jobs he could do in the meantime. It was the first time Rufus had shown an interest in doing anything other than riding in rodeos so I began to hope we might be heading in a new and better direction.

Rufus rode back and forth to work with his new friend which gave me the freedom to use our car for shopping and to go to my own job. The neighbor who owned PeeWee's mother gladly took care of my pup while I was at work, but the rest of the time I kept him with me.

I saw another newspaper article about Autry and decided just for the hell of it to call his bluff about contacting him if I ever came to California. I stopped off for a few minutes at the Cameo Productions where I had been offered a contract, actually just an option for a contract, two years before. I hoped I might get a chance to say "Hello" to Cliff Sanforth, but was told he was directing a movie at one of the other studios, so I went on to Republic mainly out of curiosity to see what would happen.

Exactly as I expected, a uniformed guard stopped me at the front gate.

"Wish to see someone, miss?" he asked.

"Yes, I do," I replied. "Gene Autry asked me to come over sometime today, so if you'll let him know I'm here."

"Certainly," he smiled. I thought this was too easy, and then he added, "As soon as Mr. Autry okays it, you can go right in."

He took out a pencil and pad. "Name?"

As a joke, I was tempted to give him the name of a movie star, or I could simply back my car out of that lane and head for home. Instead, I mumbled, "Jane Burnett," and waited for the axe to fall.

The guard was already on the phone and I was feeling embarrassed about the rejection I would receive in a minute or so. There was no reason to believe Autry would remember my name, considering the number of people he came in contact with every single day, but I had hoped to prod his memory if I saw him face to face.

The guard replaced the phone and said, "Go right in, Miss Burnett. Mr. Autry is expecting you."

As per his directions, I parked my car and walked through the gate and passed by several sound-stages until I came to an outdoor set. I still expected someone to chase after me, yelling that there had been a mistake, but I reached the shooting area unnoticed. I stood off to one side and watched as the director called out instructions to Autry and Smiley (Frog) Burnette just before the cameras began to roll. In a couple of minutes, the two men raced into town in a cloud of dust and brought their horses to a sliding stop in front of the saloon. They both dismounted, guns in hand and disappeared through the swinging doors.

I assumed the filming would continue right on into the next scene so I was surprised when Autry and Smiley strolled out through those same doors, followed by a group of technicians.

As soon as he spotted me, Autry came over and gave me a quick hug before introducing me to Smiley. He explained about my riding broncs at his rodeo in Minneapolis, and I was about to answer a question that Smiley asked about my bronc riding, when they were told to go back into the saloon for the next scene. Smiley offered me his canvas chair and draped a hand-towel over the last "E" in his name so it would simply say BURNETT.

I was thoroughly enjoying myself when the filming began again. I watched as one of the bad guys was tossed out through the swinging doors and before I realized what was happening, PeeWee jumped off of my lap, trotted across the board walk and stood right in front of the doors, yipping like mad!

About forty people yelled, "CUT! CUT! CUT!"

The director screamed, 'Where the hell did that thing come from?"

An assistant director said, "Who's it belong to?"

An assistant to the assistant said, "Okay! Come here right now!"

Assuming he meant me, I said, "Yes, sir," and brushed dust from my clothes that had accumulated when the horses skidded to a stop in the earlier scene. "I'm sorry."

Just then Autry stepped back outside and just stood there looking at the culprit who had disrupted the entire scene. He picked up said culprit and walked over to place him back on my lap.

I was so embarrassed, my only option was to make a joke of the situation.

“I don’t suppose you could leave that scene in. Right?”

He just shook his head, and then started to laugh. The director was not laughing.

Naturally, they had to re-shoot the scene and most of the crew except for the director thought what happened was really funny. At various times in the future, Autry would tell people about this incident whenever I was present.

What could easily have been embarrassing turned out to be great fun for me. I lunched with them in the commissary and watched them shoot several of the indoor scenes. I was surprised that the saloon was not behind those swinging doors as I expected, but was on a set in another area of the lot.

I was surprised, and delighted to see that Cactus Mack was working that day and I had a chance to chat with him whenever he was not in that particular scene. He wanted to know what I had done since leaving California two years before, and I mentioned the highlights which mainly centered around Chicago, Minneapolis and Madison Square Garden.

“You planning to hang around Hollywood again, or are you just rodeoing?”

“I’m always hoping to do a little of both, but don’t know if it’s possible.”

He told me it would be worthwhile for me to have a Guild card if I planned to be in the area very long.

“You want to get a B-card, though,” he explained. “That’s the bottom of the ladder, but it lets you work not only as an extra but on any job over and above that. You don’t want to be limited to speaking parts only, when you’re just getting started. A lot of rodeo people pick up jobs now and then during their off-season ”

I thanked him for his suggestion and he gave me a business card so I could let him know if and when I got into the Guild.

On my way back to the apartment, I told PeeWee how pleased I was at the outcome of my little escapade. Except for the part he played in disrupting the whole set.

PeeWee jumped up and down on the car seat and yipped his approval. Smart dog.

“I can’t wait to tell Rufus.” I began.

All of a sudden I remembered that Rufus was not privy to my plans to find work in western movies, even if only at the very lowest level. Today's episode had been strictly spur-of-the-moment, mainly because I was certain I would never get past the front gate at Republic, and also because I felt sure he would object to my having gone there alone.

"On second thought," I sighed, "I guess I can wait."

The following Monday morning I drove over to the Screen Actor's Guild. The girls in their front office reminded me of some of the clerks at the courthouse in Lewistown. They all huddled together around one desk, gossiping and giggling, and they glared at anyone who interrupted. That's where I came in.

"Excuse me," I apologized. "Could I have an application form, please?"

A tall, bony girl broke loose reluctantly and came toward me. Her upper lip kept catching on her buck teeth, giving the impression that she was about to snarl.

"What'd you say?" Actually, she did snarl.

"I want an application for a Class B card."

Apparently this was funny. When she laughed, she had to disengage her upper lip with the fore-finger of her right hand.

"I imagine you would," she giggled. "And so would half the population of L.A.!"

"What is it, Hilda?" a pleasant-voiced woman with gray hair asked.

"I want to apply for a Class B card," I repeated, "but it seems there's some kind of a joke here that's over my head."

The older woman glared at Hilda and said, sternly, "I'll take care of this. After all, we do accept applications." She turned to me. "It's just that so many Guild 'extras' are out of work these days, an agreement was made with the Motion Picture Producers Association to keep new B-memberships to a minimum. The Board meets once a month to consider applications, but out of the thousands that will come in this year, they figure less than 100 will be approved. However, you're welcome to take one of the forms home with you."

"Can't I just fill it out here?"

"Certainly. But it may take some time." She handed me several pages and a pen before she rejoined the huddle.

The entire questionnaire consisted of inquiries about the applicant's talents: "Can you act? Check YES or NO. Give complete details of former experience." Then the same with singing, dancing, archery, fencing, swimming, tennis, boating, and anything else an 'extra' might be called upon to do. I zipped through page after page because I was not hampered with such items as "details of former experience." All I had to do was check the NO column. I did hesitate for a moment when I came to "swimming," but decided my dog-paddle did not place me in the expert category. Next to the word "fencing" I was almost tempted to write, "I'm one hell of a hand with barbed-wire or pine fence posts," but I had the feeling they would not appreciate my weird sense of humor. When I finally reached the crucial section listed as "horsemanship," I made a great big X by the YES, and added that I could either drive teams of horses, or ride.

I signed my name and gathered the papers together.

"Is there anything else?" I called out in an attempt to get some attention.

Hilda glared again, but was forced to help me because the older woman was taking time-out from her time-out, at the drinking fountain.

Hilda picked up my application and thumbed through it quickly, a knowing smile snagging her upper lip again.

"It is kind of pitiful, isn't it?" I asked.

Her answering grimace agreed.

I had brought a copy of my scrapbook with me, hoping to corner a Guild officer and show him pictorial evidence of my riding ability. I was now aware there would not be an opportunity to do this, but I thought the clippings and photos might at least wipe the smug look off the face of old snaggle-tooth.

"I'd like this to accompany my application." I shoved the scrapbook across the narrow counter. "I'll just pick it up when I come after my card."

With this little display of bravado, I walked out.

The next couple of weeks dragged on with both of us working, and although Rufus liked the welding part of his job, it was not in his nature, or mine, to stay away from rodeos for very long. One thing that kept me anchored was the prospect of obtaining a guild card because I would be able to use it every winter, if I wanted to, even if we kept on rodeoing. I called the SAG office to inquire about the proposed date of their next meeting and was told not to expect word for at least three more weeks due to a postponement of their monthly meeting.

Exactly six weeks later, we were eating breakfast one morning when there was a knock on our door.

"I'll get it," I said shakily. "It's probably Mrs. Moody. She's taking both dogs to the vet for their shots."

A Western Union messenger was standing on our doorstep.

"Jane Burnett?" he asked.

"Yes."

"Telegram."

Since he had used my maiden name, my first thought was that something had happened to my parents. I tipped the boy and closed the door before tearing open the envelope. The wire stated: Application approved. On payment of fifty-dollar fee you will receive Class B card. Signed, Screen Actors Guild.

For a minute or two, there was silence.

"Honey!" Rufus sounded puzzled. I guess when I just stood there, he realized that my message was not bad news. "Your mouth's open."

He removed the telegram from my limp fingers.

"I know." Tears were streaming down my face.

"This is great, girl!" he grinned. "I don't know how they found you but maybe if we ever run into Autry again, he might even help you get a job."

His response surprised me for two reasons. I suddenly remembered I had not told him about my visit to Republic Studios and there was also his attitude toward Autry at the Minneapolis rodeo. This was not the time to bring him up to date so I just sat there, silent.

The first thing I did after Rufus went to work the next morning, was to leave messages for Cactus at the number on his business card and with Stuart Hamblen. I left my home number and the one for the soda fountain, and asked that he call me. I was anxious to share my good news.

One of my old habits that had carried over from the days when I was solely responsible for my own livelihood, was a $20 cache. It would be hidden at various locations depending on the situation at that particular time and place. When this was added to my paycheck from the previous week, I had sufficient funds to pick up my SAG card so I headed out as soon as Rufus left for work.

I had one malicious thought about changing most of the $50 into nickels and dumping them onto the counter for Hilda to count but thought she might somehow delay the procedure so I talked myself out of it. Actually, I did not have to resort to such drastic measures because the shocked look on Hilda's face when I handed her the telegram, was satisfaction enough.

"And could I please have my scrapbook?" I asked in a snooty tone of voice (after the B card was safely tucked into my billfold).

"Just a minute. I'll see," she replied.

Before long, Hilda motioned for me to follow her through a doorway and into an elaborate office where a man I recognized as Noah Beery, Sr. was seated behind a desk, leafing through my scrapbook. He explained that he was sitting in for the current head of that division of SAG.

"This is very impressive," he said, smiling. "It isn't often we have an applicant with talent along these lines—a woman, that is."

"Thank you."

"But that is not what I wanted to tell you."

"Oh?"

He flipped the leather album closed and handed it to me. "As you no doubt already know, we rarely issue B-cards any more—but we made an exception in your case."

"To tell you the truth," I laughed nervously, "I didn't really expect it. I can't do anything but ride a horse."

"That's just the point," he interrupted. "If you had indicated even one other talent, you would have been a tentative threat to other Guild 'extras' and we could not have approved your application!"

"Well," I beamed, "in that case, I'm glad I didn't try to run a bluff on you."

He nodded in agreement. We shook hands and I left.

As I strutted past Hilda in the outer office, I tipped my hat forward onto the bridge of my nose, in a Clint-like gesture, and began whistling, "I'm Just An Old Cowhand."

With Rufus working days most of the time, this gave me the opportunity to make the rounds of the studios two or three mornings each week. Even though he had appeared pleased about my guild card, I was always careful about discussing any activities that included my contact with others of the male species.

My first break came much sooner than I dared expect, when Cactus returned my phone calls and told me who to contact at Monogram Pictures where they were producing a series of westerns that featured Ray Corrigan, Johnny King, and ventriloquist Max Terhune as the gun-toting trio named the "Rangebusters." Their entire operation was just small enough to offer an excellent opportunity to a beginner with my special talents, or lack of same. I could be a face in the crowd at the schoolhouse scene, then double for the leading lady in a runaway-wagon, or race across the prairie on a trusty steed to "fetch the Rangebusters in the nick of time."

After a couple of cattle calls and an interview set up by Cactus, I finally had some good news to take home to Rufus.

That evening when he returned from work, he barely stepped through the doorway when I bombarded him.

"I think I've got a job in the movies!"

He had seemed happy when I was able to get a guild card, but I was always aware of any facial expression that might indicate his disapproval. This time I could hardly stop in mid-stream so I kept babbling.

"It's a series—eight or ten pictures. I can probably work in most of them. They're leaving for Tucson on Monday to film some shots of the rodeo there, for background. I'll double for the leading lady in the scene where she's supposed to be a bronc-rider." I finally ran out of breath.

"Suits me," he said stoically. "So we leave for Arizona on Monday. Right?"

"What about your job?"

His eyes squinted almost closed and the muscles in his jaws bulged as he chewed each word before spitting it out. "You know damned well you ain't going to no rodeos without me."

"Right! Like you said, we leave Monday."

What I had neglected to mention to Rufus was that my working in the picture in Tucson depended solely on whether or not the rodeo committee allowed me to ride a bronc. I assumed with Monogram shooting the action scenes as they occurred, the officials would allow me do the stunt.

Wrong.

Plans were to accumulate a lot of free footage to which closeups of the real stars could be added at a later date. With the rodeo promoters still adamant about not allowing women's saddle-bronc riding, it became necessary to film a short, slender cowboy in woman's rodeo garb making the exhibition ride.

When I knew for certain they were not going to allow me to do the stunt, I was forced to admit to Rufus that the trip had been mostly speculation on my part. No work. No pay. Fortunately, he was in a good mood after winning some money in the bull riding, and later on after a lot of nagging on my part, I was finally allowed to make an exhibition ride on a bareback bronc. I was thrown after about four jumps out of the chute and was never able to understand why the powers that be decided this was better than letting me ride the saddle-bronc. This was hardly a victory for either the rodeo committee or me, but I made a few bucks, anyway.

Next to the last day of the rodeo, Rufus was not scheduled to ride so I talked him into driving out to a small ranch where the rest of the Monogram group was on location. I had barely stepped out of the car when Ray Corrigan spotted me and let out a war-whoop as he raced by on his horse and swooped me up onto the back of his saddle. He made a complete circle of the set before putting me down beside Max Terhune. Fortunately, I had left PeeWee in the car.

"Hi, there, honey!" Terhune said, with the words coming out of his dummy, Elmer. "How's my favorite cowgirl?"

I saw Rufus coming toward us and even from that distance I recognized anger in the way he walked.

"I'm just fine, Max. See you guys later, okay?"

I intercepted Rufus before he reached us, and grabbed him by the arm.

"What say we leave? They're through shooting for today, anyway."

Rufus bucked off of his last bull so we both collected our money at the rodeo office and headed for Compton. I only had $5 coming for the bareback ride and the cowboy who did the saddle-bronc riding in my place was paid considerably more by Monogram.

We arrived back in Compton the next day, and I was relieved to learn that Rufus still had his job. It seemed the foreman on his shift was an ex-rodeo hand who usually covered for the boys if they took a few days off to go to a show. Some of his leniency was due to manpower shortage, too, with more men being drafted every day.

As soon as Monogram began filming their next picture, "Wrangler's Roost," I worked for three days straight before my budding career hit a temporary setback.

My hours were such that I could leave after Rufus went to work each morning and return before he did at night, so I kept the whole thing to myself for two days even though I was bursting to tell someone about the schoolhouse scene where I had four or five closeups while standing or sitting among the main actors at the "box social." Then, the third morning, I woke Rufus to go to work, and he blandly informed me he had been switched to the night shift. I had no choice but to admit I was due at the studio in two hours.

"That's okay," he said, without any change of expression, "it won't take me long to get ready."

I knew better than to argue. All I could do was make the best of it—and pray. Apparently I used a poor selection of words in the silent pleas for Outside Help, because nothing could have been more agonizing than the eight hours that followed.

When we first arrived at the studio, I tried to bluff my way out of the situation. I climbed out of the car and said, "Thanks for bringing me over here. I can just take the bus home after work and you won't need to make this long trip again."

Without giving any indication that he heard me, Rufus stepped out of his side of the car, slammed his door, and marched right beside me as I entered the main gate. I showed my I.D. and the guard moved to stop him.

It was a temptation to not intercede, but I said, "He's with me. It's all right for my husband to come in for a few minutes, isn't it?"

As the guard smiled and stepped back, Rufus said in a semi-joking way, "If I don't go in, she sure as hell don't!"

The guard and two or three "extras" who were coming through the gate raised their eyebrows knowingly. I felt embarrassed but continued walking.

"I'll have to go over to 'wardrobe' for a few minutes, I whispered to Rufus. "Why don't you just wander around and look things over?"

For several uncomfortable seconds he stood, arms crossed, and glowered at me. A hard knot formed in my stomach muscles as I awaited his decision.

Then he nodded, and walked away.

It took me nearly half an hour to put on the long, old-fashioned dress and bonnet because my hands were shaking so badly, and I had to ask another girl to help with my hair.

"What's the matter, honey?" she asked shrilly, in between each open-mouthed chew of her gum. "You sure are nervous. Your first day?"

"Yeah," I lied. "That's right. My first day."

I busied myself with the high laced shoes in order to avoid further questioning. As quickly as possible, I headed for the set, even though they were not ready for me that soon. Rufus was there, mentally tapping his foot, when I arrived.

He was barely civil when I introduced him to various members of the cast, and I knew he was capable of just about anything the first time Corrigan walked past and gave me a quick impersonal hug like he always did.

All during filming that day, I was so tense and watchful, I never knew exactly what I was supposed to do. I avoided talking or joking with other members of the cast and I kept an eye on Rufus because

I was aware of each time he "froze" when a director or someone else called me honey. When I had a few free seconds, I slipped over and explained the Hollywood over-use of the word, and let him know the person in question did not even know my name.

Had it been necessary to work one hour longer that day, I know I would have burst into tears right in front of everyone. As it was, I thought I was hiding my uneasiness pretty well until the director asked me to step into his office after we finished shooting.

"Please, just wait for me in the car," I begged of Rufus. "It'll only take a minute to find out if I work tomorrow or not."

"Okay," he replied, sulking. "But you'd better not be any longer than that."

I was nervous, embarrassed, and ashamed all at the same time. I was certain the director wanted to discuss Rufus' attitude.

"Jane," he began, kindly, when I closed the office door behind me, "I hope you won't be offended."

"I think I know—and I understand."

"If you were an established star it would be different, but we can't put up with this jealous-husband routine with one of our extras. You see that, don't you?"

I just nodded, and stared at the pattern in the carpet.

"There's no more work for you on this particular script, anyway, but if we can use you on the next one, we'll give you a call. If you can straighten things out in the meantime, we'll see what we can do. You understand?"

"Yes, I'm afraid I do."

Just then the door burst open and there was Rufus, spraddle-legged, arms crossed over his chest.

"Thought you was comin' right out."

"I am," I replied wearily. I walked out the door without even looking back. I wanted to say thank you, or something, for the few days of work but I just nodded to him and walked out.

Ray Corrigan had purchased some real estate in Simi Valley where he developed a multi-purpose movie location that was open to the public. They staged "shoot-em-ups" for visitors and Corrigan produced and directed a few films of his own. I did not feel quite so bad when I knew the Range Busters thing folded shortly after I made my brief appearance in one of their films, but that was little consolation during those days immediately following my conversation with the director.

For over a month I hardly left the apartment at all. I had sieges of pacing the floor like a caged animal, then spells of depression when I sat for hours, huddled in a corner staring at nothing.

I finally went to a movie one afternoon and when I returned, I stopped at the front office to check for mail or phone calls, since there were no lines to the individual apartments. The secretary said there were two messages, one from Gene Autry's office and the other from Central Casting. This news momentarily brought me out of my shell until I returned the calls.

At Central Casting I was told, somewhat impatiently, that they simply went through their roster of "extras" when they received a call for mob-scenes, and if they did not make instant contact, they went right on to the next name on the list. She said in a few weeks they might get back to my name again. Or not. . .

At Republic, Autry and company had reportedly just gone on location—for a month.

"At least I'm consistent," I mumbled.

"What's that, Miss?" the switchboard operator at Republic asked.

I did not bother to answer.

# Chapter Eighteen

Robbie, the Texas cowboy, came to the apartment one evening to see how Rufus was doing after his accident at the jackpot rodeo. He brought some beer and a bottle of tequila so after we drank and talked rodeo for several hours, the three of us agreed that it was the time of year when all good rodeo cowboys took to the highways.

It surprised me that Rufus had also been thinking along those lines because I was getting restless, myself, and we had not discussed it. I figured my newly acquired guild card would be good every winter if I wanted to take advantage of it, as long as I paid the dues, and it was silly to sit around all summer waiting for a call that may or may not come when they had their random drawings.

Cheyenne was mentioned during our late-night discussion but this did not excite me very much because they had not hired women bronc riders at their rodeos for quite some time. However, any move would be welcome as far as I was concerned. One of my worries was our Ford that we bought as a used car in Texas before the trip to Minneapolis. At the present time, it needed a lot of work on the engine and the tires were so bad that a Cherokee who worked at the Rogers' ranch in Palm Springs had said several months before, "That's the only car I ever saw that left moccasin tracks!"

I realized it would not be long before we headed for one rodeo or another, so the next afternoon, I headed for Hollywood with PeeWee jumping from one side of the car to the other as we traveled north. I decided to leave a message for Cactus and bring him up to date on the results of his recommendations, and also to thank him for his help. I omitted my final discussion with the director from Monogram because I was ashamed that I had allowed Rufus' interference to jeopardize any connection with them in the future. I also wanted to let him know we were probably going back to rodeoing, at least for the summer, but would contact him again if and when we returned to California. Stuart Hamblen did not broadcast in the afternoon but he had a mailbox at the radio station so I left an envelope with the note to Cactus and I headed home.

I was still thinking about our car problems when I saw a huge banner over the entrance to a used-car lot that said: PUSH YOUR CAR IN AND DRIVE ONE OF OURS OUT! WE TAKE ANYTHING THAT MOVES.

The Ford just barely qualified but I made a quick change of lanes that nearly caused two collisions and drove right under the huge sign. I explained to the car salesman that we owed very little on the car but wanted something a little newer because we both needed transportation to work. I saw no reason to mention that our work might be any place from Wyoming to Texas, so the only information I gave them was the name of the welding company where Rufus worked.

Thirty minutes later I was behind the wheel of a three-year-old yellow Buick convertible with the top down and that beautiful California sun shining in my face. Before the deal could be closed, Rufus would also have to sign the papers, but I had no doubt that he would be as pleased with the transaction as I was.

I was not used to driving a convertible and as I cruised along with the top down, it did not occur to me that any dialogue between me and someone else in a convertible would be just like sitting beside someone on your sofa at home. When a sun-tanned young man in a Cadillac convertible cut in front of me, changing lanes, I yelled, "Watch out, you stupid son-of-a-bitch!" It came as a total shock to me when he started laughing and saluted me as he pulled away! I would have to be careful what I said if I continued to drive in that "land of convertibles."

I parked near the entrance to the building where Rufus worked, and I only had to wait about thirty minutes for his shift to end. Using PeeWee as a "stand-in" for Rufus, I rehearsed what I would say about the purchase of a new car. I thought I was quite convincing so I was a trifle annoyed when he curled up and went to sleep right in the middle of the best part of my argument.

When Rufus finally came out of the exit with a horde of other workers, he just stopped and stared when he recognized me in that shiny almost-new convertible. After several minutes he approached, hesitantly, as though he thought his eyesight was playing tricks on him.

"Where the hell'd you get that thing?" He was right next to the door on my side by that time, and reached out to touch the car as though he needed reassurance that it was real.

"This is our new car," I could hardly suppress a delighted giggle. "All we need is your signature and information about your job here, and this beautiful machine is ours!"

He listened to the details of the transaction, including how the car-lot would make those last two payments to GMAC, and we would now be making $40 a month payments on this new car for the next three years.

"Isn't that great?"

He still looked puzzled.

"Anything wrong?"

He nodded.

"What?"

"I told my boss today I was quitting and would be leaving in two weeks. What'll those yokels at the car-lot say when they hear I don't have a job any more?"

Now I was the one to just sit and stare.

Finally, Rufus told me to wait for him, and he went back inside of the building. It was nearly thirty minutes when he returned, but he looked much happier than when he walked away before. He explained that his foreman, the one who used to be a rodeo cowboy, said his actual period of being one of the unemployed would not begin until the end of his two weeks' notice, so there should not be a problem.

I started to move over so Rufus could get behind the wheel but he went around to the other side and crawled in, after moving PeeWee to the center of the front seat. We drove back to the car lot and after another forty-five minutes we were the proud almost-owners of that gorgeous automobile.

We rode in silence the rest of the way to our apartment. When I parked out in front, Rufus blew a puff of air onto a single spot on the dashboard and polished it with his shirt sleeve.

"Man, oh man!" he chuckled. "Won't them cowboys sit up and take notice when we come wheeling into Cheyenne in this big yellow buggy?"

"You bet!" was all I could say.

I was happy that we would be headed for another rodeo before long, but also a bit sad because I realized that our particular lifestyle could not possibly provide a happy home for PeeWee. I finally solved this by leaving him with Mrs. Moody for the time being, and tearfully promising to send for him as soon as possible.

Rodeos as large as the one in Cheyenne understandably have to sign their contract performers several weeks prior to the show. I knew they had a history of not hiring women bronc-riders for the past several years but there was always a chance that I might find someone who would let me use their horse for the barrel races. It so happened that I knew very few of the contestants so was unable to make any such arrangements.

Rufus placed second in one go-round and tied for third in another. I was happy for him but as always, when not performing or doing any side jobs, I was restless and grumpy. Even though my marriage was running smoothly at the moment, I had already decided to bail out once we participated in some Colorado rodeos and Rufus had been hand-delivered back to his Mom in Beaumont.

After the final performance in Cheyenne, Rufus collected his winnings. Even after we sent our first car payment two weeks ahead of time, we were still in better financial shape than we had been for some time.

"How about this, girl?" Rufus beamed. "Money in every pocket." He patted his right hip where his billfold (usually empty) had worn an outline in the denim, then indicated every remaining pocket as he added, "In fact, if I find one with nothing in it, I'll cut it off!"

By that time, it was so late that we decided to stay one more night before making a definite decision about where we should go next. We wandered from bar to bar and were about to return to our room. We were several blocks from our hotel and I needed to use the restroom before we left the bar.

As soon as I entered said room, I saw a short, stocky, redheaded girl who had propped herself in a corner so she would not topple over while she struggled with the zipper on her black frontier pants. She could have been quite attractive, but by applying far too much make-up, her slack expressionless features took on the appearance of a grotesque hallowe'en mask.

"Need some help?" I offered.

She glanced up and the mask cracked at the bottom into a rather cute crooked smile that disclosed small, shiny-white teeth. I wondered why she caked her long lashes with so much mascara, when I saw what an effort it was for her to lift her eyelids.

After a few seconds, this girl tipped her head back against the wall and forcibly popped her eyes open, blinking once or twice, as though in an attempt to see what I looked like. Her eyes were a beautiful amber color, flecked with brown. This analysis was done rapidly because her eyes were only open for a matter of seconds.

She finally nodded her head as if to indicate that I had passed the test, and mumbled, "All right. You can help me."

"Gee, thanks," I had to laugh because the sarcasm was wasted.

"Y'welcome."

She managed to hold the sides of the zipper together with her stubby, scarlet-tipped fingers, while I inched the center-fastener upward. Her cheap perfume was a brand that professed to be "the scent of orange blossoms" but actually, on her, smelled more like orange-gin, and was almost making me sick. If I had not held my breath for the last few moments of the zipper repair, I never could have made it.

"I'm Betty." She made the announcement, then collapsed into the corner.

I stood and looked at her for a minute. She did not appear to need immediate attention as much as I did, so I uncrossed my legs and hurried to complete my original mission.

I returned shortly and said, "I'm Jane."

This sounded so much like something out of an old Tarzan movie that I had to laugh.

Betty began to snore, so I reached over and took a burning cigarette from her limp fingers. I had just finished tossing it into the toilet when she awoke and started to cry. Instead of feeling sympathetic, I watched the tears roll down her cheeks, and wondered if they were eighty or ninety proof.

"That dirty so-and-so," she mumbled. "I'll never speak to him again. Not as long as I live."

"If he's really that bad, how come you don't come right out and say so?"

Betty's eyes popped open again and she looked genuinely shocked. "Because I don't cuss," she stated indignantly, then passed out again.

It took fifteen or twenty minutes of these spasmodic conversations before I pieced together enough information to understand that she, too, was a bronc-rider. She was from California. She had been traveling with a man named Huck, and he had just given her the old heave-ho.

"So what now?"

"I don't know," she sniffled. "I'm broke. Don't know nobody. An' that so-and-so already left town."

I knew Rufus was probably due to start banging on the door and I started to walk away. Then I turned back.

"That's simple," I told her. "You can travel with us"

"Thanks." She started to collapse again.

I struggled to pull her upright so she could walk through the swinging door with me. Before Rufus realized I was not alone, he glared at me. I glared back.

"What the hell you been doing?" he snapped. "You been gone thirty minutes."

"Just visiting. And look what I brought back with me."

I let go of Betty to make a sweeping gesture in her direction and she would have fallen on her face if Rufus had not grabbed her.

"Who is she?" he demanded.

"Says her name's Betty. She rides broncs. She's been stranded by some guy that's a son-of- a-bitch but she won't say so 'cause she's too nice a girl." I had to chuckle at the absurdity of this statement. "And she's going with us."

"Like hell she is. We're headin' out now. Alone."

"I am not leaving this poor girl stranded," I stated this with slow deliberation. "She is going with us."

Rufus stared at me for a minute. His voice was filled with disgust when he finally said, "Oh, all right. Bring her along. But let's go."

How could I have been so stupid?

Although I was generally quite fortunate in my selection of stray dogs and cats that I chose for adoption, this time I came to regret bowing to my maternal impulses.

Many of the contestants went on to Boulder, Colorado for their PowWow Days held each year right after Cheyenne but the three of us headed for Pine Bluffs, Wyoming, instead. We arrived there late at night, and the only vacant room in the entire town had bare floors, ragged curtains, one water tap (cold) in the corner, one bed, and it had the same moldy alcoholic smell as scotch-whiskey (and seemed damned near as expensive at the time). We were so thankful to find any place to stay, the three of us crawled into the only bed and went to sleep.

I awoke early. Because I was unable to rouse the other two, I left them in bed while I went to the rodeo headquarters.

I managed to promote bronc-riding jobs for Betty and me. I also entered Rufus in the bull-riding and bareback-riding, then returned to our room just before noon. Rufus and Betty were just leaving to go have breakfast.

Looking back, it is hard to understand how I could have been so naïve, or for want of a better word: stupid.

The conversations I had with Terry, the trick-rider in Florida, should have made me aware of the various reasons for affairs without love, namely incompatibility within the marriage, or excessive opportunity and convenience outside the marriage. So what the hell could be more convenient for a man than to have his wife "bed him down" with another female, then thoughtfully depart for five or six hours?

Neither Rufus nor Betty was very talkative that morning during breakfast, but they had little opportunity to be, as I chattered on and on about how fortunate we were that all of us could work the Pine Bluffs show. Betty finally mentioned that she had no reins, hobbles, chaps or spurs. I took off in a cloud of dust again, to request that our rides be split up on the program so that one of us would be through with my gear in time for the other to use it.

Betty rode before I did that afternoon. She actually did a much better job than I, even though she admittedly had no particular ambitions about becoming a famous bronc rider. As I watched her on a wiry bay gelding, and listened to the deafening applause, I was as proud as though I had done it myself. Rufus retrieved my gear before he made his bareback ride, because my bronc was to be put into the chutes soon after that. He also made a good ride, but "goose-egged" out of the chute. The judges of the riding events stand right outside of the gate, on either side. If the cowboy does not spur the bronc in the shoulders when he first leaves the chute, the rider get a zero from that judge and is disqualified from that entire go-round.

The Pine Bluffs arena was situated inside the oval of the race-track. There was a narrow foot-gate leading from the arena to the track, so anyone could go back and forth to the concessions under the grandstand. As soon as my bronc came out of the chute, he bucked straight toward the grandstand, and although I was too busy to notice at the time, someone had left the small gate open and we were headed straight toward it. I divided my reins when the whistle blew and held one in each hand. Before I realized what was happening, two pickup-men rushed in, one on each side, and snatched both reins away from me. I grabbed the saddlehorn and was taking a terrific beating when my bronc reached the foot-gate and bucked right through it out onto the track. Naturally, there was not enough room for more than one horse at a time to go through the narrow opening, so the pickup-men had to let go of the reins. My bronc hit the race-track and began running instead of bucking. I could see my reins flopping on the ground and knew that any second the bronc might step on them. If he did, he would flip end over end. The pickup-men were also on the track by this time and were again racing along beside me. Now there were three horses that might step on the reins!

"Get back!" I yelled. "Just try to head him off."

I am not exactly sure how I expected them to accomplish such a feat without going completely around the track and heading me off when I approached from the other direction, but I did know they were scaring me to death the way they were already going about it.

Apparently these men knew of only one way to handle the situation, because they kept chasing my bronc around the track. The pick-up-man on my left finally crowded in. I kicked my feet loose from my stirrups and made one wild leap into his arms. The very second he caught me in midair, he pulled his horse off to the right and set me on the ground.

I had no sooner cleared the saddle than the bronc stepped on the reins and turned a complete forward somersault. The saddlehorn and cantle were smashed.

"Want a ride back to the chutes?" the other pickup-man asked as he rode by.

I was so shaken watching the bronc struggle to his feet, I could hardly answer.

"No thanks," I said hoarsely. "I'll just rest here for a few minutes."

I leaned against the track-railing and drew as much air into my lungs as I could. I tried to calm myself before heading back and when I felt a little better, I started walking.

Because our three-horse chase around the race-track had taken us almost full circle, I chose the shorter distance by walking the final eighth of a mile to the the rear gate of the bucking chutes. Just as I stepped into the arena, I saw Rufus and Betty walking toward the grandstand. I ran to catch up with them.

"Hey!" I hollered. "Wait up, you two."

They gave me time to catch up and Rufus said, "You all right, hon?"

"Sure, I'm fine." Nice of you to ask.

"Gee, that's good," Betty sighed. "I was so afraid!"

"Me, too!" Rufus nodded.

Rather than mention that it was damned near as tough on me as it was on them, I changed the subject.

"Where you headed?"

Rufus grinned. "Betty needed a drink, so we thought we'd just wait for you over at the beer stand."

I muttered to their backs as they walked ahead of me, "You really shouldn't have worried so."

The second day of the show, which was also the final day, was pretty much the same as the first. This time my bronc stayed in the arena, but the pickup men seemed overly anxious to do a good job, and one of them plowed into me on the right side, partially dislocating my knee cap. Unaware of my injury, the other pickup-man lifted me from the bronc, set me down in the middle of the arena, and rode away looking quite pleased with himself. The fact that I was facing north and my right foot was pointing southeast should have given him a clue that there was a problem.

Fortunately, Rufus was watching. When I did not move toward the chutes, he rushed out to me.

"What's wrong, girl?"

"My knee. An old injury. Happens sometimes."

"Anything I can do?"

I just nodded, and gestured for him to move me over to the pole fence. The pain was rough, but I wanted to get out of the middle of the arena until somebody could jerk the knee back into place. A big cowboy named Harvey suspected what had happened and came over to help.

When we reached the fence, Harvey and Rufus unbuckled my chaps and I eased down so I could lie flat on the ground.

"Can you take it?" Harvey asked, motioning toward my twisted leg.

"You mean I have a choice?"

"I mean, do you want a doc—or should I put it back?"

"Have at it, boy," I told him. "I'd just as soon not wait any longer."

Before I finished speaking, Harvey had grabbed my right foot. With a deft twist and a hard jerk, he popped my knee-cap back into place.

"How's that?" he asked, smiling.

I wiped the sweat off of my forehead and my upper lip before I answered. "I feel better with both boots pointing in the same direction. Can you guys get me back on my feet?"

As soon as I stood up the muscles in my leg began to twitch. At least there was not as much pain as there had been before. Not quite.

Rufus looked at me with a puzzled expression on his face.

"I don't get it," he said.

"Get what?"

"You." He shook his head. "You start blubbering over every little thing that don't mean a damn, and then when you really get hurt, you don't cry at all. I just don't get it."

"Tears have nothing to do with guts," I explained as I limped toward the gate. "With little hurts, or injured feelings, you have time to feel sorry for yourself. With a big hurt, you don't. Get it?"

"Nope," he muttered, "cain't say that I do."

In a few minutes he helped me into the car, and went to find Betty so we could return to our room. While I was sitting there alone, Harvey went by. I called him over to thank him.

"Glad to do it," he replied, smiling. Then he looked more solemn as he added, "It's none of my business, but if you figure on riding any more broncs for awhile, you better not walk around on that leg much for a few days. An' you ought to wear an elastic bandage when you do ride. Them damned trick-knees can be a hell of a thing if you don't take care of 'em."

"I'll try to remember. And thanks."

"Any time." He touched the brim of his hat in kind of a saluting gesture, and walked away.

I watched as car after car pulled away, and thought once about asking some of the cowboys for a ride into town. I probably would have tried driving our car, but Rufus had the only set of keys.

My leg was swollen, and throbbing a lot, when Rufus and Betty finally returned an hour-and-a-half later. They approached the car, laughing and joking with each other.

"Hurry up, will you?" I called out to them. "I'd like to lie down for a couple of hours before it's time to take off again."

"Take it easy, girl," Rufus teased, "an' you'll last longer." Then he added, to Betty, "You'd better sit in the middle so Jane can keep her bum leg stretched out better."

Betty avoided looking at me as she crawled into the car. Assuming she was simply ashamed for keeping me waiting, I complimented her on her bronc-ride to make her feel more at ease.

After we reached our room, Rufus left to collect all of our money, while Betty packed. Within two hours we were on our way to Golden, Colorado, with Rufus driving, Betty next to him, and me eating aspirin. I watched, fascinated, while the leg of my levis inflated until it looked more and more like a pulsating balloon.

It was much farther to Golden than what the map said.

It was a cold, rainy night when we arrived. As usual, we had very little choice of rooms. We rarely called ahead for reservations because most of the time we did not decide until the last minute which rodeo we thought would work out best for us. After several stops, Rufus and Betty managed to get the last vacant room in a walk-up hotel. My leg did not bend too well by then, but with their help I climbed the stairs. One glimpse of our room and I was not convinced that it was worth the climb. I felt secure, though, when I saw a coiled rope by a window at the end of the hall. One end was tied to a radiator, and there was a large sign attached that said: FIRE ESCAPE!

The room was cold and damp, with one cot, bunk-beds, a three-legged chair, and a small dresser with mis-matched drawers. There were no curtains on the only window, just a dirty green shade that rolled to the top with a loud bang and went "clap-clap-clap-clap" every time I limped past.

While Rufus unloaded the car, Betty helped me undress. I hobbled down the hall to the bathroom where I took a hot bath for about thirty minutes. Sort of shock therapy with the shock due to finding hot water in such a crummy hotel. However, I was able to move around better by the time I returned to the room.

Rufus was already asleep in the top bunk, and Betty on the cot, so I crawled into the lower bunk, and despite the chill of the room, I went to sleep almost immediately.

In the morning when I awoke, I started to get up. When I rode broncs every week, my arms, legs, and back were almost always sore and stiff the first thing in the morning, but this time it was ridiculous. I could barely move. My knee was still swollen, and each muscle in my body felt like I was the victim of day-old knife wounds when I tried to flex my leg even a little bit.

"Keerist, but I'm sore," I moaned. Then I sneezed. "Besides that, I've caught a cold."

I waited for someone to speak, even if it were only a "Shhhh!" No sound was forthcoming except two harmonious snores. If I had not been too lame to stand up and fight, I probably would have thrown something at each of them.

Before I had time to feel too annoyed, I remembered the rodeo. I tried to waken Rufus and Betty but they just groaned and mumbled, so I struggled into my clothes and drove over to the rodeo headquarters by myself.

This time when I returned to the room, the other two were still sleeping soundly. I had all three of us lined up for the show, and I had purchased a can of ether and an elastic bandage for my knee.

I would pour the ether on my knee to freeze it if the pain became too severe. As it happened, I managed to get by without such extreme measures but once or twice when the bronc leaned against my right leg in the chute, I almost came out over the top of the gate without the horse. There was a drizzling rain all afternoon and I kept hoping they would postpone the rodeo for a day or so, but they did not.

Right after the show I asked Rufus to take me to the room. I was afraid to take another hot bath for fear my cold might get worse so I went straight to bed and Rufus brought me a half-pint of Jim Beam whiskey so I could have a couple of hot-drinks. More accurately, luke-warm drinks, since I was using tap water. When he brought the whiskey, he mentioned that there was going to be a street dance that night, now that the rain had stopped, and he wondered if I would feel like going to it later on. Surely he already knew the answer.

"I sure as hell don't feel like dancing," I told him, "but you two go ahead if you want to."

"I'd hate to go without you, girl, but we might as well look things over for an hour or so."

I had been acting as the "company banker," so now I held back a $2O bill and gave them the rest of our money. "I'll just put this twenty in the dresser drawer under my underwear and socks, so we'll be sure to have eating-money in the morning. Okay?"

"Sure thing," they both nodded.

"We've got more'n we need here, anyway," Rufus added, without returning any money to me.

The whiskey made me drowsy and I was asleep as soon as they left the room.

The following morning my leg was better and my cold was worse. I was not going to waken the other two until I had some breakfast because I figured they had probably been out late. After I dressed, I checked the dresser drawer to retrieve the twenty dollars, and it was gone.

"Hey, you two! Who took my twenty dollars?" I yelled loud enough to wake up everyone on that floor of the hotel, but at least I got a reaction from Rufus and Betty.

"What happened, hon?" Rufus mumbled.

"The twenty. It's gone. You guys take it?"

"Hell, no," Rufus sounded sincere. "We wouldn't do that without telling you."

I was still fuming. "How could anybody come in here without waking me.?"

"Gee, I guess we shouldn't have left you here alone," Betty sounded sincere. "But I never dreamed somebody'd come right into our room."

I looked from one of them to the other. I really hoped it was not Rufus who took the money but in any event, there was nothing I could do about it now. I felt worse about being lied to that I did about the loss of cash.

"No use griping, I guess." This time I felt a pain that was different from my bad knee. "We'll have to go out and borrow some money, so we might as well start now."

They mumbled in agreement, and before long we had each hustled enough cash to carry us over until we could draw some of our own money at the rodeo headquarters.

I was angry all day. What made it worse was the knowledge that I had been betrayed. Strangely enough, this incident bothered me more than what I could see was going on between Betty and Rufus. In the latter case, it was almost a relief to have his attention diverted in a different direction.

By the time the rodeo ended that afternoon, I had decided to act like the twenty dollars incident had never happened. I collected some of our wages, paid for our supper, and then waited to see if anyone suggested going out again that night. No mention was made of the street dance. We all went to our room, presumably to sleep.

We had one more day to go before the rodeo ended and we could collect the rest of our money, but I had no intention of losing what was left of the eating money we had borrowed. Each of us downed a couple of hot drinks in our room, and I was trying to decide how best to protect myself from another "robbery" on that final night in Golden.

I made a big issue of placing our money under my pillow and I rolled over, facing the wall, and pretended to fall asleep almost immediately.

What I needed was a hiding place that would not occur to either or both of them in case they were plotting a midnight sneak-out with the rest of the cash. I thought of a sure-fire solution. It was at this point that I remembered an old stunt Clint sometimes pulled on one of his not-too-trustworthy gambler friends and it would fit the present situation perfectly. I almost spoiled my plans by laughing out loud.

I managed to stay awake until I was certain both of them had fallen asleep. As always, Rufus had stepped out of his Levis and dropped them in a heap beside the bunk-bed. I very cautiously eased the money out from under my pillow, folded in into a neat little packet, and tucked it into his own watch-pocket. Then I lay back, smiling smugly, and went to sleep.

I had no idea how long I had been asleep when I felt a hand moving under my pillow. I lay perfectly still as it pawed around for a minute or so, then stopped.

"Find anything?" Betty hissed.

"No. Did you?"

"No. I looked through her clothes, suitcase, dresser drawers, and everything."

Rufus whispered as he climbed back into the upper bunk, "Guess we might as well forget it. I thought she said she'd put it under her pillow, but maybe I'm wrong. She musta spent all of it on supper. Or the whiskey."

"I guess so."

I woke up fairly early, and lay in bed staring at the lumpy mattress of the bunk above me as I grinned to myself. After awhile I reached over the edge of the bed and leisurely picked up one of my boots. I held it at arm's length, then dropped it. Even the sound of the boot was not as shattering as the Clap-clap-clap-clap of the window shade.

"What the hell was that?" Rufus sat up and looked around.

"What happened?" Betty's usually heavy-lidded eyes were now wide open.

I stretched languidly and crawled out of bed. "Just thought we'd go eat. Okay?"

"We got no money," Rufus grumbled.

"Oh, we must have something," I said. "Let's look around."

Both of them seemed bored as I checked through my pockets, under the pillow, and the entire route they had tried the night before. Then I stepped over and began rifling through Rufus' Levi pockets. I watched him out of the corner of my eye, and when I reached into his pocket and pulled out that wad of bills, I thought he'd fall out of that top bunk.

Betty snapped to attention, too. She and Rufus stared at me, then at each other, while I calmly tossed the money onto the dresser and started to get dressed.

"Where the hell did that come from?" Rufus asked weakly.

"Damned if I know," I tried to sound as innocent as possible. "Guess you didn't spend as much as you thought the other night."

"Well, shit!" Betty glared at Rufus.

He wore an extremely pained expression.

I pulled on my boots, and reached for a towel.

"I'm going to wash up and then go have some breakfast. You two don't need to get up yet unless you want to."

"I'm ready," Rufus grumbled. "I cain't sleep now, anyhow."

Betty also grumbled, "Me neither," and crawled out of bed.

As soon as our gear was loaded into the car, Rufus motioned for me to climb in beside him. For the first time in days, he asked, "You feelin' better, girl?"

I glanced from his grim expression to Betty's scarlet, pouting mouth, and did not try to hide a grin. "Much better, thank you."

All during our trip to Monte Vista, I was aware of the strained relationship between Rufus and Betty. She chatted incessantly about the cowboy named Huck, the one who had deserted her in Cheyenne, and continued to mention the different cowboys she had lived with in the past couple of years.

At one point when we had stopped for gas in a small Colorado town, Betty went inside for some cigarettes and she was barely out of the car when Rufus exploded.

"We gotta get rid of that little chippie!" he snapped. "She's plumb rotten, and you might as well admit it."

"You could be right." I tried to sound like I needed to be convinced. "Betty's not really such a bad sort, and she can be a lot of company for me. I've missed having a woman to shop with, or exchange nail polish and stuff like that."

Betty crawled into the car and we took off so fast my head snapped back, flipping my hat into the rear seat. For the rest of the trip, Rufus grumbled, Betty pouted and I enjoyed the scenery.

We pulled into Monte Vista just after dark and went straight to the rodeo headquarters. Rufus entered the bull-riding, and Betty and I were assured we could each ride one bronc at every performance. We were at the bar-and-café a few minutes later when Rufus placed his order and stomped away to go have a drink at the bar while our food was being prepared. He was still sulking.

I recognized Betty's friend Huck as soon as he came through the front door, and at first it looked as though he might be coming to our table, but then he shoved his way past the crowded bar to a booth where he sat by himself.

Betty's mouth twisted into a bitter grin.

"There's that so-and-so now," she grumbled.

"So why don't you go over and say hello?" I teased.

"Who, me? You'll never catch me within thirty feet of that so-and-. . ."

"Wanna bet?"

"What d'you mean?" She assumed that same wide-eyed, innocent pose I had noted when I asked about my missing twenty dollars.

"What I mean is, a man named Shakespeare once said something like 'he who doth protest too much is as close to being a cinch bet as you'll ever find'!"

She glared at me.

"I'll bet you my twenty to your ten that you end up in bed with Huck before this show's over!"

"You're joking."

"Take it or leave it."

Her smirk looked so genuine I felt a bit uneasy, but I shook her hand and she said, "You're on!"

Rufus arrived at our table about the same time as our food. He was still irritable.

I ate most of my steak but the dismal atmosphere gave it a tainted flavor, so I slipped over to the bar and had a drink with Muscles Pearson. He was about to get into a fight, and although he could be a bit obnoxious when he was drinking, the gunsel he was squabbling with seemed at fault this time. I butted in a time or two and suggested they forget their differences, and then I heard Rufus quarreling with someone at the other end of the bar and I hurried away to offer him the same advice.

For nearly thirty minutes I charged back and forth, trying to pacify people. It seemed to be one of those times when everyone was spoiling for a fight. The job of "peacemaker" was a taxing one especially when it was out of character for me, and I finally stopped to lean against one of the booths directly behind Muscles. While I rested and analyzed the situation, Muscles' opponent, a burly-looking man whose jacket logo indicated that he was a miner, looked over his shoulder at me.

"Hold this a minute?" He handed me a full bottle of beer. I nodded and reached for it when I realized he was preparing to "cop a sneak" on Muscles, who had turned away for a second to ward off a blow from a different direction.

Just as the miner squared off to hit Muscles in the back of his head, I poured the entire bottle of beer over his head and it ran down into his eyes before he completed his swing.

That turned into the only real "free-for-all" I ever saw. Cowboys seemed to come out of the woodwork and each of them found a gunsel all his very own to clobber.

Once I had backed away from the man with the beer running down his face, I stayed out of things pretty much, except for once or twice when I took a poke at a waitress who was trying to interfere with a perfectly good fight.

Sometime later, the police arrived. It took them a considerable length of time to get the place quieted down, and when they did, they immediately lined up all of the cowboys (and not one single town boy), and prepared to march them off to jail.

"Who started this, anyway?" a sweaty-faced policeman asked.

The waitress I tangled with pointed at me, and said, "She did!"

Without a word, I fell in at the end of the line.

The cowboys were marched down the street in columns of four, with me at the tail-end in a column of one. The line was about one-fourth the length of a football field and all of us were booked and held overnight without bail. The sheriff called it a sobering-up period and no-one would be released until that feat was accomplished. The police were in a quandary because they had no facilities for such a mass arrest, and also because there were not any cells separate from the others where they could stash me.

"If you're full," I suggested, "I can always go back to my hotel."

"You sit right there by that desk," the sergeant snapped, "until we think of something."

It became apparent that they were not very fast thinkers, because I sat in that same chair all night, with first one policeman and then another pacing the floor and glaring at me. The only time I was allowed to move was whenever I needed to go to the restroom.

I knew Rufus had to be someplace in the mass of faces but I could not find him. Soon after we were marched to a local café for breakfast the following morning, some members of the rodeo committee paid our fines and we were released. I tried to offer my thanks, but one of them informed me, coldly, that their action had been entirely a desperation measure, as there were not enough rodeo hands outside of the jail to put on a show. Even one rodeo judge was locked up with us!

As soon as we returned to the hotel, I remembered Betty. She was not in her own bed, so I phoned the desk to inquire about the location of Huck's room. It was just four doors away from us.

I went down the hall and knocked on his door. I rapped several times before a man's voice said, "Yeah? Who's there?"

"It's Jane," I answered. "I'm looking for Betty. It's almost rodeo time."

There was complete silence for three or four minutes, then the door opened slowly. A whiff of orange-gin-perfume drifted into the hallway. A bare arm reached out and the stubby scarlet-tipped fingers handed me a single ten-dollar bill before the door quietly closed again.

That partial exposure, as she paid off her bet, was all I saw of Betty until the Monte Vista rodeo ended. I invented some rather vague excuses to explain to the rodeo committee why she did not ride her broncs, but finally ended up telling them she had a fever and would be bed-ridden for several days. That sounded about as near the truth as anything I dared say.

The next big rodeo was Durango, Colorado. Betty and Huck had split up again and when I found out she and I could not work there, we headed north to Estes Park in the Buick while Rufus went south to Durango with some bull-riders.

We had a miserable trip. I have always been famous for taking short-cuts that turned into disasters and the one I mapped out for us this time was no exception. While we waited for the service station attendant to fill the tank with gas, check oil, water and tire pressure, I spotted a terrific short-cut on their wall map next to the cash register. This route, indicated by a pencil-thin line, would take us over the top of a small mountain as opposed to the longer route along the foothills to the same destination. I estimated we could cut our traveling time by at least one hour, to say nothing of the reduction in gas consumption.

Right.

I soon understood the pencil-thin line on the map when I was nearly forced into the ditch to allow an approaching car to get by. It was the last vehicle we saw that night.

With no warning, about 2 a.m., our car lights shut down. Not bright to dim, but bright to black! I jammed on the brakes and sat there for a few minutes, shaking. Betty was curled in a ball on her side of the front seat, snoring peacefully and I had no intention of facing our disaster alone so I woke her.

We discussed our options, which were almost nil. We could sit there until daybreak but I had no idea how far we were from Estes Park and since we had no prior arrangements with the rodeo committee, we needed to get there as soon as possible. We sat there in the dark for thirty minutes or so until I finally put the top down and we decided to try creeping along with Betty directing the beam of my small flashlight onto the road just ahead of the car. An occasional flash of moonlight through the trees helped to a certain extent and we finally pulled into Estes Park at daybreak.

For awhile it appeared that neither of us would be allowed to ride in their two-day rodeo. Their allotment of funds for contract riders had already been assigned to other acts but they agreed to furnish us with bucking stock if we could somehow handle the money part of it by ourselves.

We finally took off with me on one side of the street and Betty on the other. Both of us were able to get various shopkeepers and businessmen to sponsor our rides. Everyone, including a couple of lawyers who were new in town, seemed eager to get in on the deal and we got carried away with our promotional scheme. Before we finished, we were advertising almost every establishment in Estes Park! The poor announcer was required to rattle off twelve or fifteen individual blurbs for these sponsors each time Betty or I rode, but at least we would leave town with some cash in our pockets after we paid for our room and the headlight problems on the Buick.

While we were waiting to collect the last of our money on Sunday evening, I found a pay phone nearby and placed a call to Durango. I planned to leave a message for Rufus at the rodeo headquarters to let him know we were leaving for Loveland the next morning, but he happened to be at that number while waiting to get paid so I gave him the message myself.

I explained why he should catch a ride and meet us in a day or two. With Durango at the opposite corner of the state from where we were headed, it would be pointless to handle it any other way. He had won over $150 but lost "a few bucks" in a crap game. He said he would head north as soon as he collected his rodeo winnings and paid off his crap-game losses and would see me in Loveland.

Betty's and my money from the local merchants was already in a money pool that had been paid ahead of time so we were able to collect as soon as the rodeo ended.

Rufus arrived at Loveland with three other cowboys, including our friend Robbie whose beer and jug of wine in California had been partly responsible for our final decision to hit the road again.

At both Loveland and Sterling, I was able to arrange one bronc ride on Saturday afternoon and one on Sunday with Betty on one and me on the other. When the time came, we decided which one would ride at which performance. Rufus won a little over $100 total at the two shows.

It was impossible to understand what was going on in his mind. In Sterling, we all stayed in the same room with one double bed and a folding cot. Although Rufus and I slept together, it was difficult to decide which of us he was married to. At certain times, he and Betty would be laughing and joking. They even held hands on occasion, until she flirted or joked with some cowboy and Rufus would come storming back to me and insist we get rid of that dirty little bitch. During those spells, he fussed over me to the point where I felt disgusted and was actually embarrassed for him.

I had no intention of altering my plans for a divorce as soon as we reached Texas soil. I would keep the car because seeking any alimony would be ridiculous, and for the time being, I could tolerate almost anything in order to put an end to my marriage.

On Saturday, with one final performance remaining for either Betty or myself, I told her I'd like to ride that afternoon. Since I made most of our decisions, she usually went along with whatever I suggested and it was fortunate that she did because I would have been unable to do much of anything the following day.

The three of us went to a dance in the local gymnasium. Rufus spent most of his time with Betty, which was great as far as I was concerned because my bronc that afternoon had been fairly tough and I looked forward to a hot bath and a good night's sleep.

I was headed outside for some fresh air when I saw one of the local cowboys cut in and whirl away with Betty in his arms leaving Rufus in the middle of the dance floor by himself. I had no intention of going to his rescue and even chuckled to myself at his embarrassment.

I stepped aside to make room for some incoming couples and bumped into Robbie who was also pushing his way through the crowd.

"Where you headed, Janie?" he asked. To avoid the onslaught of bodies heading in and out of the gymnasium, he took me by the arm and pulled me over to one side. He leaned over to say something to me and because of the loud music and the hordes of people, we were almost nose-to-nose when I started to reply.

Before I said a word, I was jerked away from Robbie and slammed against the outside wall of the gymnasium.

"Come on, Bitch," he screamed in my ear. "We're gettin' out of here."

Robbie started to say something and I shook my head to indicate it was best to just let us leave. Rufus kept screaming at me all the way to our room and even though I realized his embarrassment at the gymnasium was responsible for his anger and not really anything I had done, his anger was out of control to the point where I was more afraid than usual when he parked and dragged me out of the car.

He unlocked the door and slammed me across the room, still cussing and accusing me of trying to leave the gym with Robbie. I knew he was going to hit me and all I could think about was to remind him that he had promised me, in California, that he would not hit me in the face ever again.

He was acting really crazy at that point. He reached over and grabbed the front of my shirt and literally tore it off of my body with one hand while undoing his western belt with the other. I covered my face with both hands and then realized what he planned to do. He began hitting me across the back with the metal-tipped end of his belt while he grabbed a handful of my hair with his other hand so I could not get away.

After three or four blows, the door burst open. It was Betty and Robbie.

"What the hell you doin', Rufe?" Robbie yelled at him. "You nuts or something?"

Betty had reached out to keep me from falling and she grabbed a jacket from the closet and draped it around my shoulders. When she saw how painful it was for me to have any clothing touching my back and shoulders she held it in front of my chest and helped me to sit on the edge of the bed.

Rufus slumped into a chair and covered his face with his hands. He did not speak for several minutes, and then he finally looked at me, and then at Robbie.

"Guess I kinda went crazy." he began.

"You sure as hell did!" Robbie glared at him. Then he turned to me. "You okay? You want to see a doctor or anything?"

Betty was still hovering over me.

"I'll take care of her," she said. "You just get that son of a bitch out of here."

Even as much as I was hurting, I could not resist a comment. "Thought you didn't cuss!"

She grinned. "Only when someone deserves it."

While Robbie was still there, Betty drove to an all-night drug store and came back with some medication and bandages. When the two men left, she doctored the areas on my back that were still bleeding where the metal tip had sliced into the flesh, and covered them with pads and adhesive tape. She stayed with me the rest of the night.

Neither Robbie nor Betty could believe I was going to make the trip to Texas with Rufus. I tried to explain that I saw no advantage in walking away at that point and that I intended to head south as soon as we collected our money that night. Robbie was going to Texas with us, and I think he was more concerned with my welfare than he was in finding transportation back to Houston.

Betty moved on to a different cowboy and I never saw her again.

On our way south, we were going to by-pass Denver but we saw some posters indicating a celebration of some kind and thought we would look it over as long as we were already in the area.

We stopped off at the arena and were wandering around the building to check it out when Robbie noticed two cowboys from Texas that he wanted to say hello to while we were there. I walked on ahead and as I passed one doorway that was slightly ajar, I noticed Autry's Flying A brand over the entrance. Going on the assumption that this was a private room for his riding equipment or something, I decided if he happened to be there, I would stick my head in the door and say hello while I waited for Rufus and Robbie. I tapped on the door.

Autry said, "Come on in, George. My saddle's in the corner."

Just as I stepped into the room, he looked up.

"You're not George." He frowned almost accusingly. He looked so serious, I started to laugh.

"Nope," I replied. "I haven't been, all day today."

A glow of recognition replaced the confused look in his eyes.

"Janie!" he exclaimed. "How the hell are you?"

"Great!" I stepped forward to shake his hand, but instead, he put his hands on my shoulders and kissed me on the cheek.

There was no clinch, and in fact there was nothing personal in the kiss at all, except as a greeting. He quickly released me and a prickly feeling along the back of my neck made me look toward the door. There was Rufus in the doorway, standing spraddle-legged with his arms crossed. His usual pre-battle stance. Robbie and another cowboy were behind him.

I was so afraid of a scene, I muttered to Autry, hastily, "I know you're busy, so I'll see you some other time." I hurried toward the door.

"Sure. Sure. See you later." He sounded a bit anxious himself. He nodded to Rufus just as I pulled the door closed behind me.

Rufus grabbed the front of my blouse and snatched me over to him, our noses almost touching.

"What the hell you trying to do? Make a damned fool out of me in front of everybody?"

For once, I glared right back at him. "You're doing a good job of that all by yourself!"

He raised his hand as though he was going to slap me. Robbie pushed him aside and I just shook my head to let him know everything was all right.

I was glad we would have someone with us on the long road back to Texas.

# Chapter Nineteen

It was a long, miserable trip from Denver to Beaumont. Robbie, Rufus and I took turns driving and I only spoke to Rufus when it was absolutely necessary. As he often did after one of our fights, he acted as though nothing were wrong.

We dropped Robbie off in Houston and Rufus drove the rest of the way to his mother's house in Beaumont. He parked in front of the house and went around to unlock the trunk.

"Just leave my things in the car," I told him when he began unloading. "I'm going to get a room down town until I decide what to do."

At first I thought he was going to argue with me, or even order me to get out of the car, but I think he saw something different in my expression and decided it was best to let me go for the time being.

"Tell your mother I'll call her later when I make up my mind."

"Yeah. You just do that, girl." He took his one suitcase out of the trunk, slammed the car door and walked away. He did not look back.

I spent a couple of days in a small hotel in downtown Beaumont, while I made inquiries about filing for a divorce. There was no need for me to have a lawyer because the Texas legal system for that procedure was really quite simple. I learned it would only take twenty-one days from the date of application until the decree was granted, providing it was not contested, but in order to expedite things I would need to remain in the area.

Before I actually went to the court house to set things in motion, I decided to find a job to pay my own expenses during that three-week period and still have some "get-out-of-town" money once it was over. In my pre-marriage days, I would simply have wired to

Montana for cash, but I felt this disaster was of my own doing and I needed to resolve it by myself.

With very little job experience other than rodeos, I had no idea where to start. There was a HELP WANTED sign in the window of a small millinery store and I decided I might as well face my first rejection there so I took a chance. I no longer owned any dresses but I was wearing a nice pair of black gabardine bell-bottomed rodeo pants with the least decorative blouse I owned, and hoped it would be acceptable. Apparently, because my clothes were cleaned and pressed and I spoke English, that was all they required because I was told to start work at nine a.m. the very next day. This was Thursday and I waited until Monday to file for divorce.

Lillian Denton and her mother came into the hat store on the second or third day of my employment. I remembered her from some small rodeos the year before, and she was so excited about seeing me again that they invited me to have dinner with them that evening. Lillian was a rodeo "groupie" although I am not sure they had such a descriptive title in the 1940's and to her, the very thought of taking a professional bronc-rider out to dinner was so exciting to her that I could not resist accepting their offer.

She wanted to hear all about California and any rodeos where I had performed since the last time I was in Texas. I told her about my little dog, PeeWee, and said I had been thinking about having him shipped to me but with my particular lifestyle, I thought it was best to leave him where he was. Maybe later on I could send for him.

When I mentioned that I was staying in Beaumont only long enough to get a divorce, she was shocked that anyone would want to get out of a marriage to a cowboy.

When they realized I was staying in a local hotel, her mother insisted I move in with them for the present. I agreed, but with the understanding that I pay them something for my room and board.

I had been thinking about PeeWee again, and I made a brief call to Mrs. Moody to discuss sending him to me as soon as I could afford to pay shipping costs. That was when I learned my little pal had died of distemper.

What next?

I already had two weeks of the twenty-one-day waiting period behind me the next time I saw Rufus. My lawyer said he had seemed surprised when the papers were presented to him for his signature but considering his short-term memory in the past, I knew it was quite possible he thought I would not go through with the divorce.

The day I did talk to Rufus, I was just returning to work after my lunch hour. I parked on Pearl Street, near the hat shop, and started to get out of the car, when he stepped up to the window on my side. For a second it startled me, because I remembered some of the threats he had made in the past whenever I said I was leaving him.

I was surprised at his nonchalant tone of voice when he spoke.

"Hi, girl!" he said. "Wha'cha know?"

"Not much." I closed the door. "And you?"

The muscles at the corner of his mouth twitched.

"About the same." He seemed to be shuffling his feet around. He looked away for a minute, and finally mumbled, "There's a great little show over at Port Arthur next week. Wanna go?"

For the first time, he looked straight at me. I hated to see the sadness in his eyes, especially since I felt responsible.

I shook my head. "No."

"Even if I promise. . ." he added almost inaudibly.

I could not answer for a second or two. I studied the cars approaching from the opposite direction as though analyzing every inch of every car was the only reason I had been placed on this planet.

I shook my head no, but I replied, "We'll see."

"Okay, girl." He put his hand on my arm, and squeezed so hard it hurt. Then he added softly, "See you 'round. Hear?" He walked away.

"You bet," I tried to swallow the lump in my throat. "See you around."

We both knew we were lying.

Except for a rodeo in Cleveland, Ohio, many months later, that was the last time I ever saw Rufus. For him at nineteen, and me at twenty-one, a bad dream had ended and it had taken part of our youth with it.

The day I received the final decree for my divorce, the Buick was loaded and ready to go when I came out of the Jefferson County

Courthouse. Lillian had permission from her mother to go to a couple of rodeos with me before I left for Montana, so when I walked toward the car, she already had the motor running and our luggage in the trunk. With the Buick radiator ornament pointed northwest, I climbed in and nodded and we drove away.

We did not talk very much on our way to Liberty, Texas, about forty miles from Beaumont. I kept expecting a feeling of elation that I assumed would accompany a divorce, but when I felt nothing except an ache in my chest and a deep sense of failure, I stopped trying to hold my head so high and sagged against the car door and cried quietly.

Liberty was the nearest rodeo, and besides, that was as far as my bankroll would take us. My job at the hat store did not provide much of a bankroll. I knew Lillian would be an added expense for me, but until I was used to the idea of traveling alone again, I decided her companionship was worth what little extra she might cost.

Lillian was a cute little 17-year-old blonde with big brown eyes, a pixie face, and a tiny mouth that curled up at the corners when she smiled. She was completely smitten with rodeo people. Other than her desire to rub elbows with each and every person who had anything to do with our profession, there was no reason whatsoever for her to hang around the arenas or rodeo headquarters, but she had a talent for "name dropping" that was unbelievable. Lillian called all of the top contestants by their first names and she could quote statistics about who did what in half of the rodeos around the country. The fact that she had never competed in any rodeos, and had actually only attended a few, in no way hindered her enthusiasm. By eavesdropping on cowboys' conversations she had learned enough information to recite dates, riders, livestock, and arena conditions that even the contestants themselves had forgotten. Even though I had been around most of the top rodeo performers at one time or another, it would never occur to me to refer to them by their first names if I happened to be discussing them with someone else.

Not so with Lillian.

"Are Cobe and Gene putting on the Garden show this year?" she would ask blandly. "They've sure got good bucking bulls. Y'all should've seen them at New York last year."

This from a gal who had yet to step foot out of the state of Texas.

Even when someone replied dryly, "I did see them," it never fazed her. She just grinned happily and said, "Weren't they just great?"

This love of rodeo was what prompted Lillian to go with me in the first place, but she certainly earned her own way before we got out of Texas.

At Liberty, Fred Alvord staked me to one of his horses and I placed first on Saturday and second on Sunday in the barrel-race. After giving Alvord his share, the balance of the prize money added very little to the bankroll I needed for the long drive to Montana. I planned to take Lillian back to Beaumont and start working my way north.

We checked out of our hotel and I was going to have the gas tank filled when a highway patrolman walked over to my side of the car and arrested me for not having current license plates on the Buick. He made me leave the car right there next to the service station, and he took both Lillian and me to appear before a local justice of the peace. I insisted Lillian was in no way responsible for the Buick and I simply wanted to pay my fine and be on my way.

I had almost $15 in my pocket. The fine was $12.50. When I asked them how much a license plate would cost he said $13.75.

The solution seemed obvious. Instead of the fine, why not let me just pay for the license and be on my way? The law does not work that way.

Lillian and I walked back to where the car was parked. At first, the same officer refused to let us retrieve our luggage until I explained that we would need our clothes if we were going to earn enough money for a new license, so he reluctantly allowed us to retrieve our things and then he put my keys back in his pocket.

All of the rodeo people had moved on, so there was no-one in town that we might borrow from. During my marriage, and especially during the divorce, I refused to call or wire back to Montana for cash. I needed to solve this problem alone.

At least that was the way I felt until Lillian grabbed my arm as we walked back to our hotel.

"I've done waitress work a few times," she began,"and I'll bet it wouldn't take too long to get enough for your license if I could just get a job."

"You don't need to do that," I argued, but did not protest too much. "That car's not your responsibility."

"It would be," she grinned, "if Mom says I can go to Montana with you!"

"I'll have to think about it." I grinned right back at her. "For now, we'd better find us a couple of jobs. Okay?"

Across the street from where the Buick was parked, there was a bus stop. We ate one or two meals there during the rodeo and had joked about the WAITRESS WANTED sign in the window, saying we might be needing that job before the show was over. We thought we were joking!

Anyway, we were now on our way to that same bus stop to see if they were still hiring. We would be able to keep an eye on the Buick from there, so no-one could strip it.

We pooled our money and with Lillian's 37 cents we had the huge bankroll of $2.87 so I told her, "We don't want these people to know how broke we really are, so we'll have to split a hamburger. I'll order it, with my glass of milk, and you just order your drink. Understand?"

"Why?"

"They'll make the terms of the job that much tougher if they know we're desperate."

"Okay. I'll remember," she promised. "I don't order food. Just a drink. Right?"

I nodded, and we went in. We climbed up on the stools at the counter, and decided to eat before we talked job to anyone. A waitress approached and I held my breath until Lillian said, "Just a small Pepsi for me."

I tried to sound casual, as though I could pay for anything I wanted on the menu. "I guess I'll have a plain hamburger, and a glass of milk."

I sighed with relief when the waitress turned toward the kitchen, but I relaxed too soon. Just as she put her hand on the swinging door at the rear of the room, Lillian called to her (the full length of the counter), "Hey, there! Put onions on half of that hamburger, okay?"

I started looking for a hole to crawl into until I glanced at Lillian. When I saw the wide-eyed innocence and knew she had no idea she had given away our big secret, I almost fell off of the stool, laughing.

While each of us polished off our half-hamburger, a man that I assumed was the boss, walked past. I asked if they still needed waitresses.

He was a dark man, and his black hair lay in sweaty ringlets on the rolls of fat at the back of his neck. A combination of sour-disposition and folds of flabby skin drew the corners of his mouth down into the shape of a horseshoe. As soon as he spoke, I had a feeling things were going to be tough, whether he knew we were broke or not.

"Yah!" he barked. "I neet two girlz. Twelf hour shiffs. One meal a day an' plaze to sleep. One buck a day wages."

"One dollar?" I gasped. "For twelve hours?"

"So you gotts a place to sleep, und one meal a day. Take hit or leef hit." He started to walk away.

Lillian and I looked at each other, then glanced out the window at the Buick, baking in the sun all by itself.

"We'll take it," we both spoke at once.

The boss did not look back, but he heard us, because our waitress came over in a minute and said she'd show us where to sleep. She led us to a tiny cabin in the back yard. It was skirted by four more shacks of the same vintage. Early South Africa. When she pushed the door open, I noticed the same vegetable-soup and disinfectant smell as in the café, and the heat that slapped us in the face was like the blast you feel when you are too close to a branding-fire. There was one narrow cot along the wall of the curtainless, rugless shed. A shower stall in the corner (without the stall), was just a sunken drain in the floor beneath a faucet high enough on the wall that you could squirm under it if you were sufficiently agile. Luckily, the faucet put out about sixty drops a minute, or the room would have flooded each time someone bathed.

"Where's the other bed?" I asked the waitress. "In another cabin?"

"Nope," she replied in a bored, exhausted tone, "two to a bed. One of ya works midnight to noon, the other noon to midnight. I ain't crawled into a cool bed for damned near six months now."

She started to leave, then added, "Each of you gets one uniform. Wash it yourself." She wrinkled her face into an exaggerated wink, and added, "If the boss could figger a way, he'd have us strippin' off our uniform on the way out'a here, and handin' it to our room-mate, so's she could get dressed on her way to work. Save money on uniforms that way. Hope to Christ he don't think of it."

She pulled the door closed behind her.

"Wow-eee" Lillian said, as she looked around the room. "Don't this beat all?"

I just nodded. I was too disgusted to reply.

The waitress was not exaggerating about the boss. He not only stood his ground about the one meal per day, but he kept such close tabs, no one even had an extra slice of bread without paying for it.

Part of my first twelve off-duty hours was spent soaking my feet in a bucket of water. I was trying to decrease the swelling so I could get my only pair of dress shoes on again for my next shift. My ankles and feet were so puffy and distorted, they looked like red rubber gloves inflated into balloons. Those twelve hour shifts on cement floors, were something a bronc-rider's feet should never be forced to experience.

It was fortunate we had the license money by the end of a week, because both of us were fired on our seventh shift. Just before noon on that day, I was hobbling around, praying for the next few minutes to pass so I could get off of my feet. I had waited on three men and a soldier who were obviously not bus passengers. The men appeared to be businessmen, and from their conversations, I gathered the soldier was a hitch-hiker. I gave them extra attention, hoping they might leave a tip, which was unheard of with our regular customers. About five minutes to twelve I looked over, and from where I stood behind the counter I could see one of the men place a half-dollar beside his plate. I would have jumped over the counter right then had it not been for my swollen feet and my natural inability to jump, but instead, I hurried as fast as I could waddle around the end of the counter and pushed through the crowded tables for my tip. Fifty cents! Six hours in this sweat-factory.

The men were already on their way out, and just as I reached the table, the soldier ducked back, grabbed the half dollar, and stuck it in his pocket.

That was when I threw a catsup bottle at him. It was kind of a glancing blow and not too serious except for the fact that he got away with my tip. And also, of course, when the boss saw him run through the door with catsup on his face and uniform, I was fired on the spot.

"Well," Lillian consoled me, when we crossed paths at the cabin door, "at least I can work a couple of more days, and we'll have enough to buy one good meal someplace along the line."

Famous last words. At midnight that night, I had just put some cool water in my foot-bucket when I heard a loud thump, some foreign phrases in a tone of voice indicating they had to be cuss words, then silence. I jumped, upsetting the bucket, and sloshed toward the door. When I jerked it open, the light from our room showed Lillian and the boss, both scrambling around on their hands and knees, picking up objects scattered all over the ground.

In a minute, the boss looked at Lillian while they both tugged on something that resembled a coffee-cake, and shouted, "You—you teef! You're tru work here! You hearrrr me? You boff fired."

"Y'all made your point," Lillian drawled. "We got enough for our license, anyhow."

She scrambled to her feet and came toward me.

When Lillian entered our room, I expected her to show some concern over both of us being fired but instead, she was giggling almost hysterically.

"What happened?" I asked, as soon as I could get her to settle down.

I realized she looked a bit plump and saw the reason when she walked over to the cot and started dragging food out from under the blouse of her uniform. Wrapped half-sandwiches, a donut, cheese, and even the coffee-cake. She had actually wrestled it away from the boss.

"I was gettin' powerful hongry," she grinned in an exaggerated Texas drawl. "I'd have made it with the rest of the loot, too, if that nasty old man hadn't charged through the kitchen door just as I was charging out! Y'all should-a seen the loot I had before he made off with half of it."

In between laughs, we hurriedly ate as much of the evidence as we could in case the boss came back. He didn't, so we finished eating, and picked up our day's pay. It was customary to collect at the end of each shift in case he'd think of a new deduction before the next day. If we waited any longer he would deduct for Lillian's "haul."

We had never really unpacked because we either wore our one assigned uniform or we slept, so now we grabbed our two small suitcases, walked across the street, and slept in the Buick until dawn. The cop did not know about my spare key!

The next morning, as soon as I had a receipt to prove my license fee had been paid, we were allowed to go on our way. We barely made it to the next rodeo in time after making a quick stopover in Beaumont to get permission for Lillian to travel to Montana.

At the first show I was not only hired to ride broncs but after a couple of phone calls, managed to get a job at another rodeo forty miles away. One of the towns had matinee performances only and at the other one the shows were at night. By driving back and forth, I managed to ride two broncs a day on Saturday and Sunday!

The last night of the rodeo, with Lillian cheering me on, I won $18 shooting pool, so we were home free. Lillian phoned her mother to let her know we were on our way to Montana, and I added a few words to tell her not to worry, and that we would keep in touch.

While I was still standing by the pay phone at Harry's Billiards, I made one last call to Rufus' mother. I apologized for not calling sooner and told her I was sorry the way things turned out, but it was all for the best. She told me she understood, and we promised to keep in touch. We did, in fact, exchange Christmas letters for the next ten or twelve years and then they stopped. I assumed she had passed away.

My folks had no idea I was on my way home. We hit right in the middle of a rain storm. The car got bogged down at a creek crossing about two miles from the ranch, and Lillian and I straggled in at daylight, exhausted and covered with mud.

Clint greeted me at the front porch with a calm, "What the hell'd you two do, walk all the way from Texas?" Mister Sympathy himself.

"Nope," I sighed. "Just the last hundred miles."

Lillian and I stayed at the ranch for several months. I was beginning to outgrow a little of the numbness I felt after my divorce, and my long hours of driving a team on a buckrake left me too tired to mourn over lost causes. I rode broncs in a couple of shows around Central Montana, besides announcing some rodeos and county fairs on weekends, but when haying was nearly over and the hectic pace began to slow down, I got squirmy again.

One day when my Buick was in the garage for repairs, Lillian and I rode to Billings with a friend of my parents. We each took a small suitcase and planned to spend a few days before returning to the ranch. While there, Lillian latched onto a stray cowboy for a few minutes of rodeo talk and that was how we heard about a rodeo in Forsyth, Montana, 100 miles east of Billings. Result: an eastbound bus ride instead of the north-bound to Lewistown.

A man named Sid Vollin was putting on the show in Forsyth. He hired Bobbie Brooks and me to ride saddle-broncs during the three-day rodeo. Bobbie was used to riding big old rank wild-horses out on the range, and she was one of the few professional women bronc-riders who did not hobble her stirrups. Because she had no hobbles for me to borrow, we had to do some fast scrounging to duplicate the gear I had left behind.

Duffy Crabtree was there, so he helped with the hurry-up job of obtaining new hobbles and small stirrups and got one of his friends to braid some new reins for me.

On the first day, I drew a miserable black and white pinto that bucked a few jumps out of the chutes, reared so high in the air that he fell over backwards with me still in the saddle. I had often worried about what would happen in such a case, because I might not be able to think or act fast enough to get out of the way. From what I was told later, as soon as the horse toppled the rest of the way over backwards after being poised in the air for a split-second, I kicked my feet out of the stirrups, put the heel of my right hand against the saddlehorn, and shoved myself away from the horse just as we toppled backwards and crashed against the ground together. I fell clear, but I hit so hard on my left shoulder, my collarbone was cracked and my head whipped against the ground, knocking me goofy. In the 1940's, there was no such thing as protective helmets, padded vests or any of the equipment that finally surfaced in later years and our bodies suffered because of this.

According to Lillian, to all outward appearances, I was conscious and unhurt. She said I got to my feet, brushed myself off, and walked away. One problem. The next thing I was aware of, was me sitting on the running-board of someone's pickup truck, listening to the voices of the cowboys inside.

"How's it going for you, drawin' rodeo pictures on café windows?" one of them asked.

"Fine. Just fine," another replied. "I get to a town ten days ahead of the show, and make fifty or sixty bucks just paintin' pitchers! But I ran into a funny deal here."

"Yeah?"

"Yeah. When Vollin sent me here a couple'a weeks ago, he said I was supposed to just hang out and look over the lay of the land."

"So what happened?"

"Hell, man, I couldn't even find out who she was!"

Lillian and Duffy Crabtree started laughing, and that was the first I realized they were sitting on the running-board next to me.

"Say, Duff," I said, nudging him with my elbow. "When will my bronc be in the chute? It must be almost time."

I thought Duffy looked at me kind of funny, and when I turned to Lillian, she wore the same puzzled expression.

"Better take her back up town," Duffy told Lillian, as though I were a small child. "I'll check with you as soon as I get through roping."

"Now hold on just one damned minute!" I interrupted, "I'm not going any place till I ride my bronc."

It must have been quite an ordeal for those two, trying to convince me I had already ridden, but it was also difficult for me to absorb that information. I finally realized I did not even know what town we were in, or how we got there.

Lillian spent all that day recalling the past forty-eight hours for me, and gradually some of it came back. Not all of it, though. To this day, I do not remember one single minute of the time period starting when we left Billings and ending when we were seated on that running-board.

The doctor said there was not really any way to bandage the injured area and I just needed to keep my arm strapped down for a week or so to give it a chance to heal. He put great patches of adhesive tape across my back and some across my chest. None of the bandages lessened the pain and as long as I did not try to raise my left arm, I could do anything I wanted.

I had Lillian remove the tape on my back but the part that remained across my chest kept my left arm in place where it would not cause further damage.

I insisted on going out to the rodeo grounds because my pain had lessened somewhat, and I thought I should ride that afternoon. I was so adamant, she and Duffy drove me to the arena rather than argue with me.

As soon as I checked one of the programs, I saw that I was scheduled to ride the pinto again. I walked over to stare at the horses that would be used for the next go-round. I could swear the pinto winked at me!

I leaned against the fence, suddenly feeling dizzy.

Sid Vollin came over.

"You ain't thinking about riding today, are you?".

I tried to sound as normal as possible. "Not today, Sid. But tomorrow for sure."

I was glad when Lillian and Duffy arrived right then to lead me to his car. My mind was doing crazy things.

After acquiring some pain pills, I managed to get twelve hours of good sound healing sleep. The next afternoon, we road out to the rodeo grounds with Duffy and I found it hard to believe that they still had me scheduled to ride the pinto. There he was in the chute, waiting for me. The only reason I felt I could ride in spite of my injury, was because my left arm remained tight against my body when I held the reins in my left hand.

A bronc rider that I did not recognize suggested leaving the cinch a little looser that day. He said my bronc would be less apt to go over backwards so we took his advice. It turned out that the cowboy was correct on that score, but the pinto had a change of plans and bucked straight across the arena where he tried to crawl over the top of a six-foot fence!

With both of the bronc's front feet on top of the fence, I had a few seconds to jump off to the side before he crashed backwards right beside me. At some point in the confusion, a weak spot in the bronc's halter gave way, and when I stepped off and walked toward the chutes, I discovered I still had the reins in my hand and I was dragging the halter along behind me.

Sid Vollin raced over to me on his horse.

"You okay, Jane? You all right?" he asked nervously.

"Of course!" I grinned. I held the reins and halter where he could see them. "Notice how I did this? I'm working on an act for next year when I'll unsaddle my own bronc in the arena, too."

He just shook his head. "It wouldn't surprise me one bit," he chuckled. "Not one little bit."

After Forsyth, Lillian returned to the ranch and I went on to Pine Bluffs, Wyoming. I meant to go back for her and the Buick in a week or so, but I never made it. She surely realized I was not coming back to the ranch when I called the Montana Tavern and left word for her to ship me a suitcase full of clothes in care of the rodeo headquarters in Elsie, Nebraska. That would be my next stop.

I learned later that Lillian was a lot of company for Mother and it was also a great experience for her to spend some time on a real cattle ranch. She stayed there for several more months, and when she finally decided to go home, Clint paid her bus fare back to Texas.

Although we corresponded for years, I never actually saw Lillian again. Like my friendship with Rufus' mother, I regretted that it continued only by mail.

I joined four cowboys who were headed for Pine Bluffs, Wyoming, in a car belonging to Hugh Ridley, a man with two amazing talents over and above his rodeoing abilities. He was able to go indefinitely without sleep, and he could tell jokes day in and day out without ever repeating a single one! Hugh allowed no one to drive his car, so the rest of us slept most of the time during the entire trip. I can remember waking up when we stopped for coffee, and Hugh would cut off a joke right in the middle of a sentence. On returning to the car a few minutes later, he settled himself behind the wheel and continued the joke without missing a single word.

I rode saddle-broncs at Pine Bluffs, then we went on to Elsie, Nebraska, with most of the same group.

This time Bill Linderman was with us. He and I had not met several years earlier when I rode two steers and a buffalo in his hometown of Red Lodge, Montana, but we became good friends through the years and I followed his career when he became the first man in professional rodeo history to win three world championships in one season. He held six world titles that included the "all around cowboy" for bareback bronc-riding, saddle-bronc-riding and steer wrestling and was the president of RCA from 1951 until he refused to be nominated again in 1958.

The rodeo in Elsie rained out for the first five days. By then, most of us were running out of money and Ridley suggested everyone pool their remaining cash and buy the giant one-gallon bottle of Jim Beam whiskey that was on display at the liquor store. The cowboys formed a line and walked past Ridley, handing him their cash. Everything went smoothly until one bull-rider held back a couple of quarters, and when he started to walk away, they rattled in his pocket. Ridley calmly picked the boy up by his boot-heels, shook him, head down, until the fifty-cents fell to the floor. He set the boy back on his feet and went on with the collection. Everyone who donated to the whiskey fund, and a few who had been unable to, brought their own little flasks to Ridley's room whenever they needed a refill from the community jug. We were all literally "on the Beam" the rest of the week.

I rode two broncs when we finally managed to have a rodeo. My suitcase had arrived and I was glad to have extra clothes for a change. With one day remaining, I wandered alone around the carnival area while I was trying to decide where I would go when this show ended, and I heard a "barker" from one of the concessions shouting about how easy it was to win $5 cash with three shots from a 22-rifle.

Being a pretty fair shot at small game on the ranch, I could not resist the temptation of taking a shot (literally) at that much cash.

The target was on a small track and after the barker showed it to you, up close, he then slid it away for what I would estimate was a distance of about ten or twelve feet. There were various small circles on the cardboard and if you could totally eliminate any one of them with just three shots, you won the five dollar prize. What I did realize was that no matter how well the tiny circle had been eliminated, he could always rub the back of the target just enough to force a tiny section of black to reappear when viewed from the front.

I took my three shots, and it seemed to me that I had, in fact, wiped out the little circle I aimed for. When the barker pulled the cardboard forward to where I was standing, he tried very hard to find a tiny section of the target that was still visible. Finally he located a tiny speck. Surprise!

"Sorry, girl. You almost did it, but not quite."

Just then, an arm reached past my shoulder and a hand grabbed the barker by the front of his jacket, lifting him straight up in the air.

I looked around, and it was Bill Linderman! I never asked him how he happened to arrive at just the right time, but the little man at the rifle concession certainly did not hesitate to give me a nice new five-dollar bill.

I offered to buy a drink to thank Bill for his help, but instead we wandered over to a billiard parlor across the street from the carnival. It was one that I had noticed during our "rainout" but stayed away from because of everyone's lack of funds. This time, I mentioned that I would like to play a couple of games and although Bill said he was not a pool player, he would stay around and watch.

They had a snooker table, the first one I had ever seen, and I just observed for a while before deciding to try that strange game on a 6x12-foot table where they played with a whole bunch of little red balls and six numbered balls. I did better than I expected and was a bit too cocky when it was hinted that I might want to place a small bet on a game against any one of their local players.

Clint would have warned me, but he was nowhere around. I am convinced I would not have been so gullible if my opponent had not been a wizened old man who practically had to be helped over to the table when it was his turn to shoot. They explained to me that it was necessary to make a red ball before you could shoot the next numbered ball to add that it to your score. An additional rule was that you could re-spot the six ball after you knocked it into one of the holes, and then shoot at it again without being required to make a red one first. I saw no reason to be concerned about that particular rule, so I bravely placed my new five-dollar bill on the table and the game began.

I made one red ball, then a number-three, which gave me the first score. Then I missed my next shot.

My opponent made a red ball, then a six. Once it was spotted on the table, he made the six again. He made the six again. He made the six again.

As far as I know, he was still shooting that damned six ball when we drove out of town the next day, except he was probably tired by that time and already spending my $5 bill.

I went to Cleveland, Ohio, from Nebraska while Ridley, Bill and the others all went in different directions. Autry was producing the rodeo in Cleveland, so I had no problem getting a job, even though I had not contacted him ahead of time.

Rufus was competing there, and he nodded at me once when I finished my ride, but we never spoke. From there, I caught a ride to Elk City, Oklahoma. I had been there the previous year but it was a good thing I arrived a few days early because it took every minute of that extra time to convince the Beutler brothers to give me a job. Along with many of the other rodeo promoters, they were shying away from women's bronc riding most of the time. It was partly due to the Turtle regulation requiring a minimum $20 per ride for our exhibition, and there was always a chance we might be injured.

That particular annual rodeo had a reputation for being one long party from start to finish. As was generally the case, the cowboys began celebrating as soon as they hit town but for a change, I did not join in. I was gradually becoming aware that it is not possible to simply get a divorce and return to your original single status. Most of the rodeo people treated me fairly well, but it seemed like a few of them felt that since I had been married for awhile, I must be really hurting without a man. One of them actually said that to my face.

The snide little remarks, and uncalled-for passes really bothered me. I spent more and more time alone and possibly my sobriety and self-imposed seclusion influenced the Beutlers in their decision to hire me. Whatever the reason, they were very kind, and I even spent a few days at their two homes during the week.

They were moving some cattle to a different pasture one day while I was there and I asked if I could go along. I sensed their reluctance but I mentioned that I was raised on a cattle ranch so they allowed me to tag along. I handled the stock exactly as I would at home, everything low key, with no quick moves that might startle the cows or their calves except when one single quick move to head something off would actually prevent a problem rather than cause one.

During dinner that evening while they were discussing that day's work, Lynn Beutler said, "You can tell Jane's a cowhand, at heart. She knows the right way to move a herd."

I tried to pretend I was not flattered by the remark but I am sure it was obvious.

It was only two or three days until the rodeo would begin. Lynn Beutler assured me they had two horses at the ranch that had been used for women's bronc-riding before. He said both of them were showy but not dangerous in the chute or in the arena. Problem solved.

Wrong! The rodeo stock, including the final selection of my broncs, was in the hands of a square-jawed, dark-faced bronc-rider named Eddie Curtis, who helped with Beutler bucking stock at various rodeos. He was noted for his attitude about women's bronc riding and it was no secret that he considered the event to be a damned nuisance that did not belong in professional rodeos.

For whatever reason, he did not bother to bring the two specified broncs from the ranch. Instead, he took it upon himself to select Hooper-Dooper and CBC out of the men's string for me to ride. I seldom saw anything even remotely resembling a smile on Eddie's face, but the day he informed me which horses I was to ride, he appeared almost happy.

I was fortunate to acquire the help and expert advice from Fritz Truan and Larry Finley, two great bronc-riders. Fritz won the All Around Cowboy chamionship in 1940 and I was flattered when these two men took the time to get me out on my bronc each day. They both knew I was overmatched, and I think it may have bothered them a little that Eddie chose those two broncs for me to ride, when it would have been just as easy to bring the selected ones from the ranch.

I made the whistle on Hooper-Dooper the first day. Just barely. When the pickup man took me off and hauled me back to the chutes, I smiled at Eddie (gloated, may be a better choice of words) as we rode past him.

The next day, everyone was so drunk that I worried whether they would be able to help with my bronc at all, but Fritz and Larry were right there, ready to saddle CBC and set me down on him. I would have liked to ask Fritz if he thought my particular clothing that day would bring me luck because it was common knowledge that he was almost a fanatic in the belief that certain items of his own clothes were good luck when he rode broncs, and he never varied from that belief. I was afraid to bring up the subject because all I knew about this particular quirk of his was that some of the cowboys joked about his superstitions, but only behind his back. I did not want to take a chance that he might be offended.

Anyway, as he belted me down on my bronc, Fritz said, seriously, "Jane, you been riding too far forward in the saddle. You do that on this sonofabitch, he'll murder you."

"He will?" My voice was barely a squeak.

"Yup. When the gate opens," he went on, "just try to hit him on the ass with the back of your head. Then, just maybe, you'll be back far enough."

I nodded for the gate.

When it swung open, Fritz yelled, "Fall back!" and that's what I tried to do.

CBC lunged out of the chute, kicked high, and tucked his head between his front legs that first jump. I had made such an effort to "fall back," he took all the slack out of my reins and snatched me forward again, just in time to slam my face against the top of his head as he reared and lunged the second time. I must have hit a buckle on the top of his halter, because something cut a deep gash in my lower lip. Blood also spurted from my nose, but that smack in the face was all I needed to make me rear back again, and finish my ride.

Eddie, himself, swung me off of CBC and started to set me on the ground out in the middle of the arena so I would have to walk back to the chutes, but I grabbed ahold of him and stayed there, right behind his saddle, forcing him to give me a ride whether he wanted to or not.

I stepped off of Eddie's horse right beside Fritz and Larry. Just as Eddie rode away, he almost grinned. "Didn't think you could do it."

"Damned good ride," Fritz was smiling. "You'll sure be ready for New York this year."

"Didja see Ed's face?" Larry asked. "I guess you proved something, huh?"

I nodded. "Besides that, I bled all over him. That's why I made him give me a ride back here."

Both of the Beutlers rode over and asked if I was all right. Lynn thought I should see a doctor about the gash in my lip, but I wiped away most of the blood with someone's handkerchief, and when the bleeding appeared to have stopped, I took a swig of the whiskey-and-coke Fritz handed me. I puffed out my lip and asked if any whiskey leaked out.

"Nope, just blood," Lynn answered.

"Then it's not cut all the way through! No doctor required."

Jake Beutler patted me on the shoulder and said, "I guess you'll live. But you better get washed up. It's bad publicity when our contestants are covered with blood!"

By the next day, my face looked terrible. Both eyes were black, my nose was swollen and spread all over my face, and my mouth was so sore I could hardly talk. That was how I looked when I reached Kansas City, so it was no wonder the rodeo promoter said, "Jane, if you and Rufus are battling again, I can't use you for this show. There's no place in our rodeo for that sort of thing."

Luckily, I had witnesses from the Elk City show who vouched for the legality of my wounds, and I was hired to ride four broncs sometime during the seven-day show.

When I left the rodeo office, I checked in at the one-story Stockyards Hotel where many of the rodeo people stayed. As evidenced by the name of the hotel, there were still lingering odors from the location of the hotel's namesake at the time this arena was built.

The rooms were small and stuffy, but convenient to the stadium. I learned I was not to ride during the first three days so I stayed in my room most of the time, experimenting with various new Max Factor products that covered most of the remaining discoloration. I had one or two drinks in the hotel bar and for variety I caught a cab to the Wyoming Bar to see if there might be a familiar face somewhere in the crowd. When my plan failed, I went back to my hotel in the same taxi and returned to my room.

I think it is safe to say that was one of the wildest few days I ever experienced.

Not the rodeo. The Stockyards Hotel.`

About thirty first-story rooms, on level with mine, had windows overlooking a row of glass panes set in steel and cement that formed a skylight over the hotel lobby. When I first raised my window to allow some fresh air into the sweltering room, I peeked out and saw that the fifteen along my side were also open, as were the fifteen facing us across the "glass-bottomed-patio." Every word uttered in any of the rooms echoed in and out of the other twenty-nine, gaining momentum with each bounce. Most of the rooms were empty except when their occupants were sleeping but a man-and-wife battle next door kept me entertained for the first forty-eight hours. Even that became more annoying than amusing.

One of the highlights in their conversation was when the man said, gloatingly, "These gals around here shore do like cowboys. All I did was walk into that bar next door, and about five of them sweet young things charged me!"

The wife's dry reply of, "How much?" caused quite a commotion. Then came sounds of flying objects.

Due to the lack of ventilation, and the fact that I prayed for the fight-noises to sail on through my room instead of bouncing off of the walls, I left my door slightly ajar. There were no keys for the rooms anyway, so there was no reason to keep it closed.

On the third night, I had just crawled into bed and turned off my light, when I heard the sound of someone running down the hall. I automatically pulled the sheet over myself, just as my door was slammed open. A silhouette wearing a cowboy hat rushed past my bed, climbed through the window, and could be heard tiptoeing along the cement edge of the skylights. I sat up, clutching the sheet even tighter, when a second person dashed along the same route. In the confusion I had not noticed if the second speedster wore a hat or not, so I switched on the bed light just in time to see a cowboy boot disappear over the window sill.

More sounds approaching. I hopped out of bed, grabbed my Levis and shirt, and jumped back under the covers where I struggled to get dressed. There was no time to close the hall door. While I was squirming into my clothes, I missed seeing the third person enter my room until he was almost all the way through the window. By that time I was able to get a "gate count" and saw one uniformed policeman crawling through with a second one awaiting his turn. I wondered if our glass patio could handle that much traffic.

"Just what the hell's going on?" I demanded. "This place is worse than Grand Central Station."

The policeman on standby, awaiting his turn at the window took the time to reply, "Two cowboys ran out without paying their checks at the café downstairs. But we'll get 'em."

Then he was gone.

"I'm sure you will." I did not mention that the two culprits had just that minute slipped past my door, running down the hall, giggling like naughty children! I recognized them from the clothing they wore as they raced through my room, even though I never saw their faces.

I learned later that the cowboys, Pat Parker and my friend Larry Finley, had pulled the whole thing as a prank, and had already paid the café check by the time the frustrated policemen went back downstairs.

As soon as the excitement died down, I wearily removed my Levis and climbed back into bed. Just then, outside my window, I heard sounds of someone being sick—a crash of broken glass—and a muffled, "Help!"

I jumped out of bed, again, and stumbled across to lean out of my window. On my right was what appeared to be the backside of Slugger Sloan. I assumed it was Slugger because he had the room next to mine on the other side from the quarreling couple. Positive identification was impossible since the party who had been leaning out of his window had lost his balance and fallen partway through the skylight, head first.

While I scrambled into my clothes again, I tried to decide whether to rush into the next room and try to pull him back, or should I go for help? I decided to hurry downstairs and notify the desk clerk about the accident, in case they needed more than one person for the rescue.

I reached the lobby, still buttoning my shirt. I knew immediately there was no need to notify anyone.

They already knew.

There was Slugger's red head jutting out of the ceiling like a furry, carrot-colored chandelier, and he was still throwing up! The hotel manager and the night clerk kept running in circles, wondering if they should save Slugger first or clean up the mess, but apparently someone from upstairs took care of the former problem, because the spewing chandelier gradually disappeared upward, out of sight. I was never quite sure why Slugger's throat was not cut when he fell through the glass. Or, for that matter, why the manager of the hotel did not cut it for him later.

I was still barefooted and my shirt-tail was hanging out, but my sleep project had been defeated completely, so I made a square-knot out of the front shirt-tails and went into the Cowboy Bar.

As I crawled onto a stool, a slim cowboy with a pointed chin, friendly smile, and laughing eyes stepped over to me and said, "Where you been, little cow-mama? You look like you had a rough night."

My face was still not completely healed, my hair not combed, I was barefooted and clad only in Levis and shirt. He was putting it mildly.

"Can I buy you a drink?" he asked, grinning.

I smiled as much as my sore lip would allow, and said, "You sure can."

At that moment, I doubt if he had any more idea than I did, that he was to be my next husband!

# Chapter Twenty

While the cowboy beside me ordered our drinks, I examined his clean-cut profile and deliberately-casual attire. I was convinced he knew exactly how far back to flip his expensive Stetson so it would not fall off but would still allow a few locks of brown wavy hair to escape. Likewise, the slightly askew bright neckerchief and the pantlegs half-in and half-out of elaborate yellow boots, seemed a bit too staged to be accidental. The overall picture was a pleasing one, though, and even the dour bartender responded to this cowboy's contagious grin with a twitch-of-the-lip that was not quite a smile but closer to it than anything he had demonstrated so far.

The bar was so crowded we still had to wait several minutes for our drinks in spite of the slight improvement in the bartenders' attitude.

"I'm Jack Couch," the cowboy announced with only a trace of a drawl. "And you?"

"Jane Burnett."

Although everyone else in the place was either too drunk or too busy to notice my disheveled appearance, I felt I should offer some sort of explanation to my new acquaintance.

"I don't always look like this. In fact, I've even been known to wear shoes—and on special occasions, I comb my hair."

"Little cow-mama," he interrupted, laughing. "You suit me just fine the way you are."

When he talked, I tried to determine the color of his eyes. One second they appeared to be grey. Then green. Then hazel. Getting a clear view of eyes that darted excitedly from place to place sharing the fun of strangers as well as friends, was like capturing a firefly between your thumb and forefinger.

“Wanna come over to our booth?” he asked.

I glanced down at my clothes and made a helpless, sweeping gesture from collar to waist with my fingertips, as though I could brush away the knotted shirt-tail, and magically don a whole new wardrobe.

Jack took me by the arm without waiting for an answer, and led me through the crowd. He walked so jauntily, springing up on his toes with each step, that I found myself absorbing some of his exuberance.

“I feel like having fun for a change,” I said, with more enthusiasm than I actually felt, “so lead on, Couch.”

Just saying the name, I realized it was tailor-made for punsters, but at that moment I could only wonder how come such a restful-sounding tag was hanging on such an animated product.

We reached the booth then. I noticed the minute Jack introduced me and we sat down, the four young cowboys and their tittering girl-friends gulped the last of the whiskey they had been nursing along, and they waited for Jack to order more. With a grin of sheer pleasure, he paid for that round of drinks and two more that were inhaled as though a return of prohibition might be threatening to go into effect at midnight. An older cowboy and I were the only ones to refuse the last two drinks. Actually, it was none of my business how Jack spent his money, since he seemed to have plenty of it and enjoyed throwing it away on those whiskey-leeches, but I could not keep the annoyance out of my voice when I interrupted the fourth order.

“I’ll pay for this one myself,” I said, not too congenially. I looked from one to the other of the flushed, eager faces around the table. “Don’t you guys think three re-rides on the same bronc is carrying things a little too far? You could ride a good horse to death, you know.”

If I expected to see any signs of remorse, I was certainly disappointed. For them, it was enough that Jack had appeared in time to bear part of the load when an older man pushed his chair back from the end of the table and was preparing to leave. His eyes disclosed that he liked the situation even less than I did. Apparently he had been hustled for a few rounds before we joined them.

"I ain't had much sleep the past few nights," he explained. "Think I'll hit the hay. See y'all."

As soon as he was gone, Jack said, "Joe's a good old boy, you know that, little cow-mama?"

"He seems to be. But he's sure in for a surprise if he thinks he's going to get any rest in that 'cowboy's madhouse' upstairs. I just escaped from there, myself."

My narration of the evening's events kept Jack entertained long enough for the others to start getting thirsty again. Apparently each of them lived by the rule to "be one, rather than buy one," because they toughed it out until my filibuster ended, then three of them spoke at once, suggesting that Jack accompany them to the Wyoming Bar. Right away.

The invitation obviously did not include me, so to avoid any embarrassment, I said quickly, "I really should go upstairs, anyway. After all, I'm still barefooted."

"You'll do no such a thing," Jack said with feigned seriousness. "Where I go, you go. And if you'd feel any better about it, I'll take off my boots and socks, too!"

"Thanks, but that won't be necessary. If you're sure."

"We're sure. Aren't we, men?"

The others did not share his enthusiasm, and the response of two or three who sullenly agreed, was barely audible. I decided to ignore their hostility so I scrambled out of the booth and headed for the front door.

"Where you going?" Jack asked, hurrying to catch up with me.

"I saw a cab stand in the front end of this place, so we won't have to wait for a taxi."

He looked puzzled and the other cowboys had the same expression on their faces.

Jack smiled, "Well, okay. If you say so." Then to his friends, "See you soon. Right?"

I thought it was funny they weren't going with us, but assumed there was a reason. I received a sour, knowing look from each one in turn, as Jack and I climbed into the taxi parked at the curb.

We arrived at the Wyoming Bar, shortly, and elbowed our way to a small space where we could order a drink. I glanced around and saw we were surrounded by the same cowboys and girls we had left a few minutes before.

One of them looked as surprised as I felt, and said, "What the hell you doing here? We figgered. . ."

He was interrupted by the bartender. Things were a bit hectic for the next hour, what with shoving and being shoved. I never did get a chance to compare notes with anyone, and find out what it was they had "figgered."

It was almost closing time an hour later. Everyone looked quite drunk and I wanted to return to the starting-gate so I could get back to my hotel. When I phoned for a taxi, the others piled in with us this time, with a sort of grim determination. Each of them wore the triumphant expressions of a winning team when I said good-night and went upstairs alone.

It was all too confusing for me after such a crazy day and I was soon asleep.

Beginning the next day, I rode a saddle-bronc at each performance. The bar-to-bar routine remained unchanged except for the attitude of Jack's little group, who, by the way, were not even entered in the rodeo, but had come from Oklahoma with him "just for the ride." They were a little less hostile as soon as they realized I had no intention of absconding with their meal-ticket. (Whiskey ticket?)

After my ride the last day, Jack was waiting for me at the chutes. He said that after the show he would have to help someone out on his bull, a re-ride, but wanted me to meet him at the Cowboy Bar and we would go someplace for supper.

I returned to my room long enough to bathe and change clothes, then went on down to the bar. I became restless after a couple of drinks and caught a cab to our other haunt, the Wyoming Bar. I was still sipping my first beer in that place when two bronc-riders and their B-girl friends invited me to their table.

"Thanks, anyway," I told them, "but I'm supposed to meet Couch at the Cowboy."

"Fine!" one of them said congenially. "We'll all go!"

When the four drained their glasses, stood, and started toward the back door, I followed. I thought I might as well ride over with them. I was the last one to step out into the narrow alley, where I saw nothing but a few garbage cans, a set of small railroad-type tracks laid as far as I looked in either direction, and a doorway directly across from me (about twenty feet) where the others disappeared one by one. Out of curiosity, I looked up at the sign above that entrance, and it said: COWBOY BAR!

I just stood there with my hands on my hips, and said, "Well, I'll be damned."

After a minute or two I stepped over the tracks and went in to join my friends for a drink.

Jack arrived soon and I asked him, "How come you never told me these two places were right across the alley from each other?"

"I don't know," he laughed. "At first I thought maybe you didn't want to walk on the gravel and broken bottles on account of being barefooted but then I decided you just liked to ride in taxies!"

"Oh, no," I moaned. "When I think of all the whiskey-money we've wasted in the past three days. . ."

"Never fear, little cow-mama," he teased, "there's plenty more where that came from." Then he interrupted himself, "Which reminds me, I have to cash a check. Be right back."

He disappeared into the crowd. As soon as he returned a few minutes later, I knew something was wrong. It was the first time I saw him without a smile on his face. Although Jack had bulges in his lower cheeks that somehow reminded me of how a cute little pocket-gopher might store a few days' supply of food, this in no way detracted from his good looks when he grinned. Now, as I watched him, I noticed this particular facial characteristic had a tendency to draw the corners of his mouth down and he appeared "pouty" when his smile was gone.

"Let's get out of here," he said sullenly. "I got to find Parker."

"Sure!" In an attempt at lightness, I added, "If we're going to the Wyoming Bar, what say we 'rough it' and hike over?"

He replied, "Yeah! Sure."

I felt he was not listening to me at all.

When we reached the other saloon, Jack made his way through the crowd to where Pat Parker, a calf-roper friend of his, was seated on a bar stool, looking dejected.

"How's chances to borrow a few bucks, Pat?" Jack asked, as quietly as he could and still be heard above the usual din. "Just enough to do me till I cash a check."

"If I had a few bucks," Pat muttered morosely, "do you think I'd be sitting here without any booze in front of me?"

I elbowed my way in between them and said, "I've got enough cash for one round."

Before I had a chance to say more, a gleam came into Pat's eyes that was unrelated to my offer to buy a drink. I looked behind me, but I saw nothing special except for about twenty "dudes" seated around one long table that was made up of three smaller ones shoved together. The dude group in all their fur-and-jewel finery kept staring at the cowboys as though they were animals in a zoo. Little did they know that one of the animals was also casing them.

One tall, slouching, tweedy, horn-rimmed man with a tiny blond mustache ordered three consecutive rounds of drinks for his group. Mostly martinis. He did this so rapidly, there were squeals of protest, and delight, from the others who claimed they had not yet finished their first drink.

All this time, Pat's smile grew broader and broader. I was about to explode with curiosity. Then, just as I decided to come right out and ask what he had in mind, Pat crawled off of his stool, strolled on past the "dude table," grabbed a poor unsuspecting gunsel out of one of the booths and punched him in the nose.

I had no time to register anything but amazement. A regular free-for-all ensued and everyone I saw looked too big for me to fight, so I dived behind the bar for protection. The bartender had selected the same refuge and was taking a swig out of a bottle of whiskey when I hit the floor beside him. He wiped his mouth and the top of the bottle with his sleeve, then handed the bottle to me.

"Might as well help yourself," he said, grinning. And while I took his advice, he asked, "How come the cowboy to hit that fellow? The old boy's just a day-laborer over at the old stockyards."

"Damned if I know," I replied in between drinks, "but I'll take a quick look and see if I can figure it out."

The fight sounds were nearly as loud, but the dude noises of scraping-chairs and screaming, fur-clad women had subsided, so I peeked over the edge of the bar. What I saw explained the entire episode and I motioned for the bartender to come on up and share the view.

Pat's knowledge of human nature convinced him the dudes would vacate at the first sign of trouble, which they did as soon as he hit the gunsel and set off the battle-fuse. Then, while some other cowboys finished what he had started, Pat calmly seated himself in one of the empty dude-chairs, put his feet up on the table, and proceeded to lap up every drink within arm's length. He finally leaned over and touched Jack on the arm, where he was sitting on top of a local man who had been knocked down during the heat of battle.

"Say, Couchie," Pat chuckled, "when you get through there, would you mind handing me a couple of drinks from that other table? I can't reach 'em without getting up."

It took about thirty-seconds for that last statement to register in the minds of the scrappers around the room. When it did, they stopped as though someone rang a bell to end the round, and they all turned to glare at Pat. I was afraid of what they might do to him but he headed off any such calamity by gesturing toward the thirty or so drinks on the two tables and invited, "Have one on me, boys!"

Most of the crowd laughed off the incident, although a few of the gunsels, including the one Pat hit in the first place, did not seem to think it was very funny. We were fortunate they settled for free drinks and let it go at that.

To relieve any remaining tension, Jack went into great detail, telling everyone who would listen about my "taxi-mania," as he called it. By the end of his story the battle-lines had more or less disappeared and I came out from behind the bar.

Likewise, the bartender.

"I needed a break, anyway," he announced, congenially, and went about his business as though nothing unusual had happened.

Jack and I slipped away from the Wyoming Bar as soon as we could. I did not think about food until he reminded me we had forgotten to eat.

"I know a night club that serves the best steaks in K.C.," he said, "and I feel like I could eat three of them by myself, right now."

I wondered briefly what he was going to use for money, but I had to assume everything was under control, so I told him, "I'm with you, Couch. Lead on."

When the taxi driver stopped in front of a ranch-type building with neon tubes outlining the eaves and a lighted steer-head hanging above the front door, Jack reached forward and slapped the man on the back.

"Come on inside for a minute, will you, Mac?" He was his usual smiling self once again. "I'll pay you as soon as I cash a check."

I felt uneasy, but only briefly. Jack, as he had promised, cashed a large check, paid the cab fare (including a ridiculously large tip), and it seemed he was in the chips again.

The hostess called Jack by name. She led us to a secluded table where we were served by a waitress and bar-maid, both of whom acted much too chummy toward him. I watched him deftly conning each of these women, and something about the way they fussed over him convinced me their interest was personal as well as mercenary.

Because of his attitude toward the women, and theirs toward him, I was completely taken by surprise when Jack finally leaned across our table, took my right hand in both of his, and said seriously, "We make a hell of a pair. You know that, little cow-mama?"

"But. . ."

"Now don't get all shook up till I finish," he interrupted, "but I been thinking about this for the past five days—ever since we met. We could live there in Nowata on my folks ranch. I buy and sell cattle all week, so we'd always have money in the bank and then we could rodeo on weekends. There's enough shows right in the state of Oklahoma to keep us busy year around."

"But. . ."

"—and I can get you a job at every single one of them."

He was forced to pause for a breath. A series of pictures flashed through my mind: traveling from show to show alone, listening to the too-personal remarks and innuendoes, never knowing where my next job would be, and never having enough money. When he finally spoke again, and asked, "Janie, will you marry me?"

I answered, "Why not?" almost before he finished talking.

On our way to Nowata, Oklahoma, I had a great deal of time to think about my forthcoming marriage. The whole idea of making such an important decision with so little knowledge of what I might be letting myself in for, seemed ridiculous. But I had agreed. Maybe everything would be all right, anyway. Maybe his family would object. There was nothing to do but wait and see.

I was in for two disappointments when we reached the Couch residence. For one thing, Jack's mother, who handled the family finances since her husband's death, told him that $300 worth of bad checks from his trip to Kansas City, were being held at the local bank. She said she refused to pay off any more of his insufficient-funds checks, and he would have to go to work and earn his own way for a change. He promptly borrowed what cash I had, then wheedled enough out of each of his brothers to cover the $300 over-draft at the bank.

The second jolt came when I realized the entire Couch clan was delighted at the prospect of someone marrying Jack and "making a man of him!" This news drove me into the bedroom where I locked the door and wrote three nasty letters to my parents. In the hastily scribbled poisoned-pen notes, which I tore up as always, I berated both Dad and Mother for raising a child who was idiot enough to get into such a mess.

"How can I go through with this?" I moaned by pen. I deserved it, of course, for being swayed for the first time ever by the idea that someone with plenty of money would make my life easier while I continued to have my "rodeo-cake" and eat it, too. That put me in a class with those other leeches—maybe even worse. And now (I wrote), I'm about to take another bull-rider to raise. Dammit, I've already been there!"

I shredded the letters, then went into the living-room and tried to tell Jack how I felt.

"I think we ought to wait a few weeks," I began. I wanted to be kind, yet firm. "We barely know each."

"But honey," he said in a whiny voice I had not heard him use before. "Mom and Sis already made the arrangements. We're getting married on Sunday."

I was standing by a large picture window that overlooked a green meadow surrounded by tall cottonwood trees. A dozen head of cows grazed peacefully while three or four young fall-calves romped around them. I tried to absorb some of the tranquility of the scene in the hope that it might loosen the hard knot of frustration in the pit of my stomach, but a numb feeling of depression turned out to be my only pain-killer. I knew Jack was waiting for me to say something. I felt very, very tired.

"All right, Jack." My voice was so low I could barely hear it myself. "Sunday it is."

My marriage to Jack Couch was like my steer ride the time the surcingle was too loose. I nodded for the gate, but I knew I was bucked off even before I left the chute. In real letters to my folks, I would make no mention of a new husband for a while. Dad's theory that a thrown rider has to try again, immediately, in order to overcome his fear, referred to horses and not husbands, and I knew he would take a pretty dim view of my latest caper.

At first Jack kept saying he would go to work with his brothers, who did extremely well buying and selling cattle, but we went rodeoing instead and before long he stopped mentioning it entirely. Neither of us made much money, although we managed as well as could be expected, and sort of coasted through weeks of Oklahoma rodeos and a bumpy marriage. I soon learned it was up to me to get my own bronc-riding jobs, just as it had always been, and because a large percentage of our funds came from my riding, it was downright aggravating to watch He's-a-jolly-good-fellow Couch spending it with both hands. Finally, as a desperation move, we agreed to stop partying for awhile when I told him I was determined to return to New York that fall and would need a great deal of cash to finance the trip.

From some place in Texas I wrote my folks that I was headed for Little Rock, Arkansas, and later to New York. When Jack and I arrived in Little Rock, there was a telegram from Clint awaiting me at the rodeo headquarters. In a lengthy night-letter, he explained that he had several hundred head of steers to gather and trail cross-country to the railroad and he needed me to come home and help.

I realized there was a real problem finding ranch-hands, because of the war, and I had trailed cattle across that fifteen-mile stretch often enough to know it was not a job to be tackled short-handed. The shipping date Dad quoted allowed me time to finish the Little Rock rodeo while I decided what to do. It was Jack Couch and New York—or me, alone, and Gilt Edge. Of course, if I could make it to Montana and finish my work there, I could still go on to New York alone.

When I told Jack about the telegram, his first question was, "What about me?"

While I contemplated that very problem, he suggested we go to the ranch together. As graciously as I could, I explained that I was not yet ready to tell my parents about having re-married so soon after my divorce and he reluctantly accepted the decision, but his childish pouting only increased my determination to escape when this opportunity presented itself.

The show would end with the Sunday matinee, so on Saturday evening I told Jack I had definitely made up my mind to leave for Montana the next night. We were in the hotel dining-room at the time and his cheek-pockets began to droop, pulling the corners of his mouth down so far I almost expected the food to leak out. He sulked from then until bedtime. And longer.

I was lying there in the dark almost an hour after we went to bed and Jack turned his back to me. A few times I almost reached out to touch him, or make some sort of verbal compromise in order to ease the tension between us but I decided it was kinder not to give him any false hope. The break had been made. Let it be clean.

When I felt the stiffness of indignation and resentment drain out of his spine, I knew he had finally fallen asleep. I was too restless to stay in bed any longer and decided to go downstairs and have a cup of coffee.

I dressed and tiptoed out. A short distance from us, across the hall, I passed a room where the party noises were so loud I could not resist peeking through the wide-open doorway. Slugger Sloan spotted me immediately from his bartending post on the other side of the room. He motioned for me to come on in.

"Glad to see you upright, Slug," I told him, grinning.

The others in the room did not know about the skylight incident in Kansas City, so we just shared the joke with each other.

Slugger magnanimously offered me a drink, some sandwiches, and two packages of cigarettes.

"Thanks, anyway," I told him, "but this party of yours must already be costing a big chunk of cash."

"Yeah, I'll bet it does," he chuckling impishly, "only I don't know whose party it is! I just happened to see the door open about two hours ago, and came in for a drink. I been here ever since!"

That was the first I noticed we were the only rodeo people in the room. "Well," I shrugged, "I don't know who the host is, either, but if he's not worried about a cowboy invasion, I'm sure as hell not. Hand me one of those sandwiches."

For the next hour or so, a few more rodeo people wandered in for the "freebies," as a result of Slugger's invitation. I was already bored so I decided to go down to the lobby and see if I could find something to read. Just before I reached the elevator, I had to detour around a couple of cowboys who had just escalated a verbal confrontation into a physical one. It appeared to be a good clean match, so I backed over to the wall, slid to the floor, and sat there cross-legged, watching them.

Sometime later the elevator door opened. The operator, an excited little man with rabbit-teeth and a bunny-tail tuft of brown-hair on top of an otherwise bald head, hopped into the hallway.

"Stop that, you ruffians!" It was a screaming-whisper. Even in his present state of anxiety, he remained hotel-conscious. "Stop it this instant!"

I was not about to sit still and let him break up a perfectly good fight, so I crawled to my feet and shoved him back into the elevator. He stumbled backwards and ended in a corner of the elevator on his butt. I reached inside the door and pushed a button that said "B" which I assumed was for the basement, and watched the door slide closed just before the elevator disappeared.

I returned to my ringside seat where I cheered for one of the combatants and then the other, determined not to show any favoritism and they eventually agreed to call it quits and go to bed.

When the two men marched down the hall, arm-in-arm, I rang for the elevator, still determined to get a cup of coffee and a magazine.

It was necessary to ring several times, but at last the door slid open and there were two burly policemen and a twittering little rabbit.

"There she is—that's her! That's the one I told you about. Right there!" His voice was so high-pitched, he had apparently forgotten about his precious hotel regulations regarding noise in the hallways. "I demand that you arrest her this instant!"

I thought he might at least mention the fighting cowboys, but he did not. Anyway, the two uniformed policemen snatched me into the elevator without a word, and I was hauled off to jail.

At half-hour intervals during the night I asked for permission to phone the hotel so Jack would not be worried about me. My requests were denied until I finally demanded the one call I insisted I was legally entitled to make.

"All right," the grumpy sergeant agreed. "We'll let you out of your cell long enough to make one call. That's all."

It took me a few minutes to straighten up after lying on that lumpy two-inch-thick mattress, but as soon as I could, I made my way to the desk and reached for the phone.

"Do you have a telephone book?" I asked politely.

"No," he growled. "Call information."

The operator connected me with "information" and I asked the number of our hotel. I can not remember the name of it now. (They kept track of their towels too well.)

I replaced the receiver while I scribbled the numbers on a yellow pad. Before I had a chance to pick it up again, the sergeant laid his hand on the phone.

"That's it," he said. "One call. Back to your cell."

"What? I just—I mean I only—I didn't. . ." I was still sputtering when the jailer led me away. About ten feet from the desk I jerked out of his grasp and spun around, determined to get a few things off of my chest, even if it cost me an extra day's freedom. As I opened my mouth to speak, the sergeant raised his ponderous frame out of the chair, just far enough to remove the Little Rock telephone directory he had been sitting on. He plopped back down, and had the audacity to turn and wink at me. It would have been worth an extra day in jail to take a poke at him but I never had an opportunity. Then, for the first time, I noticed a sly twinkle in his eyes.

"Okay," I laughed. "You win." I winked back at him and obediently returned to my cell.

At 9 a.m. I was finally allowed to make an "outside" call. Jack sounded sleepy when he answered, but as soon as I said, "Guess who's in jail?" he either dropped the phone or fell out of bed, because I heard a loud crash, then a brief period of silence before he spoke again. He was wide awake, this time.

He sounded cautious, as though he expected the line to be tapped. "What happened? Can you get out? What can I. . ."

"It's a long, long story," I interrupted. "Just bring twenty dollars to bail me out of this place, and I'll explain later."

"But when did you leave here?" he persisted. "I didn't even know."

"Later, Jack. Okay?"

"Yeah. Sure. I'll be there right away."

I returned to my cell to wait. When right away stretched into one hour, then two hours, I began to worry.

"After all," I kept telling myself, "part of that money is mine. Surely he wouldn't just leave me here." I did not realize I was talking out loud until the matron strode by and gave me a sidelong glance that seemed to indicate it was understandable that no-one wanted to acknowledge their relationship to me, but I felt she was being unfair. I had to admit $2O was a lot of cash to exchange for a female in my uncombed, unbathed condition but it was not really my fault.

The jailer approached from the other direction and unlocked the door to my cell.

"Some man come to get you out," he said in a tired drawl. His attitude also seemed to imply that he wondered why someone would bother.

"I'm ready." Then to let him know my appearance was not entirely my own fault, I grumbled, "The room service around here isn't all that great, you know."

His uncommunicative glare cut me off at that point and I followed him to the front desk without further comment.

Jack was there, placing one $5 bill on top of another and pressing the wrinkles out of each of them in turn. Since he had less concern for the all-mighty buck than anyone I knew, his deliberate manner was clearly indicative of some emotion other than miserliness. He had good reason to be annoyed with me, and embarrassed by the chore of "bailing me out of jail," but I was not aware of the ultimate cause for his discomfort until we were ready to leave the building.

A man and woman, heretofore unnoticed by me, were seated on a bench near the front door waiting for us. It turned out that they were some more of the Couch clan who lived in Arkansas, and upon learning via the family grape-vine that Jack's new bride would be with him at the Little Rock rodeo, they had decided to pay us a surprise visit while we were there.

Jack told me later that he had been on his way out of the hotel when they captured him. His prolonged delay had been due to their insistence that they accompany him to pick up his bride, and his reluctance to tell them where. They finally wore him down.

It was only natural that Jack dreaded the idea of having to "spring" his wife before he could introduce her to members of the family. However, one of my pet-peeves concerns friends and relatives who barge in without warning, so in spite of feeling sorry for Jack, I could not overlook a certain ironic-humor at the way their surprise had backfired.

After introductions, things were a trifle chilly until Jack asked, skeptically, "Just what were the charges against you?"

"Operating a vehicle without a license."

"Did you wreck you car?" the cousin-in-law wanted to know.

"Not exactly."

"But you said vehicle!"

"Well, it's difficult to explain. The vehicle was actually an elevator. I sort of sent it to the basement when I wasn't supposed to."

The three of them exchanged glances. Apparently my replies had been sprinkled with the correct proportion of truth and levity because the wrinkles between their eyes shifted around to the outside corners. Although being in jail is anything but humorous, Jack and his relatives agreed that it was not quite as criminal as it sounded at first—especially when I gave them a (doctored) blow by blow account of the events leading to my arrest.

By the time we had eaten lunch, it was time to leave for the rodeo grounds, and Jack devoted a great deal of our time telling them of his prowess as a bareback-bronc rider. I had not as yet seen him ride anything but bulls. The only bareback-bronc he had drawn at Little Rock did not buck enough to prove his ability one way or the other, so I reserved my opinion for later.

"The last three I rode before K.C., I really spurred them high," he boasted, "all the way to the whistle. You-all just watch me spur this bronc today!"

I stayed in the bleachers with the relatives while Jack went down to the chutes to get a surcingle on his bronc. For his sake, I hoped he would make a good ride because at that particular point in time, his morale was in need of a boost. I could tell something was wrong as soon as the chute flew open. Instead of the high-spurring he had promised, Jack jammed his spurs into the cinch and held them there so tightly it looked like his legs were tied down. The bronc was a miserable twisting, high- kicking, spinning little bay, and although Jack disqualified by not spurring, he did manage to stay aboard. In fact, that was the point he mentioned first when he came to the bleachers to sit with us.

He looked kind of sheepish, after all of his bragging, when he said, "I got off-balance there for awhile, and couldn't seem to start spurring." Then he turned to me almost defiantly. "But at least I didn't buck off !"

I could hardly hide a grin, because he was taking the whole thing so seriously. We were all proud of him, anyway, but he did not seem to realize that.

"No, you didn't buck off," I agreed solemnly. "However, we should face the fact that you'd have had to dislocate both hips to get loose!"

He glared at me for an instant, then burst out laughing. The others joined in, mostly because they had no idea what I was talking about, and also Jack's wounded ego was somewhat restored.

It made me feel better to see him smiling again. We had not discussed my departure for Montana at all that day, but my plans were unchanged and I wanted to leave with things on a friendly basis, if possible. By taking a later train than I intended, we were able to have dinner with the relatives and tell them goodbye before it was time for me to leave. This way, explanations were not necessary and we stayed so busy we had little opportunity to argue the pros and cons of my decision.

Jack and I divided our money equally and even as we left for the depot, he lined up a new collection of leeches, both male and female, who vowed to wait as long as was necessary for him to come back and buy them a drink! Dé jà vu!

The train was ready to leave when we bought my ticket and checked my luggage, so with a few vague promises as to the time and place of our next meeting, I headed for Montana. I was quite sure Jack would return to the hotel bar where his new group of hangers-on would be waiting.

I felt no sadness at what I suspected was the end of another marriage. In this case, it would be silly to mourn the loss of something that never really existed in the first place.

I went as far as Billings, Montana, by train, then caught a bus to Lewistown. Where the highway skirted our summer range for five or six miles, I watched for signs of the cattle roundup I assumed would be in progress. There was not only a notable absence of cowboys, but also of cows. The mystery was explained, however, when I reached Lewistown and hurried to the Montana Tavern, seeking a ride out to the ranch.

As usual, I found my folks in their own private booth. They were not assembling a crew of cowboys to gather the steers and trail them to the railroad, as might be expected, but were getting on a binge to celebrate the high price they had received for said steers when they delivered them one week before!

My anger at having been summoned 1,300 miles for an emergency that no longer existed, must have been apparent.

"I figured it was time you came home, anyway," Clint said defensively. "Seems to me you been having fun long enough and it's time you settled down and tried to make something of yourself."

There was no point in explaining that I thought I had been trying to make something of myself. Maybe not in their eyes, but in my own. A World's Championship, if and when I ever won one, certainly should not be taken lightly. And if he honestly thought my life had been all play and no work, there was no way I could convince him otherwise.

It was obvious, that first day, that the only help they needed from me was to drink my share of their celebration and summon the barmaid for another round when it was my turn to buy.

Occasionally, I caught Dad looking at me rather smugly. No doubt he considered the telegraphic SOS a touch of sheer genius. After all, it did bring me home by fair means or foul. What he did not realize was that I was secretly being smug right back at him, because I had every intention of leaving for New York the following Sunday, anyway.

It took three days of drinking to do justice to the cattle market, then we returned to the ranch. On our way out of town, Clint sent me to the grocery store for a case of tomato juice and some other get well drinks that would deal with the hangovers he knew would be prevalent. I slipped an issue of *Hoofs & Horns* into the bottom of one of the bags, but had no opportunity to read it until I was alone in my bedroom that night.

Since the beginning of time, people have predicted "the end of the world." If I had any thoughts at all regarding such an event, it was to laugh at the absurdity of the whole crackpot idea. However, that was before I understood that some individuals are allotted their own private doomsday, and it in no way jeopardizes the rest of the universe.

It would not be fair to blame the *Hoofs & Horns*, itself, for delivering the final blow. The TNT hidden between its covers had been stockpiling for years, and it was really I who flipped the page that opened the bomb-bay doors. When I did, Jane Burnett, bronc-rider and hopeful contender for a World's Championship title, was blown off the face of the earth!

There it was. A short item sandwiched in with some rodeo gossip as though it were of no great importance: "—and the producers of the Madison Square Garden and Boston rodeos have decided to discontinue Women's bronc-riding entirely. This comes as no great surprise to anyone."

They had notified all of the women they could locate, to inform them of the change. Mary Parks, and the current World's Champion, Mildred Mix Homer, were asked to stand by in case a few exhibition rides were allowed.

I barely glanced at the rest of the article.

"—no great surprise to anyone." That's what they said. Did they not realize I needed to try again? I was not really ready the other time, but if they would just give me one more chance.

I felt as though a steer had kicked me in the stomach, but I could not cry. I was hurting too much.

It was as though I had been trying to scale a mountain. Climbing, crawling, digging, falling back. Scrambling to my feet and climbing again. Until now. The summit had been hidden from me by overhanging clouds, and then just as the foggy mist began to clear away, I discovered someone had whacked off the top of that mountain and there was nowhere else to go. If I continued my struggle, the best I could do was remain at a level I had already reached, and one misstep might very well send me tumbling back to the bottom where it all began.

When I thought about the lofty goals I had set for myself in the rodeo business and western movies, I suddenly realized to what extent my life resembled a mirage. The Three Buttes, as seen from the front porch of our ranch house, appeared to be within walking distance until you got too close.

Then they would disappear.

I crawled out of bed with calm deliberation and tore the *Hoofs & Horns* into shreds. The pieces fluttered to the floor around my feet. I barely remember getting dressed or saddling my horse, but the next thing I knew I was lying in the grass at one of my favorite places in our south pasture and my horse was grazing nearby. I had not hobbled him, but maybe he somehow sensed I needed for him to stay close by until I was ready to return home.

Now that I was back at the ranch, my parents naturally expected me to step right back into the niche I had vacated ten years before. I knew the mold was too shallow for me to ever fit in it again and this had nothing to do with bust-and-hip measurements. There was a constant struggle to find a common ground where we could meet, conversationally or otherwise; since they were not really interested in hearing about rodeos, and I did not share their concern over such earth-shaking subjects as inept ranch cooks or unreliable hired men. The draft had taken a big percentage of the young ranch hands, and this presented a problem for many of the cattlemen. So?

The first phase of my reform program called for my attendance at various events that Mother thought would help me find a niche for myself in what was considered the "country club" group.

I would never have admitted it at the time, but during my high-school years I was somewhat in awe of the Lewistown elite and now that we were going to parties at the Elks' Country Club, I thought the very act of rubbing elbows with this same crowd might give me with a feeling of accomplishment that heretofore had escaped me. Even that did not work. I had only to observe this collection of fanny-patters and cheek-tweekers for about two hours before I saw them for what they were: a brotherhood of giltedged phonies (not to be confused with the town of the same name). Even the fannies they patted would be snubbed come Monday morning.

Compared to my rodeo family, the Lewistown chosen few, (who really believed they were), simply did not stack up. Conceded, some rodeo hands were wild, crude, and often downright immoral, if you considered their virtues of being good sports, generous, loyal, and above all else, honest about themselves, to me there was no comparison. Whatever they (we) were, it was right out there in the open for the world to see. No pretense. No sham.

These country-club people who rarely left their home town reminded me of an incident several years previously when I saw a herd of animals grazing in a hay meadow somewhere in Idaho. In a field by themselves, with nothing for comparison, they looked like full-grown horses until a rider on horseback suddenly appeared on the scene and began driving them toward a pole corral about one mile away. That was when I realized I had been observing a herd of Shetland ponies! Until a full-sized horse came into the picture, the size of these animals could not be determined.

I wondered how these local Shetland ponies would stack up against the big boys if and when they ever went out into the real world.

Once I had forsaken the society route, I tried hibernating at the ranch. I thumbed through my scrapbook periodically and fondled my buck-rein and hobbles like a miser with gold. Then one day I looked at myself in the mirror and said, "Okay, Burnett. You're supposed to have some guts, so it's about time you prove it. Your rodeoing is pretty well shot until the war is over, so make a clean break and forget it for now."

Two days later I was in Lewistown with Ralph (J. R.) Cunningham, and Jack Rich, when fate took a hand again. It seemed Jack had already signed part of the paper-work required for him to join the army, and in spite of the arguments J. R. and I gave him to the contrary, he insisted on going through with it. We accompanied him to the recruiting headquarters at the local post-office when it was time for him to sign his final papers, and our sole purpose in going was to dissuade him if we could. There was one hitch in our plan. We had a few drinks before we arrived and once we saw the impressive WE WANT YOU! posters, the Army sounded so great that J. R. and I also decided to sign up and do what we could to save the world.

The recruiting officer asked, in a very business-like manner, "Name?"

"Jane Burnett."

"Age?"

"Twenty-two."

He looked up from his paper and scrutinized me from Justin boots to Stetson hat, hesitating briefly on the Levi pants and jacket.

"Well, young lady," he said, condescendingly, "you're making a wise decision. By joining the WAAC's, you'll have a wonderful opportunity to travel. You'd be amazed at the places and things you'll see, once you get away from home!"

J. R. and Jack began to snicker, but I managed to keep a straight face when I replied, "Yes, sir. I'll bet I will at that."

As soon as we three recruits departed from the post-office building, we were already walking straight and tall, in anticipation of our new roles.

J. R. whispered to me, "How come you told him your name was Burnett?"

He was the only person in Montana who knew about my marriage to Jack Couch, so I shushed him right away. "Shhh! The army's too busy to keep track of that stuff. Anyway, I'll figure some way to get out of that Couch thing before anybody finds out about it."

"Speaking of your folks," he whispered, "if you look over your right shoulder, you'll see an International pickup approaching. I have a feeling the driver with the big ears has come to take you back to the ranch."

"That's okay. Now that I have something to look forward to, I can stand the boredom while I wait for the army to call me."

Clint pulled up to the curb and beeped the horn.

"So-long," I said to the boys, then added, "Thanks for the suggestion, Jack. And you know what? You just might have saved my life."

My WAAC orders finally arrived, instructing me to report to Ft. Des Moines, Iowa, in two weeks. This allowed me sufficient time to attend the Oklahoma City rodeo, first, even though I had no particular desire to do so except to find Jack Couch and tell him what I had done.

I was almost afraid my reaction to another rodeo might be somewhat like an alcoholic taking just one more drink before going on the wagon, but I was not swayed in the least, even when I placed in the prize money each day in the barrel-racing. In fact, I was almost relieved when the rodeo ended and I could begin my new life.

Jack made no effort to conceal his annoyance at my enlisting, until I pointed out, among other things, that I could not divorce him while I was in the army because of the false statement I gave regarding my marital status. Then he grudgingly conceded the WAAC idea did have some merit. At my suggestion that he join one of the services, too, he gave a rather vague excuse about "other commitments." I learned later, this was the understatement of the year.

When he put me on the train to Des Moines, he asked how soon we could get together again.

"After the war, I guess," was my evasive reply. "I'm going overseas—if there's any way possible."

Army life fit me like a pair of made-to-order boots! I liked everything about it, except of course the tetanus shots, gas-mask drills, and K.P. Prior to my arrival at Des Moines, Iowa, I must admit to a few twinges of doubt regarding my ability to cope with army routine and discipline, but the very fact that all orders were impersonal and unbiased made them acceptable without question.

Basic training was easier for me than for some because I was in excellent physical condition and had no first-time-away-from-home-blues that plagued many recruits. The most drastic readjustment for me stemmed from the hours and hours of compulsory marching. Surprisingly enough, it was not my inherited aversion to walking that presented the problem but switching from Levis to skirts in subzero Des Moines weather was really rough.

By the time I completed basic training and transferred to the Army Radio School in Kansas City, Missouri, I had learned to adjust. We still did a great deal of marching, and as sergeant-in-charge of our platoon, I organized and trained a special drill team that became so adept at the difficult routines we concocted on our own, that we performed in three separate military shows. One of my most prized possessions is a letter of commendation for our performance before a visiting army general.

Students of the radio school were housed in one of the downtown hotels and my only recreation was an occasional evening at a local billiards room on the top floor of a building near where we lived. It was very exciting for me to meet the famous pool player, Willie Mosconi, who made a personal appearance one weekend and performed various trick shots for the audience. I was especially honored when he stopped by a table at the back of the room where I was practicing by myself. He complimented me on my "strokes" and suggested ways that I could improve my game by slightly changing my "stance" when I prepared to make a shot. The next few times I practiced at that particular location the manager teased me about taking lessons from the Great Mosconi.

I had actually turned down a chance at Officer's Training School because, to me, learning to be a radio operator seemed like the shortest distance between the two points of basic-training and overseas-duty. At the completion of our short six-week radio course, I considered myself a full-fledged operator, and was ready go out and win the war single-handed. I never once suspected the European situation could be handled without me being present to relay messages to our troops overseas.

My parents came to Kansas City one weekend shortly before my graduation. They seemed extremely proud of my accomplishments up to that point, and although I was not allowed to stay overnight with them, we did get to spend some time together on Sunday. I had an opportunity to get even with Clint for some of the jokes he had played on me in the past, when we were in the bar at their hotel. Before leaving Lewistown he had gone to the bank where he withdrew several $100 bills for their trip. He had already spent his bills of smaller denomination before they arrived in Kansas City and when he bought our first round of drinks the bartender asked if he did not have any smaller bills.

Before Clint had a chance to answer, I said, "Come on, Dad! You don't have to try and impress these people. Just go ahead and pay him with one of your fives."

The bartender glared at Clint and I decided I'd better get him off the hook before we were kicked out of the bar. I finally admitted that it was all a joke and we were allowed to remain there for several hours before I had to return to my hotel.

When my instructor presented me with a special "certificate of achievement" denoting that my code speeds, in both sending and receiving, topped or equaled most of the previous records for WAACs in that particular school, I was convinced I had succeeded. That is why it was such a low-blow to be assigned to Kelly Field, San Antonio, Texas, to drive the commanding officer's Jeep!

My periodic requests for overseas duty were ignored, and it seemed I was doomed to sweat out (literally) the rest of the war in that scorching South-Texas heat.

I have since learned of the army's steadfast ruling to train a soldier for one job, then assign him to something completely unrelated, but at that time I thought my own dilemma was an isolated case. If these following events had been scattered over a period of months, I probably would have remained at Kelly Field indefinitely. I'd have griped, but I would have stayed. Instead, Fate dumped them into my lap simultaneously, and I was forced to act.

During a single twelve-hour period: I learned: (1) A law had been passed making the WAACs a part of the regular army, instead of an auxiliary organization, giving us a choice of re-enlisting in the new WAC, or applying for discharge. (2) I received word that my first furlough was to begin the following morning; and, (3) Jacqueline Cochran appeared on the post to give a pep-talk about the various branches of the service available to women.

Miss Cochran's speech was meant to promote re-enlistments among the Kelly WAACs, but she could not resist a few words of praise for her own flying school, the Women's Ferry Command at Sweetwater, Texas. Before the question-and-answer period ended, I was firmly convinced that as a combination radio-operator and Sweetwater-graduate, I would definitely be a prime candidate for a job ferrying planes overseas.

The next morning I took a taxi from Kelly Field to the San Antonio airport, where I checked into a tiny motel near one of the remote runways. By haunting the instructors from daylight until dark, and spending almost every cent I had, I logged the 35-hours of flying time that were required to enlist in the Ferry Command. It was necessary to get a two-day extension on my furlough, but I made it. On my return to the base, I applied for my discharge, mailed my application-for-acceptance to Sweetwater, and I settled back to await developments.

The three weeks' delay while awaiting my discharge placed me "in between classes" at Sweetwater, so I was advised to return to Montana where a representative would contact me, check my logged-hours and doctor's certificate, and assign me to a flight class. While another Lewistown girl, Lorraine Wilbur, and I waited impatiently for the arrival of the interviewing officer, the bottom fell out of my luck-thermometer one more time and my big scheme now registered about twenty-below zero. Jacqueline Cochran's Ferry Command was being discontinued! The current class would be allowed to graduate, then the whole thing was "kaput." In a way, it did make sense but that was no consolation to those of us who were awaiting this new assignment.

The military officials had decided it made more sense to take the pilots who had washed out of the combat flying part of their training after two or three years in the air force, and assign them to ferrying the large planes overseas instead of starting from scratch to train women for these jobs when they had no previous training at all. It made sense but was difficult to accept.

It was the old mirage syndrome once again.

I considered re-joining the Army, but while I was at loose-ends I decided to get my divorce out of the way before tackling any new projects. As soon as I contacted Mrs. Couch to get Jack's current address, I realized something was wrong. She refused to reveal any information over the phone so I went straight to Nowata to talk to her personally. She pleaded that I not let anyone know where he was but at first she would not disclose the reason for so much secrecy. Once I located him, I learned that he was wanted by the sheriff regarding a stolen cow he bought and sold at a local auction sale almost one year previously. He claimed he was unaware of any of this until the law informed him she was a "hot" cow. He used poor judgement by suggesting, as a joke, that they might try the services of a good Jersey bull. They saw no humor in his remark.

Apparently, this deal had been pending even at the time when he and I were married, so that was the "other commitment" he had mentioned in Kansas City.

I did not want to become involved or cause him any more problems, so I left without mentioning a divorce. I learned later that shortly after I left for Montana, he and several other cowboys had asked for and received permission to take part in one of the annual Oklahoma prison rodeos where they would compete against the inmates. (At the same time, the Nowata officials were attempting to arrest him but did not know where he was. No-one thought to check the prisons!)

Because I was fairly familiar with Kansas City, I returned there and went to work for North American Aircraft where I was a consultant to new employees who were hired for low-level office jobs. I had to bluff my way through but managed to get by for several months until I became restless and decided to visit my grandmother again in San Diego.

Through a lawyer friend of my aunt Gladys, I was finally able to have my marriage to Jack Couch annulled because he had not disclosed his problems with the law at the time of our marriage. This lawyer had done some legal work for the Santa Fe railroad and when he learned of my army radio school experience he mentioned that he knew of an opening for a telegrapher at the tiny station named Lenwood, about twenty miles south of Barstow. The Santa Fe Railroad always needed help because so many of their telegraphers had been recruited into various branches of the service and in fact, his brother had been one of them. He actually made the necessary contacts for me and within a few days I stepped off of the train at a tiny station named Lenwood, and wondered what in hell I had let myself in for this time.

After meeting Gloria and George Matthews, the middle-aged couple who were in charge of our fifteen-foot-square "train station," they showed me to the thing the Santa Fe people referred to as an apartment. Actually, it was nothing but a box-car, and its glorified title was based on the presence of a small wood-stove and a narrow cot with a two-inch-thick caboose-pad for a mattress. This box-car was parked on a siding, only a few feet from the main track so whenever a fast express roared by, whether day or night, I was tossed around like dice in a dice-cup.

My shift was from midnight to eight and with no fan or other means of cooling my "apartment," I was lucky if I managed to sleep as much as two or three hours when I was off-duty. Letter-writing, walks on the desert, and an occasional trip to Barstow, twenty miles away, were my only forms of recreation.

Much to my surprise, one morning when the passenger train stopped at Lenwood, a familiar sight appeared after the train pulled away. It was Clint. He had no idea that I was working in what was laughingly called a railroad station, and the look of surprise on his face must have mirrored the one on mine when we stood and stared at each other. I wondered why he had literally arrived on my doorstep, especially since he was dressed in what appeared to be an expensive gabardine western suit and bolo tie. He rarely wore a suit regardless of the occasion.

I was too embarrassed to let him see my box-car home so I suggested he wait in our mini-station while I hurried away to change clothes. For transportation into Barstow I had purchased an old Model-A pickup with no windshield and no top and when I drove around to where Clint was waiting, his only reaction to the vehicle was a slight shake of his head. He crawled into the front seat and locked his door with the piece of wire attached to the knob and by the time we reached Barstow, both of us were ready for a meal and a drink (not necessarily in that order).

Clint said he had been to a cattlemen's convention in Las Vegas when he decided to come and see me, and that explained why Mother was not with him. We had gone to a small cowboy-bar down the street from the café, and before long both of us were quite drunk. He told me about his problems hiring help for the ranch work since so many men were now in the service. When I thought about his phony desperate plea for my help at "shipping time" the previous August, I was not at all sympathetic, but my current job and living conditions were none too great either, so it was not long before I began to consider the advantages of returning to Montana.

Even as drunk as we were, everything would have been all right if I had just kept my mouth shut, but a drunk staggered against my bar stool and nearly knocked it over and I mumbled something stupid like, "Watch what you're doing, ass-hole." and he slapped me.

As I have mentioned previously, Clint was not in the habit of doing any of his own fighting. This was due, mainly, to his total lack of ability, and also to the fact that he generally had someone take care of his battles for him. This time was different. He was going to fight for his only daughter's honor, and her health, so he pulled out a tiny pen knife (blade about three inches long) that he carried for the purpose of cleaning his fingernails, and he took a swipe at the drunk with this dangerous blade.

Clint actually seemed quite pleased that he drew blood when he poked our opponent on his wrist. Neither of us expected any repercussions because we were all equally at fault, but before we realized what was happening, a deputy sheriff arrived and arrested Clint and me for fighting with a lethal weapon!

The situation was not improved when I kept giggling. In fact, we were hauled off to their jail and they would have placed us in adjoining cells except that the sheriff said there was a ruling against placing women in those cells and his only option was to haul me off to a single one-cell structure about one mile out of town. They kept me there all night with a woman guarding me who would have made a terrific linebacker if anyone could have recruited her. I had stopped giggling long before dawn.

Once Clint had paid our fines and we were released, we drove back to Lenwood where I told the Matthews that it was imperative that I return to Montana and before I packed my clothes and we caught the next eastbound train, I made them a gift of my pickup for any inconvenience my leaving might cause them. I'm really good-hearted as all hell.

Even I had to admit it was finally time for me to settle down. I would return to the ranch and decide what I should do with the rest of my life. I had taken some wrong turns—and many that I believe to be right—but only time would tell.

# Epilogue

Clint had not been exaggerating about the ranch-hand situation, and even though all of the neighboring ranchers exchanged labor as much as possible, Clint and I generally moved the cattle to the various pastures ourselves. Grandpa Burnett, at age 84, still went with us most of the time unless the trip required an over-night sleep-out and even when we were home, he generally rode horseback for an hour or so every day around the ranch.

The small town rodeos had tapered off during the war years but I still announced at a few of them when I had an opportunity. Clint bought a used pool table for me and it was set up in the center room of the long out-building that included the bunkhouse on one end and the "electric room" on the other end where it housed the equipment required to supply power for the main residence. Improving my pool game kept me occupied to a certain extent but I also spent quite a bit of time working with one colt or another of my own to train them for competing in an event that was becoming quite popular throughout the western states.

This event was called "cow cutting" and it required the rider to rein their horse into a herd of cattle in the arena, select one particular animal, and "cut" them away from the others. The object, then, was to keep this critter from getting back into the herd until the judges indicated that the job had been completed to their satisfaction. There were two parts of this performance that were particularly difficult. One handicap was that once you selected the animal, from then on you were not allowed to rein your horse or help them in any way. The second problem was staying in the saddle as your horse dodged back and forth, changing directions to keep the selected animal from getting back into the herd. Once you reached that point it turned into a game between the two animals.

Some horses just naturally have "cow sense." I had owned one such animal and worked with him off and on whenever I was home for a few weeks and it was almost like losing a member of the family when he was struck by lightning and killed during an early spring storm. When I returned to the ranch from California, I learned that a neighbor owned a two-year-old colt that was a full brother to the one who was killed and I immediately made arrangements to buy him.

This horse, Skeeter, had so much potential as a mount for the cow-cutting events that my efforts soon began to pay off and I won first or second place in almost every competition I entered in the central Montana area. Danny Frazer, a high school student whose father recognized Skeeter's potential, asked if his son could ride him in the various high school competitions. They kept Skeeter for nearly a year and Danny eventually won the National High School competition in that event.

As the young men in various branches of the service began returning home, one of them was the younger brother of my friend Sonny Smith. I had known Woody in high school and we crossed paths a few times when he was stationed near where I was appearing in a rodeo in Oklahoma. He had been a pilot in the navy and he continued to be interested in flying even after he returned to their ranch near Gilt Edge.

Woody occasionally worked at our ranch, and after a year of dating, we were married and moved to Anchorage, Alaska.

In Anchorage, there were quite a few jobs available in construction work, but any openings for a pilot just out of the service had already been filled by local Alaskans with the same credentials. We remained there for nearly a year until Grandpa Burnett became quite ill and Clint asked us to return to the ranch. He said that we would be set up with some cattle of our own in addition to wages and it sounded like an opportunity too good to ignore.

Once we were at the ranch, we worked pretty much as hired help for awhile, which was all right except for one thing. The fifty head of cows that Woody and I were supposed to own by this time always seemed to be just out of our reach. Several times we would hear of an opportunity to purchase a small herd of cows with calves, cows without calves, or young heifers that were bred and expecting but when we mentioned any of these deals to Clint he always found something wrong with each transaction and nothing would come of it.

I think he realized that we were beginning to question the arrangement that had brought us back from Alaska, so he now elevated us to the position of ranch managers. Slight increase in wages. Still no cows.

Grandpa Burnett passed away about a year after our return from Alaska and it was soon obvious that there were problems with Woody's and my situation at the ranch. There was always an "authority" problem as far as running the ranch was concerned. Clint spent a great deal of time in Billings and Sheridan, having bought into another nightclub partnership in Wyoming. He would come to the ranch just often enough to create friction between Woody and me. Whenever Clint showed up or a few days, he would call me aside and tell me what he wanted Woody to do about certain things pertaining to the cattle or other jobs around the ranch. Then, once he was gone, it was my responsibility to see that it was done. Naturally, Woody resented taking orders from me, and I resented being placed in this situation, so we finally decided we should go out on our own.

We leased a small place not too far from the Burnett ranch, bought a few cows on credit, and spent almost a year trying to make it work, but we were never really out from under the Burnett thumb.

When our lease expired, we sold the cows, paid off what we owed on the original purchase, and bought a roadside bar and café in Windham, a small town between Lewistown and Great Falls. We built an arena between the bar and the residence that was part of the property, and eventually decided to put on mini-rodeos every Sunday during the summer. Woody and I both roped calves and steers, and I kept Skeeter on hand for the cow-cutting events. I announced the shows and the bar prospered.

I even designed a hand-made rodeo blouse for women called a "Papoose Shirt" and ran an ad in the Western Horsemen, but when

I was swamped with orders and had to hire someone to help me, it took away my already-slim profits.

Woody started his own crop-dusting business in Stanford, which was only a few miles from our place, and with me running the bar alone most of the time we began to see enough profit that all of our work seemed worthwhile. By that time, we had started a family of our own, and the two children, Camille and Loren were eventually entered in their prospective grades in the Windham school.

It would appear that our troubles were over. Because the crop-dusting business took up so much of Woody's time during the summer months, it was necessary for me to hire a combination housekeeper/babysitter to cover for me when I was working in the bar.

During one brief period of time, we had spent quite a bit of money moving the bar into a larger building on the property and completely remodeling with a lunch counter and small dance floor. One Sunday when we were short of money, my one bartender wanted to collect his wages for the week. I wrote out a check and handed it to him when he got off work, but when he went around to the front of the bar and asked me to cash the check I refused.

"How come you won't cash my check?" he was both angry and confused.

"Because it's no good."

By then the other customers were listening to our conversation.

"But." he was still confused. "You wrote it yourself!"

"That's how I know it's no good!"

He had to laugh in spite of himself, and so did our other customers. I gave him enough cash out of the register to keep him happy until I could pay him in full.

We decided to let a young local couple lease the bar for a year because Woody's crop-dusting business was doing well and by hiring bartenders and housekeepers, there was little profit from my end.

I had often played the piano at our bar, and that summer I contacted the manager of Chico Hot Springs where we sometimes spent a few days to relax, and asked about a job playing a Hammond organ in their dining room for the summer guests. I forgot to mention that I did not own such an instrument but when they agreed to hire me, I immediately went to Great Falls and bought a small organ that was to be shipped to Chico three days after the children and I arrived there. Since that instrument was totally foreign to me, I would spend the morning hours playing one tune over and over until I was familiar with all of the buttons and the footwork for that particular piece of music. That evening, the poor audience was forced to listen to that one song repeated throughout the entire dinner hour. The next day, a new song. By the end of the summer, I had a pretty fair repertoire.

When we had the bar, on weekends there was generally a "round table" blackjack game in progress all evening with the deal shifting to a different person after each hand.

I began to take an interest in dealing blackjack and when a friend of Clint's offered me a job working for him in Glacier Park the next summer, I could not resist the temptation to try something new. Off and on through the years I dealt at various towns around Montana for brief spells during their celebrations, and in later years dealt blackjack in Reno for nearly eight years after Camille and Loren had graduated from high school in Scottsdale, Arizona.

Although Woody and I owned a home in Scottsdale, he continued crop-dusting and I became interested in writing. I sold some articles and a few short stories to various magazines, taught fiction and non-fiction as a substitute at two different junior colleges.

The Burnett ranch had been sold and after the death of my parents, I rarely returned to Montana.

With our interests leading us in different directions, Woody and I eventually divorced but remained good friends and our two great children kept us in close contact with each other through the years.

I had stopped drinking completely before Camille was three months old, but I issued no guarantee, nor was I asked for one, as to how long this spell of sobriety would continue. As it happened, I did not take a drink for the next ten years, and even then I seldom drank enough to feel out of control.

I have continued playing pool, and have won quite a few trophies in various competitions around the Phoenix area. Billiards in the senior olympics has helped me maintain an interest in the sport, also, and I have won a medal every year I competed.

For a woman, what else is there after rodeo? Become a full-fledged member of the "dude" crowd? Rodeo men who retire from the arena usually settle for breaking and training horses, managing ranches, teaching in one of the newly formed "rodeo schools," or even tending bar or gambling. But women? That's a different story. A wife and mother ex-rodeo or not, is supposed to behave like any other wife and mother, even if she never feels like she really belongs. She has no one to talk to who understands how she feels even after many years of trying to readjust to civilian life.

There has been a lot of satisfaction in writing about rodeos and my research has provided some fascinating information such as the fact that the first recorded bronc ride by a woman was in 1912 when a Mrs. Riordan performed this remarkable feat while riding on a side-saddle!

With rodeos becoming more popular every year, I only hope that I can make people understand the performers themselves. I want the readers to know that a cowboy bucking off a bronc or a Brahma bull is not an actor in a poorly directed show, but a man who really needs that prize-money to get his wife out of the hospital, or maybe to get the finance company off his back so he can keep his car and have transportation to the next rodeo. That same cowboy would never explain this to an outsider because he knows this information could be interpreted as self-pity, and that is the last thing he wants or expects.

I did not keep in touch with any of my rodeo acquaintances through the years except for an occasion letter from Bill Linderman. I was extremely saddened by his death in an airplane crash in Salt Lake City in 1965.

Another great loss to the rodeo world was when Fritz Truan was killed in Iwo Jima on February 28, 1945. My only personal contact with him was during the three days when he and Larry Finley helped me survive some difficult bronc rides in Elk City, Oklahoma.

My own small role in the history of rodeo may or may not be considered typical of rodeo people in general. I am kind of a "has-been who never was," but I damned sure gave it a try. And just because a man or woman never reached the championship level, maybe never even came close, is no reason to write them off as failures. There are lots of things besides riding ability and guts that determine who makes the grade and who does not. It is no disgrace to fail. The only disgrace is in not trying."

Occasionally someone will ask if I had it all to do over, would I live my life the same way?

Many of the rough parts, I'll admit, I could certainly have managed without. But I still get a tight feeling in my chest when I hear a band playing Grand Entry music, and my vision is always a little blurred when I see a carload of laughing, carefree rodeo hands heading out of town for points unknown. So there's actually only one honest answer.

"Live my life the same, you ask? You damn betcha!"

THE END

# THE AUTHOR

Jane Burnett Smith was raised on a cattle ranch in Montana, rode saddle-broncs professionally in rodeos, worked in Western movies and was a blackjack dealer in Nevada. A member of the writing organization Sisters in Crime. She has written two Western mystery novels, *Always Standing By* and *If At First. . .* She also has written a number of published short stories.

Jane now lives in Tempe, Arizona, near her daughter and family. She was recently nominated to the National Cowgirls' Hall of Fame in Fort Worth, Texas. She is a member of the Western Writers of America.

Selected titles from
***Caxton Press***

***The Lewis and Clark Trail***
***Yesterday and Today***
William Hill
ISBN 0-87004-439-7 300 pages illustrated paper $16.95

***Our Ladies of the Tenderloin***
***Colorado's Legend in Lace***
Linda Wommack
ISBN 0-87004-444-3 250 pages paper $16.95

***Necktie Parties***
***Legal Executions in Oregon, 1851 - 1905***
Diane L. Goeres-Gardner
ISBN 0-87004-446-x 348 pages paper illustrated index $18.95

***Salmon River Country***
Mark Lisk and Stephen Stuebner
ISBN 0-87004-441-9 120 pages in full color hardcover $27.95

***On Sidesaddles to Heaven***
***The Women of the Rocky Mountain Mission***
Laurie Winn Carlson
ISBN 0-87004-384-6 256 pages paper $19.95

***Holy Rollers***
***Murder and Madness in Oregon's Love Cult***
T. McCracken and R. Bloggett
ISBN 0-87004-424-9 308 pages paper $16.95

**For a free catalog of Caxton books write to:**

*CAXTON PRESS*
312 Main Street
Caldwell, ID 83605-3299

or

Visit our Internet Website:

www.caxtonprinters.com

*Caxton Press* is a division of The CAXTON PRINTERS, Ltd.